86030 being used for driver training in November 1984 in readiness for Anglia East electrification.

GW00494233

1989
(reprint
revised)
£4.00

PSL FIELD GUIDE

Railways of the

EASTERN REGION

Volume 1: Southern operating area

PSL FIELD GUIDE

Railways of the
EASTERN
REGION

Volume 1: Southern operating area

Geoffrey Body

PATRICK STEPHENS LIMITED

Title page *First of the Class 315 units while on commissioning trials.*

© Geoff Body 1986 and 1989

All rights reserved. No part of this publication may be reproduced, stored in a retrieval system or transmitted, in any form or by any means, electronic, mechanical, photocopying, recording or otherwise, without prior permission in writing from Patrick Stephens Limited.

First published in 1986
Reprinted with additional material 1989

British Library Cataloguing in Publication Data

Body, Geoffrey, *1929—*
    Railways of the Eastern Region. — (PSL field guide).
    Rev. ed.
    Vol. 1 : Southern operating area.
    1. Eastern England. Railway services: British Rail.
    Eastern Region
    I. Title
    385'.09426

    ISBN 0-85260-298-8

Patrick Stephens Limited is part of the Thorsons Publishing Group, Wellingborough, Northamptonshire, NN8 2RQ, England.

Printed in Great Britain by Biddles Limited, Guildford, Surrey
Typeset by MJL Limited, Hitchin, Hertfordshire

10 9 8 7 6 5 4 3 2 1

Contents

Acknowledgements
The compilation of this book would not have been possible without the considerable assistance afforded by the Eastern Region of British Rail. Arrangements for that assistance were readily and generously made by Public Affairs Manager Bert Porter and implemented in the most helpful way by Stuart Rankin and Andy Lickfold of the Public Affairs Department. A number of others contributed in various ways including David Wrottesley who provided invaluable advice and guidance on the Sheffield area.

Major contributions were also made by my family. From his vantage point of a railway career which spanned the Great Northern, LNER and BR eras my father, 'Jim' Body, read through the final manuscript, my son Ian represented the third generation of railwaymen in the family by drawing the maps and my wife, once a railwaywoman herself, did wonders in creating an environment in which the final work was enabled to emerge from the vast mass of reference material that this sort of book entails.

Except where otherwise indicated the illustrations have been provided by the Eastern and Anglia Regions of British Rail or are drawn from my own collection.

SECTION 1

The Eastern Region field guide

The objective of this volume remains the same as that of its predecessors—to provide all the information necessary to the understanding and enjoyment of railways in a given area. The difference is that the size and complexity of British Rail's Eastern Region has made it appropriate to deal in separate volumes with the two geographical areas into which the Region is divided for operational purposes. There is so much of interest in each that any alternative could not possibly do justice to its subject.

This first volume deals with the southern operational area of the ER, broadly that from the Thames to the Humber. It is an area dominated by the southern portion of the East Coast main line, famous for over a century for its high speed running, and by the lines of East Anglia including the Norwich main line, both now approved for electrification. Nearer London electric commuter trains serve Essex, Hertfordshire and parts of Cambridgeshire while in the north a network of local services fans out from Sheffield and Doncaster, both areas of significant freight business.

The subject treatment used previously has been maintained in this latest volume. This introduction is followed by a summary of 150 years of railway history in the area and then by a detailed gazetteer which provides an entry for every railway location of significance. The sub-heading for each entry pinpoints its location and provides its official distance based on the BR Sectional Appendix to the Working Timetable, any out of the ordinary circumstances being explained in the text which follows. The main entry then provides a summary of the origins, features, functions and facilities of the location. For these purposes physical features and train services are normally referred to in the Down direction (ie, away from London or the focal point of the original railway), information on the latter being based on the Monday to Friday service at the time of writing. Distances normally refer to a signal box where one still exists or otherwise to the central point of the location. In the case of tunnels the sub-heading distance refers to the portal nearest to London.

In the majority of cases the gazetteer section deals with points of interest on a location basis but this is varied to a line basis where the line is so much of a single entity that its fragmentation would be confusing. This applies especially to branch lines. Locations in the same town are usually dealt with in the same entry.

Following the gazetteer comes a section in which the main routes are presented, first in terms of origin, physical features and current traffic and operations and then in tabular form with the main locations, distances and reference numbers

from the gazetteer section. Subsequent sections deal with the modern railway and
its departmental activities, then with the closed lines and finally with the railway
preservation activity.

Together these sections not only provide a full picture of the origins and present
state of the railways of the Eastern Region but do so in such a way that the information is readily accessible either in the form of a gazetteer entry, by route, or as part
of one of the subject summaries. A supplementary index covers those locations of
secondary or former significance. Thus in one volume is provided all the information, data, dates and distances necessary to derive the maximum interest from a
journey, a location visit, the study of a route or a desire to know more about a
specific railway discipline or other subject.

British Rail itself welcomes an interest in its activities and will be as helpful in
encouraging that interest as is consistent with its primary task of running a
modern, efficient and safe railway system. Viewing, spotting and photography are
generally permitted, at the discretion of the local BR management, wherever
normal public access is free or available by platform ticket. BR provides a compre-
hensive service of train information and fares, with travel centres in most of the
main towns; and there are many reduced fare facilities which can be put to good
use in the pursuit of a railway interest.

In preparing this book every effort has been made to ensure accuracy and
account has been taken of changes known to be coming along during the interval
between writing and publication. Yet the railway scene is constantly changing—
new facilities being introduced, old ones abandoned, new evidence of the past
emerging, new plans being made for the future—and for the benefit of future
volumes the compiler would be glad to hear from readers about any additional or
altered items.

Abbreviations used

AOCL	Open crossing with road warning lights monitored by train crew	*LC*	Level crossing
CCTV	Closed circuit television	*m*	Miles
ch	Chains	*mgr*	Merry-go-round
DGL	Down Goods Loop	*OT*	One Train
dmu	Diesel multiple unit	*RC*	Remotely-controlled
DPL	Down Passenger Loop	*R/G*	Red/Green
DRS	Down Refuge Siding	*TCB*	Track Circuit Block
emu	Electric multiple unit	*TMO*	Trainmen-operated
ET	Electric Token	*UGL*	Up Goods Loop
HST	High Speed Train	*UPL*	Up Passenger Loop
		URS	Up Refuge Siding

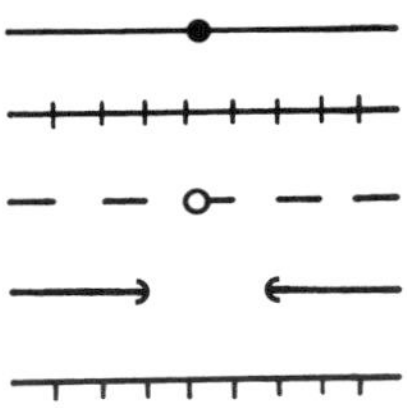

Open line and station

Freight and non-passenger line

Closed line and station

Tunnel

London Regional Transport

SECTION 2

The Eastern

The southern area of the Eastern Region dealt with in this volume was part of the London & North Eastern Railway from the grouping of 1923 until Britain's railways were nationalized on the first day of 1948. Prior to that period the area was dominated by three great companies, the Great Northern Railway with its main line to Yorkshire and the North and a host of branches radiating from it, the Great Eastern Railway which enveloped the whole of East Anglia, and the Great Central Railway whose cross-country lines served North Lincolnshire and stretched along the south bank of the Humber to Grimsby, Cleethorpes and the great port of Immingham. Various other companies penetrated the area, especially the Midland Railway with its interests in the Midland & Great Northern and London, Tilbury & Southend systems, but this area of eastern England was essentially Great Northern and Great Eastern territory and both railways guarded it jealously, not least because much of the countryside was rural in the extreme and its traffic potential was no more than modest.

Early tramways were not a feature of this part of Great Britain as they were in the more industrialized areas and the first real stirrings of railway activity did not occur until the late 1820s and early 1830s when the concept of a route from London to York via Cambridge originated. From the various rival plans all that emerged at this time was the Northern & Eastern Railway's truncated 53-mile line from Islington to Cambridge. With the same incorporation date of 4 July 1836 came the 126-mile Shoreditch to Yarmouth project of the Eastern Counties Railway—a company which, after many tribulations and manipulations, was to grow to dominate its rivals and form the eventual basis of the Great Eastern Railway.

Despite the bad financial climate work on the ECR line, which was to be of 5 ft gauge, began at the London end in 1837. It was to take six painful years to gain Colchester by which time the original enthusiasm for the project in Norfolk and Suffolk had turned to bitter disappointment.

The Northern & Eastern was faring no better. The depression had held back the start of work until 1839 by which time agreement had been reached to connect with the ECR line at Stratford instead of having a separate London terminus. The N&E opened to Broxbourne on 15 September 1840 and in three more stages to reach Bishops Stortford on 16 May 1842.

In 1843 the N&E obtained powers for another section northward (to Newport) and began discussions with the ECR. At the same period, frustration at the ECR line's slow progress had led Norfolk interests to establish their own railway activity with work starting on the Yarmouth & Norwich in 1843 and with the Norwich &

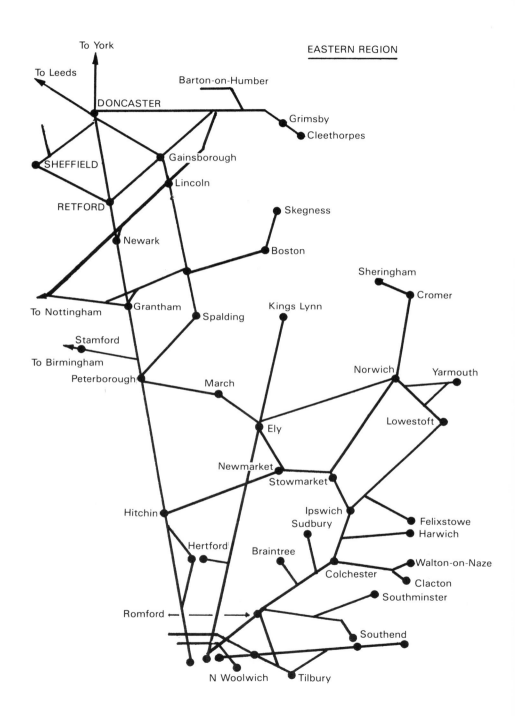

EASTERN REGION

Brandon planned as the next step. To recognize this development and solve its financial problems by getting a route for coal from the North via Peterborough the ECR leased the N&E from 1 January 1844 and on 4 July of that year obtained powers for closing the gap between Newport and Brandon and for a branch to meet the London & Birmingham at Peterborough. In the second half of 1844 the ECR system was converted to standard gauge and from 30 July 1845 trains were able to run from Shoreditch to Norwich via Bishops Stortford, Cambridge and Brandon.

The efforts of the Suffolk interests, led by J.C. Cobbold and also disillusioned with the ECR, had by this time brought about the incorporation of the Eastern Union Railway which obtained powers for seventeen miles of railway from Colchester to Ipswich in place of the lapsed ECR authority. Trains started running in 1846 and on 24 December of that year the first services ran over the metals of the Ipswich & Bury Railway as far as Bury St Edmunds. The EUR took over the I&B's Haughley to Norwich extension in 1847 and opened this line in sections to reach Norwich on 12 December 1849.

By 1849 other lines opened included the ex-N&E branch to Hertford (31 October 1843), the Eastern Counties & Thames Junction's line to North Woolwich (to Canning Town 29 April 1846 and on to North Woolwich 14 June 1847) and the Norfolk Railway group (Norwich-Yarmouth 1 May 1844 and Reedham-Lowestoft 3 May 1847 for goods and 1 July for passengers). The cable-worked London & Blackwall Railway had started operating its services designed to abstract traffic from the Thames steamers on 6 July 1840 and in 1849 was converted to locomotive operation as a corollary of the link established with the ECR at Bow.

The ECR was now in a position to dominate its area. It leased the Norfolk Railway group in 1848, acquired control of the port of Lowestoft and proceeded, through manipulation of services, tolls and fares, to make life so impossible for the Eastern Union that an agreement giving the ECR working control of the NR and EUR systems became inevitable. It began on 1 January 1854 and, coupled with the absorption of the East Anglian Railways (Kings Lynn to Ely and Dereham) on 1 January 1852 and the Newmarket Railway on 30 March 1854, gave the Eastern Counties Railway the unshakeable domination of East Anglia.

While the Eastern Counties Railway was building up its position in the Eastern Counties and George Hudson was expanding his railway enterprises to the north and west, some powerful interests in Yorkshire and Lincolnshire were polarizing into support groups for a more direct route between London and York than Hudson's lines could provide. The debate continued for ten years with three main schemes emerging, the Direct Northern (for a route via Peterborough and Lincoln), the London & York (via Peterborough and Grantham) and that of the ECR which took over the northern aspirations of the Northern & Eastern.

The Direct Northern and ECR Bills both failed, the former then joining forces with Edmund Denison's London & York the better to fight off the bitter antagonism and counter proposals of the Hudson group, now centred on the newly-formed Midland Railway. After a bitter fight in Parliament the L&Y proposals were approved on 8 June 1846 under the new title of Great Northern Railway but at the cost of alienating most of the surrounding lines and the loss of the Sheffield and Wakefield arms.

The 1846 session produced other decisions which were to shape the railways of the present ER area. In addition to authorizing the East Lincolnshire Railway's coastal route from Boston to Grimsby, Parliament approved the Sheffield &

Lincolnshire Junction and the Sheffield & Lincolnshire Extension Railways. These and associated projects came together with the Sheffield, Ashton-under-Lyne & Manchester Railway from 11 January 1847 to form the Manchester, Sheffield & Lincolnshire Railway which, in turn, became the Great Central from 1 August 1897.

Where the GNR's Sheffield plans had failed in 1846 those of the Sheffield & Lincolnshire Junction had succeeded and provided for a line extending the SA&M's newly opened Woodhead route across to Gainsborough and connecting with allied projects for links on to Lincoln and Grimsby. Sheffield had been connected to Rotherham in 1838 and had been linked there with the North Midland's Derby line two years later. Now it was further surmounting the physical barriers of its Pennine location with this Mersey-Humber route.

The terrain being easier, the GNR planned to complete its loop from Peterborough via Boston and Lincoln before the direct route via Grantham. The first Great Northern trains began operating in 1848 over the leased East Lincolnshire line, running from Louth to Grimsby and on to New Holland (GG&SJ) for the Hull ferry from 1 March of that year. Extension south quickly followed— Louth-Firsby (3 September 1848), Firsby-Boston (1 October) and Boston-Lincoln and Peterborough (17 October).

The 1848-51 period was particularly important for the MS&L, first for the opening of the Ulceby-Brigg and Barnetby-Market Rasen sections in 1848 and then, in 1849, for the Sheffield-Woodhouse, Barton-New Holland and Brigg-Gainsborough-Woodhouse lines, as well as for Parliamentary approval of the new title and absorption of the Manchester & Lincoln Union. After the GNR's plans for access to Doncaster via Rossington instead of Bawtry were rejected by Parliament an alliance with the MS&L produced the alternative of running via a link from the loop line at Sykes Junction to the MS&L at Clarborough, near Retford. Completion of the new line together with the GN's Lincoln-Gainsborough and Retford-Doncaster sections not only allowed services to develop on the loop route from 4 September 1849 but also provided the key to access to Sheffield over the MS&L line from Retford.

Many of its towns and cities, like Sheffield, were already being served by the GN's rivals—Hudson had reached Lincoln from Nottingham on 3 August 1846, while Peterborough had seen the arrival of the L&B from Blisworth in 1845, the ECR from Ely in 1847 and through trains from the Midland in 1848. Now, however, the position was to change dramatically. On 7 August 1850 the Great Northern link between London (Maiden Lane) and Peterborough was completed to provide the company with onward access to the Lincolnshire network of lines, to Grimsby and Sheffield, and forward from Doncaster over the new line between Burton Salmon and Knottingley to York.

Work on the direct 'Towns' line of the Great Northern had started in 1849 and its completion allowed main line expresses to be diverted from the loop line from 1 August 1852 (it had been opened for freight on 15 July), saving something like an hour for services between London and Edinburgh via the East Coast route. The Great Northern went on to reach Nottingham in 1855 by leasing the Grantham-Nottingham line of the Ambergate, Nottingham & Boston & Eastern Junction Railway (opened on 15 July 1850). Its trains from Grantham reached Sleaford on 16 June 1857, Boston on 13 April 1859 and Lincoln on 15 April 1867.

The main framework of the railway system in Eastern England was thus largely complete by the end of the 1850s but the Great Eastern Railway which had emerged from the ECR system on 1 August 1862 still had no direct outlet to the North. This was to be a bone of contention between the Great Eastern and Great Northern companies until the formation of the GN&GE Joint Committee on 3 July 1879 and the. vesting in it of the Huntingdon-St Ives, Needingworth Junction-March, March-Spalding and Lincoln-Doncaster lines plus a new link from Spalding to Lincoln which was opened in 1882.

One other major route was that of the M&GN Joint Committee which came into being on 1 July 1893 and stretched from Peterborough and Castle Bytham via Kings Lynn to Norwich and Yarmouth. The initial grouping had been that of the Norwich & Spalding, Spalding & Bourne and Lynn & Sutton Bridge concerns which had become the Midland & Eastern Railway on 23 July 1866. Then, on 1 January 1883, the Eastern & Midlands was formed from the Lynn & Fakenham, Yarmouth & North Norfolk and Yarmouth Union companies and in the same year enfolded the M&E and the Peterborough, Wisbech & Sutton Bridge Railway.

Many smaller lines were built in the second half of the 19th century to be followed by the rural lines prompted by the Light Railway legislation, but the efforts of the major railways turned increasingly upon better services and better facilities—bogie vehicles, effective lighting, heating and train catering, larger and more efficient locomotives and faster trains.

As early as 1857 the Great Northern had operated its fast 'Manchester Flyers' in conjunction with the MS&L and routed via Woodhead but the greatest impetus to service improvements came from the 'Railway Races to the North' between the East and West Coast routes. The first period of racing took place in 1888 and another followed in 1895. In 1898 the Great Northern introduced its first Atlantic locomotive (No 990 *Henry Oakley*) and the first of the Gresley 'Pacifics' was built at Doncaster in 1922.

The emergence of the country from the depression that followed the First World War set the stage for the great events of the 1930s, starting with *Flying Scotsman* and *Papyrus* exceeding 100 mph in 1934 and followed by the introduction of the Silver Jubilee services running non-stop between Darlington and Kings Cross at 70.4 mph in 1935. On 27 September of that year *Silver Link* thrilled the Press with

The LNER's most famous train with a set of varnished teak coaches in the 1930s.

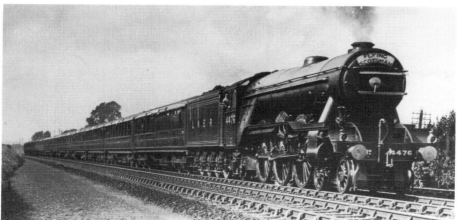

A reminder of 1935 and the LNER 'Silver Jubilee' expresses.

100 mph for 25 miles and a top speed of 112 mph on a demonstration run. In 1937 came the 'Coronation' services and in 1938 *Mallard*'s world record of 126 mph.

The Great Eastern had a long tradition of express services with trains like the *Cromer Express* and its successor the *Norfolk Coast Express*. As a final major achievement before grouping, it also astonished the railway world with the introduction of its 'Jazz' service from Liverpool Street which set new standards for the utilization and turnround of commuter services and all done for much less than the costly alternative of electrification. To keep pace with the dramatic events of the mid-1930s on the East Coast main line, the Ipswich/Norwich route got its own streamlined services from 27 September 1937 using two modified 'B17's, *East Anglian* and *City of London*, and specially designed six-coach sets.

Other GE section named trains ran in connection with the steamer services from Harwich and Parkeston Quay. The Harwich branch had opened on 15 August 1854 with the GER operating its own steamers ten years later. Parkeston Quay was opened in 1883 with extensions in 1911 and 1934, the train ferries commencing in 1924. In the north of the area the steady increase in trade through Grimsby had led to the opening of Immingham in 1912 and its subsequent rapid development as a bulk cargo port.

The new yard at Whitemoor, complete with two hump yards and mechanized route setting and retarders, was opened as part of the LNER's efforts to hold its

This scene shows an Up train passing through Peterborough, by 1973 no longer the bottleneck it had previously been.

In addition to its north-south main lines the LNER had many cross-country routes, including that of the M&GN Joint Committee whose Melton Constable station is here pictured in 1959.

freight business against the increasing road competition of the late 1920s and early '30s. In addition to the heavy traffic of the Sheffield area and the coal movements out of Nottinghamshire and South Yorkshire, the LNER carried major flows of bricks from Peterborough, fish from Grimsby and the East Anglian ports, fruit and vegetables from Bedfordshire and the Fens, agricultural produce from Norfolk, Suffolk and Lincolnshire, iron ore from South Lincs and dock traffic from the East Coast and London area ports.

Like the other main line railways, the LNER achieved incredible movement performances during the period of the Second World War and then proved remarkably resilient in its recovery to be handed over to the British Transport Commission in a workable if not ideal condition on the first day of 1948. Under national ownership, schemes halted by the war were revived and the new era saw completion of the Liverpool Street-Shenfield 1,500 volt dc overhead electrification of the bottlenecks south of Potters Bar on the ECML. From 3 May 1959 the completion of the new station and tunnel at Potters Bar set the seal on a process of track quadrupling as far as Welwyn Viaduct which had started a century earlier.

A major period of change was ushered in by the additional capital made available under the 1955 Modernisation Plan. This was to bring diesel multiple units and railbuses on branch lines, 'Britannias' on the Norwich services and 'Deltics' to Kings Cross shed, the emergence of the new BR standard stock, faster fitted freight

Refurbishing has turned out this Class 309 emu looking like new.

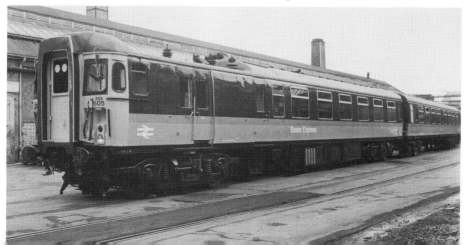

Contrast in signalling between traditional semaphore arms (and gated crossing beyond) and modern colour light signal with route and calling on extras.

services and new marshalling yards like the redesigned Temple Mills, planned to sort 1,000 wagons a shift and take over the work of the smaller East London yards. But the biggest changes came from the London suburban electrification schemes, starting with the extension of the 1,500 volt dc to Chelmsford on 11 June 1956 and on to Southend Victoria by the end of that year. The North East London scheme, inaugurated on 16 November 1960 with 6.25/25 kV ac, had all sorts of teething troubles and was not fully effective until 1963. By then it had been able to return the borrowed LT&S emus so that electric services could start running between Fenchurch Street and Shoeburyness and the original Colchester-Clacton/Walton local services had become an excellent through service to and from Liverpool Street. In parallel with the new electric services came new signalling schemes, new track layouts and new electric traction depots like the one at East Ham which took over from the tired old Plaistow loco shed. The LT&S also got a dramatically remodelled Barking to provide a new pattern of interchange with the London Transport services.

The electrification period was to be followed by the Beeching era 'Re-shaping Plan'. Most of the M&GN system had already been closed in 1959 but now many other rural lines and stations, including a major rationalization in Lincolnshire, featured in a slimming down and simplification of the physical network. Other changes were less immediately obvious but were typified by the new hump yard at Ripple Lane which was already being outdated by the rapid changeover from conventional wagon movement to trainloads of high capacity Carflats, Presflos and privately owned tank wagons. The merry-go-round scheme for the continuous, planned movement of high capacity coal trains was an Eastern Region concept which developed in this period. It made its debut in 1965 with the first Freightliner services on the ER appearing a year later.

All these traffic and traction changes had brought with them other major alterations in the railway infrastructure, revised track layouts, continuous welded rail, modern signalling and new and simplified stations. With the foundations of the 'new railway' thus laid the 1970s became a time for development and improvement, especially on the East Coast main line. In one decade the old Great Northern's main line changed from a traditional railway to an exciting modern one with the Kings Cross bottleneck remodelled out of existence, old sources of delay removed by quadrupling and easing curves, a new station and layout at Peterborough and signalling placed in the hands of three modern panel boxes.

In October 1977 Class '312' emus first appeared on the newly electrified GN suburban lines and eventually the full service pattern was operating from Moorgate to Welwyn Garden City and from Kings Cross to Royston. In addition to the changes at Kings Cross, this scheme involved the use of the old GN City line from Finsbury Park, a new flyover at Welwyn Garden City and the routing of the Moorgate trains via Watton-at-Stone. As this scheme settled down the Inter-City 125 High Speed Trains were proving their worth on the Western Region and then, twenty years after the 'Deltics' had taken on the responsibility of the ECML express services in 1961-2, the HSTs took over this mantle.

By 1984 the new passenger timetable had brought a timing of 4 hours 30 minutes and an average speed of 87.3 mph for the 'Flying Scotsman' and 75.2 mph for London-Aberdeen. Complementing the main line services were good cross-country services—Birmingham-Norwich, Nottingham-Skegness, Nottingham-Lincoln-Cleethorpes and Sheffield-Doncaster-Humberside—and increasingly

Right *ER modernization of trains and track was accompanied by wholesale improvements in ancilary facilities, in this case the Dunlop 'Starglide' installation at Stevenage.*

Below *Deltic-headed special train at Mark IIA rolling stock arriving at Kings Cross on 21 November 1967.*

sophisticated passenger ticketing, information and support systems. By this time the old type of freight wagon had virtually disappeared to be replaced by a mix of company trains, mgr coal trains, Freightliner and Speedlink services plus special distribution schemes and, with Rail Express Parcels station to station facilities, catering for the major freight areas around Sheffield, Humberside and Thameside.

The new wave of Eastern Region progress was very much in evidence as 1985 dawned with re-signalling completed to Cambridge and beyond Ipswich on the Norwich main line. Other pre-electrification work was also proceeding well, including remodelling of the layout at Ipswich, and electric trains duly started running to that point in May as the first stage of the Anglia East scheme which would ultimately electrify 76 route miles north of Colchester. The next timetable should see electrification as far as Harwich with completion to Norwich in 1987. Class 86 locomotives and Class 312 and 309 emus will meet the traction requirements and much else will change on the East Anglian main lines including control from the Colchester panel all the way to Norwich.

Practical work on the £306 million electrification of the East Coast main line was inaugurated at Peterborough on 7 February with the ceremonial installation of the first of the overhead wiring masts. Target dates envisage electrified surburban services to Peterborough (using Class 317 four-coach emus from BREL/GEC) by 1987, main line electric working to Leeds by 1989 and to Edinburgh by 1991. By then the route will be completely controlled from only seven signalling centres, at Kings Cross, Peterborough, Doncaster, Leeds, York, Newcastle and Edinburgh. In addition to the mammoth changes in power supply, track and signalling and telecommunications hardware, the ECML electrification scheme envisages 62 new electric locomotives and 324 new coaches.

1985 work on the Southminster branch, including not only the wiring but also platform lengthening and the installation of two automatic crossings, will lead to electric services on the 16½-mile line by 1986. Nearer London the freight route between Camden Road Junction and Stratford received electrification consent and from May the extension of electrification east from Dalston Junction to North Woolwich enabled the introduction of a new twenty-minute interval service through from Richmond. In addition to its £9 million contribution to electrification itself, the GLC also put money into a station modernization and reopening programme, both on the North Woolwich and Enfield Town lines—all reasonable compensation for the loss of the Tottenham-Stratford service and closure of Lea Bridge.

As the Dockland Light Railway scheme planned not only a start on track laying at Poplar, but also extension from Minories to Bank the Eastern Region was pointing the way forward with some exciting new speed records. Fifty years after the exploits of *Silver Link* in 1935 a run of the new 'Tees-Tyne Pullman' produced an average of 115.4 mph for the 286.6 miles from Newcastle to Kings Cross which included a new world record for diesel traction of a staggering 144 mph.

SECTION 3

Gazetteer

A.1   Acle—see Norwich-Yarmouth Line

A.2   Aldwarke Junctions

Sheffield-Doncaster/Pontefract lines. See text

The Midland and Manchester, Sheffield & Lincolnshire (later Great Central) Railway routes north from Rotherham made use of the Don Valley and formerly had stations at Parkgate & Rawmarsh and Parkgate & Aldwarke respectively. These are now closed but the location remains important for its South and North Junctions where the routes for Doncaster and Pontefract divide and the freight line from Woodburn Junction joins. On the latter the distances of the two junctions are 6 m 69 ch and 7 m respectively and on the Midland route 164 m 43 ch and 164 m 48 ch.

From 1983 the North East/South West Inter-City services were transferred from the Dearne Valley line to the Mexborough route and made this change at Aldwarke but the emphasis may change again to route Sheffield-Doncaster trains via the Holmes Chord and a re-opened spur north of Aldwarke.

The former Aldwarke Junction signal box stands between the physical junctions, and along the Mexborough line are the connections to BSC Thrybergh and the Silverwood Colliery branch plus traces of the curve from the former GC&Mid joint line towards Roundwood Junction. Chemical, coal and oil traffic are also dealt with locally.

A.3   Alexandra Palace—see Wood Green

A.4   Alresford—see Colchester-Clacton Line

A.5   Althorne—see Southminster Branch

A.6   Althorpe

Barnetby-Doncaster line, between Scunthorpe and Doncaster. 19 m 21 ch from Doncaster

The present station at Althorpe is a modest affair of Up and Down platforms linked by a footbridge and served by the Doncaster-Cleethorpes local trains. It is, in fact, the second station, the first one having been closed on 21 May 1916 after the present bridge (19 m 34 ch) over the River Trent replaced a predecessor located a few yards to the north. The 30 mph speed limitation on the curve approaching Althorpe is a reminder of the resultant deviation. The bridge itself has two fixed spans and a lifting span (not now used) of 160 ft and carries the A18 road in addition to the double track rail route.

The South Yorkshire Railway originally reached the Trent at Keadby, near Althorpe, in 1859 using a route along the Keadby Canal. The river was then bridged as part of a scheme with the MS&L to link up with the latter at Barnetby. The through route was opened on 1 May 1866 (1 October for passengers).

Shipping still uses the Trent wharves north of the railway but the latter's links to Gunhouse Wharf from Gunhouse Junction (20 m 22 ch) and to Keadby Wharf from Keadby Junction (18 m 14 ch) have now closed although their courses remain visible. Keadby Junction signal box still stands by Keadby Canal LC (18 m 18 ch) although the signalling is now on the Doncaster panel.

A.7   Ancaster—see Grantham-Skegness Line

A.8   Angel Road

Liverpool Street-Kings Lynn line, between

Liverpool Street and Broxbourne. 7 m 57 ch from Liverpool Street

Angel Road, a typical simplified station of Up and Down platforms with shelters, enjoys a basic half-hourly service provided by the Liverpool Street-Hertford East electric trains.

Nine years after the opening of the Northern & Eastern Railway's Lea Valley line in 1840 Angel Road became a junction when a single line to Enfield was brought into use on 1 March 1849 and got a change of name from Edmonton to Water Lane. The connection veered away on the Down side from the country end of the station (through what is now a scrap yard) but became of secondary importance from 1 August 1872 when Enfield trains started using the new route via Hackney Downs. Some passenger trains continued to link Angel Road and Edmonton Low Level via the original route until 11 September 1939 with goods facilities surviving until 7 December 1964.

Pre-rationalization Angel Road had four running lines, the branch route, an extensive goods yard on the Down side and private sidings serving a dozen assorted firms.

A.9   Ardleigh

Liverpool Street-Norwich line, between Colchester and Manningtree. 55 m 71 ch from Liverpool Street

Pre-electrification Ardleigh, once noted for its horticultural and seed traffic but closed in 1967, retained a signal box and barrier crossing. The station house remained as did the signal box at Parsons Heath (54 m) but the Refuge Sidings at Ardleigh and the signal box at Dedham (57 m 63 ch) were no more.

A.10   Arkwright Colliery

Chesterfield-Rotherham line, branch from Barrow Hill Junction.

Access to Arkwright Colliery was formerly by an 8 m 55 ch, 30 mph, One Train operation single line from Beighton Station Junction. A new curve towards Barrow Hill and linked to the Sheffield panel has permitted the closure of the old GC line via Renishaw.

A.11   Ashwell

Hitchin-Cambridge line, between Hitchin and Royston. 41 m from Kings Cross

The Royston & Hitchin Railway's line opened on 21 October 1850 and the present Up side buildings—long, low and with age overshadowing their modest decoration—may well be original. There is a traditional waiting room on the Down side and period maltings beyond the station. The half-hourly Kings Cross-Royston trains call.

A.12   Askham Tunnel

East Coast main line, between Newark and Retford. 134 m 37 ch from Kings Cross

Topping the high ground which precedes Retford the 57 yd Askham Tunnel (134 m 36 ch to 134 m 40 ch) is a modest affair with an Up Passenger Loop at the country end. There were formerly signal boxes either side at Markham and at Gamston, where there is still an emergency crossover (132 m 68 ch).

A.13   Aslockton—see Grantham-Nottingham line

A.14   Atercliffe—see Sheffield

Angel Road when it still had a rail-connected gas works.

A.15 Attleborough

Norwich-Birmingham line, between Thetford and Wymondham. 108 m 19 ch from Liverpool Street

Attleborough is a typical period railway station with a Down side signal box, traditional crossing gates and brick buildings with gables and thwarted 'Gothic' pretensions. The sites of the old Down Refuge Siding and of the former Gaymer private siding are reminders of the large volumes of apples, cider and wartime traffic once conveyed by rail. The Norwich-Birmingham line dmus still provide a passenger service for this small Norfolk town.

There is a traditional LC at Poplar Farm (107 m 21 ch) on the London side and an AHB LC at Spronces (108 m 70 m) towards Norwich.

A.16 Audley End

Liverpool Street-Kings Lynn line between Bishops Stortford and Cambridge. 41 m 55 ch from Liverpool Street

The station opened as Wenden when the link between Bishops Stortford and Brandon completed a railway from London to Norwich on 29 July 1845. The name was changed to that of Lord Braybrooke's nearby mansion three years later.

From the opening of the Saffron Walden Railway on 23 November 1865 until its closure in 1964 Audley End was a junction with a 'V' platform on the Up side from which trains ran to the market town of Saffron Walden (1¾ m). From 2 October 1866 they continued on via Ashdon (5¼ m) to Bartlow (7¼ m) where junction was made with the 1865 line from Shelford Junction to Long Melford. In addition to its push and pull services the branch, at one period, enjoyed slip coaches (detached at Newport) and later diesel railbuses and dmus. Between Saffron Walden and Ashdon a small halt was constructed to serve the Acrow works.

The branch platform area is now a car park as part of the station's role as a passenger railhead with a service derived from the Cambridge/Kings Lynn trains and the Bishops Stortford-Cambridge local dmus.

Audley End is approached via Trees LC (41 m 30 ch) and comprises signal box (41 m 48 ch), Up and Down platforms and main buildings of solid and pretentious appearance to match the influence of the great house. The line then cuts through two ridges by means of chalk cuttings and the 456 yd Audley End Tunnel (42 m 70 ch to 43 m 11 ch) and 407 yd Littlebury Tunnel (43 m

Littlebury, one of the two tunnels on the Cambridge main line's descent from Elsenham summit.

27 ch to 43 m 46 ch). The two tunnels came into being as much to protect the grounds of Audley End mansion as for civil engineering reasons and the portals of the first one reflect the same influence in the decoration. It appears again in the decorative spandrels of the station canopy supports.

B.1 Baldock

Hitchin-Cambridge line, between Hitchin and Royston. 36 m 47 ch from Kings Cross

Baldock has the same origins and style as its neighbour, Ashwell. The approach from Letchworth is beneath an overbridge, with the platforms then linked by a modern footbridge and provided with a period wooden shelter on the Up side and traditional buildings up a short flight of steps on the Down. There is a half-hourly service to and from Kings Cross.

B.2 Barking

Fenchurch Street-Shoeburyness line, junction with line from Upper Holloway and the Tilbury Loop. 7 m 42 ch from Fenchurch Street

Barking station was completely rebuilt when the LT&S line was electrified. The new station, formally brought into use on 29 September 1961, largely eliminated conflicting movements by providing a flyover to link the Tilbury and Tottenham & Hampstead lines and a combination of underpass and flyover to bring the Up

Barking station looking east.

London Transport line between the Up Southend and Down Tilbury lines. Above the four island platforms a sizeable combination of ticket office, concourse and ancillary facilities has a good position in East Street, with bus stops right outside the station.

The first station in Barking was opened by the LT&S on 13 April 1854, with major alterations subsequently taking place in 1889, 1906-8, 1932 and 1935. Today the Barking complex stretches from East Ham (6 m 19 ch), where the emu maintenance depot and stabling area commences on a site between the Up and Down lines, to Ripple Lane (9 m 7 ch) which comprises a locomotive depot, freight yard, Freightliner terminal and container depot. The yard area ends at 10 m 37 ch, just outside Dagenham Dock.

All LT&S section passenger trains stop at

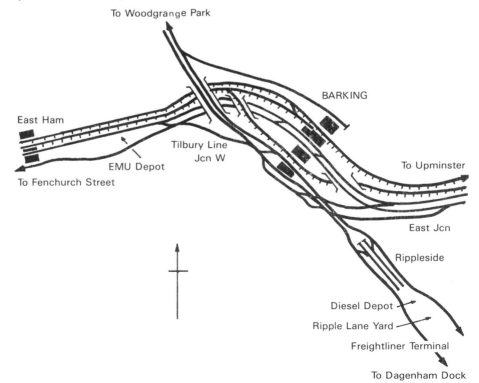

Barking during off-peak periods when the pattern consists of three main line and two loop trains each hour, with 6-9 minute connections with the half-hourly service to and from Gospel Oak.

Following the East Ham depot complex is Tilbury Line Junction West (7 m 5 ch) where the Up Tilbury joins the Up main. Then after the station and panel box area comes East Junction linking the main (8 m 11 ch) and Tilbury (7 m 60 ch) lines. Down the latter lie Rippleside LC (8 m 5 ch) and then Ripple Lane (9 m 7 ch) where Track Circuit Block applies on the goods lines (no TCB on the Up line beyond the signal box).

Although the 1961 changes left a water crane at the country end of Barking station they finally wiped away Little Ilford Yard, near the junction with the T&H, and the spur linking the T&H with East Ham— once used by East Ham-St Pancras/Moorgate trains. The work of Little Ilford was taken over by Ripple Lane where the new hump yard was designed to deal with the heavy movements of traffic off the Tilbury line. The main lines pass round the yard area which now accommodates a locomotive depot, Barking Rail Handling, Isislink, Speedlink facilities and the terminals of Freightliners Ltd, with two 30-ton Morris cranes, and Dagenham Storage, with one 35-ton Allen crane. In addition to staging traffic off the Tilbury Loop, Ripple Lane is a signing on point for trainmen and re-crews a number of freight services.

B.3 Barkston

East Coast main line, north of Grantham and junction for the Skegness line. 109 m 56 ch from Kings Cross

Barkston today comprises the main line route to the north, the single line of the Skegness branch round to East Junction (110 m 10 ch) and the 4 m 76 ch double line which joins there from Allington Junction on the Nottingham line. On 5 May 1983 the ECML bridge over the latter was replaced by two formerly used near Darlington, the track being slewed at the same time to raise it from 90 mph to 125 mph.

Barkston station, south of the junction, closed on 16 March 1955 and Barkston has also lost the spur from East Junction to the former North Junction. New or repaired locomotives on a 'running in' trip from Doncaster used to turn round here, as did *Mallard* before her world record-breaking run.

B.4 Barnetby

Cleethorpes-Sheffield line, junction with

Lincoln and Doncaster lines. 94 m 56 ch from Manchester (London Road)

Barnetby was one of the focal points of the Great Central lines in the northern part of Lincolnshire. Here the three lines from Lincoln, Gainsborough and Doncaster met before splitting again for Barton, Immingham and Cleethorpes. The surviving trackwork, coal yard and Lee Grinling & Co warehouse bear witness to the volume of goods traffic formerly received, forwarded and exchanged. Passenger interchange between the lines was also substantial.

Barnetby started life as a junction, the Ulceby-Brigg and Barnetby-Market Rasen sections both being opened on 1 November 1848. It was linked to Lincoln from 18 December of that year and to Gainsborough two years later. The route via Scunthorpe was not completed until 1866.

The approach from Cleethorpes is via Melton Ross Sidings (96 m 79 ch) where the signal box formerly controlled access to a private siding, past New Barnetby LC (95 m 79 ch) with its house and gated crossing and by Barnetby East signal box (96 m 64 ch) which stands just before the station platforms. These comprise two islands with substantial brick buildings dating from 1915, the centre fast lines being supplemented by slow lines to the outer platform faces plus an extra Down Goods line. Beyond the station the long, tall Wrawby Junction signal box (94 m 12 ch) controls the junction itself where the 94 m 6 ch of the main line becomes 33 m 34 ch from Marshgate Junction on the Doncaster route and 12 m 55 ch from New Holland on the Lincoln route.

Its junction status gives Barnetby an excellent passenger service including calls by the 'Humber-Lincs Executive' which gets passengers to Kings Cross by 09.22.

B.5 Barnetby-Lincoln Line

From Wrawby Junction, Barnetby to Pelham Street Junction, Lincoln. 28 m 48 ch

This line is the former GC portion of the present through route from Cleethorpes to Nottingham. The section involved is served by Cleethorpes-Lincoln trains, a number of which continue on to Newark, Nottingham and Birmingham New Street. The line also carries the 'Humber-Lincs Executive' which leaves Cleethorpes at 06.15 and returns from Kings Cross at 18.18.

The origins of this North Lincolnshire line go back to the Great Grimsby & Sheffield Junction Railway which became a part of the Manchester, Sheffield & Lincoln-

*Period scene at Barnetby. Note the junction signal gantry (*Lens of Sutton*).*

shire and thus of the Great Central. This genesis is still reflected in the distances on the route which are based on New Holland whence the GG&SJ operated steam ferries across the Humber. The Barnetby-Market Rasen section of the route was opened on 1 November 1848 and the Lincoln portion on 18 December of the same year.

For the most part the route runs through the flat rich farmland that is a feature of this part of Lincolnshire. By skirting the Wolds it avoids any serious gradients but is by no means featureless. With the exception of Market Rasen the intermediate stations were closed on 1 November 1965 so that despite a maximum line speed of 60 mph the route is traversed in 36 minutes. At the time of writing it was double track with conventional Absolute Block signalling.

From Wrawby Junction (12 m 55 ch) the line heads south, past the signal box, gated level crossing and gabled former station buildings at Howsham (16 m 17 ch) and on through similar locations at North Kelsey (18 m 3 ch), Moortown (19 m 34 ch), Holton-le-Moor (21 m 11 ch) and Claxby & Usselby (23 m 69 ch). There are intermediate level crossings at Smithfield (18 m 25 ch), No 18 Gatehouse (20 m 43 ch), Claxby Gatehouse (22 m 7 ch) and Walesby (24 m 26 ch) with crossovers at Holton-le-Moor and on the approach to Market Rasen.

The pattern of modest original stations with Tudor influences becomes a little grander at Market Rasen although the long

main buildings have now lost their canopy. At the London end the former signal box stands empty and the dock, loading gauge and other paraphernalia of the old goods yard are no longer used.

The situation on the northern section is now repeated as today's trains rush along the flat, straight southern section, past more combinations of signal box, level crossing and former stations of pleasant design at Wickenby (30 m 53 ch), Snelland (32 m 15 ch), Langworth (35 m 25 ch) and Reepham (36 m 61 ch). Again there are intermediate level crossings, at Buslingthorpe (29 m), Lissingley (29 m 20 ch), Stainton (33 m 60 ch) and Scothern (34 m 51 ch).

The approach to Lincoln starts with the AHB LC at Cherry Willingham (37 m 55 ch) with the modest Monks Abbey signal box (40 m 2 ch) then preceding crossovers and the final stretch to Pelham Street Junction (41 m 23 ch). The old Clayton private siding lay on this section of the route which also affords present day users an excellent view of Lincoln's cathedral, majestically situated on a hill above the city.

B.6   Barnet Tunnel

ECML between New Southgate and Oakleigh Park. 7 m 42 ch from Kings Cross

The 605 yd Barnet Tunnel (7 m 42 ch to 7 m 70 ch) forms part of the long 1 in 200 climb to Potters Bar. The separate bores for the Slow lines were constructed during the quadrupling period and are slightly higher than the original tunnel.

B.7 Barrow Haven—see Barton-on-Humber Branch

B.8 Barrow Hill—see Chesterfield-Rotherham Line

B.9 Barton-on-Humber Branch

Cleethorpes-Sheffield line, branch from Habrough Junction. 11 mm 33 ch

No sooner had it got its Act for the main line west from Grimsby than the Great Grimsby & Sheffield Junction Railway was planning to add branches, including one to New Holland. In the following year, 1846, it became part of the MS&L and two years later, on 1 March 1848, it opened the New Holland branch to link up with the East Lincolnshire company's line via Louth. The station at New Holland was on a pier into the Humber and from the floating landing stage beyond a steamer service was operated across to Hull. The section from New Holland to Barton was opened on 1 March 1849.

From Habrough Junction the branch runs as a 1 m 45 ch single line to Ulceby South Junction where it meets the double track curve from Brocklesby and the mileage changes to 100 m 31 ch from Manchester, reflecting the Great Central parentage. Under the control of the high Ulceby Junction signal box (100 m 32 ch) it then passes via the surviving platform at Ulceby (100 m 36 ch) to Ulceby North Junction (100 m 36 ch) where the Immingham line departs.

The single lead from the junction becomes conventional Absolute Block double line as the route takes a straight course across the flat agricultural landscape to the gated LC at Bystable Lane (102 m 9 ch) and then Thornton Abbey (103 m 4 ch). Still with a touch of LNER days about it, the station has a path across the fields to the abbey itself. The straight course continues on via more gated level crossings at Barton Road (103 m 12 ch) and Butterswood (103 m 48 ch) to Goxhill (104 m 51 ch), a pleasant spot with wooden signal box, gabled main buildings and a traditional gated crossing. The line from Immingham Dock via Killingholme (1¾ m), and East Halton (4½) formerly joined the Barton branch at Goxhill Junction (104 m 43 ch), 7¼ miles from its starting point. This was the Barton & Immingham Light Railway opened in 1910-11 to carry workpeople to and from Hull via the New Holland ferry, leased to

the Great Central and eventually closed on 17 June 1963.

At Oxmarsh Crossing LC (106 m 38 ch) the double track becomes single. The flat-roofed signal box with its token exchange platform also controls the gated level crossing. At New Holland (106 m 52 ch) there is just a modest wooden platform followed by an empty signal box at Barrow Road LC (106 m 57 ch) where the route to the steamer pier is now part of a fenced off area devoted to commercial purposes. The days of the paddle steamer ferries and the bustle, gleam and warmth of their open engine rooms are now but memories.

For the remainder of the route, through Barrow Haven (108 m 5 ch) to the modest terminus (110 m 19 ch) dwarfed by the nearby Humber Bridge, the line runs close to the Humber. It is worked on the One Train basis with a 'No Signalman' key token provided at the Associated Chemical Co's siding.

The branch is served by dmus to and from Cleethorpes and there is a linked bus service from Barton, over the bridge, into Hull.

B.10 Basildon

Fenchurch Street-Shoeburyness line, between Upminster and Pitsea. 24 m 48 ch from Fenchurch Street

For a time Basildon New Town had to manage with the stations at Pitsea and Laindon but it is now served by a modern facility adjacent to both bus services and shopping facilities.

The two-platform station, with ticket office at street level below, lies on the 4-mile descent from Laindon to Pitsea and has cuttings on either side, something of a rarity on the LT&S. There are three trains an hour off-peak—one calling only at Barking on its 29-minute journey from Fenchurch Street—with the service doubling in the busiest hours.

B.11 Battlesbridge—see Southminster Branch

B.12 Bawtry

East Coast main line, between Retford and Doncaster. 143 m 71 ch from Kings Cross

On the ECML north from Retford the three CCTV crossings at Botany Bay (140 m 53 ch), Sutton (141 m 55 ch) and Torworth (143 m 17 ch) are followed at Ranskill by UPL, DPL and emergency crossover (143 m 71 ch), Ranskill LC (144 m) and No 238 R/G LC (144 m 57 ch) and then Bawtry

A view from the town showing Basildon station and the new road and bridge.

Emergency Crossover (148 m 55 ch). There were formerly stations along the same stretch at Barnby Moor, Ranskill, Scrooby and Bawtry, with watertroughs preceding the latter. The remains of most can still be spotted, along with the 'Edinburgh 250 Miles' sign.

On 7 August 1901 a Light Railway Order was granted to the Tickhill Light Railway which opened a single line from Bawtry to Haxey on 26 August 1912. The section to Misson carried agricultural and sand traffic and survived until 1964.

B.13 Bayford—see Hertford Loop

B.14 Beccles—see East Suffolk Line

B.15 Beighton Junction—see Chesterfield-Rotherham Line

B.16 Bellwater Junction—see Grantham-Skegness Line

B.17 Benfleet

Fenchurch Street-Shoeburyness line, between Pitsea and Southend. 29 m 11 ch from Fenchurch Street

Signed 'Benfleet for Canvey Island', the station lies on the edge of Benfleet Creek looking over a mixture of boats towards the flat expanse of Canvey Island. The main access to the 'island's' mixture of marshes, housing and tank farms is now via the raised A130 road over East Haven Creek but the earlier access road from South Benfleet passes beneath the station and runs parallel with the line before crossing to Canvey proper.

The LT&S route is raised at this point and the Up and Down platforms are linked by subway. The present station dates from the Midland period when it replaced the original which lay nearer London and was closed

on 10 December 1911. There are traditional buildings on either side and an off-peak service of two trains an hour via Tilbury and three via Upminster. To cater for the commuters of Canvey, South Benfleet and Thundersley some peak hour services run non-stop to Fenchurch Street taking 34 minutes compared with 52 minutes for the best services in LMS days.

B.18 Bentley

Liverpool Street-Norwich line, between Manningtree and Ipswich. 63 m 8 ch from Liverpool Street

Bentley closed to passengers on 7 November 1966, having lost its freight service a couple of years earlier. Now only the gated crossing remains active although some of the station buildings were still standing in 1985.

Bentley, in fact, became a junction quite early when the Eastern Union & Hadleigh Railway opened its line towards Lavenham in 1847 (for freight 21 August, passengers 2 September). This 7 m 3 ch single line ran via Capel (2 m) and Raydon Wood (5 m) and lost its passenger service as early as 29 February 1932, freight continuing until 19 April 1965. The site of the junction and the trackbed of the Hadleigh branch is just visible at TM 124 379.

B.19 Berney Arms

Reedham Junction to Yarmouth line. 15 m 71 ch from Norwich

In 1985 five trains each way daily still called at Berney Arms, a lonely, single platform station on the long straight single line linking Reedham and Yarmouth by way of the Reedham Marshes. While Broads holiday vessels pass along the River Yare nearby there is no road access to Berney Arms station and the Wednesday postman arrives by train and departs again after his long walk around the local farms. He has a 'Bearer Pass' and BR permission to walk along the line.

To all intents and purposes Berney Arms is the Reedham Junction to Yarmouth line for it serves no other station. Worked on Tokenless Block the 60 mph route commences at Reedham Junction (12 m 29 ch) and runs straight to the junction with the Acle line where the 19 m 32 ch distance via Berney Arms changes to 17 m 15 ch.

The line via Berney Arms was opened by the Yarmouth & Norwich Railway on 1 May 1844 but it declined in importance when the more direct link between Breydon Junction and Brundall Junction via Acle was opened on 1 June 1883. Despite this the lonely route and its station have clung to life despite closure threats dating back to 1850, protected by a condition in the original sale of the land and, in recent years, by awareness of the social needs of the isolated area they serve.

B.20 Bessacarr Junction---see Doncaster

B.21 Bethnal Green

Liverpool Street-Norwich line, junction with Kings Lynn line. 1 m 10 ch from Liverpool Street

Bethnal Green station came into existence on 24 May 1872 with the opening of the first part of the Enfield Town line. The Stratford line platforms went out of use in 1946 leaving just the Up island and the Down platform, elevated and showing the burden of their years, but enjoying an excellent service from trains on the Enfield Town, Cheshunt and Chingford lines.

At Bethnal Green (1 m 20 ch) the Up and Down Suburban lines and a pair from the Up and Down Main (which become the Fast lines to Hackney Downs) turn northwards, leaving the main and electric line pairs to continue towards Bow Junction. The rounded brick signal box lies between the diverging routes.

B.22 Bevercotes Colliery Branch—see High Marnham Branch

B.23 Biggleswade

East Coast main line, between Hitchin and Huntingdon. 41 m 13 ch from Kings Cross

One of several modest towns in a rich horticultural area of Bedfordshire, Biggleswade has retained its typical GNR station comprising two island platforms with footbridge to the ticket office block. At one time the latter also had a stable portion, a reminder of the dray services, and later lorries, provided for collecting produce for loading to the London and northern markets. In LNER and early BR days such traffic was considerable, demanding rapid loading, hectic labelling and invoicing and some smart yard working to make sure the fast freight services provided did not lose their main line paths despite growers bringing their loads in at the last possible moment.

Biggleswade also controlled a Down side public delivery siding at Langford. Before that lay Arlesey station, for long a bottleneck where the four-track section narrowed to two for the passage through the station and the scene of several mishaps including a serious one on 23 December 1876, the same year as the Abbots Ripton crash.

The London commuter influence declines rapidly north of Hitchin but Biggleswade has a good and increasing traffic potential at present catered for by the Hitchin-Huntingdon/Peterborough dmus. The station is preceded by R/G level crossings at East Road (39 m 34 ch) and Holme Green (40 m 6 ch) and followed by No 42 (42 m 10 ch).

B.24 Billericay—see Shenfield-Southend Line

B.25 Bilsthorpe Colliery Branch—see Clipstone-Mansfield Line

B.26 Bishopsgate Tunnel—see Liverpool Street

B.27 Bishops Stortford

Liverpool Street-Kings Lynn line. 30 m 27 ch from Liverpool Street

The Northern & Eastern trains reached Bishops Stortford on 16 May 1842 and were extended on to Brandon and Norwich on 30 July 1845. The station became a junction on 22 February 1869 with the opening of the cross-country route via Dunmow to Braintree. Never very busy, the latter lost its passenger services on 3 March 1952 with freight closure following in stages until the Bishops Stortford-Easton Lodge section finally closed down on 17 February 1972. The triangular junction north of Bishops Stortford is no longer apparent although the rising Up side course taken by the branch trains on their 42-minute journey via Hockerill Halt (1¼ m), Stane Street Halt (4 m), Takeley (5¼ m), Easton Lodge (7¾ m), Dunmow (9½ m), Felstead (11¾ m), Bannister Green Halt (13½ m) and

Views of the main station buildings on the Down side and of the Up side entrance at Bishops Stortford.

Rayne (15¾ m) can just be spotted.

Bishops Stortford enjoyed an upsurge in importance with the arrival of the electric services and it now deals with stops by main line trains on the Liverpool Street-Cambridge-Kings Lynn service, electric services from Liverpool Street (mostly via the Lea Valley line) and the dmus serving the intermediate stations northwards to Cambridge. The last two groups turn round at Bishops Stortford where the run-round crossovers enable Up electrics to reverse from the Down line to the outer face of the Up island which makes for easy connections with the Up Cambridge-Liverpool Street trains using its inner face. The dmus to and from Cambridge use the country end of the Up Passenger Loop.

The station's two platforms are staggered and linked by a modern footbridge with exits to London Road and to the main building block on the Down side. Original and in brick the latter has a central three-storey portion and a modernized ticket hall, contrasting with the traditional canopy and decorated spandrels.

From a trailing connection between the tall signal box (30 m 22 ch) and the London end of the Down platform there is a link to the coal concentration depot where the contents of bottom discharge wagons are conveyor elevated to hoppers standing in an arc. The station also has carriage sidings on the Up side at the London end.

B.28 Black Carr Junction—see Doncaster

B.29 Black Horse Road—see Upper Holloway-Barking Line

B.30 Blidworth—see Clipstone-Mansfield Line

B.31 Bolsover—see Chesterfield-Rotherham Line

B.32 Boston

Nottingham-Skegness line. 107 m 24 ch from Kings Cross

The single line from Hubberts Bridge becomes double on the approach to Boston and the mileage changes from 137 m 6 ch to 106 m 70 ch, a reminder that until the closure of the Spalding-Boston line the route from London was over the Great Northern's original Lincolnshire Loop. Contractors Peto and Betts had started work on this back in the spring of 1847, just after the East Lincolnshire Railway had let the contract for its line on from Boston to Louth. Throughout 1848 Boston's wharves were to be busy with ships bringing in pig iron and other materials for the new railways.

In view of its link on to Grimsby and from there to New Holland and Hull the Great Northern arranged to lease the East Lincolnshire enterprise. Trains started running on the route north of Louth on 1 March 1848 with attention then turned to the section south to Firsby and Boston. Following the provision of a wooden rail bridge across the Grand Sluice at Boston the first train, a load of 25 ballast wagons, actually entered the town in June 1848. Through public services to New Holland and Hull began with the 7.35 am departure on 25 September. The following month the Peterborough-Boston-Lincoln line was opened by the GNR on 17 October although it appears that the first portion of this may actually have carried trains a few weeks earlier.

Despite plans to extend the 1850 Nottingham-Grantham line eastwards this did not happen until 1859 when the Boston, Sleaford & Midland Counties extended from Sleaford to Boston on 12 April. The remaining railway at Boston was the corporation's line over a swing-bridge into the docks, which were opened on 15 December 1884.

Boston used to be a varied and busy railway centre. Fish and timber came in through the docks, all kinds of freight traffic passed through the goods depot (extended in 1903 when new livestock facilities were also provided) and the passenger services on the four radiating routes were supplemented by extra summer trains which gave the town through services to Kings Cross and the Midlands, thanks to the holiday trade at Skegness and Mablethorpe. The main Grimsby-London trains called at Boston and gave it a best timing to Kings Cross of just over two hours.

The facilities at Boston were extensive. In addition to the main station with its two through lines as well as the platform lines there was a locomotive depot at Broadfield Lane and a large goods depot near the junction with the docks line. The many typical railway ancillary activities included a sleeper depot, an engineers' depot, a sack store and a plant for extracting gas from oil. The evidence of some of these still remains.

Following the closure of the Woodhall-Boston section on 17 June 1963 the remaining East Lincolnshire lines secured a reprieve until the end of the decade but were then cut back to the present surviving line from Nottingham and Grantham to Skegness. This now serves Boston's function as a railhead for a large catchment area with dmu services to connect with the East Coast main line at Grantham and with Midlands services at Nottingham, through services along the GN&GE joint line to Lincoln and Doncaster and extra summer trains to Nottingham, Sheffield and Kings Cross.

On the approach to Boston from the Sleaford direction the gated level crossing at Wyberton (135 m 57 ch) is followed by a change from single to double line where the Spalding route formerly joined via Surfleet (96 m 74 ch), Algarkirk (100 m 54 ch), Kirton (103 m 38 ch) and Boston High Street box (106 m 29 ch). The old Goods South Junction was here, marked by a surviving siding area and shed, and the remains of the docks branch still joins the main route as the 106 m 70 ch via Spalding supersedes 137 m 6 ch via Grantham. Next Broadfield Lane level crossing (107 m) acts as a reminder of the former locomotive depot and of the fact that Boston was the Great Northern's locomotive headquarters until 1853. Some ornate buildings survive on the Down side before West Street Junction signal box and level crossing (107 m 14 ch) which is then followed by the station comprising Up and Down platforms with original main buildings on the former. The tower of the parish church, stunted and known as Boston Stump, can be seen on the town side of the station.

Leaving the station the double line becomes single at Grand Sluice Junction signal box (107 m 41 ch) and, after Tattershall Road AOCL crossing (107 m 69 ch), sets off on its flat, straight course towards Skegness. Just 20 chains beyond Grand Sluice lay East Lincoln Junction and signal box and the start of the route on to Lincoln via Hall Hills Creosoting Yard, Langrick (112 m 12 ch), Dogdyke (118 m 23 ch), Tattershall (119 m 16 ch), Kirkstead/

Woodhall Junction (122 m 65 ch)—for the Horncastle and Little Steeping lines—Stixwould (124 m 74 ch), Southrey (126 m 42 ch), Bardney (129 m 5 ch), Five Mile House (133 m 8 ch), Washingborough (135 m 63 ch) and Greetwell Junction (137 m 10 ch).

B.33   Bottesford—see   Grantham-Nottingham Line Line

B.34   Bottesford-Newark—see   Grantham-Nottingham Line

B.35   Bowes Park—see Hertford Loop

B.36   Bow Junction

Liverpool Street-Norwich line, junction with Fenchurch Street line. 2 m 69 ch from Liverpool Street

A 62 ch, 40 mph double line section links the LT&S line with the Norwich main line, leaving the former at Gas Factory Junction (2 m 57 ch) and joining the latter at 3 m 39 ch/2 m 69 ch. Controlled by Fenchurch Street panel the route no longer carries regular services and is used for emergency diversions and stock working but when it opened on 2 April 1849 it brought the 1840 London & Blackwall Railway's first link with the outside railway world and, as a consequence, its conversion from cable to locomotive haulage.

The Bow Junction title also applied to the point at which the link from the LT&S at Campbell Road joined the North London line, the course of which passes beneath the GE main line. On the latter between Bethnal Green and Bow Junction there were once stations at Mile End, Globe Road and Coborn Road (some platform remains just visible) and Up and Down goods depots at Mile End/Devonshire Street. The Down side location had a crane for the transfer of traffic from the Regents Canal and was subsequently an MAT ferry traffic terminal, the Up side being used for the hopper discharge of sand traffic.

From Bow Junction towards Stratford there are six running lines plus the A and B Carriage Roads which commence near the junction box.

B.37   Bradway Tunnel

Midland main line, between Chesterfield and Sheffield. 152 m 49 ch from St Pancras

To open its 1870 approach to Sheffield the Midland had to bring its route up the valley of the Drone and then drive a tunnel through to a descent via the valley of the

Sheaf. The result was the 1 m 266 yd Bradway Tunnel (152 m 49 ch to 153 m 61 ch) which immediately precedes the junction with the Hope Valley route from Manchester.

B.38   Braintree Branch

Liverpool Street-Norwich line, branch from Witham. 6 m 19 ch

From a rural line originally planned to feed the harbour at Maldon, the branch has passed through the steam, railbus and railcar eras to become an electrified commuter line making a worthwhile contribution to the modern railway network. The mixture of through trains (or part trains) to and from Liverpool Street and local workings to and from Witham has brought London within an hour's journey for the users of White Notley, Cressing and Braintree stations.

The line was originally conceived by the Maldon, Witham & Braintree Railway which had become part of the ECR before the two lines outwards from Witham were opened in 1848 (goods 15 August, passengers 2 October). Braintree got a new station with the extension to Bishops Stortford in 1869 when the old one became a goods yard which still deals with fertilizers to the UKF depot. Passenger services beyond Braintree were withdrawn on 3 March 1952 although the route westwards remained open as far as Felstead to serve the sugar beet factory there until 20 June 1970.

With a maximum speed of 50 mph, the route runs north-west along the course of the River Brain. There is a 10 mph speed limit through the sharp curve from the country end of Witham Down island platform opposite which stands the panel box (24 m 15 ch) which controls the whole route. The first station, White Notley (21 m 10 ch), has a short Up side platform with a wartime pillbox, gated crossing, control cabin and passenger shelter. Continuing on through gentle arable farmland the route then comes to Cressing (19 m 75 ch) which comprises Up side platform with a ticket office now incorporated in the modest period buildings and a gated level crossing. Unlike White Notley, rebuilt in 1977, and the modernized original at Cressing, Braintree is still a typical GE section station despite its four-car emu service. The main buildings on the Up side are in brick and of pleasant design with good decoration to the canopy columns. The former Down platform is no longer used.

Braintree is 17 m 76 ch from Bishops

Stortford and although no longer part of the through route is lucky to have survived 1963 closure plans. The station now serves a pleasant and interesting town which is also a good centre for exploring some of the most attractive Essex villages.

B.39 Brampton—see East Suffolk Line

B40   Brancliffe East Junction-Kirk Sandall Line

Freight-only link between Retford-Sheffield and Doncaster-Humberside lines. 20 m 52 ch

Essentially a coal traffic route, the section north from Brancliffe Junction to Thurcroft Colliery was originally a GC&Mid joint line while the Dinnington Junction-Kirk Sandall section was a South Yorkshire initiative. Following the opening of the 17½ miles of the latter for freight on 1 January 1909, a passenger service over the whole route was added on 1 December 1910 but the Saturdays-only GCR trains from Doncaster via Tickhill (6 m), Maltby (9¾ m), Dinnington & Laughton (14¼ m), Anston (16¾ m) and Shireoaks (19½ m) lasted only until 2 December 1929.

The 25 mph Permissive Block section to Thurcroft Sidings runs via Dinnington Colliery Junction (3 m 17 ch) and its connection to Dinnington Colliery, the signal box at Dinnington & Laughton Colliery Junction (3 m 29 ch) and Laughton East Junction (3 m 40 ch) with the portion on to Thurcroft (6 m 15 ch) being operated on the One Train basis.

From Laughton East Junction, the Electric Token single line for Kirk Sandall takes a very winding course via Maltby Colliery South (9 m 33 ch) to Firbeck West Junction (11 m 20 ch) where the Harworth

Colliery Branch departs at the triangular junction and the main route heads towards Doncaster.

The Harworth Colliery Branch runs from Firbeck West Junction (11 m 20 ch) via Firbeck Junction B signal box and south Junction (11 m 45 ch) to Harworth Colliery Junction (14 m 54 ch) and then 69 ch further along the former connection to the ECML near Scrooby. The link from the branch to Firbeck Colliery over the old Firbeck Light Railway closed in 1968.

On the main route after Firbeck Junction A box (11 m 30 ch) the two-direction crossing loop commences at Firbeck East Junction (11 m 41 ch) and the links to the ECML and the GN&GE joint line are made at St Catherine's Junction (15 m 17 ch) and Low Ellers Curve Junction (15 m 55 ch). On the final section around the east side of Doncaster the line passes the airport and racecourse sites and then Markham Sidings (17 m 69 ch). Track Circuit Block operates over this whole portion as far as Kirk Sandall Junction (20 m 52 ch).

B.41   Brandon

Birmingham-Norwich line, between Ely and Thetford. 86 m 32 ch from Liverpool Street

Brandon lies in the Breckland region near the Norfolk/Suffolk county boundary. It has heath and woodland on three sides and still cherishes the ancient art of flint knapping, a process of splitting flints to provide a smooth surface outwards when used for building. At Grimes Graves, some four miles from the station, are some remarkable pits where Stone Age man mined the flints in prehistoric times.

Brandon is also of some historic significance for the meeting there of the Eastern

Brandon enjoyed a brief moment of historic importance when the ECR and Norfolk Railway lines met there to complete the route from London to Norwich.

*A view of Brigg GCR, complete with overall roof (*Lens of Sutton*).*

Counties Railway's route from London via Ely and that of the Norfolk Railway from Norwich and Yarmouth. A constituent of the latter was the Norwich & Brandon Railway which was authorized in 1844 and then became part of the new through line in the following year with an opening ceremony on 29 July and the commencement of public services on the following day.

At first Brandon was a locomotive exchange point and then in later years it came to deal with a fair amount of freight and parcels business, handling commodities as diverse as timber and pit props from the yards adjoining the station to rabbit skins for dressing. In steam days it had through trains to and from the North as well as the Norwich portions of the Liverpool Street trains. Today the passenger facilities are maintained by the Ely-Norwich dmu services and by calls by the surviving Liverpool Street-Norwich trains.

The station has staggered platforms and follows the signal box and barrier crossing (86 m 25 ch). Appropriately, the main Down side buildings are of knapped flint, just a shelter being provided on the Up. The trackwork includes a Down Goods Loop and Up Refuge Siding and along the pleasant woodland section towards Thetford there are AHB crossings at Santon (88 m 72 ch) and Two Mile Bottom (91 m 16 ch).

B.42   Brentwood

Liverpool Street-Norwich line, between Romford and Shenfield. 18 m 16 ch from Liverpool Street

For the two miles preceding Brentwood the ruling gradient is 1 in 103 with the steepest part 1 in 99, quite a struggle for the heavy trains of steam days. For these the old LNER Appendix stipulated that 'the assisting engine must cease pushing at the 19¼ mile post' which marks the end of the climb up Brentwood Bank and was formerly the site of Ingrave box. In those days Brentwood had its own loco depot but today it functions just as a passenger station, important to the local community and its commuters and with a basic semi-fast service giving three trains an hour to Liverpool Street and taking thirty minutes on the journey.

The traditional station comprises centre island and two outer platforms with stairs up to the footbridge and ticket office. Enjoying slip coach facilities at one time, Brentwood had seen its first ECR trains arrive on 1 July 1840 but it then took nearly three years before the section on to Colchester was ready for traffic.

B.43   Brigg

Cleethorpes-Sheffield line, between Barnetby and Gainsborough. 91 m 1 ch from Manchester (London Road)

Brigg was the terminus of the MS&L line from Ulceby from 1 November 1848 until the extension to Gainsborough was made on 2 April 1850. In GCR days the Manchester-Cleethorpes trains called as part of their 3½ hour journey and some Sheffield-Cleethorpes dmu workings still provide a service for the modest township.

The approach from Wrawby Junction is by way of Kettleby LC (92 m 58 ch) and the wooden Brigg signal box and gated crossing (91 m 23 ch). Brigg station has Up and Down platforms with simple shelters and the station house survives, together with a dock, siding and some old 'B' type containers. Following the station the route curves and passes over the Old and New River Ancholme, the latter followed by Brigg Siding (89 m 64 ch) and the overgrown network of the BSC factory. The whole of this section from Wrawby Junction, through Brigg and the closed station at

Scawby and then on from Hibaldstow AHB LC (89 m 3 ch) and up the climb to Kirton Lime Sidings is to be singled.

B.44   Brightside—see Sheffield

B.45   Brimsdown

Liverpool Street-Kings Lynn line, between Tottenham and Broxbourne. 10 m 61 ch from Liverpool Street

The Brimsdown Lead Company, Enfield Cable Works and the Royal Small Arms Factory were just three of the many private sidings controlled by Brimsdown station which also had a busy goods yard until the end of the 1950s. Some of the old 1884 station buildings still remain but Brimsdown was remodelled in 1969 and today is essentially a new station with a barrier crossing and up-to-date ticket office. The half-hourly Hertford East trains call to cater for the commuters of the Lea Valley and for those using the leisure facility developments of recent years.

B.46   Brocklesby

Cleethorpes-Sheffield line, junction with Barton-on-Humber branch. 99 m 33 ch from Manchester (London Road)

The railway came to Brocklesby on 1 November 1848 and the station was enlarged forty years later when the MS&L started running its trains to and from Grimsby instead of New Holland and required passengers for the latter to change trains. Despite these alterations the original station buildings have survived, their gabled style and ornate chimneys a reminder that the MS&L's chairman lived at nearby Brocklesby Hall and would not have wanted anything sub-standard for his local station.

Today the two-car dmus of the local Doncaster-Cleethorpes service call at Brocklesby, approaching over a four-track section from Barnetby, Track Circuit Block and Permissive working applying on the two goods lines. The signal box stands at the country end of the Up platform which is then followed by Brocklesby Junction (99 m 39 ch) where one set of double tracks heads north towards Ulceby South Junction (100 m 31 ch) and another continues to Habrough Junction (101 m 13 ch) and Cleethorpes, the former being used by freight trains to and from Immingham.

B.47   Brookmans Park

East Coast main line, between Potters Bar and Hatfield. 14 m 37 ch from Kings Cross

This simple, two-island platform station derives an excellent twenty-minute service from the Moorgate-Welwyn Garden City emus, extra trains running during the peaks. Off the Down Slow towards Hatfield is the Marshmoor Siding connection for Kelloggs traffic and there is an obelisk on the Up side to the south of the station.

B.48   Broughton—see Chesterfield-Rotherham Line

B.49 Broxbourne

Liverpool Street-Kings Lynn line, junction for Hertford East branch. 17 m 17 ch from Liverpool Street

Broxbourne was reached by the Northern & Eastern from Stratford on 15 September 1840. Three years later the Hertford branch was opened and by 1845, before many towns had got a railway at all, Broxbourne was an important stop on the new through route to Norwich.

Apart from a three-legged bridge on the approach to the station most of the other signs of the past were wiped away in the rebuilding which accompanied the North East London electrification. This gave Broxbourne a new ticket hall and passenger concourse with footbridge access to the two island platforms which cater for local passengers and those changing between the Hertford East and Lea Valley services. The administrative offices, power box (17 m 24 ch) and the Charringtons coal concentration depot stand beside the Down Loop and an old siding area beyond the Up Loop, the latter recalling Broxbourne's former freight business which included coal to the power station located to the north of the station. The station used to handle a great deal of produce from the Lea Valley nurseries.

Beyond the overgrown sidings of the power station comes Broxbourne Junction LC (18 m 24 ch) and then the junction (18 m 35 ch) itself, where the Hertford East trains leave the main line.

There are basic half-hourly services from Liverpool Street via Broxbourne to Bishops Stortford and Hertford East, the slower Hertford services being overtaken by the Bishops Stortford trains at Broxbourne where across-platform interchange takes place.

B.50   Bruce Grove—see Enfield Town Branch

B.51   Brundall—see Norwich-Yarmouth Line

B.52 Brundall Gardens—see Norwich-Yarmouth Line

B.53 Brundall Junction-Lowestoft Line

Branch from Norwich-Yarmouth line. 17 m 60 ch

The section of the Eastern Region's 'Wherry Line' from Reedham to Norwich was part of the line opened from Yarmouth on 1 May 1844, the year which saw the emergence of the Lowestoft Railway & Harbour scheme. Under Norfolk Railway auspices the latter produced the Reedham-Lowestoft line which opened for goods traffic on 3 May 1847 and to passengers on 1 July. In the following year the two lines became part of the growing Eastern Counties Railway empire.

Today's dmus take 45 minutes for the 23½ mile journey from Norwich to Lowestoft compared with the 56 minutes (48 minutes limited stop) of Great Eastern days. They part company with the Acle line at Brundall Junction (5 m 71 ch from Norwich) and continue along the course of the River Yare through Strumpshaw LC (7 m 11 ch) to Buckenham (7 m 65 ch). A traditional gated crossing separates the station's staggered platforms, only parts of which are now in use. The Down side signal box is also closed.

At the next station, Cantley (10 m 4 ch), there is another LC and also a sombre station house. The station is used by workers at the BSC factory which lies between the railway and the river and has an extensive rail network with 0-6-0 diesel locomotive and rail mounted crane. Ferry van and Speedlink traffic is dealt with via the BSC Sidings Ground Frame.

The route now cuts across the neck of a long bend in the Yare to come to Reedham and a view to the south of Reedham Ferry, the only road vehicle crossing between Norwich and Yarmouth. The station (10 m 4 ch) used to have a considerable trade in game and poultry and the former station house and ticket office stand on the Up side, to a pleasant gabled design in red brick with stone facings. There is a URS between the station overbridge and one near the signal box at Reedham Junction (12 m 29 ch) where the single line to Yarmouth via Berney Arms departs. The route then curves sharply south to cross the Yare by means of a swing-bridge controlled by Reedham Swing-Bridge signal box (13 m 6 ch) and displaying the time-honoured 'Bridge Will Open' board.

In the days of Norfolk's trading wherries Reedham swing-bridge would open often

for river traffic but few working vessels now come up the Yare and even fewer use the New Cut, a part of Peto's 1833 Norwich & Lowestoft Navigation and linking the Yare with the Waveney. The railway runs beside the New Cut which in summer is alive with Broads yachts and hire cruisers all, presumably, heeding the 5 mph signs. Near where the 1960 road bridge now crosses the New Cut is the site of an old BR dock and opposite this area a railwayman used to stand with a long net on the end of a pole to collect dues for using the Cut.

Haddiscoe (16 m 15 ch) has a long Down platform with cottages behind and a short Up platform. At the country end are the abutments of the bridge which carried Yarmouth & Haddiscoe Railway's line from 1 June 1859 until its closure on 2 November 1959. Part of the Y&H scheme was a spur from the Beccles direction towards Reedham, another from Yarmouth towards Lowestoft being laid in 1872 and used by a passenger service until 1903. In the following year the original station on the low level line was replaced by the present location near the high level route and became a goods depot, the old Herringfleet Exchange station being remodelled and renamed Haddiscoe High Level at the same time. Beyond it can be seen the piers of the former swing-bridge and to the south there is a portion of the route to Beccles which had been kept in use as a siding for sugar beet as far as Aldeby for some five years after the passenger closure.

The Lowestoft line is now running along the south bank of the Waveney, a long viaduct heralding the crossing of the river by means of Somerleyton Swing-Bridge (17 m 60 ch). Half a mile beyond the signal box comes Somerleyton proper (18 m) where the station is a grander version of the one at Reedham, as was only fitting for the station which served Peto's own house and village on the edge of Somerleyton Park to the north.

Across Somerleyton Marshes the railway provides a good view of the restored Herringfleet Mill and then of Suffolk's Oulton Church and Norfolk's Burgh St Peter Church, both with unusual towers. The route turns east to come to Oulton Broad North (22 m 5 ch) which comprises signal box, barrier crossing, Up and Down platforms and station buildings in the style of the line and now housing a gift shop. The station, which is quite near Oulton Broad itself, is followed by Oulton Broad North Junction (22 m 17 ch) where the Beccles line trails in for the remaining stretch to Lowestoft (23 m 41 ch).

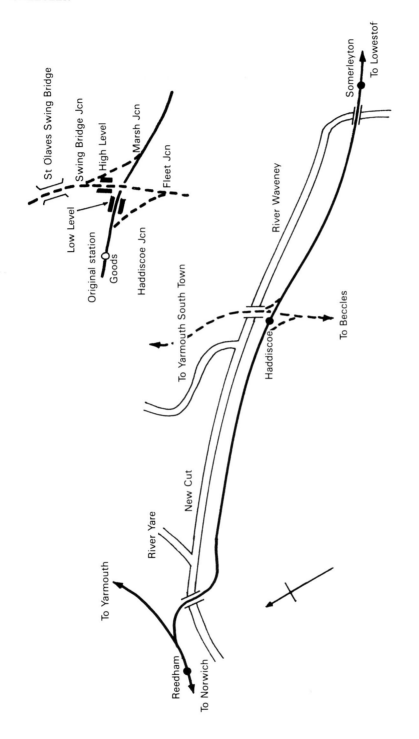

B.54 Buckenham—see Brundall Junction-Lowestoft Line

B.55 Bures—see Sudbury Branch

B.56 Burnham-on-Crouch—see Southminster Branch

B.57 Bury St Edmunds

Cambridge-Ipswich line, between Newmarket and Haughley Junction. 28 m 44 ch from Coldham Lane Junction

Not only did the Ipswich & Bury Railway construct the line whose first passengers reached Bury St Edmunds on Christmas Eve 1846 (freight on 30 November) but its architect, Frederick Barnes, built some fine stations including the one at Bury St Edmunds itself. Its most distinctive features are the two domed towers, one forming part of the arched frontage complete with Tudor-style house and ornate gables.

The link between Bury and Newmarket was completed on 1 April 1854, followed by the single line branch to Long Melford on 9 August 1865 and another to Thetford on 1 March 1876. In addition to the main Cambridge-Ipswich services, taking 2 hours 16 minutes for all-stations trains and 1 hour 45 minutes for a semi-fast, the traveller of Great Eastern days could make some interesting south-north journeys via Bury. Leaving Colchester at 8.44 am, for example, he could travel via the Sudbury branch to Long Melford (19¾ m) and then on via Lavenham (25 m), Cockfield (28½ m) and Welnetham (31½ m) to Bury (36¼ m). Arriving at 10.36 am there was then a connection forward to Thetford at 10.42 via Ingham (3¾ m), Barnham (9¼ m) and Thetford Bridge (11¾ m) which arrived at 11.10 am, in good time to catch the 11.42 am on to Swaffham and, eventually, Kings Lynn. A lot of freight workings to and from the North used to pass via Bury and it was quite a busy spot until the branch passenger services were withdrawn, on the Thetford line on 9 June 1953 and to Long Melford on 10 April 1961.

Although Bury St Edmunds no longer has the benefit of a portion of 'The Fenman' to give a through Liverpool Street service, it does enjoy a number of through services (including 'The European') and it has good connections at Cambridge and Ipswich off its local dmus. The elevated station is slimmed down these days but retains a goods yard, engineers yard and grain terminal. There are two signal boxes, Bury St Edmunds Yard (28 m 33 ch) and Bury St Edmunds Junction (28 m 60 ch), the latter between the station and the former BSC factory connection, where the two branches used to diverge.

B.58 Bury Street Junction—see Enfield Town Branch

B.59 Bush Hill Park—see Enfield Town Branch

C.1 Cambridge

Liverpool Street-Kings Lynn line, interchange point for Hitchin and Newmarket routes. 55 m 52 ch from Liverpool Street

In addition to today's routes Cambridge used also to have services to Bedford/Bletchley, via Haverhill, to Huntingdon/Kettering, to Ely via St Ives and on the Mildenhall branch. This great variety meant that there was always something of interest to see, engines from GN, GE, LNW and Midland stables, rolling stock from every corner of the main line system and a continuous activity in all the railway operating spheres—stock movements, signalling, goods traffic and so on. Even as late as June 1952 a typical day saw on the shed 'B17/1' 61623, *Lambton Castle;* 'J15' 65477; 'J17' 65512; 'J69' 68530; 'J19/2' 64646; 'B17/1' 61604, *Elvedon* and 'D16' 62618.

The long, single main platform at Cambridge showing the central double crossover.

GAZETEER

Cambridge was to have been a focal point on the Northern & Eastern Railway's trunk route to the North and it did become part of the growing railway system quite early with the opening of the Eastern Counties Railway's route to Norwich on 30 July 1845. The area then became the centre of a number of rival ambitions for new lines which might have seen the Royston & Hitchin extending to meet the Newmarket Railway's 1848 link from Great Chesterford to Newmarket with an extension forward to the Norfolk Railway at Thetford. However, the Newmarket enterprise was eventually overpowered by the ECR and its line south of Six Mile Bottom was closed when the connection from that point to Cambridge was brought into use on 9 October 1851. The link on to Bury St Edmunds and Ipswich was opened on 1 April 1854.

The opening of the main line in 1845 was followed two years later by the line from Chesterton Junction to St Ives which reached the latter point, together with the Ely & Huntingdon line, on 17 August 1847. Extension to March came in the following year and from 1866 Midland trains started to work to Cambridge via St Ives, the route eventually being used for through excursion trains via Colchester to Clacton.

The ECR system at Cambridge was linked with the Royston & Hitchin line from 1 April 1852. The arrival of LNWR trains over the Bedford & Cambridge route from Sandy ten years later (passenger services 7 July) gave the GNR the possibility of access to Cambridge this way and this helped in the tortuous process which eventually brought a Great Northern take-over of the ECR's lease of the Royston & Hitchin and full GN access to Cambridge.

Cambridge was linked with the local lines to the south-east when the Great Eastern branch to Haverhill opened on 1 June 1865. Twenty years later trains were also running out to Mildenhall when the 2 June 1884 branch to Fordham was extended on. In the 1930s this branch carried only four trains each way daily, taking 54 minutes to cover the 20¾ miles and calling at Barnwell (1½ m), Fen Ditton Halt (2½ m), Quy (4½ m), Bottisham & Lode (6 m), Swaffhamprior (8 m), Burwell (10 m), Exning Road Halt (10¾ m), Fordham (13½ m), Isleham (16¾ m) and Worlington Golf Links Halt (20 m).

Passenger services from Cambridge to Mildenhall were withdrawn on 18 June 1962, to the Colchester line on 6 March 1967, to Bedford on 1 January 1968 and to St Ives on 5 October 1970.

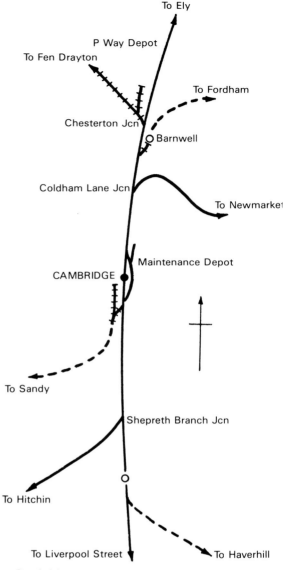

Cambridge has changed from being a traditional railway centre to being a modern one and one of the most significant dates in this process was 30 April 1981 when the modern panel box took over the whole area bounded by Ely, Royston, Bishops Stortford and Fulbourne. The new panel replaced traditional signal boxes including the old Cambridge North and South boxes which had themselves been ahead of their time when commissioned in 1926. The station ticket hall has been modernized but the station proper remains much as originally built with a long single platform and a round arch *porte-cochère* with fifteen bays fronting the main block and the work of either Sancton Wood or Francis

Above *Local dmu sets wait at Cambridge before working forward to Bishops Stortford and Royston.*
Below *The country end of Cambridge station.*

Thompson. Outside there are bus interchange facilities.

On the approach to Cambridge from the south two of the previous four routes survive and are united at Shepreth Branch Junction (53 m 4 ch) but trains no longer arrive from Bletchley and Colchester and the station's London end bays are quite adequate for the Bishops Stortford and Royston dmus using them. The latter provide a link with the Kings Cross suburban electric service but are not quite in the same class as the former 'Cambridge Buffet Car Express' trains. Developed from the first Great Northern through expresses to Cambridge of 1897, by the late 1930s and under the label 'Garden Cities and Cambridge Buffet Express' these were providing five daily workings each way with a best time of 72 minutes for the 58 miles via Hitchin. The buffet car services to London are now concentrated on the former Great Eastern

route and give a basic hourly service with a best time of 62 minutes.

The old LNW approach to Cambridge is now part of the access to a Charrington oil terminal and coal concentration depot, with the new panel box also situated on the Down side. The latter makes light work of the two-way working and central crossover complex of the single 1,200 ft platform although the old Appendix instruction preventing trains setting back without proper authority remains in the modern BR working instructions as it existed in the LNER Appendix. East of the station are the through line, freight yard and the old goods area where demolition began in 1984.

North of Cambridge lie the carriage servicing area and then Coldham Lane diesel maintenance depot which from September 1958 took over the traction operations formerly scattered over the whole area. The Newmarket line then leaves at Coldham

Lane Junction (56 m 24 ch) followed, 63 ch on, by the site of Barnwell Junction where the Mildenhall branch connection is now part of the link to a small oil depot and a camping coach still stands adjacent to the old Barnwell station.

The principal services leaving Cambridge from the north end of the main platform are for Kings Lynn and from the adjacent bays are the services for Ipswich and Peterborough, although some of the latter are extended on to Birmingham or the GN&GE joint line.

C.2   Cambridge Heath

Enfield Town and Chingford lines, between Bethnal Green and Hackney Downs. 1 m 61 ch from Liverpool Street

This station, once the way the garment makers of the area got to and from work, was opened with the line in 1872 and closed for a period of three years from 1916 to 1919. With elevated platforms to the suburban pair of lines only, it is served by the Enfield Town and Chingford trains.

C.3   Canning Town—see North Woolwich Branch

C.4   Canonbury Junction-Finsbury Park Line

Link between East Coast main line and former North London Line. 1 m 22 ch

After opening at the end of the previous year North London trains began providing passenger services over this GN spur from 18 January 1875. For some twenty years after the Second World War it was used as a route for Eastern Region services to and from Broad Street but this came to an end

The tide is high as an Up Fenchurch Street train passes between Chalkwell and Leigh-on-Sea.

with the development of the Moorgate line electric service. From Canonbury Junction (3 m 11 ch) the 30 mph double line, still in existence in 1984 but little used, passes through the 545 yd Canonbury Tunnel (3 m 21 ch to 3 m 45 ch) and becomes single before splitting again to rise either side of the ECML at Finsbury Park (4 m 33 ch).

C.5   Cantley—see Brundall Junction-Lowestoft Line

C.6   Carlton

East Coast main line, between Newark and Retford. 126 m 25 ch from Kings Cross

This former station lies on a level section of the main line as it uses the Trent valley north of Newark. Nowadays it is significant just for the CCTV crossings at Norwell Lane (123 m 38 ch) and Cromwell (124 m 55 ch), for Carlton LC (126 m 25 ch), the adjacent Up and Down passenger loops and old signal box, for the emergency crossover (126 m 32 ch) and then for R/G pedestrian crossings at Eaves Lane (127 m 2 ch) and No 195 (127 m 8 ch). The former Crow Park station, Grassington Lane LC (128 m 30 ch) and Egmanton CCTV LC (130 m 29 ch) follow as the line starts its 1 in 200 rise to Tuxford.

C.7   Chadwell Heath

Liverpool Street-Norwich line, between Ilford and Romford. 9 m 79 ch from Liverpool Street

The station comprises three platforms with four faces to the main and electric track pairs and stairs up to the footbridge and ticket office. Speed restrictions of 25 and 30 mph apply through the facing crossovers which lie on the Romford side.

The present station dates from the turn of the century when it replaced an 1864 predecessor. The Liverpool Street-Gidea Park all-stations trains give it a basic 20-minute service.

C.8   Chalkwell

*Fenchurch   Street-Shoeburyness   line,
between Leigh-on-Sea and Southend Central. 34 m 2 ch from Fenchurch Street*

This western area of the Borough of
Southend grew rapidly in the early years of
this century and the estates of that period
are still apparent from the railway. The
present station, exhibiting many signs of
the 1930s, caters for a large residential area
and the adjacent seafront with large numbers of passengers making both local journeys and longer trips to and from London.
There is an excellent basic service of four
Shoeburyness trains each hour plus two via
Tilbury, the fastest bringing Fenchurch
Street within 42 minutes journey time.

C.9   Chappel & Wakes Colne—see Sudbury Branch

C.10   Chelmsford

*Liverpool Street-Norwich line. 29 m 65 ch
from Liverpool Street*

Chelmsford got its first passenger trains on
19 March 1843 before the Eastern Counties
Railway lapsed into temporary exhaustion
after reaching Colchester. Over the next
100 years the railway contributed much to
the growth of the county and market town
with a new station in 1856, slip coaches in
1872, a GER bus service from 1905 and
considerable freight activity, including
private sidings for the electrical and
mechanical engineering activities of the
town. The progress continued with the
extension of overhead electrification from
Shenfield on 11 June 1956. The most recent
development is a £1 million remodelling
scheme for the station and its travel centre.

The Eastern Region main line to Norwich
takes a high level course through Chelmsford, crossing the river and then continuing
through the station's elevated Up and
Down platforms by means of a powerful
Victorian brick viaduct. Beyond the
modern station, near the site of the original
island platform, is the incline (limited to 15
SLUs) which leads down to the Down side
Lower Yard where the traditional bustle of
goods wagons and cartage vehicles has now
been replaced by use for Railfreight high
capacity wagons plus some remaining coal
traffic. There are Up and Down Goods
Loops.

Around 16,000 passengers use Chelmsford daily, encouraged by the fast Clacton
electrics which put Liverpool Street only 34
minutes away and by the service to inter-

mediate stations provided by the Braintree
and Colchester trains.

C.11   Cheshunt

*Liverpool Street-Kings Lynn line, junction
with Churchbury Loop. 14 m 1 ch from
Liverpool Street*

The original Northern & Eastern station at
Cheshunt dated from 31 May 1846 but this
was replaced in 1891. Further remodelling
in 1970 produced the present station which
comprises two platforms plus Down side
bay and with a modern ticket office 'cell'
capsule within a glazed circulating area.

The Churchbury Loop, opened first in
1909 and again in 1915 and 1960, joins the
main line at Cheshunt Junction (13 m 71 ch)
with its trains then running into the bay
under the control of the traditional London
end signal box, complete with decorative
barge boards. There is a CCTV crossing at
the country end of the station, with Slipe
Lane LC (15 m 62 ch) following.

Instead of the former steam trains picking up passengers plus packages of Lea
Valley greenhouse produce, Cheshunt now
has an excellent emu service. It turns round
two trains an hour via Southbury, the Up
departures leaving after calls by an Up Fast
from Bishops Stortford and an Up Slow
from Hertford East. Both of these are
routed via the Lea Valley, with the former
calling just at Tottenham Hale and taking
21 minutes to Liverpool Street.

C.12   Chesterfield

*Midland main line. 146 m 20 ch from St
Pancras*

Chesterfield's famous crooked spire is visible to the thousands of rail travellers who
use or pass through Chesterfield either on
the former Midland Railway's main line
from London to Sheffield or on the cross-
country trains of the North-East:South-
West route. HST sets have now brought
Chesterfield within 2 hours 19 minutes of St
Pancras—compared with the 2 hours 47
minutes achieved by the 'Thames-Forth
Express' in 1938—and the station also
enjoys a call by 'The European', as well as
its links to all the main cities between Ply-
mouth and Newcastle.

In 1938, of course, Chesterfield also had
local and London services via Nottingham,
and LMS services to Mansfield via Staveley
and to Sheffield over the original 1840 route
via Rotherham. The LNER had inherited
from the Great Central the service to and
from Lincoln which commenced at Chesterfield's Market Place terminus and then

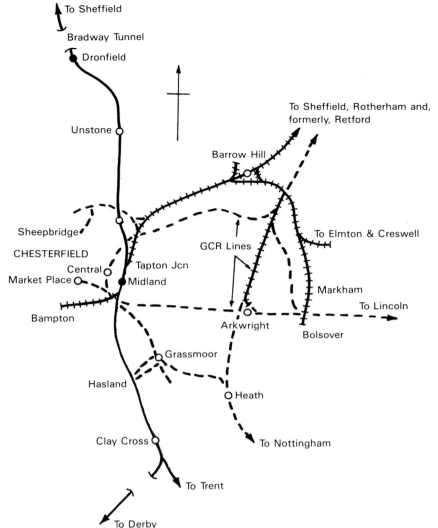

To Sheffield

Bradway Tunnel

Dronfield

Unstone

To Sheffield, Rotherham and,
formerly, Retford

Barrow Hill

Sheepbridge

CHESTERFIELD

GCR Lines

To Elmton & Creswell

Central

Tapton Jcn

Market Place

Midland

Markham

To Lincoln

Bampton

Arkwright

Bolsover

Grassmoor

Hasland

Heath

Clay Cross

To Nottingham

To Trent

To Derby

ran via Arkwright Town (3¼ m), Bolsover (5¾ m), Scarcliffe (8 m), Shirebrook North (9¾ m), Warsop (12¼ m), Edwinstowe (16¼ m), Ollerton (18¼ m), Boughton (20¾ m), Tuxford Central (24 m), Dukeries Junction (25 m), Fledborough (28¼ m), Clifton-on-Trent (30 m), Doddington & Harby (33¼ m) and Skellingthorpe (36¼ m) to Lincoln (39½ m). On the ex-GC main line there was a local service between Sheffield and Nottingham via Chesterfield and the latter also enjoyed through coaches from the South Coast as well as links eastwards as far as Cleethorpes.

The original North Midlands Railway route from Derby via Chesterfield to Rotherham had been opened on 11 May 1840 and the direct approach to Sheffield followed thirty years later. Chesterfield's first MS&L service began on 4 June 1892

with the loop to Heath being completed in the following year. Four years later the LD&ECR's Lincoln line was opened but became part of the Great Central in 1907. The latter finally ceased operation on 19 September 1955 (after Market Place station had closed in 1951), Chesterfield then losing the GC Central station on 4 March 1963, although both continued to deal with goods traffic for some time longer. Chesterfield did, in fact, have a significant freight activity with a number of private sidings, several off the Brampton goods branch.

On the Midland main line the Eastern Region takes over at Horns Bridge. Then comes Hasland Sidings (143 m 32 ch) where the Trent box hands over to the Sheffield panel and once the starting point for lines to Grassmoor. The two main lines are accompanied by TCB goods lines through the station as far as Tapton Junction (146 m 59 ch) where some siding connections remain and the 1840 route via Barrow Hill departs. The station itself, moved slightly north in a rebuilding in 1870, was modernized in the mid-1960s.

C.13 Chesterfield-Rotherham Line

From the Midland main line at Tapton Junction to Masborough Station Junctions at Rotherham. 15 m 45 ch

To secure the easiest gradients the North Midland Railway's 1840 line from Derby bypassed Sheffield to the east and took the Rother Valley route to Rotherham from whence a connection was provided to Sheffield Wicker via the 1838 line of the Sheffield & Rotherham Railway. The Great Central main line later became a companion route from Staveley northwards and places like Eckington & Renishaw enjoyed a Sheffield-Rotherham service on both.

Today the original main line acts as a diversionary passenger route to Sheffield via Beighton Junction and Woodhouse and also as a through route for freight. It is also of considerable importance as the access to the network of coal traffic lines which lie east of Barrow Hill.

The route commences at Tapton Junction (146 m 59 ch) immediately north of Chesterfield and, until relatively recently, had connections here to a number of sidings, including the Sheepbridge complex. Now, however, it heads straight for Barrow Hill South (148 m 76 ch) and the Barrow Hill locomotive depot and sidings.

On the Rotherham line Barrow Hill North Junction (149 m 46 ch) and Foxlow Junction (150 m 64 ch) form the base of a triangle which has Hall Lane Junction (150 m 56 ch) as its eastern apex. Beyond the latter is the new connection to the One Train line to Arkwright Colliery which allowed the closure of the old GC line via Renishaw. Further east comes Seymour Junction (152 m 20 ch/155 m 6 ch) where the route divides into the Bolsover Colliery Line (Seymour Junction 7 m 61 ch, Markham Colliery Junction 7 m 5 ch, Markham Colliery Sidings 7 m and Bolsover 5 m 21 ch) and the Electric Token single line to Elmton & Creswell Junction (149 m 37 ch) via Oxcroft Junction GF (154 m 15 ch) and its one-mile, One Train branch to Oxcroft Opencast Colliery.

Back on the 1840 line, Renishaw Park

Colliery stands on the Down side and then comes Beighton Junction (155 m 47 ch) where the One Train 3 m 21 ch single line Westhorpe Colliery Branch joins and the diversionary route turns west via Woodhouse and Darnall to Sheffield. Most of the Chesterfield-Rotherham line is on the Sheffield panel but there are signal boxes at Beighton Junction and then at Treeton South (158 m 35 ch) and Treeton Junction (158 m 62 ch). The former stands adjacent to Orgreave Colliery and Coking Plant and the latter controls the triangular junction (Treeton S Junction 158 m 65 ch and N Junction 159 m 19 ch) which leads to Tinsley Yard and Brightside. On north from Canklow Goods Junction (160 m 6 ch) via the BSC connection at Masborough Sorting Sidings South Junction (160 m 61 ch) to Masborough Station South Junction (161 m 73 ch), Rotherham (162 m) and Masborough Station North Junction (162 m 24 ch) the control of the route is back on the Sheffield panel.

C.14 Chingford Branch

Liverpool Street-Kings Lynn line, branch from Clapton Junction. 5 m 75 ch

This double-line electrified London suburban commuter line leaves the Cambridge main line, crosses Walthamstow Marshes to Walthamstow proper and then curves sharply north to Chingford and the edge of Epping Forest. The sharp curve is a surviving reminder that the route was built in two halves, just as the 'through station' design of the terminus at Chingford is evidence of the plans that once existed to extend the line on to High Beech.

There were several early schemes for serving Walthamstow and the areas beyond but nothing happened until the Great Eastern Railway entered its first expansion period. Then, after some equivocation, a spur was opened from Lea Bridge to Shern Hall Street, Walthamstow and started carrying a passenger service from 26 April 1870, despite the fact that the Parliamentary proceedings for the acquisition of land had not then been completed.

On 22 June 1872 the line from Hackney Downs to Copper Mill Junction was opened plus a connection from Clapton Junction to Hall Farm Junction to link up with the 1870 line. The extension on to Chingford came into use on 17 November 1873 and the single line was doubled five years later. In the early years Epping Forest excursion traffic was as important as the commuter business but now the latter is the main feature of the route which became all-electric on 21 November 1960.

Clapton Junction (4 m 38 ch), where the Cambridge direction trains leave the Chingford route to join the Lea Valley line, follows a crossing of the River Lea by a single span steel bridge. The branch continues across Walthamstow Marshes, over the old main line from Tottenham Hale to Stratford and then past the sites of Hall Farm East and West Junctions where the spurs from the Tottenham and then the Lea Bridge direction joined. The former was used by Chingford-Gospel Oak services and the latter survived to be electrified but was abandoned seven years after.

Past the water filtration beds and over a flood relief channel the Chingford branch takes an elevated course to St James Street (5 m 55 ch) where the station was given wooden extensions at the country end to cope with the nine-car electric sets and had a complete building reconstruction in 1973-4. From a modern version of the old LNER 'Passimeter' type of ticket office stairs rise to the simplified waiting and staff accommodation on the platforms.

On the section on to Walthamstow Central (6 m 16 ch) the branch passes over the Tottenham & Hampstead line and the latter's Queens Road station can be seen to the south. Central deserves its change of name from a former Hoe Street suffix and has substantial brick buildings, direct links with the LT Victoria Line services to and from Brixton and an interchange facility with LT bus services. The goods yard, closed to public traffic on 2 November 1964 and now a car park, had a siding connection to the power station beyond.

A 1 in 78 gradient leads through a cutting, where one of the overbridges collapsed in 1978, to the 71 yd Hoe Street Tunnel (6 m 49 ch to 6 m 52 ch) and then over Shernhall Street where the old station was closed on 17 November 1873 when the route was extended and curved round to the present Wood Street (7 m 7 ch). This was quite an important station at one time with some services starting and terminating, a rake of carriage sidings for train stabling and an engine shed and controlling signal box at the country end. The station was modified in the 1973-4 reconstruction period and provided with a combination of canopy and separate waiting units beneath.

The route now heads north past the old Wood Street locomotive depot site, over the modest River Ching, across the barrier LC (8 m 45 ch) preceding Highams Park

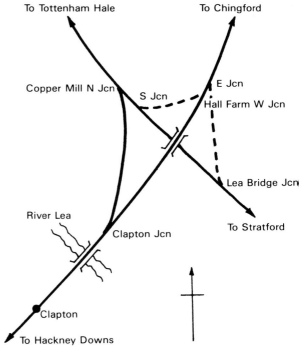

and into the station itself (8 m 52 ch). Variously named Highams Park, Hale End or both, the present single-storey buildings on the Up side date from 1900 and the subway from 1909. The Up side signal box now controls only the crossing but at one time also embraced the goods yard which stands overgrown and unused behind the Down platform.

On the approach to Chingford four carriage sidings descend towards the connection with the Down line and a parallel line with washer installation. This is followed by a further group of six sidings, also equipped with raised walkways and controlled by the 1920s Up side signal box (10 m 17 ch). This group terminates in the dock area behind Chingford station (10 m 33 ch) Down platform.

The original wooden Chingford Green station was near the Kings Road bridge about half a mile in advance of the present site and was broadly marked until the 1970s by the signal box controlling the old Down side goods yard. The present site dates from 1878 and the station was built with an extension of the line to High Beech in mind. Until the Up bay track was removed in 1971 the layout was that of two through platform faces, each with a bay. In fact, the through lines led only to the engine coaling and watering area, and since electrification the two platforms have been connected behind the buffer stops and surviving engine release ground frame. The main buildings, two-storey, substantial and in red brick, are on the Down side.

The branch service pre-war enjoyed a timetable description 'at frequent intervals throughout the day', the first train leaving Wood Street at 02.06 hours and the last train getting back to Chingford at 01.06. On Sundays trains from the North Woolwich line brought hundreds to enjoy a day away from the docks amid the greenery of Epping Forest. The branch journey time was 31 minutes compared with the 24 minutes of 1985's basic twenty-minute emu service. Class '315' sets made their appearance on the branch in 1984.

C.15   Chippenham Junction

Cambridge-Ipswich line, junction with Ely line. 16 m 4 ch from Coldham Lane Junction, Cambridge

At Chippenham Junction the line opened between Bury St Edmunds and Newmarket on 1 April 1854 becomes single for its eastward passage through Warren Hill Tunnel. The later route, that opened to Ely on 1 September 1879, continues double as far as Soham. Chippenham Junction signal box stands at the junction itself and used to have a companion at Snailwell Junction, towards Ely and where the former spur from Warren Hill Junction (15 m 22 ch) joined at a point recorded as 1 m 56 ch from Newmarket Old Station.

C.16   Churchbury Loop

Link from Bury St Junction, Enfield Town Branch to Liverpool Street-Kings Lynn line at Cheshunt. 5 m 8 ch

When the Great Eastern Railway opened the line on 1 October 1891 it provided an excellent service of 24 trains a day calling at Churchbury, Forty Hill and Theobalds Grove but the route fell victim to the Waltham Cross tramway and was closed on 1 October 1909. A second opening came on 1 March 1915 when a 'Y65' Class 'Crystal Palace' tank was put on with two coaches to operate a push-and-pull service for munition workers. On 2 July 1920 the line was closed to passengers for the second time, the Down line continuing in use for freight with the Up used for wagon storage.

A new lease of life began with the establishment of a depot at Carterhatch Lane for the North-East London electrification and the line itself got its third opening in November 1960 with the stations more appropriately named Southbury, Turkey Street and Theobalds Grove. These are now served by the half-hourly Liverpool Street-Cheshunt emus.

The route commences at Bury Street Junction (9 m 20 ch from Liverpool Street) and is double throughout. Southbury (10 m 32 ch) used to have a sizeable freight activity but now comprises just the ticket office on the overbridge with substantial platforms below. There are several more overbridges on the section on to Turkey Street (12 m 16 ch) where the platforms are elevated above the small ticket office with its highly pretentious chimney stack. After Park Lane LC (13 m 18 ch) comes the third station, Theobalds Grove (13 m 45 ch), with high platforms and substantial but careworn buildings on the Up side. Carterhatch Lane, formerly a Down platform at 12 m 16 ch, was closed in 1919 and not reopened, while the former signal box at Theobalds Grove became redundant when control of the line was put on the Enfield Town panel.

C.17   Clacton

Terminus of the Colchester-Clacton line. 69 m 52 ch from Liverpool Street

The Class '309' and '312' sets on the through fast services from Liverpool Street now give Clacton a basic hourly service with the journey taking 1 hour 20 minutes. Between these a local service to and from Colchester is provided with Class '308' and '313' sets. The present regular timing for the through London trains is five minutes faster than that of the former 7.56 am Up 'Essex Coast Express' and thirty minutes faster than the 'Clacton Buffets' in the 1960s. At that period Clacton itself was issuing 145,000 tickets a year and collecting around 700,000.

Much else has changed at Clacton too, for the days of steam were a nightmare on summer Saturdays when 10,000 intending passengers might be queuing across the concourse and out into the street. Inside the barriers the process of releasing incoming engines, running round stock and getting crews to their right outwards trains was hard work if things went well and exhilarating madness on the days when the first incoming train was late enough to upset the whole carefully planned operation. At that time trains came from many Midlands centres as well as from London and many times a last minute change of locomotive or crew meant that the former was the wrong route availability or the latter did not 'know the road' for the next working.

Neighbouring Walton was a Victorian seaside resort long before there was any development at Clacton and was reached by the former Tendring Hundred Railway on 17 May 1867. That company's engineer, Peter Bruff, also built the Clacton-on-Sea Railway but severe drainage problems delayed its opening until 4 July 1882. At that time Clacton had a population of about 650 but this soon started to grow and by the end of the century the line had a late Saturday 'supper car' train from London. Its first Pullman service came in 1920 and the station was rebuilt in its present form in 1929. The section from Thorpe-le-Soken to Clacton, the 4¾ miles the local company had opened back in 1882, was doubled in 1941 with local electrification coming in 1959 and through emu services to and from Liverpool Street four years later.

Approached via Burrs Road LC (68 m 9 ch), Clacton station area commences with the signal box (69 m 35 ch). There are three pairs of lines terminating at the concourse, with two platforms and four faces between them. On the Down side stands the old goods shed and, opposite, a modern electric traction maintenance depot which was opened on 17 July 1981. The depot, which cost £2 million, has a three-line main shed with stabling and washing plant beyond and is responsible for the maintenance of around 250 motor and trailer vehicles.

C.18   Clapton

Liverpool Street-Kings Lynn line, between Hackney Downs and Clapton Junction. 3 m 78 ch from Liverpool Street

After the Cambridge main line separates from the Enfield line at Hackney Downs, trains on the former slow to 40 mph to pass through the 445 yd Queens Road Tunnel (3 m 19 ch to 3 m 39 ch) beneath the Downs themselves and then through the 284 yd Clapton Tunnel (3 m 53 ch to 3 m 66 ch). The Great Eastern Railway had once considered a station between the two tunnels but, more recently, they were in the news when the 6.25 kv section was standardized to 25 kv in uprating works carried out between 30 July and 21 August 1983.

Earlier in 1983 Clapton station (3 m 78 ch) had been given a major facelift as part of one of the GLC:Hackney/Islington partnership inner city renewal schemes. In addition to general refurbishing and better lighting Clapton received a new train indicator, a public address system and a new, glass-fronted ticket office.

After the reverse curves of the tunnels

and passing beneath the skew bridges over the station, the main line crosses the River Lea by a single span steel bridge and then takes a 35 mph curve from Clapton Junction (4 m 38 ch) to the Lea Valley line at Copper Mill North Junction.

C.19   Clarborough Tunnel and Junction

Cleethorpes-Sheffield line, between Gainsborough and Retford. Tunnel 67 m 48 ch and junction 68 m 32 ch from Manchester.

East of Retford the trains on the old MS&L/GC main line to Cleethorpes pass through the 658 yd Clarborough Tunnel (67 m 48 ch to 67 m 79 ch). The straight, wet tunnel is followed by Clarborough Junction (68 m 32 ch) where a portion of the former route to Sykes Junction and Lincoln survives as the access to Cottam Power Station. This is reflected in the distances as the 3 m 47 ch branch runs via Leverton AHB LC and former station (70 m 16 ch) and Westbrecks AHB LC (71 m 22 ch) to the power station itself (71 m 79 ch). The route is double and the power station has both coal hopper and oil discharge facilities.

C.20   Claydon

Liverpool Street-Norwich line, between Ipswich and Stowmarket. 73 m 46 ch from Liverpool Street

Although Claydon's passenger station closed on 17 June 1963 the location remains important for an aggregate plant on the Up side of the main line and the Blue Circle cement works on the Down. The latter has mgr coal discharge facilities and stands on the approach to the old station and its surviving signal box and barrier crossing. An AHB crossing at Baylham (75 m 17 ch) follows the siding area north of Claydon.

C.21   Cleethorpes

Terminus of Cleethorpes-Sheffield line. 112 m 37 ch from Manchester (London Road)

Cleethorpes lies right at the mouth of the Humber with a view out to Spurn Head and the North Sea. Its sands and seaside entertainments make it a popular resort for the people of South Humberside and Lincolnshire with many more visitors coming in summer from South Yorkshire and the East Midlands. To convey them, and the all-year-round regulars, Cleethorpes enjoys trains services on four routes—to Barton-on-Humber, to Doncaster via Scunthorpe, to Sheffield via Retford and to Nottingham via Lincoln.

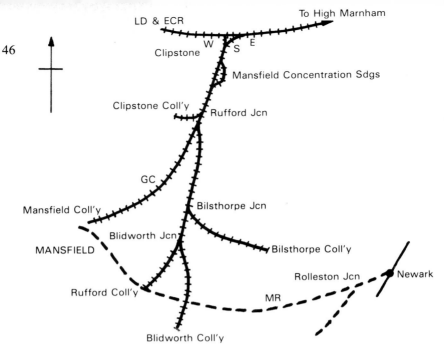

Cleethorpes got its first railway link from Grimsby on 6 April 1863 and was at one period planned to have a route south to Mablethorpe. This did not materialize but considerable investment by the MS&L at the end of the last century helped to fashion the shape of the resort and its present facilities.

The approach from Grimsby is via the two long platforms and 15 mph speed restriction at New Clee (110 m 79 ch) which is served by the morning and evening Barton-on-Humber dmus. The carriage siding and washer area precede the signal box (112 m 23 ch) on the seaward side of the route which then terminates at two platforms with four platform lines. Beyond stand the new station buildings provided at the beginning of the 1960s and leading to the sea itself and all the paraphernalia of a typical British seaside town. The previous station buildings still stand on the inland side of the station area and are used for trainmen's and operational purposes.

C.22   Clipstone Junction(s)-Mansfield Line

Branch from High Marnham branch. 4 m 57 ch

At one time Mansfield had three stations but now its only railway is this colliery branch which leaves the former LD&ECR main line at a triangular junction at Clipstone (10 m 74 ch) and runs as a double line via the signal box at Mansfield Concen-

tration Sidings (9 m 76 ch) to Rufford Junction (9 m 8 ch) and then on as a single One Train line to Mansfield Colliery (6 m 32 ch). The route started life as the independent Mansfield Railway with its first movements of coal in 1913 and passenger traffic lasting from 1917 to 1956.

A former part of the GCR system, the line has a 48 ch branch to Clipstone Colliery (9 m 56 ch) from Rufford Junction which is also the starting point for the freight line to Bilsthorpe Junction (1 m 8 ch from Rufford Jcn). From here a single OT line runs for 3 m 31 ch to Bilsthorpe Colliery and another to Blidworth Junction (1 m 40 ch) where there is a Key Token Instrument for the portion on to Rufford Colliery (2 m 5 ch). Another single line runs south from Blidworth Junction towards the former MR Mansfield-Rolleston Junction-Newark line and today serves Blidworth Colliery (4 m 11 ch).

A considerable volume of coal traffic originates on these lines which, in many cases, are extended by the NCB's own routes and systems.

C.23   Colchester

Liverpool Street-Norwich line, junction for Clacton line. 51 m 52 ch from Liverpool Street

Colchester had been delighted with the passing of the ECR's Act of 1836 which would put it on a main railway line to Nor-

Colchester station showing the Up Passenger Loop and staggered Up side platforms.

wich. It was even more pleased with the formal ceremony on 11 June ten years later which marked the arrival of Eastern Union trains from Ipswich and a revival of the hopes which had evaporated soon after the ECR had reached Colchester on 29 March 1843. By the end of 1849 the main line was open through to Norwich, Colchester was connected with the Stour Valley by the line from Marks Tey to Sudbury and it had a goods branch to the wharves on the River Colne.

By the end of the next decade thoughts had turned to extending the rail links eastwards. A connection between the Hythe branch and the small port and shipbuilding centre at Wivenhoe was brought into use by the Tendring Hundred Railway on 8 May 1863 and the same company linked the Hythe line with a new station in Colchester, St Botolphs, on 1 March 1866. By 1876 THR trains had reached the Essex coast at Walton-le-Soken. In 1882 the then small town of Clacton got its first trains, the THR being sold to the Great Eastern in the following year.

Over the years Colchester grew and pros-

pered, its trains got faster and increased in number and its station was several times altered and expanded. A new era of expansion began at the end of the 1950s with a major station remodelling linked to the commencement of local electric services to Clacton and Walton on 13 April 1959 and the through London services which began on 17 June 1963. Major features of the new layout were an underbridge for Down Clacton line trains, easing of the curves through the station and a modern ticket and information office. In 1981 work started on another piece of modernization, a new signal box and a revised track and signalling layout, the former destined eventually to link up with the area covered by the Cambridge panel and control the main routes of the whole of the eastern side of East Anglia.

On the main line Colchester derives a non-stop service to and from London from the Norwich trains which get to Liverpool Street in 49 minutes. In between, the hourly Clactons make two stops and take fourteen minutes longer. The local emu service to Clacton also runs hourly, via St Botolphs, and there is a dmu service via Marks Tey to

The operating floor of Colchester panel box, at this stage only controlling Colchester but due to have the main line on to Norwich added.

Sudbury surviving from a former through service to Cambridge.

The approach from the Marks Tey direction is via Chitts Hill LC (49 m 41 ch) and the adjacent Up side wiring depot. At the London end of the Colchester complex two TCB goods lines veer off to pass behind the Down side locomotive and carriage depot area at the north end of which the old signal box still stands beside its modern replacement (51 m 43 ch). The station area then comprises a Down side island with main and loop lines around it and, on the Up side, a two-section long platform 'stepped' so that the Up loop serves the country end and the main line the London end. The main entrance for bus, taxi and car passengers is on the Down side with subway access to the Up. Opposite the Up access stands the former Victoria Station Hotel, now a hospital.

The Clacton lines descend and turn east from the main line at Colchester Junction (51 m 65 ch). The Down Avoiding Line passes beneath the main lines and joins the Up side route at 52 m 65 ch. The latter, just a single reversible line from the bay to 52 m 33 ch, then doubles.

Along the Clacton line the old signal box still stands at East Gate Junction barrier crossing (53 m 14 ch) where the St Botolphs route curves back towards the town via Colne Junction (53 m 30 ch). It continues double to the site of the former signal box (55 m 63 ch), now derelict at the end of the single platform, but is single for the section along the platform which limits reversing trains to 530 ft. Opposite the traditional station buildings and decorated canopy the goods yard now stands empty, a stark contrast with the days when Colchester initiated a portion of the East Essex Enterprise express freight service, serviced an Ind Coope siding at East Gate and despatched substantial quantities of Colne oysters.

From Colne Junction the local emus which have reversed at St Botolphs cover a 22 ch curve back to the Clacton line at

Hythe Junction (53 m 36 ch). Hythe station and barrier crossing (53 m 49 ch) then follow the old line across the creek and the access to the coal concentration depot. There is a substantial station house of THR design and beyond the station a section along the River Colne still reveals how much Colchester owes to its status as an inland port.

C.24   Colchester-Clacton Line

Liverpool Street-Norwich line, branch from Colchester Junction. 17 m 67 ch

On 13 August 1859 the Tendring Hundred Railway secured an Act for a 2½ mile line from Hythe to Wivenhoe and opened this on 8 May 1863. In the previous year another Act had authorized extension to Colchester and on 13 July 1863 the THR secured its powers to link the Wivenhoe end of its new line with the modest Victorian seaside resort at Walton. The recently-formed Great Eastern Railway subscribed £28,000 of the £33,000 capital authorized by the THR's 1863 Act.

The section immediately beyond Wivenhoe station was to have been built by the Wivenhoe & Brightlingsea Railway under an Act of 11 July 1861 but that company had run into financial difficulties which compelled the THR to take powers to build the section from Wivenhoe to the Brightlingsea branch junction themselves. This

The frontage of the ER terminus at Clacton-on-Sea.

done, the route was opened to Weeley on 8 January 1866, to Kirby Cross on 28 July of that year and to Walton on 17 May 1867.

The initial THR scheme for a branch from Thorpe-le-Soken to the then tiny Clacton not having evoked much interest it was left to the Clacton-on-Sea Railway to revive the idea with an Act of 2 August 1877 and opening on 4 July 1882.

The Great Eastern Railway worked the Tendring Hundred lines from the outset and took them over completely from 29 June 1883. The railway brought growth and prosperity all round and by the end of the century the original single line had been doubled as far as the junction at Thorpe. Through services to London and the growth of the resorts brought increasing

Clacton electric traction maintenance depot.

traffic in this century which electrification in 1959/63 has developed a stage further.

At Wivenhoe (56 m 4 ch) a goods shed still stands in the old yard and there are substantial station buildings on the Up side. The Station public house looks down on the route as it passes via a cutting to the site of the former junction for Brightlingsea. Heavily supported by the GER, which had acquired the W&B shortly after its opening on 18 April 1866, the modest branch had run for 5½ miles along the north bank of the Colne over a swing-bridge and into a modest terminus at Brightlingsea. Trains took twelve minutes for the 5 m 4 ch journey and mainly ran through to or from St Botolphs and Colchester. The line was closed for ten months after the 1953 floods but, rather surprisingly, reopened and continued at work until 15 June 1964. The trackbed is still visible.

Alresford (57 m 62 ch) has another good example of THR station buildings with cen-

A Clacton train has just passed under the Norwich main line at Colchester.

tral two-storey portion where the ticket hall leads to the platform via a shelter area. It also has a gated level crossing of which there are further examples at Colchester Road (58 m 2 ch) and Thorrington (59 m 51 ch) where platform remains are still visible from the station that closed to passengers on 4 November 1957. After Frating AHB LC (59 m 70 ch) comes Great Bentley station, again with a gated crossing (60 m 4 ch), THR buildings and the old goods yard area which used to deal with the station's coal and agricultural traffic.

A caravan park near Weeley (62 m 73 ch) acts as a reminder that the line is part of a holiday area. The station itself has another THR building on the Down side, a concrete footbridge and a glazed shelter on the Up platform.

Although there is a Down platform at Thorpe-le-Soken (65 m 4 ch) trains normally use the island platform. For many years trains split into Clacton and Walton portions here but nowadays the Walton sets arrive at the Up face of the island platform, draw forward for the through Clacton trains to use it and then set back after they have left for Colchester, ready to connect with the next Down Clacton. Movements are controlled by the signal box which actually stands on the island platform whose Great Eastern origins are still apparent in the canopy support spandrels. The traditional maltings buildings of Albrew Malsters stand on the Down side.

The single line to Walton continues parallel after the station and crossovers and then rises as it departs at Thorpe-le-Soken Junction (65 m 12 ch), leaving the Clacton lines to continue via Burrs Road LC (68 m 9 ch). A spur was authorized between the two routes but never built.

The Clacton line has a few minor summits but is as easily graded as one would expect from its coastal plain location. Although the days of the 'Essex Coast Express' and the Clacton interval service have gone, today's train pattern gives an even better coverage based on hourly local and through fast services with additional trains in the peaks.

C.25 Coldham Lane Junction—see Cambridge

C.26 Collingham—see Newark-Lincoln Line

C.27 Conisbrough

Doncaster-Sheffield line, between Doncaster and Mexborough. 18 m 13 ch from Woodburn Junction

After the Doncaster Avoiding Line joins the former GCR line to Sheffield at Hexthorpe Junction (20 m 76 ch) the latter heads through a deep sandstone cutting and then crosses the River Don. Next comes the 237 yd Conisbrough Tunnel (19 m to 18 m 69 ch) above which once passed the mainly coal Dearne Valley Railway. There is then an Up Goods Loop between the tunnel and Conisbrough station (18 m 13 ch) and the present line from Cadeby Colliery connects with it. The station itself has substantial brick buildings on the Down side and is well served by calls by both the local Doncaster-Sheffield dmus and some of the Humberside-Sheffield/Manchester trains.

Beyond the station is the former colliery access connection and the CCTV barrier crossing at Denaby (17 m 12 ch), the route now being under the control of the Sheffield panel.

C.28 Copenhagen Tunnel—see Kings Cross

C.29 Copper Mill North Junction

Liverpool Street-Kings Lynn line, junction with Stratford line. 4 m 74 ch from Liverpool Street

The junction came into being on 22 June 1872 when the line from Hackney Downs was linked with the original N&E route north from Stratford. The junction signal box used to control four tracks together with a spur round from South Junction to Hall Farm West Junction on the Chingford line. It was a busy location with passenger services from Palace Gates to Stratford and North Woolwich as well as on the main line, and large numbers of freight trains heading for Temple Mills reception sidings, but today the points are set for the main line most of the time as its trains save the 2 m 19 ch compared with their early predecessors which reached Liverpool Street via Stratford.

C.30 Cottam Power Station Branch—see Clarborough

C.31 Cressing—see Braintree Branch

C.32 Cromer—see Sheringham Branch

C.33 Crowle

Barnetby-Doncaster line, between Scunthorpe and Thorne Junction. 9 m 41 ch from Doncaster

The original South Yorkshire line opened on 10 September 1859 and subsequently became part of the GC system. Crowle's second station, some way to the north, was on the Isle of Axholme Light Railway which was opened from Reedness Junction to Crowle on 10 August 1903 and then on south to Haxey Junction on 2 January 1905 after the completion of Crowle swingbridge. Under L&Y and NER management this line carried a service from Goole via Reedness Junction (5¾ m) to Crowle (8¾ m), Belton (13 m), Epworth (14¾ m), Haxey Town (17¾ m) and Haxey Junction (19½ m) until 17 July 1933. Goods traffic continued until 5 April 1965.

Approaching via Godnow Bridge LC (14 m 17 ch), the Doncaster-Cleethorpes dmus call at Crowle's modest platforms alongside the canal and then continue past the surviving embankment and bridge piers of the light railway.

C.34 Crouch Hill-see Upper Holloway-Barking Line

C.35 Custom House—see North Woolwich Branch

D.1 Dagenham Dock

Tilbury Loop, between Barking and Tilbury. 10 m 49 ch from Fenchurch Street

Dagenham Dock owes its name to an 1855

Ford's plant at Dagenham with one of the company's steam locomotives marshalling wagons for the Halewood train in 1963.

A Ford Dagenham-Halewood train at Dagenham Dock.

Act of Parliament which authorized the construction of a dock on the site of an old breach in the bank of the Thames. The dock never materialized and instead the area was infilled with London refuse and became the site of the vast jetty and storage complex operated by S. William & Sons. This industrial estate had some 25 miles of private sidings with traffic passing to and from a host of tenant firms. On the opposite, east side of Chequers Lane the Ford jetty was built with a huge pig iron plant behind it and then, north of the railway line, the main Ford manufacturing plant.

The LT&S line through Dagenham to Tilbury was opened on 13 April 1854 and

the railway has shared in the growth of the area over the years. It still carries a large volume of workers to and from the Ford plant although the station is a simple one of undistinguished period buildings behind sombre canopies. At the country end is the level crossing and signal box (10 m 55 ch) and then, on the Down side, the goods yard where the buildings have been modernized and car ramps built as part of the process of catering for the considerable volume of Ford business.

While the movement of cars was still controlled by the individual dealers and steam locomotives were still bustling about the vast Ford internal rail network BR set about

A reminder of the extensive private siding activity along the north bank of the Thames; one of Ford's industrial locomotives.

building up its share of the car movement business. Between 1952 and 1953 carryings went up 53 per cent and continued to rise until the volume warranted Ford's taking control and the provision of special Cartic wagons. After the opening of Halewood in 1963 the Eastern Region began moving palletized traffic in scheduled trainloads as part of the production line process. Movements to other factories and to and from Europe were subsequently added and although today the private siding is only modest compared with its former extent the volume of rail business is anything but. On 7 July 1981 the loading of the 2 millionth car was celebrated with the name of 47158, *Henry Ford*.

D.2 Darsham—see East Suffolk Line

D.3 Decoy Junctions—see Doncaster

D.4 Derby Road—see Felixstowe Branch

D.5 Dinnington—see Brancliffe-Kirk Sandall Line

D.6 Diss

Liverpool Street-Norwich line, between Haughley Junction and Norwich. 95 m 4 ch from Liverpool Street

Diss lies on the section of the Eastern Union Railway opened from Finningham to Burston on 2 July 1849 and completed to Norwich later the same year to give a new through route to London. Today the station survives as an Inter-City calling point serving the town of Diss itself and a large hinterland. The alternate hourly Liverpool Street-Norwich services call plus some extra morning and evening services. The station also has a Post-Bus link to Gislingham.

On the Up side of the straight, rising main line a long approach road leads to the station which has partially staggered platforms and the main ticket office and station house block on this side—gabled red brick buildings relieved by the gables and some decorative brickwork. Beyond the platform is the goods yard with a grain loading facility and UKF depot. The signal box is on the Down platform.

The AHB crossing at Palgrave (94 m 4 ch) lies on the London side of Diss and on the Norwich side is the gated crossing and house at Ardley End (97 m). Next comes the AHB LC at Burston (97 m 42 ch) where there are still some remains of the station closed to passengers on 7 November 1966 and, after that, Gissing gated LC with its

house painted entirely in black.

D.7 Doncaster

Junction of East Coast main line and Sheffield, Wakefield and Humberside routes. 155 m 77 ch from Kings Cross

Doncaster has always been a great railway meeting and interchange point where passenger lines exchanged their human cargoes and freight consignments were loaded, re-marshalled or exchanged between companies. The town itself owes much to the railway influence and for many years 'The Plant' was the dominant factor in the employment situation. Much of the detail of the past has changed but overall Doncaster remains an important interchange point between the east-west routes and the East Coast main line—especially now the North-East/South-West services are routed this way—and it is still of considerable significance for freight, especially coal.

Doncaster is essentially a meeting point of the former Great Northern and Great Central systems although a number of other companies served the area, either directly or by means of running powers, at one time or another. South of the town the GN&GE joint line meets the GN main line beneath the old South Yorkshire's route to Kirk Sandall, south of the station the Kings Cross and Sheffield routes join and then north of it, at Marshgate Junction, the Wakefield and South Humberside routes fan out again and leave the ECML to continue to Shaftholme Junction where the former North Eastern took over. The other main feature is the Avoiding Line from Hexthorpe Junction to Bentley Junction which carried the GC trains behind the plant area and over the north-south lines.

The formative period of Doncaster's railway history was a short period between 1848 and 1852. In just four years the then small town graduated from a few local services out of a temporary station to main line junction status.

As work on building the GN was progressing, agreement with the Hudson interests provided for the Great Northern trains to reach York via Askern Junction, the Wakefield, Pontefract & Goole line to Knottingley and then on via York & North Midland metals. Some services to the north began operating from a temporary Doncaster station in 1848 while the following year brought the link south to Peterborough via Lincoln and the opening from Swinton of the South Yorkshire, Doncaster & Goole Railway's line, destined to become part of

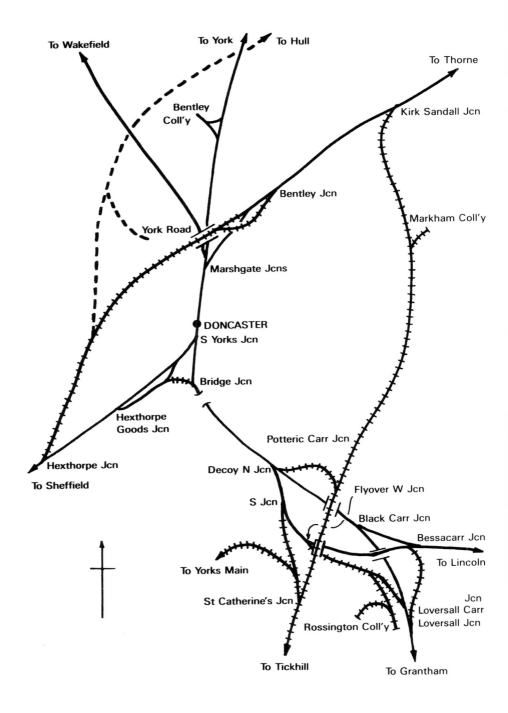

To Wakefield

To York   To Hull

To Thorne

Kirk Sandall Jcn

Bentley
Coll'y

Bentley Jcn

Markham Coll'y

York Road

Marshgate Jcns

DONCASTER
S Yorks Jcn

Bridge Jcn

Hexthorpe
Goods Jcn

Potteric Carr Jcn

Hexthorpe Jcn

To Sheffield

Decoy N Jcn

Flyover W Jcn

S Jcn

Black Carr Jcn

Bessacarr Jcn

To Lincoln

To Yorks Main

Jcn
Loversall Carr
Loversall Jcn

St Catherine's Jcn

Rossington Coll'y

To Tickhill

To Grantham

the MS&L from 1846. The 1850-52 period then brought the opening of a permanent station, slightly south of the original, the first Great Northern trains from London to York, the decision to establish a locomotive works and the completion of the direct line from Peterborough.

The South Yorkshire made faltering steps towards the Humber in the 1850s but completion through to Hull and Cleethorpes had to wait for the next decade and the MS&L era. The direct line to Wakefield dates from 1866, the direct NER line from Shaftholme to Chaloners Whin from 1871 and the GN&GE Joint Committee, when authorized in 1879, took over the Doncaster-Gainsborough line which the GN had opened twelve years earlier. The broad route pattern was completed in this century by the GC's 3¼ mile Avoiding Line and the Hull & Barnsley & GC joint goods line down from Aire Junction to Doncaster York Road, opened in 1910 and 1916 respectively.

On the main line the approach to Doncaster is via Rossington CCTV LC (151 m 29 ch) where the station house survives, Loversall Carr Junction (152 m) and Loversall Junction (152 m 36 ch). On the connection from the former to Flyover West Junction with the GN&GE joint line (at 153 m 19 ch) lies Rossington Colliery Junction (152 m 12 ch) from which a single 10 mph line runs to Rossington Colliery (153 m 20 ch). At Black Carr Junction (153 m 18 ch) the ECML is joined by the Up spur from the joint line at Bessacarr Junction, at Potteric Carr Junction (154 m 2 ch) by the Low Ellers Curve spur from the South Yorkshire line which has just passed over the top, and at Decoy North Junction (154 m 13 ch) by the joint line proper.

There are now additional Up and Down running lines as the Fast pair continue between Decoy and Belmont Yards to Sand Bank Junction (155 m 34 ch) which gives access to the yards at the north end. The 95 yd Balby Tunnel (155 m 34 ch to 155 m 39 ch) is followed by Bridge Junction (155 m 38 ch) which provides the Down link with the Sheffield line and South Yorkshire Junction (155 m 58 ch) which completes the triangle. The panel box which has controlled the main line all the way from Stoke then follows (155 m 65 ch) and, immediately after, the platforms of Doncaster station (155 m 77 ch).

Exceptionally convenient for the town centre, Doncaster station has a long frontage in the functional style of the 1930s and this houses the main offices, travel centre and ticketing facilities. The whole area is enclosed by the town on one side, the plant on the other and overbridges at the north and south ends. Inside are the two sizeable island platforms, the Up comprising two full length platform faces and one (formerly two) London end bay, with four lines separating it from the Down side where the position is similar except that there is a country end bay with two platform lines and a third between.

A footbridge passes across the station to the BREL works area and BR maintenance depot. The former, together with the Carriage Works, came into being in 1853 and came to cover 84 acres, employ 3,000 men and operate over 600 machines. It produced such famous locomotive types as Stirling's 8 ft 'Singles', the Ivatt 'Atlantics' and the succession of great 4-6-2 types from Gresley, Thompson and Peppercorn. A view of the works and station area taken from the air and showing the old engine turntable and the goods yard opposite is on view, along with other steam era photographs, posters and similar items in the Great Northern bar of the Danum Hotel in the town.

The six passenger and two freight lines through the station reduce to a total of six running lines at Doncaster North Junction (156 m 9 ch) and then at Marshgate Junction (156 m 28 ch) the Humberside and Wakefield lines depart and the Northern Area takes over the main line itself.

On the joint line the approach to Doncaster is on a rising gradient through a sandstone cutting and then at 50 mph maximum past Bessacarr Halt R/G LC (115 m 48 ch) to Bessacarr Junction (115 m 72 ch), Flyover East Junction (116 m 20 ch), Flyover West Junction (116 m 46 ch), Decoy South Junction (116 m 71 ch) and Decoy North Junction (117 m 46 ch).

From the Sheffield direction the railway uses the course of the River Don and then plunges into a deep cutting on the approach to Hexthorpe Junction (21 m 10 ch) where the 3 m 24 ch double track freight route, operated on Track Circuit Block and with a 50 mph maximum speed, veers north for Bentley Junction on the Thorne line. There are additional goods lines between Hexthorpe Goods Junction (20 m 76 ch) and St James West Junction (22 m 35 ch) where the Up spur from the ECML joins and the passenger lines become single on to St James North Junction (22 m 50 ch) and South Yorkshire Junction (22 m 57 ch).

Leaving Doncaster on the Humberside line Marshgate Junction (3 ch) follows a

*Doncaster in GNR days (*Lens of Sutton*).*

crossing of the river and precedes Bentley Junction (1 m 3 ch) where the Avoiding Line has direct and flyover connections. The section on between Bentley Common and the canalized river was formerly four-track but the extra Slow lines do not now start until Kirk Sandall Junction (3 m 27 ch). Here, too, is the link with the Track Circuit Block single line which originated 20 m 52 ch away at Brancliffe East Junction and in the Doncaster area has passed via St Catherines Junction (15 m 17 ch), Low Ellers Curve Junction (15 m 55 ch) and Markham Sidings (17 m 69 ch) to reach Kirk Sandall Junction (20 m 52 ch).

Evidence of Doncaster's continuing importance in connection with BR's coal business is very evident from the number of hopper wagons to be seen at the various surviving yards. Passengers still come to enjoy the St Leger, to change between the 24-hour pattern of services or just to pause briefly on their way between London and the North. Full of interest and never still, Doncaster is a part of railway history which is still contributing in full measure to the BR network.

D.8   Dore

Midland main line, junction with New Mills Central line. 154 m 20 ch from St Pancras

Preceded by Dore South Junction (153 m 73 ch) and followed by Dore Station Junction (154 m 50 ch) the simplified, four-platform station at Dore lies on the north-south leg of the triangle with the Hope Valley line and on the 5-mile descent at 1 in 100 from Bradway Tunnel. The service is provided by the Hope Valley local trains which travel by the

third point of the triangle at Dore West Junction (154 m 16 ch).

D.9   Downham

Liverpool Street-Kings Lynn line, between Ely and Kings Lynn. 86 m 4 ch from Liverpool Street

Downham, formerly Downham Market, lies on the first section of the Lynn & Ely Railway to be opened. Trains started running between Kings Lynn and Downham Market on 27 October 1846 and on to Ely on 26 October of the following year. Recently landscaped and provided with more car parking space, Downham remains an important railhead now served every two hours by Buffet Car trains from Liverpool Street to Kings Lynn.

Downham itself comprises Up and Down platforms preceded by a barrier crossing and controlled by the wooden Down side signal box. The main buildings, on the Up side, have Dutch gables, tall chimneys and traditional leaded windows. In addition to the Up side granary and 1878 corn store behind the former dock area, the grain connection is maintained by a simple gantry loading point behind the Down platform.

South of Downham the route heads for Denver LC (84 m 38 ch) and Denver Junction (84 m 32 ch) where the signal box had previously controlled access to the Stoke Ferry Branch. In 1984 singling was taking place on the main line here and the connection to the branch had been cut although the rails had not then been lifted. Denver station (84 m 44 ch), closed between 1 February 1870 and 1 July 1885 and then from 22 September 1930, could still be identified by the remains of its platforms.

The Stoke Ferry branch was opened on 1

August 1882, lost its passenger service from Kings Lynn and Downham Market to Denver (1½ m), Ryston (3 m), Abbey (5½ m) and Stoke Ferry (8¾ m) on 22 September 1930, but then continued to handle freight until 1965 and sugar beet for the Wissington BSC factory even after that. The connection from Abbey & West Dereham to the factory had, at one time, been part of the Wissington Light Railway which had started life on 30 November 1905 and grown to become a large, if unsophisticated network serving dozens of farms, an ammonia factory and even with prospects of a through link to the Ely-Norwich line. The system, a nightmare to work because of its many sidings and branches, was kept alive during the last war by Ministry of Agriculture support and with the LNER acting as the operating agents. It closed in 1957 through lack of support and because the dearth of fenland roads which had originally brought it into being had been remedied.

D.10   Drayton Park—see Moorgate Line

D.11   Dronfield

Midland main line, between Chesterfield and Sheffield. 151 m 44 ch from St Pancras

After closure in 1967 Dronfield has now been reopened again and has a peak hour passenger service provided by the local Chesterfield-Sheffield trains. The simple station, once serving an SPD depot, lies on the steep 1 in 100/102 climb to Bradway Tunnel.

D.12   Dullingham

Cambridge-Ipswich line, between Cambridge and Newmarket. 10 m 54 ch from Coldham Lane Junction

The Cambridge-Ipswich dmus pass through Brinkley Road LC (7 m 78 ch) and Westley Road R/G LC (8 m 74 ch) to come to Dullingham's combination of short Up and long Down platform. The location has a gated crossing and a brick signal box, the latter controlling the single line sections in both directions.

E.1   East Suffolk Line

Liverpool Street-Norwich line, branch from Ipswich to Lowestoft. 46 m 67 ch

Marketed as the Lowestoft Line but known traditionally as the East Suffolk Line, this route sprang from the Halesworth, Beccles & Haddiscoe Railway which opened its line linking the two Suffolk inland ports with the Norwich-Lowestoft line in 1854 (goods

20 November, passengers 4 December). Earlier in that year the company had become the East Suffolk Railway with powers to extend southwards to meet the Eastern Union at Woodbridge. It became part of Sir Samuel Morton Peto's plans for a new route to Lowestoft and was leased to him, joining and later amalgamating with his Lowestoft & Beccles Railway and Yarmouth & Haddiscoe Railway enterprises. Operated by the ECR to protect its existing routes, the new line opened through from Ipswich on 1 June 1859.

Although Yarmouth and Lowestoft always contributed traffic to the route it runs through a very rural part of Suffolk and despite an excellent through and local train service over the years the East Suffolk was scheduled for closure in the Beeching Report. Economies, including conductor guard working, were announced at the beginning of 1964 and by the September of the following year the East Anglia TUCC was hearing the closure proposals. A recommendation to retain the route was upheld and twelve months later came the start of the basic railway concept involving minimum track, buildings and simplified signalling. Operating costs were progressively reduced but by the early 1980s were still running at some 40 per cent above the annual revenue.

Further rationalization was in hand by the middle of 1983 and the former Down line was cut between Wickham Market and Melton as part of a process of track singling which could now be tied in with the introduction of radio-controlled signalling. The contract for a radio-controlled electronic token signalling system was awarded to GEC-General Signal Ltd in 1984 with the expectation of introduction of the scheme in the following year. This would enable all operations to be controlled from a single signal box in radio contact with each train and using a computer-controlled solid state interlocking system to ensure that only one token was issued for each train.

The route remains double for the first section after leaving the main line at East Suffolk Junction (69 m 40 ch) and passing around the northern outskirts of Ipswich as far as Westerfield (72 m 20 ch). This portion is shared with the Felixstowe branch trains, Westerfield Junction (72 m 25 ch) following the gated level crossing and station with its London end brick buildings and Up side signal box near the junction itself.

From the junction the Lowestoft line descends in a straight line heading east to the point where Martlesham Creek joins the

The simple terminus at Aldeburgh prior to closure.

River Debden. Bealings station was closed to passengers in 1956 leaving only the level crossing (76 m 6 ch) active but the attractive station house, goods shed and signal box all continued in existence. Woodbridge station (78 m 8 ch) has another good station house on the Down side and the brick goods shed, surviving from freight closure on 18 April 1966, stands at an angle to the Down line. The platforms are staggered and the boats behind the Up platform are not only picturesque but also a reminder of Woodbridge's past as a port and of the former horse tramway to a quay up river.

On the next section to Melton four minor roads to the river, each with a gated crossing (Ferry 79 m 2 ch, Haywards 79 m 7 ch, Lime Kiln 79 m 27 ch and Sun Wharf 79 m 31 ch), typify the problems of creating a basic railway. The station's own crossing follows at 80 m 40 ch and Ufford LC at 81 m 60 ch. Melton closed to passengers on 2 May 1955 but continued in use for coal traffic and as a token exchange point, then being reopened on 3 September 1984 under a joint scheme of co-operation between BR and the local authorities. At this period Melton still had its old cattle pens and other features of a period railway station.

Wickham Market (84 m 43 ch) is still signed 'Wickham Market for Campsey Ash' although the reverse would be more accurate for Wickham Market is two miles away along the B1078. The latter crosses the long Down platform on which a large two-storey station house still stands. An old brick goods shed also survives, together with traces of former bays and docks.

The branch from Wickham Market to Framlingham, opened at the same time as the East Suffolk's main line, ran inland from a junction 45 ch beyond the station and still visible on the Down side. The 5 m 52 ch route served simple stations at Marlesford (1¾ m), Hacheston Halt (3¼ m) and Parham (4 m), the journey taking 20 minutes. Its passenger services ceased on 1 November 1952 although freight continued until 19 April 1965.

The next junction came 2 m 60 ch further on and is also visible, but on the Up side. From Snape Junction a 1 m 39 ch route ran to the maltings near Snape Bridge with a signal box near the junction, then a 10 ch loop followed by single line thence to the buffer stops at Snape Goods, sited near the wharves on the River Alde. Although originally intended to have a station at each end the branch handled only goods traffic from its origins as part of the ESR package to its closure on 1 March 1960.

On this section of the East Suffolk line there are gated crossings at Blaxhall (86 m 31 ch), Beversham (87 m 15 ch) and Rendham Road (91 m 2 ch). Then comes Saxmundham (91 m 8 ch), complete with substantial buildings, surviving goods shed, gated crossing, signal box and 'The Railway' public house. On 1 June 1859 an ESR branch was opened from Saxmundham to Leiston and extended on 12 August 1860 to the coast at Aldeburgh, a total of 7 m 72 ch. It had a passenger service calling at Leiston (4 m) and Thorpeness (6¼ m) until 12 September 1966 and then continued as a 25 mph, One Train operation freight-only line from Saxmundham Junction (91 m 40 ch) via TMO LCs at Knodishall (92 m 49 ch), West House (93 m 32 ch), Saxmundham Road (94 m 2 ch) and Leiston station (95 m 15 ch) to the final one at Sizewell (95 m 79 ch) giving access to the power station.

The route towards Darsham (95 m 36 ch), the next ESR station, rises at 1 in 89 to North Green gated LC (93 m 26 ch) and, after Middleton LC (94 m 54 ch), drops again at 1 in 80. At Darsham, which has a squarish two-storey building on the Down side, all Up trains must stop in advance of the R/G crossing and marker boards are provided to enable Down trains to call at the station without the rear end obstructing the highway.

On the next section there are more ups and downs and more gated crossings—Willow Marsh (96 m 9 ch), Bramfield (99 m) and Wenhaston (99 m 20 ch). Not all the crossings on this route are manned but many still have their original cottages adorned with a diamond-shaped motif in the end wall.

Halesworth signal box (100 m 47 ch) precedes the station (100 m 53 ch) which serves the 3,530 people of this pleasant Suffolk town and the many more in the large area for which it is a railhead. The Up platform is longer than the Down and there is still evidence of the movable section which once formed part of a level crossing. An old grain warehouse adds to the period atmosphere but scrub covers the site of the 3 ft gauge Southwold Railway's station. Opened on 24 September 1879, this was a line of considerable character with four daily trains taking some 37 minutes for the 9-mile journey along the course of the River Blyth via Wenhaston (2½ m), Blythburgh (5 m) and Walberswick (8 m) to the coast at Southwold. If the Mid-Suffolk had ever reached Halesworth or the Southwold-Lowestoft line been built, things might have been different but as it was the Southwold Railway closed on 12 April 1929 although its hardware survived to be used for munitions in World War 2.

Another of the main route's short sharp rises follows Halesworth, one mile at 1 in 97 leading to the gated LC at Westhall (103 m 47 ch) and then the lonely station at Brampton (101 m 45 ch), just platforms, gated crossing and a few cottages. More traditional crossings follow at Weston (106 m 30 ch), Cromwell Road (107 m 43 ch), London Road (107 m 69 ch), Ingate Street (108 m 60 ch) and Grove Road (108 m 70 ch).

The signal box at Beccles South (109 m 2 ch) is followed by the station at Beccles (109 m 13 ch), a town ravaged by fire in the 16th and 17th centuries but now a summer host to holidaymakers' boats on the River Waveney. The station is heralded by a descent at 1 in 87 from the site of the old Beccles Bank box at which assisting engines for Up trains came off. It comprises Down side platform with main buildings and gabled house and an Up side island where the loop to the outer face is no longer in use.

Five chains beyond the station the old Waveney Valley line turned west to follow the course of the river and one of its tributaries for 19 m 30 ch to Tivetshall on the Ipswich-Norwich main line. It ceased to affect Beccles when the section from Ditchingham closed on 19 April 1965. By that time the former main line, over Beccles Swing-Bridge and on to Yarmouth South Town (121 m 66 ch) via Aldeby (112 m 43 ch), Haddiscoe (114 m 58 ch), St Olaves (115 m 28 ch) and Belton & Burgh (117 m 74 ch) had been closed for six years leaving just the Lowestoft line to continue on from Beccles North Junction (109 m 31 ch).

The route stays south of the Waveney as it crosses marshes for five miles. There are two operational LCs, the AHB one at Beccles By-pass (109 m 48 ch) and a gated one at Dawys (114 m 38 ch), but seven others retain their gates and cottages. Oulton Broad South station (115 m 42 ch) is of interest for its Up side buildings with all round canopy, the line then passing via Victoria Road gated LC (115 m 60 ch) to come to Oulton Broad Swing-Bridge and its signal box (116 m) and then to the north side of the estuary and Gravel Pit LC (116 m 11 ch) and the Oulton Broad North Junction (116 m 27 ch) with the line from Norwich. Just visible before the swing-bridge is the route of the former freight line to South Side (117 m 44 ch) and Kirkley Goods (117 m 5 ch).

When the transformation of the East Suffolk route is complete, track maintenance costs will be reduced by singling between Woodbridge and Darsham and between Halesworth and Oulton Broad South, 22 crossings will be open and activated by the passage of the trains and overall control will be from a new radio centre at Saxmundham.

E.2   East Tilbury

Tilbury Loop, between Tilbury Riverside and Pitsea. 25 m 7 ch from Fenchurch Street

Lying on the 7 June 1854 extension of the original LT&S line to Tilbury proper, East Tilbury was, until recently, just a period station with two platforms, old-fashioned wooden buildings and level crossing gates. A facelift during 1983-4 has, however, provided it with a new ticket office, ticket hall

An early impression of Elsenham station derived from the Illustrated London News.

and staff accommodation building which has transformed the station.

Near the Bata Shoe factory and with a half-hourly train service, East Tilbury is preceded by Low Street signal box and barrier crossing (24 m 11 ch) and followed by Mucking LC (26 m 40 ch) and Thames Haven Junction (26 m 41 ch).

E.3   Eccles Road

Birmingham-Norwich line, between Thetford and Wymondham. 104 m 39 ch from Liverpool Street

Eccles Road, another example of the use of local flint in its buildings, comprises Up and Down platforms, small signal box and out of use sidings. It has four adjacent level crossings, Heath No 58 (104 m 9 ch), Heath No 59 (104 m 10 ch), one just beyond the platforms (104 m 44 ch) and the AHB crossing at Hargham No 1 (105 m 30 ch).

At one time Eccles Road forwarded cider produced at Banham but now it just deals with the passengers on the Cambridge/Ely-

Norwich dmu service. Snetterton Motor Racing Circuit lies near the main line as it crosses Eccles Heath on the approach to the station.

E.4   Elmswell

Cambridge-Ipswich line, between Bury St Edmunds and Haughley Junction. 37 m 11 ch from Coldham Lane Junction

The station stands on a mini summit on a long, straight part of the line originally opened on 24 December 1846. Close to Elmswell village and enjoying a dmu service on weekdays and Sundays, the station comprises Up and Down platforms, gated level crossing and signal box.

E.5   Elmton & Cresswell—see Sherwood-Shireoaks Line

E.6   Elsenham

Liverpool Street-Kings Lynn line, between Bishops Stortford and Audley End. 35 m 49 ch from Liverpool Street

A pleasant rural station mainly served by the Bishops Stortford-Cambridge dmus but with some through London services for commuters. There are attractive period buildings, a level crossing and signal box and the remains of a goods yard on the Up side north of the station. Elsenham is also the summit of this route, standing on a short level section which follows the 1 in 107 end of a climb that started back in the Lea Valley at Tottenham.

Some traces are still apparent in the goods yard of the Elsenham & Thaxted Light Railway. The 5 m 66 ch standard gauge single line, although authorized in 1906, was not opened until 31 March 1913 and then lasted until passenger services ended on 15 September 1952 and goods on 1 June of the following year. There was a triangular junction at the Elsenham end and the trains, limited to 25 mph and 16 tons per axle, then ran via Mill Road Halt (1 m), Henham Halt (1¾ m), Sibleys (3 m), Cutlers Green Halt (4½ m) and, finally, came to the station at Thaxted which was very badly situated for the town. The branch tank engines were stabled at Thaxted overnight and carried a rope for shunting at Sibleys.

E.7   Elsham

Barnetby-Doncaster line, between Barnetby and Scunthorpe. 31 m 33 ch from Doncaster.

A modest station with staggered platforms and signal box and mini-summits either side. Served by the Doncaster-Cleethorpes dmus.

E.8   Elton & Orston—see Grantham-Nottingham line

E.9   Ely

Liverpool Street-Kings Lynn line, junction for Norwich, Peterborough and Bury St Edmunds lines. 70 m 30 ch from Liverpool Street

Hereward the Wake undoubtedly knew all the best sites in the marshes adjoining the River Ouse at Ely. The cathedral chose one of them but the station opened by the Eastern Counties Railway on 30 July 1845 was on a moister patch and its costs rose accordingly. Even so, the ECR had completed a railway route to Norwich by its opening of the link between Newport and Brandon and within two years there were lines on to Peterborough (goods 10 December 1846, passengers 14 January 1847) and over the Lynn & Ely Railway's line to Kings Lynn (26 October 1847). The other major route from Ely, that to Newmarket and Bury St Edmunds authorized in 1847, was not opened until 1 September 1879. Mean-

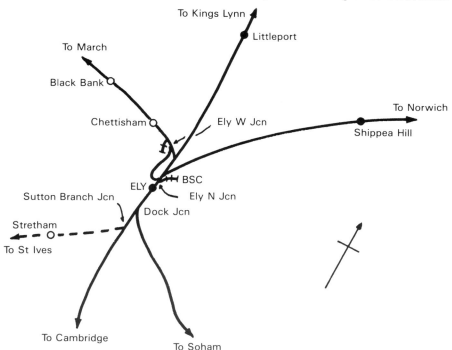

The original 1845 ECR station at Ely.

time a local line had been opened to Sutton on 16 April 1866 and extended to St Ives on 10 May 1878.

Although it no longer splits and combines trains on the Kings Lynn and Norwich routes, Ely has retained most of its services with the exception of that to St Ives. In Great Eastern days this line only warranted four trains a day, serving Stretham (2¾ m), Wilburton (4¾ m), Haddenham (5¾ m), Sutton (7½ m), Earith Bridge (12 m), Bluntisham (14 m) and St Ives (17¾ m), and the LNER ended regular passenger services on 2 February 1931 although agricultural and horticultural traffic continued until the 1958-64 freight closure period.

Ely station has an imposing, but gloomy, frontage of uncertain pedigree, the ticket hall leading to subway-linked Down and Up island platforms separated by the two

Up dmu running into Ely.

main lines plus Down Platform line and with the Up Platform and Up Goods lines passing outside the Up island. The approach from Cambridge is via Ely West River LC (68 m 29 ch) with a view of the bridge that brings the Bury St Edmunds line to join the main line at Ely Dock Junction (69 m 79 ch) which is 6 ch beyond the signal box. Station South box (70 m 22 ch) is on the Up island platform and Station North (70 m 38 ch) on the Down, the latter also controlling the level crossing. An alternative means of crossing the line is provided by the low headroom underbridge after which the line continues north, with a view of holiday cruisers and the cathedral beyond, to Kiln Lane LC (71 m 35 ch). The various junctions north of Ely are detailed in the map, control resting with Ely North Junction box (71 m 65 ch) which is followed by the junction itself (71 m 72 ch).

Ely's freight facilities have now been withdrawn and the wartime depot behind the station is no longer busy with rail traffic

but van traffic continues to be dealt with via the connection at the BSC factory. In passenger terms, in addition to the main line services to and from Kings Lynn/Liverpool Street, Ely forms a point of interchange with the Norwich line dmus and the Cambridge-Peterborough services. It is also a call for the through Harwich-North Country workings.

E.10 Emerson Park—see Romford-Upminster Line

E.11 Enfield—see Hertford Loop, Enfield Lock and Enfield Town Branch entries

E.12 Enfield Lock

Liverpool Street-Kings Lynn line, between Tottenham Hale and Cheshunt. 11 m 65 ch from Liverpool Street

The station at which the half-hourly Hertford East emus call comprises footbridge-linked platforms, modern brick ticket office and a barrier crossing. It is the modern successor to the 1855 location opened on the Northern & Eastern's original route and called Ordnance Factory because of its proximity to the home of the Enfield rifle. The present name dates from 1886 and there was a move to the opposite side of the level crossing in the early 1890s.

E.13 Enfield Town Branch

Liverpool Street-Kings Lynn line, branch from Hackney Downs. 7 m 51 ch

Palace Gates train approaching Seven Sisters from South Tottenham, headed by an L1 tank.

After Enfield interests had secured an Act in 1846 for the Enfield & Edmonton Railway this was taken over by the Eastern Counties and built as a single line from the Lea Valley route at Old Edmonton (Water Lane/Angel Road). It was opened on 1 March 1849 when the contemporary comment, 'the costs of construction of the line through country principally cultivated with market gardens must necessarily be large but the chief item of expenditure has been the making of a deviation of the Turnpike Road at Edmonton'.

The branch remained the principal rail access to the centre of the Borough of Enfield until 1872 when a double line was opened from Bethnal Green to Stoke Newington on 27 May, extended to Lower Edmonton on 22 July and connected with the earlier line on to Enfield Town on 1 August of that year. However, the single line via Low Level came back into its own as traffic levels grew on the more direct route and in the early years of this century it carried a peak hour service to and from Stratford with, later, five special ticket 'limited expresses' to relieve the early morning workman demand. The original Enfield branch was closed to passengers on 11 September 1939 and to freight on 7 December 1964.

Essentially a commuter route, the Enfield Town branch has always enjoyed an excellent service, taking 42 minutes for the 10¾ miles in Great Eastern days, 41 minutes in the 1930s and 29 minutes at the present time.

From Hackney Downs North Junction (3 m 4 ch) trains run via Rectory Road (3 m 64 ch), Stoke Newington (4 m 16 ch), the 60 yd Stoke Newington Tunnel (4 m 19 ch to 4 m

Seven Sisters, looking along the route of the closed Palace Gates branch.

22 ch) and Stamford Hill (5 m 3 ch) to Seven Sisters Junction (5 m 42 ch) where the spur from the Tottenham & Hampstead route joins. All these stations have been simplified and/or modernized.

At Seven Sisters (5 m 48 ch) there is a traditional signal box on the Up side at the London end while on the Down side the stub of the old Palace Gates branch can still be seen, a reminder of the trains that ran via West Green (6½ m) and Noel Park (7½ m) to Palace Gates (7¾ m) until 7 January 1963 and of the service between Palace Gates and North Woolwich. Seven Sisters station has been modernized to give it facilities commensurate with its importance as an interchange point with the Victoria line.

Edmonton Low Level looking north, in 1967.

Bruce Grove (6 m 28 ch), White Hart Lane (7 m 11 ch) and Silver Street (7 m 75 ch) all retain much of their original appearance, as does Lower Edmonton (8 m 45 ch) which has some excellent canopies with ornate spandrels. On the Up side the area of landscaping, waste and a district heating scheme was formerly the site of the Low Level station.

On the final section of the route the Churchbury Loop departs at Bury Street Junction (9 m 20 ch) and the Enfield line continues via Bush Hill Park (9 m 69 ch) which received a new ticket hall and other modernization following a bad fire in August 1981. Lincoln Road LC (10 m 25 ch) then precedes the signal box (10 m 40 ch) and modest terminal (10 m 55 ch). The latter is close to the shopping centre and has been reconstructed several times, notably for the introduction of the Jazz services and for today's electric trains for which it also has stabling accommodation.

E.14   Essex Road—see Moorgate Line

F.1   Fambridge—see   Southminster
Branch

F.2   Felixstowe Branch

*Liverpool Street-Norwich line, branch
from Ipswich. 12 m 10 ch from Westerfield
Junction*
There was very little at Felixstowe to justify
the faith of the original railway and dock
promoters but the town and its branch line
have prospered, partly by a willingness to
change which can still be seen in the present
railway route along the north shore of the
Orwell estuary. It was opened back in 1877
(1 May) by the Felixstowe Railway & Pier
Company which had its own station at
Westerfield until the Great Eastern took
over operation on 1 September 1879, and
then bought the line eight years later. The
first route followed the present course to
the docks but on 1 July 1898 the GER
opened a branch from it to the present passenger terminus. Trains reversed there to
get to the original Pier station and the
section across the top of this triangle was
closed.

Until recent years the docks had a modest
amount of traffic, a modest internal railway system and a complicated agreement
with the main line railway, but since the
1960s expansion has been rapid. The
closure of Pier station to passengers on 2
July 1951 and of Beach on 11 September
1967 was compensated for by the reopening
of the original direct access on 13 May 1970
to provide a freight route for the increasing
docks traffic. Another measure of the
growth was the advent of a Freightliner
facility on 28 November 1972, a second
terminal subsequently raising the level of
traffic handled to 125,000 containers a
year.

From No 1 platform bay at Ipswich the
twelve daily trains to Felixstowe take the Up
Loop to East Suffolk Junction (69 m 40 ch)
and then curve round the north of Ipswich
to Westerfield (72 m 20 ch) where the 1877
wooden station is still standing behind the
Up platform of its Great Eastern successor.
The course of the original route passed
behind Westerfield Junction signal box (72
m 25 ch) where the dmu drivers now collect
the token for the ET section to Derby Road
(74 m 67 ch). There is a passing loop at
Derby Road which has traditional main
buildings on the Down side, a small signal
box and a continuing siding tradition,
nowadays serving a coal concentration
depot and a loading point for scrap to
Sheerness.

*Edmonton Low Level looking towards
Angel Road.*

In LNER days Felixstowe had through
services to Liverpool Street and even to
Sheffield, plus a motor boat link across to
Harwich, but even in those days some trains
did not call at Orwell and the station there
closed on 15 June 1959. It can still be
spotted before a succession of three level
crossings, Routes No 8 R/G (77 m 36 ch),
Levington No 6 (80 m) and Thorpe Lane
AHB (81 m 40 ch), all with houses. Trimley
(82 m 67 ch) is another passing loop with
level crossing and signal box and pleasant
single-storey brick buildings with steeply
pitched roof and decorative canopies.

The docks can be seen to the south as the
dmus cover the final portion of the branch
into the terminus at Felixstowe Town (84 m
35 ch). The 1898 station designed by W.N.
Ashbee in the Queen Anne style and with
striped gables is being preserved as part of a
supermarket development, the surviving
rail track of the four previous platform
lines being cut back and using shortened
platforms to release it. On this last section
the docks line veers off from Felixstowe
Beach Junction (83 m 57 ch) to follow the
course of the 1877 route for 1 m 2 ch to the
level crossing and signal box at the point of
transfer to the docks lines. The route of the
spur between this line and the terminus is
still visible.

F.3   Fenchurch Street

*London terminus of Fenchurch Street-
Shoeburyness Line*

The London & Blackwall Railway was built
to cater for traffic between London and the
developing dock and residential areas along

The main station buildings at Felixstowe were being preserved as part of a supermarket development when this photograph was taken in 1984, leaving just one platform for the dmu service to and from Ipswich.

the north bank of the Thames. It had its eye on the business carried by the Thames steamers and quite soon after opening on 6 July 1840 was operating some vessels and co-operating with others to provide a service by rail from the Minories terminus to Brunswick Wharf at Blackwall and then on down river by steamer. The L&B was cable-worked and this system was perpetuated when the line was extended to Fenchurch Street on 2 August 1841. Carriages ran by gravity as far as the Minories winding engine where the journey began in earnest and a complicated system of attaching and detaching vehicles at intermediate stations was in force.

Cable working lasted until 1849 when the L&B's ambitions led to links with both the Eastern Counties and North London

companies and to their trains working into Fenchurch Street. Widening to Stepney in 1854 was followed by the first of the trains on the newly-opened LT&S line to Tilbury. NLR trains were increasingly diverted to Broad Street from 1865, the year in which Parliament approved the lease of the L&B to the newly-formed Great Eastern Railway, and the opening of Liverpool Street in 1874 affected the level of GER services but Fenchurch Street traffic levels continued to expand and further station improvements were made in the period 1879 to 1883. By the early years of the present century Fenchurch Street was handling most of the LT&S trains together with Great Eastern services from Chelmsford, Ilford, Newbury Park, Ongar and Woolwich. It did, however, lose its original Blackwall

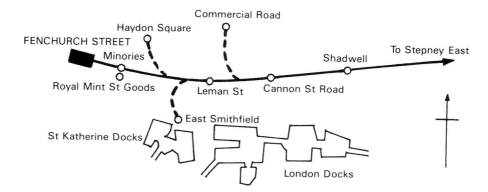

passenger services in the strike period of 1926.

The most dramatic changes at Fenchurch Street came on 6 November 1961 when the first new electric trains appeared, albeit late and only running off-peak in steam timings. The ageing 'Tilbury tanks' were not the locomotives they were in the 1930s when up to fourteen trains were moved into and out of Fenchurch Street in the busiest hours, and the operators were glad to see the full electric service come into operation on 18 June 1962.

For its modest size, just two platforms and four faces, Fenchurch Street has always handled high volumes of passenger traffic. Prior to the resignalling and other improvements from a £¼ m scheme of 1932-35 only one platform had been long enough to handle the massive trains demanded by the Southend excursion business. As part of the 1.5 kv electrification it had been planned to operate a shuttle service to Stratford and, although this did not materialize, the wiring, kept clean by empty trains, came in useful in 1953 when an electric service from Fenchurch Street to Shenfield with steam connections on to Southend Victoria provided an alternative service while embankment washouts on the LT&S route were made good. Today the service seems routine and undramatic but in place of the fourteen trains of the 1930s 22 trains now arrive in a comparable period and the Southend commuter can get home in 43 minutes instead of the 67 of that period.

In 1984, prior to its alterations, Fenchurch Street had four platforms and a concourse with the usual facilities, including a buffet adorned with share certificates and other items demonstrating the station's link with the City. Stairs led down to the ticket hall below, carrying its age rather less well than George Berkeley's frontage where the clock and single curved pediment brought grace to the functional entrance below them. The 1854 roof extended for three coach lengths, the canopies as far as the second entrance/exit to Savage Row. There was a short service platform opposite No 1 and a vintage 3 ch marker on the wall beyond.

Fenchurch Street signal box spans the track 20 ch from the buffers while on the Down side is the housing of the old wagon hoist to Royal Mint Street depot, opened in 1858 as part of the L&B's expanding goods traffic to and from the docks. Haydon Square, still visible on the Down side of the four-track route, was already open by then and soon further goods depots came into

use at East Smithfield and Commercial Road, the latter used as part of an agreement to bring Tilbury traffic into London at terms which would enable its shippers to compete with the nearer docks and wharves. Minories station has long disappeared as has Cannon Street Road which was near the coal drops at Cable Street, but traces remain of Leman Street and Shadwell both of which finally closed on 4 July 1941.

The various remains of the past tend to humanize the functional efficiency of today's station and its electric trains. The little passageway beneath the station, called French Ordinary Court, helps to bridge the gap between those who fled the French Revolution, the cable trains of the London & Blackwall Railway and today's 2 × four-car Class '302' and '308' sets filled with commuters longing for the cleaner airs of the Thames Estuary. Soon passengers will use the new station deriving from a £28 m development by the BR Property Board and the Norwich Union Insurance Company but, happily, the alterations provide for the retention of the present frontage, a reminder that the City did not want the original railway too close but soon had the good sense to change its mind.

In addition to these changes at Fenchurch Street the elevated route out to Stepney East seems also likely to accommodate the London Docklands Light Railway, a modern rapid transit development over the route of the original London & Blackwall line.

F.4 Fen Drayton Branch

Liverpool Street-Kings Lynn line, branch from Chesterton Junction. 4 m 62 ch

Part of the former passenger route from Cambridge via St Ives to March and Huntingdon/Kettering survives to serve an ARC terminal at Fen Drayton. Operated on a One Train basis, the line is single throughout, limited to 25 mph and has TMO crossings at Milton Road (58 m 38 ch), Histon (60 m 29 ch), Girton Road (61 m 39 ch) and Oakington (62 m 37 ch).

The route towards Huntingdon dates from 1847, with the March line opening in the following year to provide an outlet to the sea via Wisbech. There was a further route from St Ives to Ely (see Ely entry) and the Great Northern v Great Eastern rivalry produced a branch from Somersham to Ramsey which only carried passengers from 16 September 1889 to 22 September 1930 although some freight continued until

1964. On the main route, once busy with seasonal fruit traffic and freight to and from Whitemoor, the Kettering service ended on 15 June 1959 and the Cambridge-March trains on 5 October 1970.

The stations on the main March line were Histon (4¼ m), Oakington (6¾ m), Long Stanton (9¼ m), Swavesey (11½ m), St Ives (14¾ m), Chatteris (25½ m), Wimblington (29¼ m) and then March (33¾ m). The five daily Great Eastern trains on the Ramsey branch stopped at Warboys (4½ m) on their way to Ramsey High Street (7 m).

F.5   Finsbury Park

East Coast main line, junction for Moorgate Line. 2 m 41 ch from Kings Cross

As Inter-City 125 High Speed Trains gather momentum for their long journeys north and the latest emu sets take commuters to their Hertford Loop or Cambridge line

destinations it is difficult to imagine the old Finsbury Park. In the days of dense London fogs even the seasoned traveller got confused as the Down expresses got out of course, no one knew a late Hertford from an identical arrival for New Barnet and it could be a frozen hour before the double headed Peterborough/Cambridge train arrived, an hour in which the climb up the spiral stairs from the Underground could have been taken more slowly and a warming draught have been savoured in the 'Silver Bullet' bar opposite the station entrance. Other periods would have added the Highgate line services to the confusion or perhaps a few Broad Street trains.

Yet all this had very modest beginnings on 1 July 1861 when the simple Seven Sisters Road station was opened to give access to the woods and tea gardens which later became Finsbury Park. This new name was taken a couple of years after the Edgware branch had been added to the main line services on 22 August 1867 and just before the 1872 spur to the North London at Canonbury and the High Barnet (1 April 1872) and Muswell Hill (24 May 1873) branches. The latter was to provide access to Alexandra Palace and its history was about as turbulent, with passenger closure finally coming on 5 July 1954, but the other lines were part of the pre-war transfer package to London Transport although the LNER/ER retained a freight service, with a Commercial Agent at Finchley Central, until 1962.

Finsbury Park got a goods depot in 1865. Its own wagon load business never grew beyond a small yard on the Down side, later taken over by Macfisheries, but there were London traffic depots for Down side marshalling at Clarence Yard and at East Goods on the Up. Scrap and similar traffics were dealt with at Highbury Vale and Ashburton Grove off the Canonbury spur, and from 'The Vestry' came train loads of London refuse using former brick traffic wagons.

The Great Northern & City line of 14 February 1904 was part of an attempt to increase suburban business. The route to Moorgate (see Moorgate Line entry) passed to the Metropolitan Railway in 1913 but has now come back into the main line railway fold to realize its original objectives.

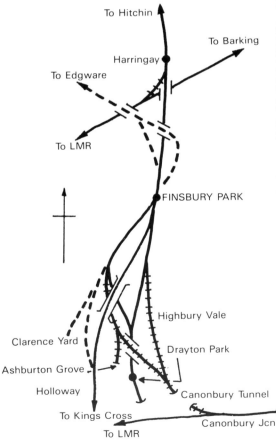

To Hitchin

To Barking

Harringay

To Edgware

To LMR

FINSBURY PARK

Highbury Vale

Clarence Yard

Drayton Park

Ashburton Grove

Holloway

Canonbury Tunnel

To Dalston

To Kings Cross

Canonbury Jcn

To LMR

From the direction of Copenhagen Tunnel the pairs of fast and slow lines and the two goods lines are joined by pairs of Moorgate-plus-Canonbury lines on each side on the approach to the multi-platform station. Near Clarence Goods Yard and where the Down joining lines pass under the main line is Finsbury Park's diesel maintenance depot which cared for the dmu fleet until the completion of electrification. The station itself retains its old platforms and buildings although these have been simplified and modernized and considerable improvements have been made in the ticket office area below. On the Up side beyond the station the route of the Highgate lines used to rise to cross the main line by means of a skew bridge and the sidings between the two were the stronghold of a group of characterful lady carriage cleaners.

Trains on the 'Northern Heights' branches served Stroud Green (3¼ m), Crouch End (3¾ m), Highgate (4¾ m), East Finchley (5¾ m), Finchley Church End (7¼ m), West Finchley (8 m), Woodside Park (8¾ m), Totteridge (9½ m) and High Barnet (11¼ m). From Highgate some of the Finsbury Park trains went via Cranley Gardens (5½ m) and Muswell Hill (6¼ m) to Alexandra Palace (6¾ m) and from Finchley a branch service operated via Mill Hill East (1 m) and Mill Hill (2¾ m) to Edgware (4 m).

F.6   Firbeck Junctions—see Brancliffe-Kirk Sandall Line

F.7   Firsby—see   Grantham-Skegness Line

F.8   Forest Gate

Liverpool Street-Norwich line, junction with Upper Holloway-Barking line. 5 m 21 ch from Liverpool Street

Forest Gate station had a chequered history under the ECR after its opening in 1840, was then expanded in the Great Eastern era and was extended by the LNER in 1946 when electrification revived the location after six years of closure. It is now served by the Liverpool Street-Gidea Park electrics, with extra services and extension to Shenfield in the peaks, and comprises centre island plus two outer platforms.

The 1854 connection to the LT&S route leaves the GE main line beyond the crossovers at 5 m 63 ch and then runs to Woodgrange Park Junction (6 m 14 ch) where the Tottenham & Forest Gate line crossed over the main line to join the LT&S from 9 July 1894. Forest Gate signal box is near the

junction and the old goods yard is nearby.

Fenchurch Street-Ilford trains served Forest Gate at one period and a mixture of regular and emergency services have operated over the spur at various times.

F.9   Foxton

Hitchin-Cambridge line, between Royston and Cambridge. 50 m 73 ch from Kings Cross

Foxton lies on the section opened by the ECR on 1 August 1851 to link the Royston & Hitchin's line with Cambridge and thwart the GNR's plans for separate access to that point. It is now served by the dmus which connect with the electric service at Royston and consists of two platforms with traditional buildings, signal box, barrier LC and surviving goods shed. There is also a 1½ mile connection from the Down line to the Rugby Cement works at Barrington, formerly Eastwoods and, as the Barrington Light Railway, authorized by an order of 15 July 1920.

Harston station closed on 17 June 1963 but still has an AHB crossing (52 m 45 ch), another following at Hauxton (54 m 1 ch).

F.10   Frinton—see   Walton-on-Naze Branch

F.11   Fulbourne

Cambridge-Ipswich line, between Cambridge and Newmarket. 4 m 43 ch from Coldham Lane Junction

On the 1851 'branch' from the former Newmarket main line to Cambridge, Fulbourne survived passenger closure on 1 January 1967 as a block post with level crossing and Down side grain loading terminal. The station remains, still evident, are preceded by Teversham LC (3 m 44 ch) which was provided with automatic half barriers as part of the singling rationalization of this section of the route.

G.1   Gainsborough

Junction of Cleethorpes-Sheffield and Spalding-Doncaster lines. Gainsborough Central is on the former, 74 m 42 ch from Manchester (London Road) and Lea Road on the latter, 98 m 9 ch from Huntingdon.

The first railway to reach Gainsborough was the Great Northern's line from Lincoln. This came into use on 9 April 1849, with the line from Grimsby following on 2 April 1850 and the link through to Sheffield on 16 July of that year. The line from Lincoln was out of use for three years prior to completion of the section to Doncaster on 15 July 1867, this becoming part of the GN&GE joint line from 1888.

Lea Road station is heralded by semaphore signals and a crossover controlled by the signal box at the end of its long platforms, slightly staggered. On the Up side there is then a connection to a BP fuel installation and a grain terminal, but the old wooden goods shed nearby is no longer in use.

After Lea Road, which lies to the south of the town, the GN route turns west and joins the GC line at Trent East Junction (98 m 56 ch). After crossing the Trent by a substantial two-span bridge, the two routes part again at Trent West Junction (98 m 69 ch).

On the Cleethorpes line the long straight section from Kirton Lindsey is now single line with a passing loop at Northorpe (82 m 14 ch) which also has a signal box, level crossing, gabled station house and brick goods shed. An attractive station house also survives at Blyton as the route continues to Gainsborough via Swinedyke R/G LC (81 m 38 ch) and Bonsall Lane LC (80 m 23 ch). Then the line turns south round Castle Hills to come to the simple platforms and shelters of Gainsborough Central, once a station of some substance but now with just the signal box (74 m 36 ch) and an oil terminal operational, although the brick goods shed still stands.

Trent East Junction signal box (73 m 24 ch) controls the junction with the GN&GE line, with Trent West Junction (73 m 11 ch) following the river crossing and then West Burton (71 m 40 ch). The signal box at the latter point controls the double line access to West Burton power station which receives mgr trains and also has a fuel oil terminal point.

G.2   Gasworks Tunnel—see Kings Cross

G.3   Gidea Park

Liverpool Street-Norwich line, between Romford and Shenfield. 13 m 41 ch from Liverpool Street

The all-stations service to and from Liverpool Street is dealt with at Gidea Park's two island platforms. Beyond the station are the carriage sidings and then crossovers either side of Gidea Park Junction signal box (13 m 63 ch), the first a Down side to Up side ladder and the second main to electric line links.

The location started life as Squirrels Heath & Gidea Park on 1 December 1910 and to cater for new estates in the area. It also came to be important for the Down

side wagon sheet depot, now used by the Railstore distribution firm.

G.4   Gonerby Tunnel—see Grantham-Nottingham Line

G.5   Goodmayes

Liverpool Street-Norwich line, between Ilford and Romford. 9 m 23 ch from Liverpool Street

Goodmayes used to have busy Up and Down marshalling yards until their work was taken over by the new hump yard at Temple Mills and the 'Goodmayes empties' trains were no more. A few sidings are still in use in the Up yard, for engineers' wagons and as a Foster Yeoman stone terminal, and there is a signal box on the Down side (9 m 36 ch) although the old Down yard itself has now largely disappeared under a light industry development.

The station, centre island and two outer platforms, is served by the Liverpool Street-Gidea Park locals. It was brought into use on 9 February 1901, about the time of the opening of the yard, and there are some good decorative spandrels beneath the long awnings.

GER boundary stone across the road from Goodmayes Yard.

G.6   Gordon Hill—see Hertford Loop

G.7   Goxhill—see   Barton-on-Humber
Branch

G.8   Grange Park—see Hertford Loop

G.9   Grantham

*East Coast main line, junction for Notting-
ham and Skegness lines. 105 m 38 ch from
Kings Cross*

In steam days changing at Grantham for the
Nottingham, Lincoln or Boston lines was
no hardship, for across from the south end
of the Down platform stood the steam
shed, home not only of engines for the
branch workings but also for 'A4's and
other big engines used on the main line. The
allocation of the latter was not great so that
if the locomotive of an Up train failed or
was not likely to be able to lift its load up
Stoke Bank the task might easily fall to a
'V2', an 'Atlantic' or even a 'K3', with the
consequent performance likely to be anything from astonishing to abysmal.

The Lincoln Bay on the Up side is now
filled in but Grantham still acts as a major
interchange point between trains on the
ECML and the dmu workings between
Nottingham and Skegness. The latter use
either the outer face of the Down island or
its bay at the country end, leaving the main
line platforms for the excellent HST service
which puts this Lincolnshire market town
within about 70 minutes of Kings Cross.

The station at Grantham, a typical GNR
red brick effort with a long severe main
block on the Up side and then a footbridge
to the Down island, acts as a railhead for a
large area. The approach from Stoke Summit is via the sites of the old Saltersford,
South and Yard boxes with Up Slow and
then reversible goods and Slow lines on the
Down side of the main pair. Beyond the
station the Slow line continues via Nottingham Branch Junction (106 m 8 ch) to then
veer off and double at the former Barrowby
Road Junction where the signal box used to
control access to the 50 ch line to Ambergate yard. The raised route of the main line
leaves the Nottingham branch behind and
plunges through the brick and stone capped
portal of the 967 yd Peascliffe Tunnel (107
m 65 ch to 108 m 29 ch).

G.10   Grantham-Nottingham
Line

*East Coast main line, branch from Gran-
tham. 13 m 49 ch to boundary with LMR*

Nottingham's aspirations for a main line
east from the city were met by the authori-

zation of the Ambergate, Nottingham &
Boston & Eastern Junction Railway in
1846. The financial constraints of the
period reduced the project to the portion
from Grantham to the MR at Colwick
opened on 15 July 1850 and with trains
using the Midland's station at Nottingham.
The strategic position of the new company
inevitably made it the centre of conflict
between the Midland and Great Northern
companies, including the well-known
physical confrontation between the two at
Nottingham in 1852.

The route was to become the basis of the
Great Northern's bid for the London-
Nottingham traffic, with through services
such as the 16.05 ex-Kings Cross (the 'Mark
Lane') taking just under three hours for the
128 miles and lasting well into BR days. The
line was also the foundation of the GN
expansion into the Nottingham and Derby
coalfields and coal trains still use the route,
along   with   the   Skegness/Grantham-
Nottingham dmus and some through trains
such as the Glasgow-Harwich 'European'
and   a   summer   Yarmouth-Chesterfield
working.

The double track route leaves the ECML
at Nottingham Branch Junction (106 m 8
ch) and heads past the site of Ambergate
Yard, the canal basin, the former Barrowby
Road signal box and adjacent sidings and
warehouse and then curves west between
Gonerby Hill and Stubbock Hill. Emerging
from the 506 yd Gonerby Tunnel (107 m 27
ch to 107 m 52 ch), a deep cutting is followed
by Allington Junction signal box (108 m 70
ch) from which a double line 4 m 7 ch
connections leads to Barkston East Junction, once kept polished by dozens of excursion trains to and from Skegness and
Mablethorpe but now relatively little used.

On the next stretch Sedgebrook's station
house is still visible on the Up side and further on, but on the Down, can be seen the
trackbed of the 1863 branch to the ironstone area around Denton and of the former trackwork at Belvoir Junction. The
ironstone branch, closed on 14 June 1965,
enjoyed a brief revival in 1976 but this
section now accommodates only the R/G
crossing at Sewerston Lane (110 m 69 ch).

Bottesford station (112 m 68 ch) comprises staggered platforms with house and
main buildings in brick on the Down side,
followed by the gated crossing (112 m 75 ch)
and its dwelling house. Normanton AHB
LC (113 m 10 ch) precedes the signal box at
Bottesford West Junction (113 m 78 ch) and
the RC barrier crossing at Orston Lane (114
m 16 ch) where the Up Goods Loop ends.

The GN&LNWR joint line, opened from Newark to Melton Mowbray on 30 June 1879, on to Welham Junction on 15 December of that year and from Harefield Junction to Leicester on 1 January 1883 passed beneath the Nottingham line at Bottesford. East-South Junction and North-West Junction spurs provided for Newark-Nottingham and Grantham-Leicester passenger services with the route also carrying large quantities of coal and ironstone.

Of the two routes north and south from Bottesford that to Newark, opened on 1 July 1878 in advance of the through line to Melton Mowbray, survived various stages of passenger closure in 1917, 1939, and 1955 to continue in use as a freight route. From Bottesford West Junction there is a single line ET section to Lowfield (7 m 12 ch) and double line thence to 22 ch before Newark South Junction (9 m 23 ch). The Newark-Nottingham service used to call at an intermediate station at Cotham and that from Grantham to Leicester at Sedgebrook, Bottesford, Redmile, Harby & Stathern, Long Clawson & Hose, Scalford, Melton Mowbray, Great Dalby, John O'Gaunt, Lowersby, Ingersby, Thurnby & Scraptoft, Humberstone and Leicester. Along the Newark line lie the Kilvington Blue Circle cement works and the Staunton works of British Gypsum and the closed southern line is likely to get a new lease of life with the Belvoir coalfield development.

Returning to the Grantham-Nottingham line, this now continues to Elton & Orston (115 m 34 ch) which once boasted a siding worked by the station staff but now has only platforms and shelters. Aslockton's gated crossing (117 m 20 ch) is followed by Aslockton station (117 m 22 ch) where a coal business survives in the Up goods yard and where the station buildings include a V-shaped ogee observation window, a feature which appears again in the house at Scarrington Lane LC (117 m 73 ch). Bingham station (119 m 39 ch) is in the London Midland Region.

G.11   Grantham-Skegness Line

East Coast main line, branch from Grantham/Barkston. 52 m 55 ch

The Skegness branch is a significant rail artery linking the ECML with the Lincolnshire coast and passing through a rich agricultural area. It is seen as an important part of the 'social railway' and, as such, receives positive support from the Lincolnshire County Council, especially in the sphere of level crossing rationalization. The route is made up of the Grantham-Boston line, that part of the Peterborough-Grimsby route surviving between Boston and Firsby Junction and what was formerly the Skegness branch from there to the coast. The line intersects the GN&GE joint line at Sleaford and carries a through dmu service from Nottingham. Most of the regular traffic is local plus passengers changing at Grantham and Nottingham for longer distance journeys but holidaymakers swell the numbers in summer and some excursion and charter trains still run in the path traditionally taken by East Midlanders seeking the sands and sun at bracing 'Skeggy'.

Sleaford, looking east and with Sleaford East signal box on the right.

A wet day at Skegness (Lens of Sutton).

After leaving the ECML the branch is single from Barkston South Junction (109 m 56 ch) to Barkston East Junction (110 m 10 ch) where the signal box controls the junction with the 4 m 7 ch cut-off line from Allington Junction. Then, via Hough Lane LC (111 m 8 ch) and Frinkley Lane LC (111 m 52 ch), it comes to Honington LC (111 m 72 ch) which, with the signal box and platform remains, survives from the former junction station. From 15 April 1867 the Boston, Sleaford & Midland Counties Railway's line (opened from Grantham to Sleaford on 16 June 1857 and on to Boston on 13 April 1859) got a branch companion along the foot of the wold to Lincoln. Trains from Grantham called at Honington (6½ m), Caythorpe (9¾ m), Leadenham (12½ m), Navenby (16 m), Harmston (19 m), Waddington (20¾ m) and Lincoln (24¾ m) until the line was closed in favour of access to Lincoln via Newark from 1 November 1965.

Back on the Skegness line Sudbrook LC (113 m 72 ch) gated crossing has an attractive cottage and is followed by the first station, Ancaster (114 m 48 ch). This consists of just platforms, shelters and signal box, its old name boards and GNR notices contrasting with the Up siding activity where the high capacity wagons of Scottish Malt Distillers are loaded. Two AHB crossings, Wilsford (116 m 59 ch) and Kelbey Lane (117 m 47 ch), come after the route has cut through a limestone ridge and are themselves followed by Rauceby station (118 m 39 ch) with platforms, modern shelters,

gated crossing, GN-type signal box still signed No 5 and overgrown dock. There is another AHB LC at Quarrington (118 m 79 ch).

Sleaford, at the centre of a fertile agricultural area and meeting place of the Boston and 'joint' lines, is dealt with in a separate entry. On the section which follows singling work was begun in 1983 with the Up line being retained and the crossings at Kirkby Laythorpe (122 m 52 ch), Burton Lane No 1 (123 m 55 ch) and Burton Lane No 2 (125 m 5 ch) being modernized under a scheme deriving from the BR/Lincs CC partnership.

Heckington (125 m 54 ch) is heralded by the sight of a great eight-sailed windmill near the gated crossing and its adjacent signal box. The station itself is in traditional style with brick buildings on the Down side and the old goods shed still standing. The Great Hale Drove crossings follow—No 1 (126 m 27 ch) and No 2 (127 m 24 ch)—as the countryside becomes wholly a rich flat plain drained by rivers and dykes like the South Forty Foot Drain which becomes the railway's companion as it reaches the simplified station at Swineshead (130 m 25 ch) and its preceding AHB crossing.

A road, rail and river combination arrive together at Hubberts Bridge (133 m 42 ch) which has a gated crossing, shelters and a modern signal box plus, of course, the bridge which gives the location its name. Already singled, the railway moves on to the former block post at Wyberton LC (135 m 57 ch) and then what was Sleaford Line Junction where the mileage changes from 137 m 6 ch to 106 m 70 ch which is the distance from Kings Cross via Peterborough and the original Great Northern loop line.

Boston, which is dealt with in a separate entry, lost a lot of its former junction importance in the East Lincolnshire closures of 1970. The 1848 loop line had given it a service to Lincoln (61¾ m from Peterborough) via Langrick (35¾ m), Dogdyke (42 m), Tattershall (42¾ m), Kirkstead/Woodhall Junction (46½ m), Stixwould (48½ m), Southrey (50¼ m), Bardney (52¾ m), Five Mile House (56¾ m) and Washingborough (59½ m). This route had been linked back to the East Lincs line by two east-west lines and from Woodhall Junction a 7½-mile line had been opened via Woodhall Spa (½ m) to Horncastle by the Horncastle Railway (opened 11 August 1855, closed 13 September 1954). All these local routes plus the Grantham line and Boston's service of Grimsby-Kings Cross and Skegness/Mablethorpe-East Midlands trains made it a railway centre of high significance and interest.

The Great Northern Railway leased the East Lincolnshire Railway which had also opened its line south from Grimsby to Louth and then to Boston in 1848. The southern section came into use by through trains to New Holland on 25 September of that year, Today's single line, now controlled by Boston West Street box, departs via the old Grand Sluice Junction signal box which used to control East Lincs Junction (107 m 51 ch) where the Lincoln trains departed. After Tattershall Road LC (107 m 69 ch) the route passes over the river and lock entrance by a two-span bridge and then sets off over the flat, rich coastal plain via crossings at Red Cap Lane (108 m 27 ch), Maud Foster (108 m 69 ch), Willoughby Road (108 m 69 ch), Pilleys Lane (108 m 76 ch), No 13 Wells Lane (110 m 15 ch), High Ferry Lane (111 m 4 ch) and High Ferry (111 m 23 ch). In addition to the working signal box (112 m 7 ch), the former station house survives at Sibsey where the route doubles again 7 ch in advance of the gated crossing. Old Leake station is now marked just by the South and North crossings (113 m 57/8 ch) which precede it, more crossings following at Simmon House (114 m 11 ch) and Boston & Spilsby Road (116 m 24 ch). Eastville LC (116 m 78 ch) follows the former station site where the signal box and goods shed are still standing.

The East Lincs line now comes to Bellwater Junction (118 m 56 ch), no longer a physical junction, but still with a signal box, level crossing and, what is more, a traditional Great Northern somersault signal. The line from Woodhall Junction via Coningsby (4¾ m), Tumby Woodside (7 m), New Bolingbroke (9¼ m), Stickney (11¼ m) and Midville (14 m) was opened as late as 1 July 1913 and in addition to trains to Firsby and Skegness carried through Lincoln, Sheffield, Manchester and Wadsley Bridge services. It closed on 5 October 1970.

Little Steeping still has its station house and both crossing and signal box (120 m 2 ch) are active, even if the latter does lean a little. At the former Firsby South Junction (122 m 2 ch) the line turns towards the coast over the route opened by the Wainfleet & Firsby Railway in November 1871. The spur from the south to Firsby East Junction (22 ch/26 ch) was not put in until ten years later but has survived the other lines at Firsby, which included the single line to Halton Holgate Goods (2¾ m) and Spilsby (4¼ m) opened on 1 May 1868, bought by the GNR for £28,333 in 1891 and closed on 11 September 1939 (freight, 1 December 1958).

The East Lincs line from Firsby (15¼ m from Boston), continued on through Burgh-le-Marsh (17¼ m), Willoughby (20¼ m), Alford Town (23¼ m), Aby (26½ m), Authorpe (27¾ m), Legbourne Road (31 m), Louth (33¾ m), Fotherby (36¼ m), Utterby (38¼ m), Ludborough (39 m), North Thoresby (40½ m), Grainsby (41½ m), Holton-le-Clay (42½ m), Holton Village (43¼ m), Waltham (44½ m), Wealsby Road (46¾ m) and Hainton Road (47 m) to Grimsby Town (47½ m). There were two routes which joined the East Lincs at Louth. One was the 1866 Louth & Lincoln Railway which opened on 1 December 1876 and ran from the junction at Bardney via Kingthorpe (13¼ m), Wragby (15¼ m), East Barkwith (18 m), South Willingham (20 m), Donington-on-Bain (23 m), Withcall (26 m) and Hallington (27¾ m) to Louth (30¾ m from Lincoln). The other was the loop through through Mablethorpe and Sutton to Willoughby which originated with the Alford & Sutton Tramway (2 April 1884), developed as the Sutton & Willoughby Railway's ambitions to serve docks at Sutton but became a reality due to the potential of Mablethorpe. Opened 1886-8, closed north of Mablethorpe in 1960 and totally in 1970, the loop ran from Louth via Grimoldby (4¼ m), Saltfleetby (8 m), Theddlethorpe (10 m), Mablethorpe (12¾ m), Sutton-on-Sea (15½ m) and Mumby Road (19½ m) back to the ELR main line at Willoughby (22½ m).

Returning to the present line, this passes Lymn Bank LC (1 m 46 ch) and then another GN somersault, this time controlled by the signal box at Thorpe Culvert (2 m 21 ch) which also has platforms with shelter and a level crossing. Two more gated crossings, Brewster Lane (3 m 6 ch) and Matt Pitts Lane (3 m 62 ch), bring the line to the market town and former port of Wainfleet (4 m 18 ch). The station, with signal box and gated crossing, was the terminus of the Firsby & Wainfleet Railway until it was extended, with GNR operation, to Skegness. This took place on 28 July 1873 and the traffic developed sufficiently to warrant doubling of the route in 1900.

Havenhouse station (6 m) follows Chain Bridge Lane LC (4 m 47 ch) and has short platforms, gated crossing and signal box, the latter with more somersault signals. Seacroft LC (8 m 2 ch) then marks the former station there and brings the route, past Skegness box (9 m 5 ch) to its terminus at Skegness (9 m 17 ch). The station still deals with a fair number of passengers, especially in summer, but it now uses only

This early Illustrated London News *view of Chesterford shows the substantial station buildings which still survive there.*

one of the six platform lines, the old Down side carriage sidings are not needed and the spacious concourse and generous buildings beyond never quite reach the heights of colour and excitement they did in the 1930s when LNER advertising plus Billy Butlin's blandishments brought holidaymakers in their tens of thousands.

G.12 Grays

Tilbury Loop, junction with Upminster line. 19 m 70 ch from Fenchurch Street

The LT&S line from Forest Gate to Tilbury opened on 13 April 1854, passing through the small town at Grays situated on the low lying land on the north bank of the Thames. The long connections with the river bore increasing fruit following the advent of the railway and Grays came to have a considerable number of private sidings forwarding flint, soap powder and cement traffic. The latter came from Tunnel Cement on the Down side and Wouldhams on the Up, both with their own motive power and with loading facilities at riverside wharves.

The line from Upminster was opened on 1 July 1892 and linked to Romford in the following year. The original Act had been obtained in 1883 more to exclude the Great

Eastern than because of enthusiasm for the traffic prospects but the route has survived to fulfil a useful function and it joins the main Tilbury Loop at West Thurrock Junction (19 m 1 ch), 7 ch beyond the signal box and level crossing of the same name. There is an additional, two-direction line from the junction to the bay platform at Grays station.

The centrally placed station at Grays has an Up side single-storey main building of brick, wood and tile with a barrier crossing at the country end and controlled by Grays signal box. Charringtons' 'The Railway' nearby depicts an early locomotive on its sign. Surviving among the fascinating industrial archaeology of this area are modern rail movements of steel (Bruce's Wharf, Grays), oil and petrochemicals (Unitank, West Thurrock) and coal and general traffic (Proctor & Gamble, West Thurrock).

G.13 Great Bentley—see Colchester-Clacton Line

G.14   Great Chesterford

Liverpool Street-Kings Lynn line, between Audley End and Cambridge. 45 m 56 ch from Liverpool Street

The Eastern Counties opened its Newport-Brandon line on 30 July 1845 and on 3 January 1848 (passengers from 4 April) Great Chesterford became the junction for the Newmarket Railway. It might also have had a link with the Royston & Hitchin but the various inter-company rivalries fell out otherwise and, indeed, lost the station its Newmarket link when that company's main line was closed in favour of the route via Cambridge on 9 October 1851.

The station lies on the descent from Littlebury Tunnel and has large and solid station buildings, much in the style of Audley End and Cambridge and probably by Francis Thompson. The Bishops Stortford-Cambridge dmus call.

There is still some residual rail activity in Great Chesterford's Up side goods yard and then beyond the station lies Ickleton Road LC (45 m 76 ch) with a good example of an early crossing house. AHB crossings follow at Hinxton (47 m) and Duxford (47 m 60 ch), the latter near the siding connection to Ciba Geigy's chemical works.

South of Great Chesterford two telephones are located on the bank up to the tunnel for use if freight trains fail on this section.

G.15   Great Coates

Cleethorpes-Sheffield line, between

Grimsby and Brocklesby. 107 m 19 ch from Manchester (London Road)

A modest station with signal box, gated crossing and platforms with brick shelters and served by the Barton-on-Humber branch dmus.

G.16   Grimsby

Cleethorpes-Sheffield line, Grimsby Docks 110 m 12 ch and Grimsby Town 109 m 20 ch from Manchester (London Road)

Grimsby began a revival of its traditions as a port at the beginning of the 19th century and the docks company was closely involved with the Great Grimsby & Sheffield Junction and East Lincolnshire railway projects which were to give the town its first railway links, to New Holland and to Louth opened on 1 March 1848. Soon these had been extended into the Manchester, Sheffield & Lincolnshire Railway's main line route to Sheffield and the Great Northern's south via Boston and Peterborough to London.

The railways brought more and more expansion to Grimsby and the MS&L, in particular, invested heavily in the area. The opening of the Royal Dock in 1852 was followed by a rail link to the docks and Pier station in the following year (1 August) and then by the opening of the Fish Dock in 1856. By this time there were regular steamer services to Northern Europe.

The extension of the railway from Grimsby Docks to Cleethorpes in 1863 was followed by another round of expansion in the 1870s. The opening of No 2 Fish Dock in 1877 was followed two years later by the new Alexandra Dock which had its own branch access from a triangular junction east of Great Coates and opened on 27 March 1879. In the first half of the 1880s the total turnover of fish increased by 23,000 tons.

The opening of Immingham at the beginning of this century had a considerable effect on the profile of the docks activity at Grimsby but it continued to expand its floating timber trade and the opening by the Corporation on 4 October 1934 of a third fish dock brought a further rise in Grimsby's fish tonnage. By the outbreak of World War 2 Grimsby had a dock system offering 139 acres of deep water, 6 miles of quays and berths and 500 acres of adjoining land. Its fishing fleet, following the herring shoals down the East Coast, totalled 500 vessels with a catch of around 190,000 tons a year. From the iced holds of all these vessels came hundreds of crans of fish to be

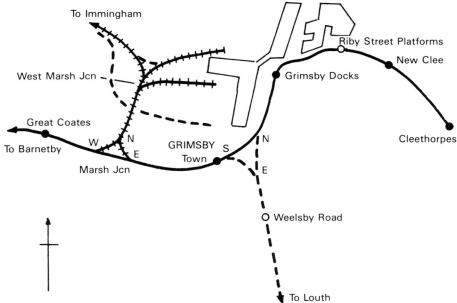

To Immingham

Riby Street Platforms

New Clee

West Marsh Jcn

Grimsby Docks

Great Coates

Cleethorpes

To Barnetby

W

N

GRIMSBY

N

E

Town

S

Marsh Jcn

E

O Weelsby Road

To Louth

sold in the covered fish market and then loaded to rail vans for Class 'C' express freight train movement to London and provincial destinations.

The character of Grimsby and its port has changed much in recent years and its railway has changed too, the freight connection to the docks now being concentrated on Marsh Junctions (East Junction 108 m 8 ch, signal box 107 m 77 ch and West Junction 107 m 69 ch). From Marsh West Junction the route runs to Marsh North Junction (108 m 5 ch) where the 14 ch spur from Marsh East Junction joins. It then continues via Great Coates No 1 box (108 m 34 ch) to the docks boundary (108 m 44 ch) and on to West Marsh Junction (108 m 73 ch). The connection on to the Immingham rail network was authorized as Grimsby & District Light Railways by a Light Railway Order confirmed on 15 January 1906. This carried a passenger service until 1912 but in recent years has been the freight link to Courtauld's factory and the Immingham freight and steel terminal. From the docks boundary (4 m 33 ch) the line runs by way of Pyewipe Road LC (4 m 19 ch) and its signal box, AHB crossings at Woad Lane (3 m 36 ch) and Marsh Lane (1 m 25 ch) and then the Kiln Lane LC where trainmen preset the operational controls and the barriers lower after the train has passed. A further 51 ch brings the end of the light railway and a change to 106 m 50 ch with Immingham East Junction (106 m 34 ch) following.

Passenger services on the Great Coates and Grimsby & District Light Railways lines ended in 1912 with the opening of the electric railway from Corporation Bridge to Immingham. Another railway enterprise, the Grimsby & Immingham Electric Railway was a busy route with a half-hour service, main stops at Yarborough Street, Stortford Street, Cleveland Bridge and Immingham Town and several intermediate request stops. The seven-mile line was closed between Corporation Bridge and Cleveland Bridge on 1 July 1956 and throughout on 3 July 1961.

The approach to Grimsby Town from the west is by way of the signal box and gated crossing combinations at Littlefield (108 m 73 ch), and Friargate (109 m 3 ch), Wellowgate signal box (109 m 14 ch) then controlling the barrier crossing which precedes the station. The main buildings are on the Up side with footbridge access to the Down island and its Permissive Down Platform lines. The complex is covered by an overall roof.

Beyond Grimsby Town station the route continues to Garden Street Junction signal box and level crossing (109 m 27 ch) which was 154 m 71 ch from Kings Cross over the East Lincs line whose trackbed is still apparent. The former goods yard area then precedes Pasture Street signal box and barrier crossing (109 m 48 ch) and the link which led to the Royal and Fish Dock area and to Pier station. Next comes Grimsby

Docks station (110 m 12 ch) with its long Up and Down platforms, then Fish Dock Road signal box and gated level crossing (110 m 32 ch) and after that an excellent view of the fish docks and the docks system's 306 ft hydraulic tower.

Although Grimsby has lost its route south via Louth it still has rail services on the Lincoln, Gainsborough and Doncaster lines, together with the local dmu service on the Barton-on-Humber branch. These services give excellent connections saving an hour on the journey to Manchester compared with LNER days and half an hour on the average journey time to Kings Cross. The daily 'Humber-Lincs Executive', in fact, reaches Kings Cross in under three hours.

G.17   Gunton—see Sheringham Branch

H.1   Habrough

Cleethorpes-Sheffield line, junction with Barton-on-Humber branch. 101 m 13 ch from Manchester (London Road)

A typical MS&L country station with its buildings showing some Tudor design features and with excellent services on the Barton-on-Humber, Doncaster and Sheffield routes.

The approach from Cleethorpes is via Roxton Siding signal box and level crossing (102 m 55 ch) with those at Habrough then following. The junction at which the branch single line turns away towards Ulceby Junction (1 m 45 ch) lies a further 6 ch along the main line section to Brocklesby Junction which makes up the base of this triangular junction layout.

H.2   Hackney Central—see North Woolwich Line

H.3   Hackney Downs

Liverpool Street-Kings Lynn line, junction with Enfield Town branch. 2 m 78 ch from Liverpool Street

Situated near the park of the same name, Hackney Downs comprises centre island platform and Down Enfield and Up Chingford platforms reached by subway and stairs from the ticket office below. It came into existence on 27 May 1872 with the first portion of the new line to Enfield and was then connected to the infant Chingford branch and the original N&E Lea Valley main line. Trains previously routed via Stratford were transferred to the Hackney Downs route and the station enlarged in 1876.

The present station layout dates from the end of the last century but recently a facelift has cleaned up the brickwork and replaced the old canopies. The signal box (3 m 2 ch) is located at the country end of the island platform and the junction two chains further on.

Even off-peak Hackney Downs has two Cheshunt, three Chingford and four Enfield Town trains each hour.

H.4   Hackney Wick—see North Woolwich Line

H.5   Haddiscoe—see Brundall Junction-Lowestoft Line

H.6   Hadley Wood Tunnels and Station

East Coast main line, between New Barnet and Potters Bar. 10 m 21 ch from Kings Cross

The original station of 1 May 1885 was completely replaced in 1959 when quadrupling north to Potters Bar was based on an additional separate tunnel for the Down direction lines. The location now comprises the 384 yd Hadley Wood South Tunnel (10 m 21 ch to 10 m 39 ch), the 1959 four-platform station served every twenty minutes by the Moorgate-Welwyn Garden City electrics and the 232 yd Hadley Wood North Tunnel (10 m 60 ch to 10 m 70 ch), all part of the 1 in 200 climb from Wood Green to Potters Bar.

H.7   Halesworth—see East Suffolk Line

H.8   Harling Road

Birmingham-Norwich line, between Thetford and Wymondham. 101 m 38 ch from Liverpool Street

Set in the heart of Norfolk, Harling Road station is served by the Cambridge/Ely-Norwich dmus and comprises Up and Down platforms with brick buildings, gated crossing, signal box, crossing house and a short Down siding. At the country end 'The Railway' public house sports an 'A4' on its sign while at the London end the old wartime camps and stores depot is a reminder that the station was once busy with freight traffic.

H.9   Harlow

Liverpool Street-Kings Lynn line, between Broxbourne and Bishops Stortford. Harlow Town is 22 m 59 ch and Harlow Mill 24 m 36 ch from Liverpool Street

Until the development of Harlow New Town the local trains to Bishops Stortford called at Roydon, Burnt Mill and Harlow, but on 13 July 1960 Burnt Mill was replaced by a new station called Harlow Town and the old Harlow became Harlow Mill. The latter continued as the block post with a small modern panel but the station itself is a very modest affair compared with its neighbour—just staggered platforms and nondescript buildings.

Harlow Town has the two main lines, plus island platforms with footbridge to a spacious ticket area and car park, and Up and Down Passenger Loops. Both Harlows are served by the Bishops Stortford electrics but Town has some additional peak services, the best of which provides a 31 minutes non-stop journey to Liverpool Street.

H.10   Harold Wood

Liverpool Street-Norwich line, between Romford and Shenfield. 14 m 76 ch from Liverpool Street

Harold Wood lies on Brentwood Bank and has the standard configuration of centre island plus two outer platforms. It originated on 1 February 1868 but was considerably altered in the mid-1930s. The service is provided by the Southend trains with some peak period extras.

H.11   Harringay

East Coast main line, between Finsbury

The signal box at Mistley, pure Great Eastern, will be closed under electrification.

Park and Wood Green. 3 m 32 ch from Kings Cross

The original Harringay was opened, along with several other GNR suburban stations, in 1885 but it was completely altered in a 1976 reconstruction as part of the GN suburban electrification programme. The alterations provided a new ticket office on the footbridge and involved using only the outer faces of the former island platforms.

The Fast and Slow lines through the station are supplemented by an Up Goods and by Down Slow No 2 and there is also a single line TCB connection from the Tottenham & Hampstead line below. This runs for 22 ch from Harringay Park Junction to the west side of the ECML at Harringay West Junction (3 m 29 ch).

Each hour three Moorgate-Hertford Loop and three Welwyn Garden City trains call at Harringay.

H.12   Harringay Stadium—see Upper Holloway-Barking Line

H.13   Harwich Branch

Liverpool Street-Norwich line, branch from Manningtree. 11 m 18 ch

Pretty well all the estuaries and small ports of the East Anglian coast had periods of ambition when it seemed that the local railway scheme or that of a major established railway would lift the area concerned away from small traditional rivalries to a position of pre-eminence. Those places which got a railway connection to boost their coastal

shipping activity then saw the increasing
change from sail to steam furthering their
growth in the business of conveying passengers, goods and mail across the North Sea.
More hopes foundered than flourished but
the Harwich branch, although a late starter
compared with Lowestoft and Yarmouth,
now receives the final triumph of electrification to cement 130 years of steady
growth in traffic and importance.

The Eastern Union received powers for a
line to Harwich back in 1847 but the route
was not opened until 15 August 1854. Nine
years later the steamer links to Antwerp and
Ipswich gave way to the Great Eastern's
own steamers to which the railway added a
hotel at Harwich soon after. By the beginning of the 1870s the Great Eastern was
intent on further expansion in the shape of a
completely new port to take over from the
cargo pier at Harwich. This was Parkeston
Quay which opened in 1883 and also involved the doubling of the branch from Mistley and the diversion of part of the original
1854 route.

Development continued over the years,
including the addition of the Harwich-
Zeebrugge train ferry from 1924 and a
variety of Pullman, Restaurant Car and
Through Carriage train services with titles
like the 'Antwerp Continental', 'Flushing
Continental' and 'Hook Continental'. By
1939 the LNER was constantly reminding

*Harwich Town station on a wet day in
1985, prior to electrification.*

potential users of 3,920 ft of deep water
quay, the cranes, capstans and coaling
appliances, the customs cages and transit
sheds, 'quay bonded and general warehouses, stables and garage, marine and
engineering repair workshops, stores etc.'
A new passenger station, Parkeston Quay
West, had been opened on 1 October 1934
and other facets of the railway activity
included a motor boat service across the
estuary to Felixstowe and a local service
between Harwich and Parkeston Quay to
cater for local people and the summer visitors to Dovercourt Bay.

Like most other lines the branch has had
some rationalization in recent years including the closure of Bradfield in 1956 and the
working of the portion beyond Parkeston
East as a single line from the beginning of
1968. Further disruption came in 1984 but
only in the form of foundation and wiring
trains to take the first steps for the eventual
introduction of electric trains in 1986.

The pre-electrification service on the
branch was maintained by dmus working
from the bay platform at Manningtree plus
a few Ipswich and Colchester through services and the named 'Day Continental',
'Hook Continental' and 'European'.

From Manningtree South Junction LC
(59 m 43 ch) the Up line of the branch is bi-
directional to cater for access to and from
the bay at the junction station but this ends
at Manningtree East Junction (59 m 67 ch)
where the 25 mph single line spur from
North Junction joins. The double line

branch then heads for Mistley, which
figured in several plans for lines towards
Clacton (including one on which work
actually started), the station being preceded
by a Down side grain siding and followed by
a line down to estuary level. Mistley station
itself (61 m 11 ch) is much in the style of the
Tendring Hundred stations, with a traditional signal box retaining its barge boards
and continuing to control traffic pending
the transfer of signalling to the Colchester
panel.

The former Bradfield station is marked
by the surviving level crossing (62 m 40 ch)
and a rise and fall in gradient is then followed by the short platforms of the former
Priory Halt which served a WD depot just
beyond.

Wrabness station has its small wooden
signal box (65 m 3 ch) at the London end of
the Down platform but the Up Loop and
Down Refuge lines have been gone some
time. The main buildings, on the Up side,
are again in the THR style and there is an
overbridge at the country end of the
station. On the next section there used to be
a Primrose signal box and siding and it is
still possible to spot the line of the original
route behind the golf course but now the
next feature is the box at Parkeston Goods
Junction (68 m 11 ch) where the route to the
car jetty and freight yard diverges. This
continues as a single line with a passing section to West Quay (69 m 23 ch) while the
passenger line heads past the sidings of Cartic and tank wagons to Parkeston West LC
(68 m 56 ch).

Beyond the busy crossing lies Parkeston
Quay station (68 m 73 ch) given a new ticket
office in 1984 and where the branch itself
becomes single and uses the north face of
the Down platform, leaving boat trains and
specials to use the Up platform immediately
across from the shipping berths. The
massive two-storey station block, conceived by H.H. Poswell and named after
the Great Eastern's chairman of the 1882
opening period, is more imposing than elegant but its facilities have been made very
convenient and its square clock tower
makes it a notable landmark. The Freightliner terminal is located on the quayside
following the CCTV crossing at Parkeston
East (69 m) and the port, with its Sealink
and DFDS ships, also has Speedlink ·
services.

Branch trains are using the Up line on this
final section, with the Down remaining in
situ as a through siding which gives access to
Harwich and the ferry terminal there. The
Down side signal box and platform at

Dovercourt Bay (70 m 19 ch) have thus been
abandoned in favour of the Up platform
which has traditional buildings and
canopy. A short distance further on comes
Alexandra Road LC (70 m 39 ch) and then
Harwich Town box and crossing (70 m 61
ch).

The old wooden Harwich station in
George Street burned down and the present
one dates from around 1865. The passenger
services use the Up platform and its traditional brick buildings, two adjoining lines
being used for car loadings. Beyond these
the old goods shed stands with the line to the
ferry terminal passing beside it to the
holding yard and then to the lifting bridge at
the ferry berth. The final movements
between yard and vessel are made by
Trackmobil vehicle. Harwich is an ancient
town and port of much interest. Many sites
carry descriptive plaques, including the
Victorian post box which the Harwich
Society maintains in the station boundary
wall.

H.14   Hatfield

*East Coast main line, between Potters Bar
and Welwyn Garden City. 17 m 54 ch from
Kings Cross*

Hatfield station has centre Fast lines and
outer Slow lines with platforms to the latter
and links between the two sets of lines on
either side of the station. The old Up side
goods yard and brick goods shed are still
standing but otherwise the modernized
station is vastly different from the rather
dingy place of late LNER days. Today electric trains get their passengers to Moorgate
in 39 minutes and HSTs dash through at
over 100 mph, all a dramatic contrast with
the days when Hatfield was an almost rural
junction with three branch lines and a grimy
loco shed to coal and water the branch
engines.

The original branch was that authorized
in 1862 to the Hatfield & St Albans Railway
and running via Nast Hyde Halt (2 m),
Smallford (2¾ m) and Hill End (4¼ m) to
three stops in St Albans, the request platform at Salvation Army Siding, St Albans
LNE (5¾ m) and St Albans Abbey LNW
(6½ m). The other two lines originally ran
to Welwyn and had even combined with the
intention of creating a physical link across
the GN main line there but after purchase
by the Great Northern they were each
brought south as a single line parallel to the
main line.

The Hertford & Welwyn Junction
Railway had opened on 1 March 1858 and

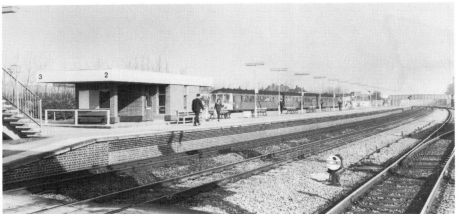

Top *Hatfield station pictured in 1969—a typical piece of GNR building.*

Above *View of the modernized Down island platform at Hatfield, taken in 1973.*

Below *Hatfield-Dunstable train at Dunstable North in 1965.*

was linked to Hatfield in 1876. Trains ran via Cole Green (6½ m) and Hertingfordbury (8 m) to Hertford (Cowbridge) station (9½ m). Its partner, the Luton, Dunstable & Welwyn Junction, reached Welwyn on 1 September 1860 and then took Hatfield as its terminus from 1869. From the LNW station at Dunstable trains ran to Dunstable Town (1 m), Luton (5½ m), parallel with the Midland main line to Luton Hoo (8¼ m), beneath it to Harpenden (10¾ m) and on through Wheathampstead (13 m) and Ayot (15¾ m) to Hatfield (20¾ m). The link with Welwyn Garden City was restored when the collapse of a bridge severed the Hatfield portion of the Luton line but by this time the other two branches had already closed, that to Hertford on 18 June and that to St Albans on 1 October 1951.

In earlier days Hatfield was the scene of some nasty accidents. In April 1860 a Manchester express was derailed; ten years later a broken wheel brought eight deaths.

H.15 Hatfield Peverell

Liverpool Street-Norwich line, between Chelmsford and Witham. 35 m 74 ch from Liverpool Street

A simple, two-platform station replacing an earlier one destroyed by fire and served by some of the Braintree/Witham/ Colchester electrics.

H.16 Haughley Junction

Liverpool Street-Norwich line, junction with Cambridge line. 82 m 79 ch from Liverpool Street

The first station at Haughley lay north of Haughley village on the line opened by the Ipswich & Bury Railway on 24 December 1846. It was replaced by the present location, east of the village, after the junction had been established there as part of the development of the new Eastern Union Railway route to Norwich via Diss. The location then lasted as a passenger station until 2 January 1967 after which it remained of significance for the junction, the signal box and gated crossing 7 ch in advance and for Wassocks LC (83 m 79 ch) along the Norwich route.

The facing junction is by a single lead off the Down line which then doubles towards Bury, Up trains using a facing crossover to reach the Up main. On the Up side of the junction the waste area in front of the old Ministry buffer depot was the site of the junction at which the single line of the Mid-Suffolk Light Railway divided to connect

Laxfield station, Mid-Suffolk Light Railway, in 1960.

with the main line and run its final 9 ch into Haughley's branch platform.

The Mid-Suffolk Light Railway was authorized by an Order of 5 April 1900 (and four subsequent amendments) to link Haughley with Halesworth on the East Suffolk route and provide a branch from Kenton to Westerfield. Freight services began running from Haughley to Laxfield on 20 September 1904 and passenger services on 29 September 1908. The ailing finances of the company allowed only small sections to be built beyond Laxfield and along the branch and it was in the receiver's hands by 1907. Rescue by the LNER in 1924 kept the enterprise alive until final closure came on 18 July 1952, only fifty years after construction work first began.

Uneconomic doubtless, but the Mid-Suffolk was a line of great character, even down to its highly individualistic station nameboards. The three daily trains of the 1930s served Mendlesham (4½ m), Brockford & Wetheringsett (6 m), Aspall & Thorndon (8½ m), Kenton (10 m), Worlingworth (12 m), Horham (14 m), Stradbroke (15 m), Wilby (16½ m) and Laxfield (19 m) and took 79 minutes for their rural journey. A Split Train Staff system was used and Kenton was the crossing place.

H.17 Havenhouse—see   Grantham-Skegness Line

H.18 Haworth—see   Brancliffe-Kirk Sandall Line

H.19 Healing

Cleethorpes-Sheffield line, between

Grimsby Town and Habrough. 105 m 75 ch from Manchester (London Road)

The Barton-on-Humber dmus served this ex-MS&L station of short platforms, plain brick buildings and simple shelter.

H.20   Heckington—see   Grantham-Skegness Line

H.21   Helpston   Junction—see   Peter-borough-Leicester Line

H.22   Hertford

Hertford North is on the Hertford Loop (see below) 19 m 48 ch from Kings Cross and Hertford East on the branch from Brox-bourne Junction. 24 m 19 ch from Liverpool Street

With electric services on both of its present routes Hertford is very well served for access to London. These modern facilities contrast strongly with the situation in the past when the original train services came from branches from the main lines on either side to which schemes for south-north routes via Hertford had lost out. The most direct access, that from the GN main line at Wood Green was the last railway to reach Hertford and then only as part of its role as an avoiding line.

The first trains to arrive started running on the Northern & Eastern branch from Broxbourne Junction on 31 October 1843. These were followed on 1 March 1858 by those of the independent Hertford & Welwyn Junction company which later joined forces with the railway from Welwyn to Luton and Dunstable. The Great Northern and Eastern Counties companies had a period of in-fighting for the Hertford traffic but eventually came to an amicable arrangement and the western branch was purchased by the former in 1861.

The delightful 1888 station at Hertford East with its imposing entrance and highly decorated main building.

The Hertford Loop line was opened under an Act of 1898 although construction work was intermittent and through freight services did not begin until 1918 and passenger services not until 1924 (2 June). The new Hertford station, although further from the town centre, made the Hertford & Welwyn station at Cowbridge redundant so it closed to passengers on the same date and the Hatfield/Welwyn branch trains used a connection to the new station. The route on to Cowbridge and thence to Hertford East was kept open for freight with Staff and Ticket working and a shunter at Cowbridge to deal with local goods traffic. Some exchange traffic also used this route, including livestock which always seemed to need feeding and watering in the process and at the most inconvenient times.

The original N&E station at Hertford was closed on 27 February 1888 in favour of the present Hertford East complex. The buildings are in a very attractive semi-Tudor style with red brick, stone-dressed arches leading to a circulating area with pavilion roof, all the work of Wilson and Ashbee and a miniature version of what they had accomplished at Norwich two years before. Beyond the main terminal buildings are two platforms with three platform lines and the remains of an earlier platform behind the Down side wall. The awnings have decorated support spandrels, a GER seat survives and old lamp standards carry the warning lights at the end of the platform lines. Close to the Up side signal box (24 m 7 ch) is a carriage washing plant with carriage sidings nearby. It was from behind this area that the connection from Hertford North formerly joined.

Hertford North has not quite the style of the East station although there is an attractive brick building on the Down island platform. The station is approached via two viaducts and there are then carriage sidings preceding the platforms and occupying the

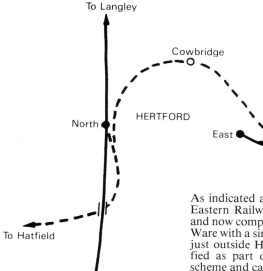

To Langley

Cowbridge

HERTFORD

North

East

To Broxbourne

To Hatfield

To Enfield

area where the H&W route trains rose from the valley floor and connected with the Loop lines until passenger services ended on 18 June 1951 and freight eleven years later.

Hertford East has a half-hourly service connecting into the Bishop Stortford fasts at Broxbourne and then continuing to Liverpool Street and Hertford North has a basic twenty-minute interval service to Moorgate.

H.23   Hertford East Branch

Liverpool Street-Kings Lynn line, branch from Broxbourne Junction. 5 m 64 ch

Buntingford terminus on 19 September 1964.

As indicated above this early Northern & Eastern Railway branch dates from 1843 and now comprises a 60 mph double line to Ware with a single section thence to a point just outside Hertford East. It was electrified as part of the North East London scheme and carries a basic half-hourly service, well patronized by commuters and those making local journeys.

From Broxbourne Junction (18 m 35 ch) the route runs past Rye House Up Sidings Ground Frame which gives access to the Dow-Mac siding and on to Rye House station (18 m 71 ch). This has a modern ticket office kiosk and glazed waiting area on the Up side and just a shelter on the Down.

Continuing up the valley of the Lea the line comes to St Margarets (20 m 23 ch) formerly the junction for the Buntingford branch. Preceded by a ferry van siding and followed by the buildings of some very impressive maltings, the station has a barrier crossing, a large Down side signal box and Up side traditional buildings with the old country end bay and yard beyond. Losing out on early hopes of main line status, Buntingford people got their own railway authorized in 1858 and opened,

Another view of Hertford East station.

with Great Eastern money and operation, on 3 July 1863. It was single with passing loops and followed the valley of the Ash and Rib rivers to Mardock (2¾ m), Widford (3¾ m), Hadham (5¾ m), Standon (9¼ m), Braughing (10¼ m), West Mill (12½ m) and Buntingford (13¾ m). In LNER days the branch had an excellent service of ten trains a day plus four on Sundays when the line was worked with a Long Section Staff and the guard of the last Up train had a special receptacle for collecting all the section staffs. The branch still had a dmu service of nine trains a day immediately before closure to passengers which took place on 16 November 1964, freight closure following in 1965.

Leaving St Margarets and the former branch junction at 20 m 30 ch the surviving line continues west to Ware, home of the Wickham Works from which many railcars, overseas and light railway units have originated. It singles just before the three-arch overbridge and former loco shed con-

nection and then comes to the station complex of single platform, barrier crossing and modern signal box (22 m 17 ch). The dark, low station buildings are probably original and the adjacent Station Hotel and maltings are other interesting reminders of 19th century Ware and its grain, timber and agricultural activities.

The final section of the route is across water meadows with a water supply canal as companion. The single line becomes double again near the point at which the Up side connection to Hertford North departed (23 m 72 ch) and the 13 ch goods yard line left on the Down side.

H.24 Hertford Loop

East Coast main line, loop from Wood Green Junction to Langley Junction. 23 m 13 ch

The double track loop line from Wood Green via Enfield and Hertford to rejoin the main line north of Knebworth started life on 26 April 1871 as a Great Northern Railway branch line to a terminus at Enfield. After a cosmopolitan period when North London Railway and LC&DR services also used the route, increasing congestion on the GN main line forced the revival of plans for a relief route and Parliament sanctioned a scheme for a link from

The original GN station at Enfield became a goods depot with the opening of the Hertford Loop.

A 1960s' view of Hertford North looking north and with the Cowbridge branch on the right.

Enfield to Stevenage in 1898. The GNR Board still had thoughts of investment in quadrupling the main line so contracts for work on the loop were not placed until 1906.

The first section of the new route to be brought into use was that from a junction south of the Enfield terminus to Cuffley & Goffs Oak. This involved the displacement of the former Enfield station by a new one on the through line, services commencing on 4 April 1910. Construction on the difficult section between Cuffley and Hertford then proceeded in fits and starts, an Act of 1914 being needed to extend the time constraints laid down in the original Act. Eventually the various viaducts and tunnels needed to get through the higher areas and reach the more level section at the northern end were completed and freight traffic was able to pass over the single line from 4 March 1918. There was still much work to do and money to be spent to double the route and finish the stations and although the loop was used for diversionary purposes from February 1920 the passenger service did not start until 2 June 1924.

The Hertford Loop was now operational and settled down to its dual role of commuter line and diversionary route. North of Hertford local traffic was sparse, despite cutting costs by using steam rail motors and railcars, and operating a permutation of services involving Biggleswade, Letchworth, Baldock and Royston as turn-round points. The two intermediate stations at Watton-at-Stone and Stapleford were closed on 10 September 1939 and the regular service north of Hertford withdrawn although it came to life again in a shadowy dmu form in the 1950s and Watton was then reopened on 5 May 1982 when the Letchworth-Moorgate emus started to call. For the rest of the route life was mainly a routine one of 'N2's thundering about with Quad-Art sets of four coaches on five bogies and coal or freight trains using the night and off-peak paths.

In the latter days of steam came 'B1's working through to Broad Street and then diesel multiple units, in turn to be ousted by Class '312' four-car electric units from 3 October 1977. The full electric service, including the section north of Hertford, began on 6 February 1978 and now gives the loop three trains an hour from Moorgate, the first one going through to Letchworth and the others terminating at Hertford.

The Hertford Loop begins at Wood Green with the Down junction at 4 m 68 ch and the Up one at 5 m 7 ch. The former involves a 1 in 55 climb to cross the main line and then descend to the island platform at Bowes Park (5 m 55 ch), at one time provided with a run-round line for reversing or access to Bounds Green carriage servicing area. The substantial traditional station at Palmers Green (6 m 50 ch) is followed by a cutting and then a similar station at Winchmore Hill (7 m 63 ch).

The route now starts to rise, the cutting giving way to an embankment before the elevated station at Grange Park (8 m 35 ch) whose signal box formerly controlled the access lines to the old terminus at Enfield. After being replaced by the new through station the terminus became a goods depot and then a coal concentration point. Freight trains descending from Enfield on the Up line used to have to stop at that point and apply the guard's brake which could only be released after passing the underbridge just south of Grange Park station.

Enfield Chase station (9 m 9 ch), again in brick, lies lower down Windmill Hill than its 1871 predecessor with the line then crossing over the main road and maintaining its elevated level on to the north Enfield station at Gordon Hill (9 m 69 ch). At one time the District Goods Superintendent (London Suburban) had his offices here in the wooden buildings on the Great Northern Athletic Association's sports ground. Pre-electrification a number of services originated from the Up bay at Gordon Hill which had a special bell code for the setting back operation.

The surroundings become wooded and rural as the route comes to Crews Hill (11 m 40 ch) on a rising gradient. Rendlesham Viaduct—405 ft long, 70 ft high and with fourteen arches—precedes the modest station and Sopers Farm Viaduct—390 ft long, 30 ft high and with eleven arches—follows it, giving some indication of why the construction process was slow and costly. Cuffley station (13 m 17 ch), with its small brick ticket office at road level below, is followed by the 1 m 924 yd Ponsbourne Tunnel (14 m 59 ch to 16 m). Decoratively portalled and with five shafts, the deepest of 105 ft, this was the longest tunnel on the Great Northern and was the subject of much dispute with the local landowner. A station at Bayford (16 m 56 ch) on the following 1 in 198 drop to Hertford was part of the settlement forced upon the railway.

On this final section to Hertford there are five catch points in the Up main, a six-span viaduct at Horns Mill, a twenty-span Hertford Viaduct and a bridge over the former Hatfield branch route. Part of the track from the Cuffley-Hertford section was lifted and sent to France in the 1914-18 war.

North of Hertford, dealt with in an earlier entry, the route passes through the 364 yd Molewood Tunnel (20 m 14 ch to 20 m 31 ch) which survived a rocket impact during the last war. Then come the sand pits which used to be served by Waterford siding and a rise at 1 in 198 to the platform remains of Stapleford station. After a dip comes Watton-at-Stone, the station nearest to Sir Nigel Gresley's Watton House home and a place with a chequered history which included repainting after the war in readiness for a re-opening that was much postponed. However, the location now has modern platforms with a small ticket office on the overbridge and the Moorgate-Letchworth services call hourly. There is also an Up side oil discharge terminal.

Past the site of the proposed Datchworth station the route comes to a crossover and the point at which the Up and Down lines separate. The former goes direct to the main line at Langley Junction (Up) (28 m 1 ch) while the latter loops below it and rises on the Down side to make its connection at Langley Junction (Down) (28 m 16 ch). It is good to see the route carrying a regular service again, keeping alive memories of Sentinel steam railcars bearing the old stagecoach names.

H.25   Hethersett
Birmingham-Norwich   line,   between

Wymondham and Norwich. 117 m 73 ch from Liverpool Street

Hethersett lost its passenger services on 31 January 1966 but there is still a signal box and gated crossing as well as the Up side oil depot connection and the remains of the former station. Towards Norwich there are AHB crossings at Intwood (119 m 47 ch) and Keswick (120 m).

H.26   Hexthorpe—see Doncaster

H.27   Highams   Park—see   Chingford Branch

H.28   Highbury & Islington—see Moorgate Line

H.29   High Marnham Branch
Cleethorpes-Sheffield line, connection from Shireoaks-Shirebrook branch. 17 m 56 ch

Oil and coal traffic secured the survival of a significant portion of the former Lancashire, Derbyshire & East Coast Railway's main line which ran from the headquarters station at Chesterfield (Market Place) through Shirebrook and Tuxford to Lincoln. Born to tap the East Midlands coalfields and with ambitions to create a major east-west route with docks on the Lincolnshire coast, the LD&EC also formed part of the Great Eastern's ambitions to gain access to coal. The LD&EC line opened on 8 March 1897 and was bought by the Great Central ten years later. It was promoted as 'The Dukeries Route' but coal was its mainstay and kept the western section alive after passenger closure on 19 September 1955.

Starting from High Marnham (27 m 48 ch) where it serves the CEGB power station the route heads west and crosses over the ECML at Tuxford (Tuxford Central West Junction 24 m 41 ch and Tuxford Central 23 m 69 ch) where there is a BP oil terminal. At Boughton Junction (20 m 15 ch) it is joined by the single line from the 1965 Bevercoates colliery. This 25 mph One Train route leads north-east from the junction, through the 350-yd Boughton Brake Tunnel (1 m 49 ch to 1 m 65 ch) to the colliery (4 m 22 ch).

There is a complicated layout at Ollerton Colliery (19 m 33 ch) which gives access to the National Carbonising Company's line and the connection from the Down main to the siding is controlled by Annetts Key issued by the signal box. The next box is then Thoresby Colliery (17 m 21 ch) where the 1 m 18 ch single line from the colliery joins. One Train operation applies and the maximum permissible speed is 15 mph.

The triangular Clipstone Junction comprises East Junction (15 m 40 ch), Clipstone signal box (15 m 20 ch) and West Junction (15 m 15 ch) and is followed by Welbeck Colliery Junction (13 m 20 ch) and its 2 m 62 ch, 25 mph One Train single line to Welbeck Colliery. On the final section to Warsop Junction (10 m 60 ch), Shirebrook South Junction (10 m 19 ch) and Shirebrook East Junction (9 m 72 ch) there is a BP terminal at Warsop Oil Sidings.

H.30   Hitchin

East Coast main line, junction with Cambridge line. 31 m 74 ch from Kings Cross

Hitchin station, consisting of traditional main buildings in red brick on the Down side, the two pairs of Up and Down lines and then the Up platform, derives an excellent service from the fast and slow Kings Cross-Royston electrics and from the Moorgate-Letchworth trains which travel via the Hertford Loop. The dmu connecting service to and from Huntingdon perpetuates a tradition of train handling which goes back through the days of splitting double-headed trains from Kings Cross into Peterborough and Cambridge portions to those early years before the Midland had its own London terminus.

It was back in 1858 that MR trains began running over the line from Bedford to Hitchin on their way to London, but the Great Northern people came to show a predictable tendency to prefer their own trains.

Down HST and Up emu trains pass at the country end of Hitchin station.

By 1862, the year of the second Great Exhibition, matters had begun to come to a head and accusations of massive delays were being made to the GNR's headquarters. By the following year the Midland had obtained powers for its St Pancras extension, the opening of which relegated the line through Henlow Camp to an ordinary branch from completion of the diversions on 1 October 1868 to its closure on 1 January 1962.

The line from Hitchin to Cambridge, one-time route of the 'Cambridge Buffet Expresses', also had a turbulent infancy. It had started life as a plan for a link from Oxford to Cambridge but only the section from Hitchin to Royston was authorized by Parliament. This was opened with Great Northern backing on 21 October 1850 and extended to Shepreth, under a subsequent Act, on 1 August of the following year. A physical connection was made with the ECR's line into Cambridge shortly after, the latter then taking a lease of the Royston & Hitchin company and only at the end of this, in 1866, giving the Great Northern full access to Cambridge.

Hitchin lies in a chalk cutting and is preceded by the site of Wymondley box and siding (29 m 70 ch) on the Down side and by engineers' sidings (31 m 50 ch) on the Up. The old loco depot stood behind the Up platform with Cambridge Junction (32 m 11 ch) then following the country end underbridge and Up and Down goods yard areas. The trackbed of the Bedford line can still be spotted on the Down side of the main line along the course of which lay the gas works siding and Cadwell crossing, box and coal siding (33 m 69 ch) on the Up side and then Three Counties station (35 m 56 ch) which had brick, lime and asylum sidings.

H.31 Hockley—see Shenfield-Southend Line

H.32 Hoe Street Tunnel—see Chingford Branch

H.33 Holme

East Coast main line, between Huntingdon and Peterborough. 69 m 28 ch from Kings Cross

From Huntingdon the main line rises for three miles at 1 in 200 to the site of Ley's box and then descends at the same gradient for four miles, past Connington South Emergency Crossover (67 m 30 ch) to Connington North CCTV LC (68 m 28 ch). Then only the main lines continue on through Holme LC (69 m 28 ch), Holme Emergency Crossover (69 m 35 ch), Holme Lode LC (70 m 22 ch) and Yaxley Emergency Crossover (72 m 50 ch) to signals P403/416 where the Slow lines recommence.

Near Abbots Ripton station (63 m 42 ch) a three-train collision on 21 January 1876 killed fourteen people due to a snowstorm freezing signals in the off position. One result was the development of the GNR's 'somersault' signal. Another isolated area, Connington, has long served as an engineers' tipping site and also had a Down side wartime marshalling yard, Holme had a branch line to Ramsey and there was a passenger station at Yaxley & Farcet until 6 April 1959.

Apart from the modern crossing box and barrier crossing, only the yard area and some railway houses are still visible at Holme where the passenger station closed on 6 April 1959. Twelve years earlier, on 6 October 1947, services had ended on the single line east to St Marys (3¾ m) and Ramsey North (5¾ m). This line had been opened originally by the Ramsey Railway on 1 August 1863 and had later been

*Holme station GNR. The Ramsey North branch trains left from the other face of the platform on the right (*Lens of Sutton*).*

acquired by the Great Northern, more to protect its territory than for any reasons of traffic potential. Plans to make a connection with the Somersham line at Ramsey East never came to anything and the Great Northern continued to work the line as a typical rural branch.

Services on the Ramsey East branch ended as early as 22 September 1930 and from 2 February of the following year trains only worked on the GN branch up to 10.15 am after which a Peterborough Electric Traction Company ominibus service was used instead.

Holme and Ramsey are part of a fenland area and at one period traffic was barged to and from the main line and the local branch. Freight continued on the latter after passenger closure, amounting to about 1,000 wagons a year of coal and seed potatoes inwards and about 300 forwarded wagons of potatoes, grain and sugar beet. The final closure came on 2 July 1973.

H.34 Homerton—see North Woolwich Line

H.35 Honington—see Grantham-Skegness Line

H.36 Hornsey

East Coast main line, between Finsbury Park and Wood Green. 4 m 4 ch from Kings Cross

South of Finsbury Park the Great Northern had little room for traffic sidings so that its major expansion took place in the areas either side of the original station at Hornsey. Here an expanded goods depot brought into use in 1885 was followed three years later by the opening of the Up and Down yards at Ferme Park, a new Hornsey Loco Shed in 1899 and a passenger station reconstruction soon after.

With the changes in the BR freight business the yards at Ferme Park have changed their function over recent years, the old loco shed has gone and, although the old

Inter-City set passing through the carriage washing plant at Bounds Green servicing depot.

Bounds Green carriage shed remains, engines and cranes have long ceased to be transferred to the Eastern Section by reversal to Palace Gates. Instead the line-side areas from the flyover south of Hornsey to Wood Green are taken up with a thirty-acre complex which embraces Ferme Park Reception Sidings, a carriage washing plant, Hornsey Carriage Sidings and the Bounds Green maintenance and servicing depot. The latter is reponsible for seventeen HST power cars and has a peak Saturday night workload of thirteen sets.

Hornsey station itself was remodelled during the electrification period and now has platforms only to the Slow lines.

H.37 Hubberts Bridge—see Grantham-Skegness Line

D9021 calls at Huntingdon in 1967 with a Newcastle-Kings Cross train.

H.38 Huntingdon

East Coast main line, between St Neots and Peterborough. 58 m 70 ch from Kings Cross

Huntingdon station provides the former county town with a local dmu service to and from Hitchin plus calls by the two-hourly HST services to Kings Cross and Doncaster. From Offord & Buckden LC (55 m 72 ch), where the old station and the restrictive curves are now a thing of the past, the main line takes a flat, straight course north, crossing its Ouse companion on the approach to Huntingdon. The station there comprises a modernized Down side and a more traditional Up side where there is a London end bay for the dmu workings. Crossovers and the old Up siding area follow as the route begins to climb at 1 in 200 towards the site of Stukeley box.

Huntingdon's goods yard and shed were on the Down side while on the Up lay Huntingdon East station, now in use as a car park although the station house survives. Planned originally as part of an East Anglian Railways expansion to Bedford, the Ely & Huntingdon Railway arrived

Above *Huntingdon East. What was once one end of the GN&GE Joint line has been reduced to a short siding.*

Below *Connection for Ilford carriage sheds towards Seven Kings and with 65467 on an Up goods.*

from St Ives on 17 August 1847 and was extended to a physical junction with the Great Northern, then newly opened, four years later. The Kettering, Thrapston & Huntingdon Railway reached the town from the west on 21 February 1866 and was soon running through services on to Godmanchester, St Ives and Cambridge. Some alterations in the layout followed the incorporation of the former Ely & Huntingdon in the GN&GE joint line in 1883 and it got a new station in 1923. By the late 1930s Huntingdon East had nine daily LNER trains and six on the LMS route but it was one of the early victims of the BR closure era and lost its trains in both directions in 1959.

H.39 Hykeham—see Newark-Lincoln Line

H.40 Hythe—see Colchester-Clacton Line

I.1 Ilford

Liverpool Street-Norwich line, between Stratford and Romford. 7 m 28 ch from Liverpool Street

At the end of 1984 work began on a £360,000 scheme to replace Ilford's street level buildings with a bright modern ticket hall and ticket office. One of the original stations on the line opened by the ECR on 20 June 1839, Ilford had then undergone major changes in the last years of the 19th century as increases in both rail facilities and local housing began a period of expansion for the area. A part of this expansion was the new Fairlop Loop which came into use on 1 May 1903 and ran from a triangular junction east of Ilford to join the 1856

Loughton line at Woodford. The 'loop' appellation derived from the service which ran out from Liverpool Street to Woodford (9 m) and returned there 98 minutes later via Chigwell (11¼ m), Grange Hill (12 m), Hainault (12¾), Fairlop (13¼ m), Barkingside (14 m), Newbury Park (14¾ m) and Ilford (16½ m)—and vice-versa.

Another round of changes came to Ilford when the pre-war electrification plans were finally realized, taking the 1,500 volt dc system through to Shenfield by September 1949 and turning Ilford into a major emu depot with a flyover to take the electric lines from the Up side to the Down. This commences just beyond Manor Park, from which point Up and Down avoiding lines are provided as far as Ilford box (7 m 17 ch). Next come the centre island and two outer platforms of the station, with the old Unigate milk siding area on the Up side. Ilford Car Sheds box (8 m 14 ch) stands in front of the depot area which includes a washer plant and has swallowed up the site of the former junction for Woodford (closed to passengers on 30 November 1947). Ilford depot will be responsible for fourteen electric locomotives under the East Anglian electrification scheme, reviving memories of *Dennis,* the former Shildon-Newport NER locomotive which used to be used for local shunting.

All local electric services call at Ilford as do the Southend Victoria and Colchester trains.

I.2 Immingham

Cleethorpes-Sheffield line, connection from Barton-on-Humber Branch. Immingham Eastern Jetty 106 m 75 ch from Manchester (London Road)

Near the village of Immingham the Humber Estuary is quite deep along its southern shore so that when all the land available for dock development at Grimsby had been used up Immingham represented a very attractive alternative site. With Great Central Railway backing the Humber Commercial Railway & Dock Company secured Acts in 1901 and 1904 and had its new dock complex ready for opening by King George V on 22 July 1912. In addition to the three lines described under the Barton-on-Humber Branch and Grimsby entries—the Grimsby District Light Railway, the Grimsby & Immingham Electric Railway and the Barton & Immingham Light Railway—there was direct access to docks from the GC main line via the Humber Commercial Railway which was opened for freight traffic on 29 June 1910, initially carrying materials for the final construction stages.

Not all the hopes for the new dock were fulfilled but by the end of the 1930s it was prospering. With a depth of 30-36 ft, the dock was the deepest on the East Coast and had a water area of 45 acres and 5,956 ft of quay length. The main traffic of the inter-war years was grain—through the 15,000-ton granary which had two elevators, each capable of handling 150 tons per hour. Timber, iron ore and coal were also important. For the export of the latter, eight hydraulic coal hoists were provided. These were capable of dealing with 700 tons of coal an hour and had backing sidings which could hold around 300 loaded wagons for each hoist, plus a total of 5,500 empties. In addition to the main dock, jetties were provided either side of the entrance, the

Oil refinery and rail sidings at Immingham.

Eastern Jetty and its adjoining passenger station handling the summer sailings of the Orient Steam Navigation Company and the Western Jetty being used for the shipment of bunker and cargo coal.

Although no longer a railway-owned port, Immingham remains important to the BR freight business especially for the movement of oil traffic from the refineries and tank farms established there. Another major traffic flow is iron ore for the BSC blast furnaces at Scunthorpe. This is moved in 2,000-tonne trains with the wagons discharged by tipper to conveyor belt at the destination. In addition to its oil and iron business, the port has an NCB coal terminal and deals with cement and other traffics. BR has a loco depot and carriage and wagon maintenance facilities there.

The route from the Barton-on-Humber Branch at Ulceby North Junction (100 m 43 ch) is double line and runs due west to Humber Road Junction (104 m 5 ch). Along this Absolute Block section lie the connections to the Lindsey Oil Company sidings serving the tank farms of Petrofina, Total and Conoco. At Humber Road Junction the route then splits into three, one arm continuing on via Immingham Reception box (104 m 30 ch) and following Permissive Block lines to Immingham East Junction (106 m 34 ch) and its box (106 m 40 ch) and then to Immingham Eastern Jetty (106 m 75 ch). Another route leads via Western Entrance CCTV LC (104 m 55 ch) to Immingham West Junction West (104 m 76 ch), with connections to the High Level, the Mineral Quay line, the Timber Storage Yard and the Dock Estate. The third arm is a One Train single line via the open crossing at New Inn (2 m 19 ch) to Killingholme (2 m 70 ch) and the further oil industry activities

Ipswich before electrification and with a Down train just arriving.

there. Connections to the loco shed and C&W shops are made off the Humber Road-Immingham East Junction section, the latter point also forming the connection to Texaco premises and to Grimsby West Marsh Junction.

I.3 Ingatestone

Liverpool Street-Norwich line, between Shenfield and Chelmsford. 23 m 50 ch from Liverpool Street

Ingatestone lies on a short level section of the descent from Ingrave summit down to Chelmsford. The complex comprises level crossing and signal box (23 m 39 ch), DPL and UGL, the old goods shed and then the station proper. The latter derives its basic service from the hourly Colchester trains. Beyond Ingatestone comes the gated crossing house at Church Lane (24 m 68 ch) and then the site of the old siding at Margaretting.

I.4 Ipswich

Liverpool Street-Norwich line, junction for East Suffolk and Felixstowe branches and for Cambridge line services. 68 m 59 ch from Liverpool Street

It says much for the astuteness of the businessmen of Ipswich that most of the railway enterprises in which they invested have survived and prospered. Indeed, Ipswich interests can claim much credit for the building of the Norwich main line, now being electrified, for they were behind the Eastern Union Railway which opened the link to Colchester on 15 June 1846 when the ECR line from London seemed to have stagnated at that point.

Already thriving and with a well-developed dock activity, Ipswich added to its railway network at the end of 1846 with the opening of the Ipswich & Bury line and then promptly started work on the link from Haughley north to Norwich, finally ready for traffic in December 1849. Ten

Unloading rails on the Down Passenger Loop at Ipswich, using a telescopic jib crane.

years later the East Suffolk line was opened with a further twenty years then adding through services to Felixstowe to the local rail network.

Ipswich was also important in terms of goods traffic and, as well as the goods depot, had a docks branch and a line to Griffin's Wharf. By the time the Railway Clearing House came to offer the 1938 edition of the 'Official Hand-book of Stations' for 10 s 6 d carriage paid, Ipswich had no less than 54 siding owners or users, ranging from the Anglo-American Oil Company to the sidings of the two Ransomes companies.

The original Ipswich station was a terminus, south of the tunnel, on a site that later became the locomotive depot and, more recently, has been used for electrification wiring trains. The tunnel was built to allow Ipswich & Bury trains to reverse into and out of the terminus, a clumsy practice that ended with the provision of a new

Class 47 with a twenty-van train passing Sproughton signal box.

station on the present site north of the tunnel and operational from 1 July 1860. As originally built the station was essentially a long single platform, in the manner of Cambridge and with an Italianate style. The Down island was added in 1883.

On the approach to Ipswich the One Train, 15 mph, 74 ch single line to Griffin's Wharf departs on the Up side from Halifax Junction Ground Frame (67 m 75 ch) to be followed by the curving dampness of the 361 yd Ipswich Tunnel (68 m 31 ch to 68 m 47 ch), now laid with slab track to give a firm, long-lasting alignment. This area was always one of some working difficulty for the nearness of the platforms necessitated shunting into the tunnel and a balance had to be struck between using the water column at the station and taking water at Halifax Junction troughs. Ipswich also had a maximum axle loading restriction of 16½ tons for Bridge No 249 over the River Orwell and special regulations governing the crossing of the swing-bridge on the docks branch. This still exists east of the station in the form of a 66 ch connection from 69 m 64 ch to a 2 m 15 ch loop on Ipswich Dock Commission's property.

Although it has lost its signal box function and the one-time District Goods & Pas-

senger Manager, Ipswich has excellent main line and branch services. The former use the two main lines and the latter either the Down Slow around the outer face of the island platform or the Permissive line into the bay. From Ipswich Goods Junction (68 m 74 ch) to East Suffolk Junction (69 m 40 ch) there are additional Up and Down Goods lines on the Up side of the main line and used for access to Upper Goods Yard which continues to deal with coal, stone, tank and Presflo traffic.

By the time this book is published electric trains will be running to Ipswich. From 13 May 1985 the Down evening 'East Anglian' will be making the run in just 60 minutes, with other services taking 62-67 minutes and passengers enjoying a major refurbishment of the station as well.

K.1   Kelvedon

Liverpool Street-Norwich line, between Chelmsford and Colchester. 42 m 21 ch from Liverpool Street

Level crossings at Motts Lane (39 m 2 ch) and Church Street (41 m 57 ch) precede the conventional station at Kelvedon which lies on a level section of the Norwich main line and is served by the hourly Colchester emus. These put the station within an hour of Liverpool Street compared with 1½ hours in steam days, when passengers also had the opportunity of spending another half hour in travelling on the single line branch east to Tollesbury. Traces of the route of this light railway can still be discerned on the Up side, north of the underbridge at the country end of the station.

Like most other East Coast estuaries, the Blackwater had cherished pretensions of growing into a major port and the Kelvedon, Tiptree & Tollesbury Light Railway, authorized by an Order confirmed on 27 February 1901, was intended to serve the local fruit industry and to revive the fortunes of Tollesbury Pier. The line was opened to Tollesbury on 1 October 1904 and extended to the pier on 15 May 1907, although the latter section carried regular services only until 17 July 1921.

The light railway was typical of its kind, taking a meandering course via Feering Halt then on to simple stations at Inworth (2¾ m), Tiptree (3½ m), Tolleshunt Knights (4¼ m), Tolleshunt D'Arcy (6½ m) and Tollesbury (8½ m). Access to sidings was by special key and there were thirteen crossings, each with a 10 mph speed restriction and each requiring a fogman during 'fog or falling snow'. No wonder

that the light railway, with its hand-me-down rolling stock, was no match for the local bus competition. The wonder is that passenger services struggled on until 7 May 1951, the Tiptree fruit and preserve business then keeping some sort of freight service going until 1 October 1962.

K.2   Kennett

Cambridge-Ipswich line, between New-market and Bury St Edmunds. 18 m 69 ch from Coldham Lane Junction

After the drop down from Higham the Ipswich-Cambridge dmus call at the simplified station at Kennett. In addition to the staggered platforms, there is a signal box—so typical an example of Absolute Block signalling that it was frequently included in the training programme of railway traffic apprentices—and a grain siding leading from the former Down dock.

K.3   Killingholme—see Immingham

K.4   Kings Cross

London terminus of the East Coast main line

In later Great Northern days the 10 o'clock departure from Kings Cross took nine hours to get to Edinburgh, the following 10.10 am was in Leeds by 2.42 pm, the 10.32 am slow got to Peterborough at 1.19 pm and the 11.30 am semi-fast was in Doncaster by 3.51 pm. Pre-war the LNER got its 10 o'clock 'Flying Scotsman' to Edinburgh two hours earlier, the 10.15 am 'Leeds/Harrogate' arrived at the former point at 2.01 pm and the 11.30 was at Doncaster by 3.40. By the 1960s another hour had been knocked off the timing of the 'Flying Scotsman', the 'Leeds' was taking about the same time but was getting to Doncaster in 3 hours 12 minutes.

In 1985 the 'Flying Scotsman', leaving at 10.20, reached Edinburgh at 15.05 and Aberdeen at 17.30. The 10.04 Doncaster train took two hours and the 10.35 Leeds, 2¾ hours. Admittedly Pullman cars and Silver Jubilee sets may have gone but the well-lit, air-conditioned comfort of the HST sets has now become the norm for ECML passenger travel.

Kings Cross station has changed quite as much as its train services. The combination of austere dignity and functional simplicity which is the keynote of Lewis Cubitt's terminal is still apparent, but it now has a modern, light, convenient entrance addition and has lost some of the unlovely extra buildings which used to house the police offices and the thousands of umbrellas and other lost property items which passengers insist on leaving on trains. The suburban station remains in partial use, albeit without its terrible buffet, but steam trains no longer labour up from Moorgate or plunge down to the Met's underworld via York Road. More important, the 'throat' layout has been simplified to cut down conflicting movements, and this is another compensation for the loss of majestic locomotives from Top Shed.

Today's drivers simply walk from the driving cab at one end to that at the other.

The Great Northern's first passenger terminus in London was brought into use at Maiden Lane on 7 August 1850, the passenger trains continuing to share the station with goods traffic until Kings Cross became operational on 14 October 1852. Approached down a 1 in 107 gradient (although contemporary railway theory preferred an up gradient into a terminal), through Copenhagen and Gasworks tunnels, the new station had an arrival platform one side, a departure platform on the other and a mass of train stabling sidings in between. The whole area was covered by Cubitt's massive double-arched roof and there were offices on either side. Extensions and alterations were quite frequent during the next 100 years, the first additional platforms dating from 1862, the year before GN trains began working over the Metropolitan route to Farringdon Street. The era of widening the approaches included the use of York Road station from 1866 and of the new local station from 1874. Platform

The great, uncomplicated facade of Lewis Cubitt's original buildings rise above the modernized approach area at Kings Cross station.

16 on the 'Hotel Curve' up from the Met dates from 1 February 1878 with the tradition of alterations, improvements and renumberings continuing right up to the new ticket and enquiry office which was brought into use on 3 June 1973.

After the links from the Great Northern to the Metropolitan lines had started carrying regular services, the latter were supplemented from 1866 by a connection with the London, Chatham & Dover Railway near Farringdon and by the addition of an extra pair of tracks known as the 'Widened Lines'. These developments led the Great Northern to open its goods depot at Farringdon Street (closed 1956 but still visible) where the District Goods Manager (London City) later came to be based. The passenger services from Moorgate Street called at Aldersgate, Farringdon Street and Kings Cross (Met) before climbing Hotel Curve to the local station and then continuing north to Hitchin, New Barnet, High Barnet or the Hertford branch.

The nearness of Gasworks Tunnel to the station, the gradients in the main line tunnels and in those to and from the Moorgate lines, plus the general space constraints of the whole area, made Kings Cross an awkward station to work. The Working Appendix made a number of special provisions to cater for its peculiar problems including Klaxon horns and a trembler bell for use when setting back out of the centre tunnel. Empty coaching stock trains of more than thirteen vehicles could be assisted as far as the South Footbridge by the engine of the incoming train and electric lights were illuminated in Hotel Curve Tunnel whenever a train was signalled into it. The sight of these also informed the knowledgeable commuter that his homeward train was coming but if the rails were greasy there might be a long interval before it arrived and an even longer one before the train could restart

from rest out of the local station platform.

Passengers using Kings Cross today can come across from the Great Northern Hotel or emerge from the Underground subways and catch their main line services from platforms 1-8. There will be no theatrical exhaust notes or wheel slipping as the HST passes the signalling panel (20 ch) which controls the whole of the ECML as far as Sandy and, with York Road on one side and the old loco on the other, enters one of the bores of the 528 yd Gasworks Tunnel (22 ch to 46 ch). At this stage the tracks are paired with No 1 and No 2 Fast on the Up side and No 1 and No 2 Slow on the Down side. Just one chain before the portals of the 594 yd Copenhagen Tunnel (65 ch to 1 m 12 ch) lies Freight Terminal Junction where the connection from the freight depot and the 34 ch single line freight link from the North London line at Camden Road Junction feed into the ECML. Next is Holloway, once provided with a ticket collecting platform, an important cattle handling point from the middle of the 19th century right up to 1964 and then a motorail depot from 1960 to 1968. The four tracks take up their conventional pairings here as a result of the Up Slow passing across the two Fast lines and the route then continues via the Clarence Yard area and the junctions on the approach to Finsbury Park.

Goods traffic was, in the past, an important activity at Kings Cross. Although not an easy depot to work it handled every kind of traffic from the large movements of Aberdeen meat, Scotch seed potatoes and Grimsby fish to such smaller flows as Yorkshire rhubarb and the thousands of 'smalls' consignments weighing under one ton. Outwards business was energetically canvassed, with the LNER offering its 'Three

General view of the new Kings Cross concourse.

Thirty Five Scotsman', 'Four Five North Eastern', 'Five Fifteen North Eastern' and 'Six O'Clock West Riding' plus other fast freight trains from Marylebone to serve the Midlands and North-West.

K.5   Kings Lynn

Northern terminus of Liverpool Street-Kings Lynn line. 96 m 75 ch from Liverpool Street

An important seaport since the time of the Norman Conquest, Kings Lynn could not afford to be left out of the wave of railway development sweeping the Eastern Counties in the 1840s. With the help of land provided by local landowners, plans for a Lynn & Ely Railway were ready by December 1844 and, laid before Parliament, these secured the Royal Assent on 30 June 1845. The authorized capital of £300,000 was to cover the main line from Kings Lynn to join the Eastern Counties Norwich line at Ely, a short Lynn Harbour branch and a longer, 9½-mile branch from Watlington to Wisbech. The plans to continue on from the latter to March and Spalding were abandoned after coming to an agreement with the ECR as the new owners of the Wisbech, St Ives & Cambridge Railway.

The year 1846 was an important one for the new railway for it brought not only the opening of the first 10 m 67 ch of the Lynn & Ely on 29 October but also of the Kings Lynn to Narborough section of the companion Lynn & Dereham Railway. Now grouped together as the East Anglian Railways, the Ely line was opened to the public on 26 October 1847 after difficulties in constructing the Ouse and Wissey viaducts had been surmounted, and in the same year the Lynn & Dereham reached Swaffham and then Sporle and the third partner, the Ely & Huntingdon Railway, opened its St Ives-Godmanchester line. On 11 September 1848 the new railway group reached Dere-

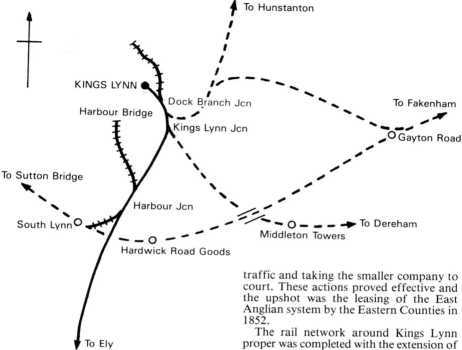

To Hunstanton

KINGS LYNN

Dock Branch Jcn

To Fakenham

Harbour Bridge

Kings Lynn Jcn

Gayton Road

To Sutton Bridge

Harbour Jcn

South Lynn

To Dereham

Middleton Towers

Hardwick Road Goods

To Ely

ham to make connection there with the Norfolk Railway's branch from Norwich via Wymondham.

With a high capital debt and very modest operating profits the EAR became involved with the Great Northern which planned to reach its new partner via Peterborough and Wisbech. But the ECR would have none of this, laying sleepers on the line to block the connection at Wisbech, strangling EAR

Bulk freight wagons at Kings Lynn.

traffic and taking the smaller company to court. These actions proved effective and the upshot was the leasing of the East Anglian system by the Eastern Counties in 1852.

The rail network around Kings Lynn proper was completed with the extension of the harbour branch in 1856, the opening of the Lynn & Hunstanton Railway on 3 October 1862, a docks branch to the new Alexandra Dock on 10 June 1870 and the advent of the embryo lines of the subsequent M&GN system between 1864 and 1886.

Kings Lynn was, and still is, one of the most interesting of railway areas. A major contributor to this was the addition of the Midland & Great Northern Joint Railway system to that built up from the original East Anglian Railways activity. The M&GN had come into being in 1893 and had had its own traffic management, based at Kings Lynn, until 1936. Its predecessor

Kings Lynn prior to modernization and displaying quite an array of finials.

had been the Eastern & Midlands Railway which had been born on 1 January 1883 from the Lynn & Fakenham, Yarmouth & North Norfolk and Yarmouth Union concerns and which, in the same year, had absorbed the Peterborough, Wisbech & Sutton Bridge Railway and the Midland & Eastern group. The latter had been formed on 23 July 1866 from the Lynn & Sutton Bridge, Spalding & Bourne and Norwich & Spalding railways.

So far as Kings Lynn was concerned, the first of the M&GN group of lines was the Lynn & Sutton Bridge which opened on 1 November 1864. The Lynn & Fakenham followed on 16 August 1879 but initially used the Great Eastern station as its terminus until, in 1886, a new direct connection was established to South Lynn. From this time the latter developed rapidly until both Kings Lynn and South Lynn had become major railway locations with loco shed, goods depot, carriage and

Locomotive of a Down train running round at Kings Lynn.

marshalling sidings.

From the Great Northern at Peterborough trains reached Kings Lynn via Wisbech (21¼ m), Ferry (23½ m), Tydd (26 m), Sutton Bridge (28½ m), Walpole (31 m), Terrington (33¼ m), Clenchwarton (34½ m) and South Lynn (37½ m), those from Manchester, Birmingham and the East Midlands travelling via Saxby, Bourne, Spalding (27¾ m from Saxby) and then Weston (30 m), Moulton (31¾ m), Whaplode (32¾ m), Holbeach (35 m), Fleet (37 m), Gedney (38¼ m), Long Sutton (39½ m) and Sutton Bridge (43¼ m). On from South Lynn the route to Yarmouth, Cromer and Norwich was via Gayton Road (5½ m from Kings Lynn), Grimston Road (8½ m), Hillington (10¼ m), Massingham (15¼ m), East Rudham (18¼ m), Raynham Park (20¼ m), Fakenham (24 m), Thursford (30½ m) and Melton Constable (33¼ m). Some services worked to or from Kings Lynn, some originated or terminated at South Lynn but many, including the extra services for holidaymakers, made connection at South Lynn with a shuttle working to and from Kings Lynn.

On the Great Eastern section the best trains from Liverpool Street in the 1930s reached Kings Lynn in about 2 hours 20

minutes. Three trains included restaurant cars and most services continued on via North Wootton (3 m), Wolferton (6 m) the station for Sandringham, Dersingham (8 m), Snettisham (9¾ m) and Heacham (13 m) to Hunstanton (15 m). Heacham had a quiet, eccentric branch line where bad weather was wont to start the telegraph single needles chattering unaided and which ran through Sedgeford (3 m), Docking (6¼ m), Stanhoe (8½ m), Burnham Market (12 m) and Holkham (16 m) to Wells-on-Sea (18¼ m). From Wells a line ran south to Dereham and Norwich and was joined at the former by the original Lynn & Dereham route via Middleton Towers (3¼ m), East Winch (5¾ m), Narborough & Pentney (8¾ m), Swaffham (14½ m), Dunham (18½ m), Fransham (19¾ m) and Wendling (22½ m).

Despite operational economies and the use of diesel multiple units the paucity of traffic which had caused financial problems for the East Anglian Railways also brought about the closure of all Kings Lynn's railway routes except that first main line to Ely. The Heacham-Wells branch, opened on 17 August 1866, lost its passenger service as early as 2 June 1952 with the M&GN system following suit from 2 March 1959. Nine years later the Dereham line closed to passengers on 9 September and on 5 May 1969 the same fate overtook the link with the seaside at Hunstanton. The pieces of railway then surviving were the docks and harbour lines at Kings Lynn, the spur round to South Lynn where there was a sugar beet factory and coal concentration depot and the line out to Middleton Towers which carried considerable quantities of sand traffic.

The 1985 main line service to Kings Lynn provided a through service to and from Liverpool Street every two hours, five out of the six trains with buffet facilities and the

Old maltings and BR bulk wagons at Kings Lynn.

best service taking just over two hours and being slightly faster than the 1960s' 'Fenman'. On the approach to the port the main line passes beneath the trackbed of the M&GN route and then comes to Kings Lynn Harbour Junction (96 m 25 ch) past the rusting sidings of the Campbells Soup premises. The line from South Lynn (35 m 27 ch) joins the main line at the junction (36 m 16 ch), surviving for its coal and sugar beet traffic but no longer the essential link between two significant railway systems.

The Kings Lynn Harbour branch departs from the Down main line at Kings Lynn Harbour Junction (95 m 31 ch) and then runs for 48 ch as a 15 mph One Train single line handling traffic for Norsk Hydro and Dalgetty Franklin. Near Extons Road LC (96 m 27 ch) there is a group of old Up sidings and then at Kings Lynn Junction LC and signal box (96 m 54 ch) comes the surviving 3 m 22 ch of the Dereham branch. This, too, is a One Train single line of 3 m 22 ch and serves the British Industrial Sand premises at Middleton Towers. The Hunstanton line also joined the main line at the same point and for the final 21 ch into Kings Lynn station.

Scheduled in 1984 for future modernization, Kings Lynn station still then retained its traditional, and not unattractive, appearance. The frontage, incorporating some French Renaissance influence, dates from 1871 and leads via ticket office and buffet to the single platform remaining in regular use, from a former total of three platform lines, one release line and an Up side bay. Behind the latter are sidings used for the storage of Scottish Malt Distillery, British Industrial Sand and van rolling stock. The fuelling point is on the Down side near Kings Lynn Junction and opposite are traditional maltings plus the connection with the 46 ch Kings Lynn Dock branch.

K.6 Kirby Cross—see Walton-on-Naze Branch

K.7 Kirk Sandall—see Brancliffe-Kirk Sandall Line

K.8   Kirton Lindsey

Cleethorpes-Sheffield line, between Wrawby Junction and Gainsborough. 84 m 64 ch from Manchester (London Road)

Kirton Lindsey's staggered platforms with their ageing brick buildings have three calls a day by Sheffield-Cleethorpes dmus. They approach past the 1897 maltings and then leave to climb at 1 in 132 and into the 1,334 yd Kirton Tunnel (85 m 10 ch to 85 m 72 ch) through the escarpment which the line has been approaching at an angle for some distance. The south portal is magnificent, round towers either side of the bore and supplementary towers beyond, but the tunnel is wet and it must have been a relief in the days of open footplates to arrive at the plainer northern end.

At Kirton Lindsey summit, the tunnel is followed by two Up side sidings and the main Kirton Lindsey Lime Works connection, all controlled by the tall wooden signal box (86 m 20 ch). The descent via Ermine Street LC (87 m 6 ch) to the broad plain had not yet been singled in 1984 and the station house at Scawby was still there on the Down side.

K.9   Kiveton Bridge and Park

Cleethorpes-Sheffield line, between Shireoaks and Woodhouse Junction. Kiveton Park is 51 m 53 ch and Kiveton Bridge 50 m 34 ch from Manchester (London Road)

Miners and other colliery workers are among those using the two stations at Kiveton which have an hourly service to and from Sheffield and running eastwards as far as Retford, Lincoln or Cleethorpes. After leaving Woodhouse Junction, the dmus on this former GCR main line cross over the Beighton Junction-Rotherham route and then climb for over three miles at 1 in 115 past Brookhouse Colliery box (48 m 12 ch) and the old Waleswood station. The two short platforms of Kiveton Bridge station are then followed by Kiveton Park Colliery which makes up mgr trains and has its own motive power.

In addition to the colliery Kiveton Park had other sidings, including one to Canal Wharf, but the station itself consists just of two short platforms with shelters, although the gabled station house remains in existence. The signal box stands near the barrier crossing after which the route descends at 1 in 40, winding through woodland, towards Brancliffe East Junction.

K.10   Knebworth

East Coast main line, between Welwyn Garden City and Stevenage. 25 m 3 ch from Kings Cross

Knebworth's island platforms are served half-hourly by the Kings Cross-Royston electrics but otherwise the station is unexceptional. It was the home of Kings Cross control during the last war, the buildings still remaining in existence, and at one time controlled Rowe's Lime Siding about half a mile to the north.

L.1   Laindon

Fenchurch Street-Shoeburyness line, between Upminster and Pitsea. 22 m 69 ch from Fenchurch Street

Until Basildon was opened Laindon shared with Pitsea the responsibility for dealing with the New Town traffic. It still deals with that portion arising at the western end of the conurbation and has a basic half-hourly service for the purpose. Non-stop services in the peak put Laindon within 27 minutes of Fenchurch Street and the station also originates and terminates business period services.

The section of the LT&S line from East Horndon to Pitsea was opened on 1 June 1888 to complete the direct route to Southend. It demanded embankments and cuttings either side of Laindon which stands at the summit of the four-mile climb needed to breast the Laindon Hills. The station itself has substantial brick buildings on the Down side encompassing station house, ticket office and staff accommodation, and the old goods yard lies behind—now part coal yard, part car park. The signal box is located on the Up island platform and there are three running lines and three crossovers to give ample turnround permutations.

L.2   Lakenheath

Birmingham-Norwich line, between Ely and Thetford. 82 m 44 ch from Liverpool Street

The Ely-Norwich dmus serve the 1845 station which retains its original brick buildings on the Down side. On the Up is a timber yard, the old wooden goods shed, a signal box and a gated crossing (82 m 49 ch) across the B1112 completing the station layout. Once noted for its chicory factory, Lakenheath is the centre of a large, rich Fenland area and is the nearest station to the USAF base of the same name.

From 1917 to 1919 there was a government line north from Lakenheath to Feltwell aerodrome.

L.3 Langley Junction

East Coast main line, junction with Hertford Loop. Up Junction 26 m 45 ch from Kings Cross, Down Junction 26 m 61 ch

At one time Langley had a goods siding, signal box and water troughs but now its importance is as the junction with the Hertford Loop which first started to fulfil its objective as a relief route on 4 March 1918. Over the years a variety of trains have left or rejoined the main line here, from steam railcars to heavy freight trains, but now the main users of the direct Up side junction and burrowing Down line are the Moorgate-Welwyn Garden City/Letchworth emus.

L.4 Laughton—see Brancliffe-Kirk Sandall Line

L.5 Lea Bridge

Stratford-Copper Mill Junction line. 6 m 25 ch from Liverpool Street

Lea Bridge passenger station marks the northern end of the Temple Mills yard complex. It was one of the stations on the original 1840 Northern & Eastern line and continued to be served by Liverpool Street-Stratford-Lea Valley trains for many years. Palace Gates-North Woolwich trains also served Lea Bridge and, more recently, there was a peak hour service to and from Tottenham Hale. At one time the location was the home of the Lea Bridge Concentration Depot for small consignments.

L.6 Lea Road—see Gainsborough

L.7 Leigh-on-Sea

Fenchurch Street-Shoeburyness line, between Pitsea and Southend Central. 32 m 43 ch from Fenchurch Street

The original LT&S line reached Leigh-on-Sea from Stanford-le-Hope on 1 July 1855 and was extended to Southend proper on 1 March of the following year. From the turn of the century the area grew rapidly and eventually became part of the Borough of Southend, now enjoying a basic emu service of three main line and two loop trains each hour. Although the steam excursions to Leigh have long since ceased and the centre reversing line between the main platforms is rarely used, a form of skip-stop working to and from the Southend stations still operates at peak periods to put Leigh-on-Sea within 34 minutes of Fenchurch Street.

L.8 Letchworth

Hitchin-Cambridge line, between Hitchin and Royston. 34 m 50 ch from Kings Cross

The original 1850 Royston & Hitchin line did not have a station at Letchworth which owes its existence to Ebenezer Howard's concept of a planned, balanced and self-sufficient township. This concept was carried into execution by Garden City Ltd in the first years of the present century, Letchworth getting a goods siding in 1904 for the receipt of inwards materials and then a temporary passenger station on 15 April of the following year. The present station was opened, just beyond the site of its predecessor, on 18 May 1913.

Pre-war Letchworth was served primarily by the 'Garden Cities and Cambridge Buffet Express' which gave it a best time to the metropolis of 47 minutes. Goods traffic was considerable, especially for and from premises linked to the First Garden City siding, these including the Country Gentleman's Association, the Letchworth Bacon Company and the Model Abattoir Siding. In place of all this and its conventional goods depot Letchworth now has carriage sidings and servicing facilities and alternating half-hourly Fast and Slow electric train services to and from Kings Cross plus one service an hour routed via the Hertford Loop.

L.9 Leyton Midland Road—see Upper Holloway-Barking Line

L.10 Leytonstone High Road—see Upper Holloway-Barking Line

L.11 Lincoln

Junction of Nottingham-Cleethorpes, Cleethorpes-Sheffield and Spalding-Doncaster lines. Lincoln St Marks is 32 m 63 ch from Nottingham and Lincoln Central 82 m 41 ch from Huntingdon.

A whole host of early railway projects included Lincoln in their north-south and east-west ambitions but by the second half of the 1840s the main trunk projects had crystallized into the meeting at Lincoln of the GN line from Peterborough via Boston with the MS&L route from Sheffield. However, Lincoln's first trains came from a typical Hudson probe, constructed at great speed in order to beat its rivals and reaching the city from Nottingham and Newark on 3 August 1846. It was then 17 October 1848 before the Great Northern arrived from Boston, Lincoln being linked with Market Rasen (and thus Grimsby and New Hol-

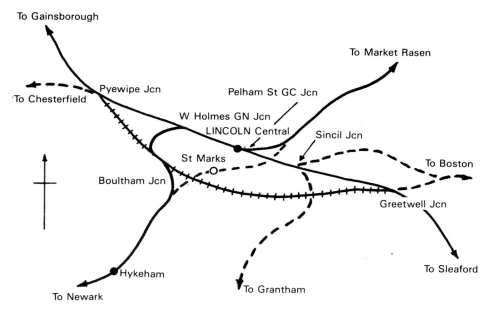

land) from 18 December of that year. By 9 April 1849 the opening of the Lincoln-Gainsborough section gave access via Retford first to Sheffield and then to Doncaster.

The more direct route to Retford came into existence on 7 August 1850 with the opening of the cut-off line between Sykes Junction and Clarborough Junction, but Lincoln's extensive rail network lost some stature with the 1852 completion of the Great Northern's 'Towns' line and then with the 1864 closure of the Gainsborough route. The latter came back into use three years later when the Doncaster-Gainsborough line was opened on the same

The bays at Lincoln, formerly used for Grantham, Boston, Skegness and Grimsby trains.

day (15 July). Three months earlier a new link from the main line at Grantham, leaving the Sleaford line at Honington and running below the escarpment to Lincoln, had been opened and this was now to contribute to the loop which had been created from Grantham to Doncaster via Lincoln and Gainsborough.

A further round of expansion of Lincoln's rail facilities was still to come. It started, modestly enough, on 1 December 1876 when the new line from Bardney east to Louth helped to improve access to the Lincolnshire coast and its aspiring ports and resorts. Some years later a new Spalding to Lincoln line was completed from Ruskington to Pyewipe Junction on 1 August 1882. With the existing lines from Huntingdon, through March, to Spalding and from Lincoln to Doncaster, the new through route became vested in the two

contributing companies as the GN&GE joint line. The GN's half share of the construction costs of the new section was just £100,000, more than they got paid for the difference in value of the existing lines contributed by the two companies; but this was still better than having the Great Eastern realize its long-cherished dream of separate access to the power and industry of the North.

The final route to reach Lincoln was that of the Lancashire, Derbyshire & East Coast Railway whose main line from Chesterfield arrived on 8 March 1897 and became part of the Great Central system ten years later.

Over the years Lincoln derived immense benefits from its extensive railway facilities. On market days farming people arrived by train from every direction and on summer Saturdays the through platforms and bays were again filled, this time with trains heading towards Skegness and Mablethorpe. The city developed a considerable engineering activity and had sidings for firms like Clayton & Shuttleworth, Clayton Dewandre, Robey & Co and Ruston & Hornsby. In addition to its passenger stations, Lincoln had goods depots dealing with full load and sundries traffic, warehouses, a marshalling yard and other ancillary railway activities. For example, the LNER Sack Superintendent had his headquarters at Lincoln.

The one big disadvantage brought by the railways was the number of level crossings, one outside St Marks, another further along the High Street outside Central and a third to the east of that station. The remodelling of the Pelham Street area has already helped to reduce this problem and the rerouting of trains from Newark into the former LNER station will further ease the impact of trains upon the busy High Street thoroughfare.

A 1984 view of Lincoln Central from the High Street footbridge.

Of course, Lincoln deals with far fewer trains than it used to. The 1950s saw the closure of the Louth line on 5 November 1951 and the end of services on the former LD&EC route on 19 September 1955. The direct route from Honington was closed on 1 November 1965 and the final implementation of the East Lincs rationalization on 5 October 1970 took away services from the Boston direction. The cutting of the GN&GE joint line between March and Spalding has altered the service pattern on that route but it still has a dozen trains each way daily and Lincoln is well served by the Cleethorpes-Newark-Nottingham trains and the dmus to and from Sheffield. The 'Humber-Lincs Executive' puts Kings Cross within two hours travelling time compared with 2½ hours in steam days.

From the Newark direction the double track approaches Lincoln via the AHB LC at Doddington Road (30 m 19 ch), past a buffer depot and cold store near Boultham barrier crossing and signal box (31 m 17 ch) and on to another barrier crossing and box at Lincoln West (32 m 38 ch). The new connection to avoid St Marks station was being laid on this section in 1984 but services were still using that station which comprised a Down side signal box (32 m 56 ch) and two platforms (32 m 63 ch) with two centre sidings. The main Down side buildings, single storey and with fluted Ionic columns, date from the 1846 opening although they were slightly altered three years later when St Marks was linked to the MS&L's Market Rasen line. This involved the crossing at High Street (GC) (32 m 47 ch/41 m 47 ch) and a further 26 ch to Pelham Street Junction.

At Pelham Street Junction (41 m 23 ch from New Holland) the Newark-Cleethorpes route meets the one from Spalding to Doncaster and the Lincoln diesel maintenance depot is also located here. The GN&GE joint line drops steeply from the 60 yd Branston & Washington

Cross Roads Tunnel (79 m 44 ch to 79 m 47 ch), with a view of the trackbed of the Bardney line along the River Witham, and then comes to Greetwell Junction (81 m 25 ch). The signal box there controls access to the Lincoln Avoiding Line which runs via Boultham Junction (2 m 34 ch) to Pyewipe Junction (3 m 10 ch).

From Greetwell Junction the joint line comes to Lincoln Central (82 m 41 ch) via the signal box and crossing at Sincil Bank (82 m 19 ch)—former junction for Grantham and Boston—and Pelham Street box and crossing (82 m 19 ch) where the Barnetby route joins at Pelham Street (GC) Junction (82 m 29 ch) and the five platform lines commence.

Lincoln Central station (82 m 41 ch) has grey brick and stone buildings of some magnificence. They include not only an impressive crenellated tower and other decorative features but the proportions are extremely generous. Even the 'Gents' is about the size of a small country church! There are three London end bays on the main platform, formerly the starting point for the Boston, Skegness, Louth and Grantham services, with a footbridge to the Down island, but the outer platform beyond this is no longer used. All lines come together near the tiny High Street LC signal box (82 m 49 ch) to cross the main access road into the city.

Beyond the station the route runs via Brayford LC (82 m 57 ch), East Holmes box (82 m 60 ch), West Holmes box (83 m 29 ch) and the 27 ch link to Boultham Junction, GN Junction (84 m 8 ch), Pyewipe Junction (GC) (84 m 14 ch) and then on along the river towards Kesteven Sidings LC (87 m 41 ch). On this section lie the freight yard and various engineers' sidings, then West Holmes where new track has been put in for the re-routed Newark trains, the remains of the old loco area and then Pyewipe where the Avoiding Line joins, the former marshalling yard was sited, and the trackbed of the LD&EC Chesterfield route is still visible.

To complement the new £1.7 million link to Central Station, and the closure of St Marks the former has received a £20,000 clean, funded by the local authority.

L.12   Lingwood—see   Norwich-Yarmouth Line

L.13   Littlebury Tunnel—see Audley End

L.14   Littleport

Liverpool Street-Kings Lynn line, between Ely and Downham. 76 m 2 ch from Liverpool Street

Apart from the well settled ridge west of the railway, Littleport stands in an area of rich agricultural land where farm tractors bustle about between the drainage channels. A boat-filled inlet from the River Ouse lies close to the station which comprises Up and Down platforms with shelters, level crossing and the traditional signal box which controls the double to single line junction towards Denver. Like Ely, Littleport also has a limited clearance road underpass.

On the flat, straight approach from Ely there are level crossings at Queen Adelaide LC (72 m 17 ch) and Sandhills LC (75 m 35 ch).

L.15   Liverpool Street

London terminus of Norwich and Kings Lynn main lines

In 1979 the City of London Corporation added its approval to the outline planning permission already given for the redevelopment of the Liverpool Street station area. In 1982 the British Railways Board approved the overall scheme put forward by its Property Board under which a massive nine-year remodelling would be funded by the provision of 1¼ million sq ft of offices and 30,000 sq ft of shops on the 25-acre site made up by Liverpool Street and Broad Street stations.

The first outward signs of the changes to come appeared in 1983 when renewal work on the Western Train Shed began a massive scheme which would eventually replace the old pattern of separate areas with long and short platforms by a new station of uniform platforms and eight tracks out to Bethnal Green. The overall scheme also involves the closure of the adjoining Broad Street terminus and of the section of line from there to Dalston Junction in favour of trains being routed to and from Liverpool Street via a new Graham Road curve at Hackney. To all intents and purposes the only survivors among the traditional Liverpool Street features will be the renovated Western Train Shed and the Great Eastern Hotel.

As it stood at the beginning of the reconstruction work Liverpool Street had eighteen platforms fed by three pairs of lines, Up and Down suburban, main and electric. Platforms 1-8 were used by the Enfield, Chingford and Cambridge line services, 9 and 10 by trains on the Colchester main line and 11-18 by the Clacton, Southend and inner suburban services. Along the frontage to Liverpool Street stood the former LNER headquarter offices and the Great Eastern Hotel, the latter continuing

The Broad Street/Liverpool Street site prior to the redevelopment scheme.

round into Bishopsgate in which Harwich House (once the home of the shipping services administration) and Hamilton House (housing the former Liverpool Street Divisional Manager) were its neighbours.

The old station was typical of its era. The entrance from Bishopsgate, decorated with 'Great Eastern Railway' in the stonework above, led to the period east side booking office and then via a long footbridge right

The country end of Liverpool Street station.

across the station to Sun Street Passage, a complete misnomer for the dark alley running between Liverpool Street and its LMR neighbour. The footbridge enabled passengers to shorten the ground level route round the back of the two long platforms, 9 and 10, and had connections to the Underground and a passage beneath the cab road which led from Pindar Street to Liverpool Street. The main ticket office and information facilities between Platform 9 and the Liverpool Street cab road had already taken over the work of the western side ticket office.

Liverpool Street station opened for suburban trains on 2 February 1874 under Parliamentary authority obtained ten years

Spitalfields and the East London Line.

earlier. The original Eastern Counties Railway route had extended from Mile End on 1 July 1840 to a terminus first called Shoreditch and then (from 27 July 1846) Bishopsgate. The initial layout comprised five lines between two platforms with an overall roof and a turntable at each end, but the site was altered and enlarged before it closed to regular passenger trains from 1 November 1875 when the second part of the new Liverpool Street terminus was brought into use. On this same date Bishopsgate Low Level station, located on the new 1 in 70 cutting and tunnel route beneath the original line, lost its suffix and became plain Bishopsgate. The former Bishopsgate terminus reopened as a goods depot on 1 January 1881 and this great warren of activity then lasted until a spectacular fire brought its closure on 5 December 1964.

The Liverpool Street of 1874-5 was the work of the Great Eastern engineer Edward Wilson who used a lot of brickwork and little stone, achieving the main effect from the broad span, high-pitched roofs. Before the main line services joined the suburban ones in using this great Gothic structure a junction had been opened with the Metropolitan and for a few years Met, Brighton and South Eastern trains ran to and from Liverpool Street. The connecting spur was taken out of use in 1904 and later built over but its course is still apparent at the western end of the Met line station. Another route to the lines south of the Thames was via the East London line.

There have been a number of alterations at Liverpool Street in the course of its long and busy history. Major track alterations in 1890 were followed by extensions on the east side in 1894. Then came the Great Eastern's importation of Henry Thornton as general manager, its look at electrification and the alternatives and the consequent introduction of the 'Jazz' service

from 12 July 1920. For alterations costing less than £100,000 the GER revised its suburban service operation into and out of Liverpool Street based on higher capacity trains, short headways and quicker turnrounds. The methods and standards of that period were to be maintained until the Shenfield electrification of 1949 and the ac schemes which began at the end of 1960.

Eastwards from Liverpool Street, the Up and Down Suburban lines plunge into a tunnel with a brief glimpse of the platform remains of Bishopsgate Low Level which closed on 22 May 1916. On the Up side, the signal box (22 ch) is followed by East London Junction (48 ch) and a glimpse of Shoreditch station and the route beneath the river to New Cross. The connection to the East London line at Shoreditch was severed on 17 April 1974, the last parcels train having used the route on the previous day.

Continuing east, the remains of Bishopsgate are now above the north side lines, still evoking memories of the huge depot and its cavernous lower levels where every type of railway activity—storage, cellaring, sampling etc—went on. Bishopsgate goods was 53 ch from Bethnal Green West Junction, its twin access lines, crossing to the Down side of the main line where Spitalfields Granary Signal Box—now standing gaunt and out of use—controlled the access to Spitalfields Yard. Spitalfields was another busy area, a depot specializing in fish, fruit and vegetable traffic, serving Spitalfields and Billingsgate markets and with its two levels linked by wagon hoist. The goods route from Bishopsgate and Spitalfields rejoined the main lines at 1 m 6 ch from Liverpool Street, near Bethnal Green station.

Amid today's frequent and unostentatious emu operations it is not easy to visualize Liverpool Street as it used to be, filled with the Worsdell and Holden 2-4-2Ts of which the Great Eastern at one period had over 200. The 'Clauds' and 'Super Clauds', some fitted for oil burning, were regular visitors until ousted by the 'B12's and subsequent 4-6-0s and then the gentle sighing of Westinghouse brake engines was drowned by the exhaust of the 'Britannias' which did such great deeds with the Norwich trains before the diesel era came along.

L.16   London Fields

Liverpool Street-Kings Lynn line, between Bethnal Green and Hackney Downs. 2 m 35 ch from Liverpool Street

At the time of writing London Fields was closed due to fire damage. The 1872 station, which had been closed once before (22 May 1916 to 1 July 1919), has platforms to the suburban lines only and in normal times is served by the Cheshunt and Hertford East emus.

L.17   Lower   Edmonton—see   Enfield Town Branch

L.18   Lowestoft

Terminus of East Suffolk line and of line from Norwich via Brundall Junction. 23 m 41 ch from Norwich

Lowestoft has dmu services to Ipswich and Norwich, both starting from the rebuilt 1847 terminal station which stands between the south end of the shopping area and the

north end of the seafront holiday area. Across the road from Station Square is the fish dock, and the channel which leads from the sea to Lake Lothing, Oulton Broad and the River Waveney runs parallel with the railway as the latter heads inland to divide into the two routes at Oulton Broad North Junction.

The man responsible for much of Lowestoft's early growth was the notable contractor Sir Samuel Morton Peto. He owned the Norwich & Lowestoft Navigation, built the 1844 Yarmouth-Norwich line and then linked Lowestoft to it at Reedham (goods 3 May 1847, passengers 1 July). When his plans for a major route westwards were overtaken by the developments of the Norfolk and Eastern Counties systems, Peto gave Lowestoft its second major railway route in the form of the Lowestoft & Beccles Railway which opened on 1 June 1859. These two routes survive but the 1903 Norfolk & Suffolk Joint Committee line to Yarmouth via Gorleston lasted only until 4 May 1970. Until then it left the main Lowestoft approach line at Coke Ovens Junction, circled the town to Lowestoft North (1 m 53 ch) and then ran along the coast through Corton (3 m 7 ch), Hopton (5 m 14 ch), Gorleston Links Halt (6 m 21 ch) and Gorleston-on-Sea (7 m 15 ch) to Gorleston North Junction (8 m 72 ch from Coke Ovens Junction and 75 m 36 ch from South Lynn Junction) where it divided for South

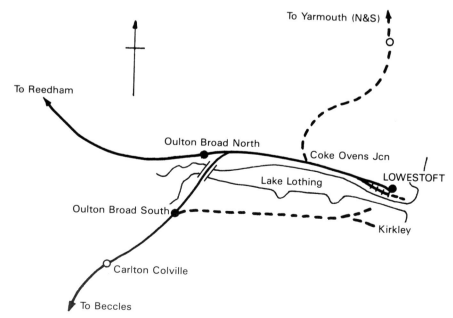

Town and Beach stations at Yarmouth.

In pre-war days, while the swing-bridge across Breydon Water was still in use, about half the Lowestoft-Yarmouth trains ran round Yarmouth to Beach Station M&GN. Before the coastal route closed some of the services from Liverpool Street got to Lowestoft over its metals but the traditional access from London was by shuttle train connection out of the Yarmouth services at Beccles or by portions split and worked forward from there. Pre-war the 4.30 pm Restaurant Car service from Lowestoft took a Yarmouth portion at Beccles and then ran non-stop to Liverpool Street on Mondays, Fridays and Saturdays, arriving at 7.15 pm.

Many of the travellers on such trains had business at the port of Lowestoft. This had first come into railway hands in 1848 and over the next ninety years had grown to 74 acres, with 6,648 ft of quay handling coal, oil, grain and timber and another 4,470 ft devoted to the fishing industry. As the herring shoals moved down the North Sea the local trawlers and drifters were supplemented by those from other ports to swell the catch landed, auctioned, packed in ice and despatched to the inland markets. From the fish dock vehicles brought load after load to the waiting railway goods and passenger vans, past the stalls of the hardy Scots lassies busy smoking some of the best tasting kippers in the world.

Despite alterations in the 1960s, Lowestoft still looks a typical small terminus with ticket office and parcels office in Denmark Street and the old buffet along the front. The public telephone still boasts 'Trunk Calls may be made from here' and the three platform lines retain their Stanton Patent Buffers and LNER lamps. The Up side bay is no longer used and the Down side lines no longer cross the road to the fish dock but there are still a number of sidings along Commercial Road, used for carriage stabling, engineers' traffic and some grain business. Opposite, the signal box stands beside the Up line (23 m 23 ch) and controls the crossovers, then further on a coal concentration depot now marks the Coke Ovens Junction area. The sleeper depot used to stand on the Down side nearby.

At Oulton Broad North Junction (22 m 17 ch) the Norwich and Ipswich routes separate, the latter to cross the waterway by a swing-bridge beyond which lay the connection to the old Kirkley goods depot.

M.1   Magdalen Road

Liverpool Street-Kings Lynn line, between

Downham and Kings Lynn. 90 m 74 ch from Liverpool Street

Contractor William Smith-Simpson started work on the easy northern end of the Lynn & Ely Railway in May 1846 and had a straight section of 10 m 67 ch ready for opening on 27 October of that year. The first trains called at Stow, Watlington and St Germans and took 35 minutes for the journey. Today the Liverpool Street-Kings Lynn trains take 18 minutes, hastening past gated level crossings at Stow Bardolph (88 m 33 ch) and Holme Road (89 m 63 ch), calling briefly at Magdalen Road, and then pushing on via the CCTV LC at Watlington (91 m 13 ch) and the traditional one with adjoining gabled cottage at St Germans (92 m 68 ch).

Magdalen Road, which was called Watlington until 1875, became a junction on 2 February 1848 when the March-Wisbech-Watlington route was completed. The trackbed of this former Fenland branch via Smeeth Road (12½ m), Emneth (15½ m), Wisbech (17¾ m) and Coldham (21¼ m) is still visible at the London end of Magdalen Road's old Down side goods yard. Just north of this is the station's short Down platform with a tall, narrow wooden waiting room and, opposite, the Up platform with the main station buildings and traces of some once-notable topiary. There is a barrier crossing and adjacent wooden signal box.

Magdalen Road was closed in 1968 but reopened in 1975 as a result of local efforts to stimulate use of the trains.

M.2   Manea

Norwich-Birmingham line, between Ely and March. 80 m 13 ch from Liverpool Street

Along this stretch Manea is the only surviving intermediate station, Chettisham (73 m 59 ch), Black Bank (75 m 30 ch) and Stonea (82 m 5 ch) having closed in the 1960s. A signal box (73 m 55 ch), barrier crossing and station house survive at Chettisham, along with an active Grainflow siding on the Down side. Level crossings at Beald Drove (74 m 58 ch) and North Fen then precede Black Bank LC, signal box (75 m 23 ch) and old Up side wooden goods shed.

On the next part of this dead straight route come three more level crossings, Second Drove (75 m 58 ch), Third Drove AHB (75 m 78 ch) and Welney Road AHB (79 m 50 ch) and the railway rises twice from its flat profile to cross the New and Old Bedford Rivers by means of tied girder bridges.

Manea itself has two short, bare platforms, barrier crossing and traditional signal box and is served by the Cambridge-Peterborough dmus.

The line rises slightly on its way to Stonea where, in addition to the signal box and gated level crossing, a wooden loo marks the site of the former Down platform! Unlike its companion at Furlong Drove (77 m 24 ch) the intermediate signal box survives at Horsemoor where there is also a barrier crossing (84 m 31 ch).

The original line was opened by the ECR on 14 January 1847.

M.3 Manningtree

Liverpool Street-Norwich line, junction with Harwich Branch. 59 m 35 ch from Liverpool Street

Manningtree is approached down a 1 in 134 gradient and the station lies just south of the point where the Stour estuary narrows sufficiently to be crossed by a conventional bridge. When the line opened originally in 1846 it was planned to build a quay here but there was no real development until 1854 when the branch to Harwich was opened on 15 August. The triangular junction was completed by the opening of the spur from the Ipswich direction on 29 August 1882 in readiness for Great Eastern's new port complex opening at Parkeston Quay.

The station at Manningtree consists of Up and Down platforms with a siding beyond the latter and a country end bay in the former. The two sides are connected by subway with the Up side buildings then housing the ticket office and buffet. To an attractive period design these brick buildings still have one room with 'General Waiting Room' in the door glazing.

There is a barrier crossing and low headroom underpass at Manningtree South Junction (59 m 43 ch) where the pair of branch lines turns east to Manningtree East Junction (59 m 67 ch). The Up line is reversible and is used by Down branch trains from the bay platform as far as the crossover at East Junction. The Up line is also reversible on the short stretch past the signal box (59 m 46 ch) to Manningtree North Junction (59 m 69 ch) from which a single line spur of 24 ch links the branch with the Ipswich direction.

Through trains from Parkeston to Ipswich and beyond use the north spur at Manningtree. All the local branch services start and terminate at Manningtree except for two services each way which run through to/from Colchester.

M.4 Manor Park

Liverpool Street-Norwich line, between Stratford and Ilford. 6 m 19 ch from Liverpool Street

The 1873 Manor Park station was one of those rebuilt in 1946 as part of the Shenfield electrification project. It lies before the Ilford flyover and comprises centre island and outer platforms, of which those to the electric lines are used by passengers travelling on the Liverpool Street-Gidea Park emus.

M.5 Mansfield Colliery Branch—see Clipstone-Mansfield Line

M.6 March

Norwich-Birmingham line, between Ely and Peterborough. 85 m 76 ch from Liverpool Street

This long, straggling town deep in the agricultural countryside of Cambridgeshire was one of many settlements which came to be dominated by the railway. In the case of March, for years many of its jobs depended on either the busy station, the large locomotive depot or the great marshalling yards at Whitemoor. The activity is now much reduced and March is just a station on the link between the railways of East Anglia and the East Coast main line at Peterborough but much of the evidence of busier days is still apparent.

The first ECR probe towards the world outside its home territory was made from Ely to Peterborough. Its opening in 1846/7 was followed by the creation of junctions at March when the Wisbech, St Ives & Cambridge Junction line opened first to Wisbech, on 3 May 1847, and then to St Ives, on 1 February 1848. The route north to Spalding, although an 1863 Great Eastern concept, was authorized instead to the Great Northern and was opened by that company on 1 April 1867. Twelve more years of rivalry then followed until the GN&GE Joint Committee was set up on 3 July 1879 and gave the Great Eastern its longed for outlet to the North once the Spalding-Lincoln gap was closed three years later.

March has now lost all its routes apart from the original Peterborough line but it used to be a very busy station, not only for passenger interchange but also with fruit and mails, and later Brute traffic. The whole area had a considerable horticultural activity with heavy seasonal loadings of fruit and vegetables at March, on the branches and at the intermediate stations on the main line towards Spalding. After passing through Whitemoor Yard, with the Up yard on one side and two Down yards on the other, the local trains called at Guyhirne (27 m 78 ch from Huntingdon), Murrow West (30 m 78 ch), French Drove (33 m 61 ch), Postland (37 m 13 ch) and Cowbit (40 m 69 ch). Just three chains beyond Murrow West the Peterborough-Wisbech M&GN line crossed the GN&GE joint line on the level, a fact that allowed links to be created from the latter east to the Eye Green and Dogsthorpe brickyard complex and west, through Wisbech North, to the 70 ch Harbour Branch. These freight lines lasted from the passenger closure of the M&GN route on 2 March 1959 until 1964 in the case of the Wisbech section and 1966 in the case of Eye Green. March-Wisbech passenger services then ended on 9 September 1968.

From the Manea direction the approach to March is via Badgeney Road LC (85 m 7 ch) and then March South Junction LC (85 m 35 ch) where the signal box controls access to the additional Up and Down lines. It is still just possible to spot the course of the former route from Cambridge via St Ives which joined at this point. On the section on to March East Junction LC and signal box (85 m 67 ch) there are the surviving sidings of the old Up and Down yards plus the former goods shed on the Down side. At East Junction the Peterborough and Whitemoor lines divide after the level crossing and then pass through the station which consists of three platforms with four faces and several Down bays. Only the Ely-Peterborough route platforms are now in use, the Down side accommodating the main ticket office buildings in red brick and to a traditional style.

Beyond the station the former Spalding lines swing north to Whitemoor Junction (86 m 11 ch) and a 13 ch spur from the latter point joins the main line at March West Junction (86 m 17 ch) to complete the tri-

angle. The Up loop and URS and DRS beyond are reminders of the amount of traffic formerly handled—freight trains waited here and at the London end for access to Whitemoor, in addition to those which came down the joint line or had to reverse off the Wisbech branch by using the station Avoiding Line. Beyond March West Junction come level crossings at Norwood Road (86 m 30 ch), Whitemoor Drove (87 m 30 ch) and Middle Drove (87 m 75 ch).

The diesel maintenance depot at March is still of considerable importance although it does not have quite the same variety as in steam days when the diagram room displayed every permutation of engine and working and the workshops were busy with every job from new firebox rivets to re-building a brick arch. Whitemoor still deals with some freight traffic and March station enjoys a good service from the Norwich/Cambridge-Peterborough/Birmingham dmus in addition to calls by 'The European'. March as a town has been pleasantly modernized but the 1982 closure of the joint line section north to Spalding ended an era during which March had as many bicycles as Cambridge but, instead of undergraduates, they were ridden by the men of March on their way to Whitemoor, the loco sheds or some other part of the railway network.

M.7 Market Rasen—see Barnetby-Lincoln Line

M.8 Markham Sidings—see Brancliffe-Kirk Sandall Line

M.9 Marks Tey

Liverpool Street-Norwich line, junction for Sudbury Branch. 46 m 49 ch from Liverpool Street

The hourly electric trains from Liverpool Street arriving at Marks Tey down the gentle slope from Long Green LC (45 m 66 ch) take just an hour for their journey. After the call at the station, which has modernized administrative buildings on the Up side and a V-platform for cross-platform exchange with the Sudbury branch on

Sudbury branch dmu draws into the branch platform at Marks Tey.

Mellis station's Up platform with the branch line to Eye on the right.

the Down side, the Colchester emus continue northwards past the branch line junction (46 m 57 ch), the Down signal box with DPL behind and then the Up Goods Loop with the two-siding sand terminal beyond it. An Up side wiring depot and crossover then precede the gated level crossing at Chitts Hill (49 m 41 ch).

On the original Eastern Union Railway line from Ipswich to Colchester, Marks Tey became a junction with the opening on 2 July 1849 of the Colchester, Stour Valley, Sudbury & Halstead company's Sudbury line which was eventually to become a through route to Cambridge, with connections to Bury St Edmunds. Today's branch trains either work through to and from Colchester or are turned round at Marks Tey. They use the short, curving branch platform which has a small hut to house the token instrument. Between this and the platform to the Down main line are the circular foundations of the station's one-time gasworks.

M.10   Marsh Junction—see Grimsby

M.11   Maryland

Liverpool Street-Norwich line, between Stratford and Ilford. 4 m 39 ch from Liverpool Street

Similar to Manor Park, described earlier, this suburban station started life in 1873 as Maryland Point and achieved its present form in 1946 as part of the Shenfield electrification scheme. The Liverpool Street-Gidea Park emus call.

M.12   Meldreth

Hitchin-Cambridge line, between Royston and Cambridge. 47 m 75 ch from Kings Cross

Meldreth lies at the foot of the seven mile descent from Ashwell, on a short 1 in 100 section which precedes the flat approach to Cambridge. This is an agricultural area

with the chalk content reflected in Meldreth's three former lime, stone and cement sidings.

On the extension of the Hitchin & Royston to Shepreth opened on 1 August 1851, Meldreth became part of the GN system from 1 January 1874 and got a new signal box three years later. Today it comprises the old brick goods shed on the Up side with the platforms, station house and ticket office with bow window on the Down side and a traditional wooden shelter on the Up, the line then continuing via Meldreth Road level crossing (49 m 37 ch). The service is derived from stops by some of the Royston-Cambridge dmus.

M.13   Mellis

Liverpool Street-Norwich line, between Stowmarket and Diss. 91 m 30 ch from Liverpool Street

On the 1849 Eastern Union Railway link from Haughley to Norwich, Mellis was once a junction with a short branch to the small but affluent Mid-Suffolk borough and market town of Eye. The passenger service was withdrawn from Mellis station on 11 November 1966 and by 1984 it was significant only for the tall brick 'Mellis Junction' signal box standing on the remains of the V-shaped Up platform, for the gated crossing 5 ch further north and for another such crossing at Thornham Road (91 m 1 ch).

Mellis had become a junction on 1 April 1867, two years after the Mellis & Eye Railway had been authorized with a capital of £20,000. Although promoted by local interests, the line was worked by the GER and from 1920 had an intermediate station at Yaxley Halt served by train steps from 'the special car' provided and with 2½d single fare tickets available from the conductor-guard to either end of the line. The single line branch was 2 m 73 ch long and lost its passenger service as early as 2 February 1931 but its buffer depot, coal and grain traffic kept the freight service going until 13 July 1964. Like most such

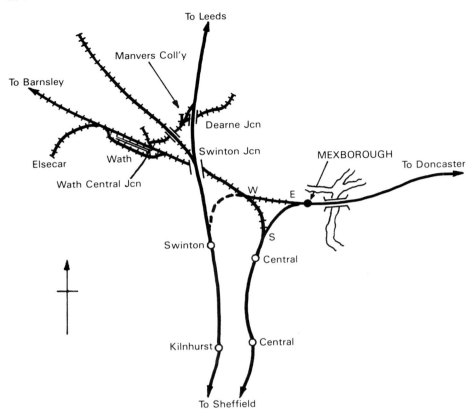

modest lines the Eye branch had its moments, including one when driver 'Juddie' took his engine through to Eye without making sure that the train was attached and another when 'J65' 0-6-0T No 249 ran through the earth drag at the end of the branch to finish up in an allotment.

M.14 Metheringham—see   Spalding-Doncaster Line

M.15 Mexborough

Doncaster-Sheffield line, junction with Barnsley line. 15 m 71 ch from Penistone

The 1840 North Midland line which used the Don Valley north from Rotherham was joined by the South Yorkshire companion route and trains from 13 March (passengers 3 April) 1871. The South Yorkshire Railway had already established an east-west route through Mexborough when it opened the Doncaster-Mexborough-Swinton link to the Midland system in 1849. Today these SY lines carry the half-hourly Doncaster-

Sheffield dmu service plus the re-routed long distance trains on the North-East/South-West route but further alterations are planned which will revive the former spur to the Midland line at Swinton and use this in preference to the SY/MS&L/GC line through the former Swinton Central and Kilnhurst Central stations.

The approach to Mexborough has waterway companions and is via the old siding connections for Denaby colliery and the following power station. The station itself retains its attractive Up side buildings, decorated in stone and provided with a splendid chimney block. The Down side platform, formerly an island, just has a wooden shelter.

At Mexborough East Junction (15 m 64 ch) the freight lines continue on to Wath and Barnsley via Mexborough West Junction (14 m 76 ch) from which a 52 ch spur provides the link from the Wath line towards Sheffield. On the SY line turning south from East Junction the mileage changes from 15 m 64 ch from Penistone to

10 m 17 ch from Woodburn Junction, Mexborough South Junction then coming at 9 m 75 ch and the route continuing on to Thrybergh Junction (7 m 73 ch) past the remains of the two 'Central' stations.

M.16   Middleton   Towers—see   Kings Lynn

M.17   Mistley—see Harwich Branch

M.18   Molewood Tunnel—see Hertford Loop

M.19   Moorgate Line

East Coast main line, branch from Finsbury Park. 3 m 69 ch

The route from Moorgate to Finsbury Park is once again part of the main line railway system after sixty years with the Underground. It started life as the Great Northern & City Railway, a GNR enterprise designed to give better access to the City of London, and was opened on 14 February 1904 from a separate terminus at Finsbury Park to another at Moorgate. Although built with tunnels large enough to allow through running to and from the main line, this dream was not realized until the GN Electrification Scheme reclaimed the route from the Underground network to which it had been transferred from 1 July 1913.

The first 2 m 52 ch from Moorgate via Old Street (45 ch), Essex Road (1 m 59 ch) and Highbury & Islington (2 m 21 ch) lies in tunnel and has a 30 mph maximum permissible speed. Then, from just beyond Drayton Park (2 m 56 ch), the Up and Down lines separate to Finsbury Park station (3 m 41 ch), the Up making a direct junction at 3 m 37 ch and the Down, after passing under the main line, at 3 m 69 ch from Moorgate.

*Newark GNR with gas lighting, stayed canopies and plenty of hoardings (*Lens of Sutton*).*

Class '313' stock is used on the line, the three-car emu sets each seating 232 passengers and being fitted to operate off the 750 v third rail system between Moorgate and Drayton Park and at 25 kv ac beyond the changeover section at that point. The basic service provides a train every twenty minutes to Welwyn Garden City, alternating with a similar pattern to Hertford North, with one in three of the latter continuing on to Letchworth.

M.20   Mountnessing   Junction—see Shenfield-Southend Line

N.1   Needham Market

Liverpool Street-Norwich line, between Ipswich and Stowmarket. 77 m 11 ch from Liverpool Street

Very gently the main line starts to rise from the Ipswich direction as it passes Coddenham Road LC (76 m 70 ch) and comes to the magnificent original station at Needham. The red brick buildings were designed in a semi-Elizabethan style by Frederick Barnes, the Ipswich & Bury Railway architect, and it is perhaps a nice touch that having lost its main line passenger service on 2 January 1967, the station was reopened on 6 December 1971 as a stopping place for the Cambridge-Ipswich dmus.

N.2   Newark

Newark Castle is on the Nottingham-Lincoln line, 16 m 78 ch from Nottingham and Newark Northgate on the East Coast main line, 120 m 8 ch from Kings Cross

The first railway to serve Newark was the line from Nottingham, born of George Hudson's attempts to satisfy the railway ambitions of the people of Lincoln. It was opened on 3 August 1846 and still serves Newark by means of the Castle station which was built in a style similar to that used at Lincoln St Marks. After coming on to the Eastern Region near Staythorpe power

station the Nottingham-Lincoln trains call at the Castle complex of traditional station, signal box and level crossing and then cross the East Coast main line on the level at Newark Crossing (17 m 69 ch). They then continue east via Newark Crossing East Junction (17 m 74 ch) where the spur from the ECML joins.

The Great Northern main line got to Newark in 1852 and served the Trent malting and brewing town from its station at Northgate. The route from Newark to Marefield was opened on 30 June 1879 and was subsequently extended to Leicester and Market Harborough but now survives only as a freight route to Bottesford. The last piece of railway to be opened at Newark was the 11 ch single line spur from Newark Crossing South Junction via Whitehouse Lane Footpath R/G LC to Newark Crossing East Junction which was put in in 1965 when the Lincoln traffic was transferred to a via Newark routing consequent upon the closure of the line from Grantham via Honington. The 'Humber-Lincs Executive' works this way, as do the Cleethorpes-Newark trains.

The approach to Newark is via crossings at Bullpit Lane (118 m 26 ch) and Barnby (119 m 3 ch) with the Bottesford line joining at Newark South Junction (119 m 73 ch) in advance of the crossovers between the main, goods and UPL lines. The Cleethorpes trains use the outer face of Newark's Up island platform with train engines running round by means of the adjoining line. The main station buildings are on the Down side, a long single-storey group with a typical GN mixture of brick plus wood and glass structures topped by standard square chimney pots and with the main uprights raised above the building line

The semi-classical frontage of St Marks, the former MR/LMS station at Lincoln.

to carry the canopy support rods. The residue of the goods yard lies on the town side of the station and includes the old warehouse building.

North of Northgate the ECML sheds the Lincoln spur at Newark Crossing South Junction (120 m 48 ch), crosses the Nottingham-Lincoln line at Newark Crossing (120 m 63 ch) and then rises to cross the Trent by a double bridge. Level crossings follow at Church Lane (122 m 7 ch), Bathley Lane (122 m 78 ch) and Norwell Lane (123 m 38 ch).

The hourly Doncaster trains serve Newark but some of the longer distance services calling have cut the time to Kings Cross to 1 hour 20 minutes, contrasting with the 2½-3 hours of the 1930s and over 4 hours taken by the stopping trains which had arrived after the calls at Barkston, Hougham and Claypole and departed to do the same at Carlton-on-Trent, Crow Park and Dukeries Junction. Most of the ECML trains give connections to the Newark-Cleethorpes line and the station has a Rail-link coach service to Mansfield.

N.3   Newark-Lincoln Line

East Coast main line, branch from Newark and part of Nottingham-Cleethorpes route. 24 m 43 ch

This double line route, opened originally on 3 August 1846 and successively part of the Midland and then LM&S Railways, is now an Eastern Region line from a point east of the signal box at Staythorpe Crossing. It carries a Nottingham-Lincoln/Cleethorpes service plus Newark-Lincoln/Cleethorpes trains and some longer distance services.

Beyond the crossing of the ECML and the following spur from Newark Northgate the route has AHB crossings at Winthorpe (19 m 1 ch), Langford (20 m 24 ch) and Cottage Lane (21 m 16 ch) and then a R/G LC at Westbrook (21 m 44 ch). It then comes to Collingham station where the modern

automatic half barrier crossing (22 m 13 ch) makes a strong contrast with the great brick buildings and their mixture of gables, colonnades and other features over-elaborate for what has never been more than a country station.

Two AHB crossings—Cross Lane (22 m 34 ch) and Swinderby Lane (22 m 46 ch)—and two R/G crossings—South Scarle (24 m 31 ch) and Mearsdall (24 m 54 ch)—precede Swinderby station (24 m 67 ch). This has a gated crossing, a Down to Up trailing connection and a rusting siding in the old goods yard, as well as the operational signal box and another set of Italianate buildings, this time to an irregular design.

Following the gated crossing at Eagle Barnsdale (25 m 64 ch) there is another at Eagle and Thorpe (26 m 53 ch), complete with cottage designed to give all-round visibility. The signal box at Thorpe-on-the-Hill LC (27 m 28 ch) stands near a disused siding and the line then passes the old Harrisons siding to Hykeham LC (29 m 44 ch) and station (29 m 49 ch). More signs of former sidings are visible as the route passes Doddington Road AHB LC (30 m 19 ch) and comes under the control of Boultham Crossing box (31 m 17 ch) on the approach to Lincoln.

N.4   New Barnet

East Coast main line, between Finsbury Park and Potters Bar. 9 m 12 ch

New Barnet, halfway up the 1 in 200 climb to Potters Bar, used to be an originating and terminating point for suburban services to Kings Cross, Moorgate and Broad Street but now the Welwyn Garden City emus call at the typically Great Northern station. This was one of the original stopping points when the line opened on 7 August 1850, although it was later rebuilt in 1896. New Barnet used to have three signal boxes and a siding connection to the large gas works on the Up side north of the station.

N.5   New Clee

Cleethorpes-Sheffield line, between Clee-thorpes and Grimsby. 110 m 79 ch from Manchester (London Road)

On weekdays the Barton-on-Humber trains serve New Clee which consists just of the two long platforms approached around a 15 mph curve from the Grimsby Docks direction.

N.6   New   Holland—see   Barton-on-Humber Branch

N.7   Newmarket

Cambridge-Ipswich line, between Cambridge and Bury St Edmunds. 13 m 61 ch from Coldham Lane Junction

Think of Newmarket, and you think of horse racing. Travel by train or road and you are likely to see horses exercising in an area that has been described as the largest cultivated lawn in the world. Indeed, the Newmarket Jockey Club was one of the supporters of the original Newmarket & Chesterford Railway, later simply the Newmarket Railway, which opened its main line between the two points named in its title on 3 January 1848 for goods traffic, and for passengers on 4 April. In later years Newmarket station(s) shared in the colour and spectacle of race days as the various 'Race Specials' arrived and departed and as late as the 1950s the horse traffic conveyed by BR involved 2,371 horse boxes in a typical year, with receipts of £27,149. Interestingly, Newmarket was also one of the last places to employ railway shunting horses, two magnificent animals who knew and did their job with very little bidding.

The original Newmarket Railway concern was not without ambitions and, even before opening, had obtained additional powers to extend on to meet the Norfolk Railway at Thetford. It also had thoughts at one time of an alliance with the Great Northern through a link up with the Royston & Hitchin but the Eastern Counties Railway, never above a few dirty tricks, so starved the Newmarket of traffic and revenue that services on the latter had to be suspended for two months in the summer of 1850. Subsequent discussions between the two railways led to an agreement under which the Newmarket's main line from Great Chesterford to Six Mile Bottom was closed on 9 October 1851 and some of its rails used to complete the Cambridge-Six Mile Bottom line which commenced operation on the same day and turned the Newmarket into an ECR branch.

Subsequent rail development in the Newmarket area included the extension on 1 April 1854 to Bury St Edmunds and the opening of Warren Hill station in 1885 to help cope with the extra business when race meetings were in progress. The grandiose terminal station of 1848 proved increasingly inconvenient as traffic grew, all trains having to reverse there before they could continue on to Bury or, from 1879, along the Ely line. Accordingly it was replaced in 1902 by a through station (paid for by private subscription) and subsequently functioned as a goods depot, with horse box traffic being unloaded to the platform sections beneath the overall roof.

From Dullingham the single line to Newmarket heads nearly due north towards Newmarket Heath and the Steeplechase course, passing Wood Ditton LC (13 m 11 ch) with its gated crossing, semaphore signals and signal cabin. Newmarket station is then just a single platform with shelter on the Down side, Horse Requisites Ltd having taken over and fenced off the decorative former station buildings. A ground frame gives access to the Dower Wood grain siding as the 25 mph speed restriction changes to 40 mph and the Tokenless Block single line heads into the 1,100 yards of the curving Warren Hill Tunnel (14 m 31 ch to 15 m 1 ch). Newmarket Yard box and the connection to the old station stood 19 ch in advance of the tunnel and Warren Hill box and the link to Warren Hill station almost the same distance beyond it. A spur from Warren Hill Junction (15 m 22 ch) used to lead round to Snailwell Junction on the Ely line and carry a Newmarket-Ely service, but today's line curves west and becomes double again as it joins the Ely route at Chippenham Junction (16 m 4 ch).

Newmarket enjoys a service of ten trains each way on weekdays and also has a Sunday service. Although the former through services from Liverpool Street have gone, train frequencies have improved and journey times are considerably faster.

N.8   Newmarket-Ely Line

From Cambridge-Ipswich line at Chippenham Junction to Liverpool Street-Kings Lynn line at Ely Dock Junction. 11 m 42 ch

The 1875 Ely & Newmarket Railway opened its line on 1 September 1879 and it came to carry a local train service connecting at Newmarket with the Bury trains plus through passenger services to and from the joint line and through freight traffic to and from Whitemoor. The local passenger service ended on 13 September 1965 but a number of through trains continue to use the line, including 'The European'.

The route is a straight, level one double from Chippenham Junction, Newmarket to the intermediate signal box at Soham and then single to the crossing of the River Ouse just outside Ely. At the former Snailwell Junction, where the spur from the Newmarket direction used to join, the mileage changes 63 ch from Chippenham Junction signal box and becomes 1 m 54 ch from

Newmarket Old Station.

The route takes a north-west direction through the flat fenland to Fordham AHB LC (4 m 64 ch). This was once a junction station with the single line from Cambridge joining 11 ch in advance of the level crossing and its continuation east to Mildenhall departing immediately beyond it. On the section on to Soham come Cockspin Road AHB LC (5 m 10 ch) and Mill Road LC (7 m 28 ch), with Soham signal box (7 m 61 ch) then following and still providing a reminder of the early hours of 2 June 1944 when a devastating ammunition train fire and explosion occurred despite the courage of the footplate crew in trying to detach a blazing van and draw it clear. Middlemere R/G LC (8 m 25 ch), Tiled House Farm R/G LC (8 m 66 ch) and Barway Sidings AHB LC (9 m 76 ch) precede the doubling of the line at 12 m 6 ch on its approach past Ely Dock Junction signal box (12 m 27 ch) to the junction itself (12 m 33 ch).

N.9   Newport

Liverpool Street-Norwich line, between Bishops Stortford and Audley End. 39 m 69 ch from Liverpool Street

To ward off the threat of revived rival schemes for railways to the North, the Northern & Eastern obtained powers to extend its line from Bishops Stortford to Newport in 1843. By the time this was opened on 30 July 1845, as part of the link up with the Norwich & Brandon Railway, the more powerful position of the Eastern Counties Railway had resulted in it leasing the N&E.

Lying in a dip between Elsenham and Audley End, Newport is approached via Ugley LC (37 m 13 ch) and followed by an AHB crossing at Trees (41 m 30 ch). Newport station itself has substantial brick buildings and the adjacent maltings are much in keeping with the whole period character of the small, pleasant township. The rail service is provided by the Bishops Stortford-Cambridge dmus.

N.10   New Southgate

East Coast main line, between Finsbury Park and New Barnet. 6 m 35 ch from Kings Cross

The working lifespan of many a commuter will encompass the change from GN Quad-Art sets to the comfort of today's Moorgate-Welwyn Garden City emus which serve New Southgate. The station, with its footbridge access to two island platforms, remains fairly traditional and dates from an

1890 reconstruction of the 1850 original named Colney Hatch & Southgate. The location, on the 1 in 200 rising gradient between the Wood Green and Barnet tunnels, used to have a substantial freight activity with a five-ton crane in the goods yard and sidings for Colney Hatch Mental Hospital, New Southgate & District Gas Company and Standard Telephones & Cables. Two Up and two Down signal boxes were needed to deal with the traffic from Wood Green Tunnel box to the south and Cemetery box to the north.

N.11   North   Elmham   Line—see Wymondham

N.12   Northorpe—see Gainsborough

N.13   Northumberland Park

Liverpool Street-Kings Lynn line, between Tottenham Hale and Broxbourne. 6 m 73 ch from Liverpool Street

Although it was one of the original Northern & Eastern stations, then known as Marsh Lane, Northumberland Park was simplified and modernized in a reconstruction completed in 1970. In Great Eastern days, and when known just as Park, Lea Valley trains via Clapton and via Stratford called at the station, a function taken over by today's Liverpool Street-Hertford East emus.

There is a level crossing at Northumberland Park and the elevated signal box survives, but the extra pair of Up side lines is no longer needed for freight and the Northumberland Park Yard's secondary marshalling activity was surrendered to Temple Mills with the opening of the new yard there.

N.14   North Walsham—see Sheringham Branch

Customs House station. When the photograph was taken the footbridge gave direct access to the docks.

N.15   North Woolwich Line

Dalston Western Junction to North Woolwich. 8 m 17 ch

This is one of London's fascinating cross-city rail routes which offers the user a sort of metropolitan land cruise. The portion from Dalston Western Junction to Victoria Park Junction was part of the North London Railway's route to the Thames at Poplar while the remaining portion in Great Eastern territory developed from G.P. Bidder's 1844 Eastern Counties & Thames Junction project which was to lead him to launch the Victoria Dock Company six years later. All sorts of service combinations have used the line, including the regular Palace Gates-North Woolwich workings via Lea Bridge, but from 14 May 1985 a twenty-minute interval Richmond-North Woolwich emu service began calling at the modernized stations along the ER portion of the route. This followed completion of the £9 million GLC-funded electrification and replaced the previous Camden Road-North Woolwich dmu workings.

The section of the line from Dalston Western Junction (1 m 71 ch) to Broad Street will first of all be cut and provided with a temporary terminus and will then be closed altogether under the full Liverpool Street redevelopment scheme. The Broad Street-Richmond/Watford trains are likely to be routed from Liverpool Street via a new connecting curve at Graham Road, Hackney. This will leave only the top leg of the Dalston triangle in use but on that leg the old Kingsland station, which the North London Railway opened on 9 November 1850 and closed on 1 November 1865, came back to life again on 16 May 1983 when Dalston Kingsland was opened by Dave Wetzel of the GLC, with a little help from a German oompah band. The attractive new station, with a ticket office in Kingsland Road and stairs down to the platforms below, cost £650,000 and was paid for by the GLC and a Department of Transport grant.

Co-operation between BR, the GLC and London local authorities has brought station reopening and improvements to the former North London line and its GER continuation to North Woolwich.

The route east as far as Victoria Park at one time carried an intensive service of North London/LMS trains via Hackney, Homerton and Victoria Park to Bow and Poplar but these ended on 23 April 1945. Now it has come to life again and, after passing the site of Hackney Downs (Graham Road) coal depot—where the connection towards Bethnal Green is planned—and under the GE Cambridge main line, comes to Hackney Central (2 m 65 ch). This is in the style used for the other new or rebuilt stations on the line with a light brick used to provide pleasant but functional ticket office and waiting facilities.

In addition to three stations on the Hackney site there was a coal depot at Mare Street with nine coal drop arches on the Down side. The remains of these were still visible in 1984 as were those of Homerton station. The latter had had a substitute bus service between 15 May 1944 and the 1945 closure but after twenty years it was to come back into service under a Hackney Partnership scheme and with funding of £440,000 by the GLC and DoE.

Just beyond Hackney Wick goods and coal depot site comes Victoria Park Junction (4 m 1 ch) where the erstwhile stations preceded the separation of the Poplar and Stratford routes. Slowly the former had diminished until even the remaining 2 m 46 ch One Train operation single line lay rusting and out of use by 1983, a sad end for the once-busy railway through Old Ford (4¾ m), Bow (5¼ m), past Bow Works and Foundry, Devons Road yard, C&W shed and loco, Lea Cut coal chute, South Bromley (6 m) and Poplar (East India Road) (6½ m) to the yard, quays, sheds and even stables of Poplar Dock.

New distance figures now take over from the North London mileages as the route heads for Stratford via Victoria Park Junction (3 ch), through another new station at Hackney Wick (20 ch), past Lea Junction (51 ch), Channelsea North (64 ch) and South (65 ch) Junctions, the old Fork Junction and under the Norwich main line by means of the 77 yd Stratford Low Level Tunnel (1 m 16 ch to 1 m 20 ch) to come to Stratford Low Level station (1 m 20 ch). On this section, which is dealt with more fully in the Stratford entry, the line uses two bridges to cross Hackney Cut and then the River Lea.

Leaving Stratford Low Level, past the elevated Southern Junction signal box (1 m 28 ch) on the Down side, the route has another change of mileage at Stratford Southern Junction (1 m 30 ch to 4 m) where it takes the distance from Liverpool Street via the 'Western Curve' from the main line. This was the route of the line known as 'Bidder's Folly' because there was very little development in the area when the Eastern Counties & Thames Junction Railway opened the stretch from Stratford to Thames Wharf on 19 April 1846.

The first station along the North Woolwich branch proper was Stratford Market. This was opened on 14 June 1847 when the route was completed to North Woolwich. Known initially as Stratford Bridge, it was replaced in 1892 by a station slightly nearer Stratford. Closed to passengers on 6 May 1957, the derelict station buildings still remain at street level above the island platform which once divided the pairs of Thames Wharf and North Woolwich lines. Nearby, fruit and vegetable boxes litter the Stratford Market goods depot area, once the destination of hundreds of consignments daily from the provincial market gardening areas, some by parcels van, some in vanfits and others arriving by cross-town cartage. Stratford Market (4 m 50 ch) has

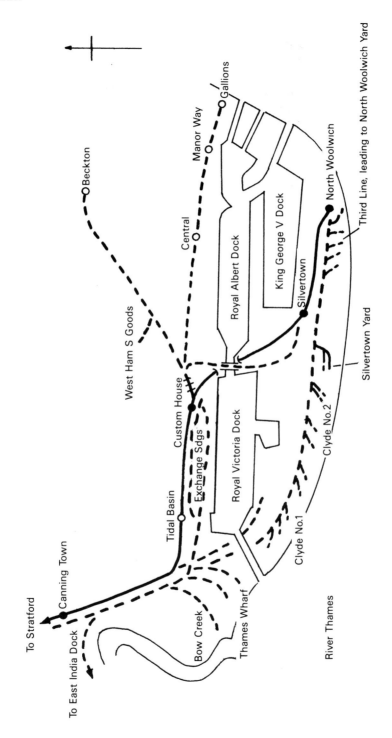

North Woolwich station in 1967.

kept its place in the working timetable as the physical junction for the separate but parallel line to Bow Creek (6 m) with its private siding link to the Berk Spencer works.

After the North Woolwich line passes under the LT&S it is still just possible to spot the old 1 m 20 ch connecting spur from Upper Abbey Mills Junction on the LT&S to Abbey Mills Junction and signal box on the four-track GER route. Today the signal box (5 m 6 ch) follows the new West Ham station (4 m 70 ch) which consists of an island platform reached by a modern footbridge from a combined entrance with the LT station.

The remainder of the route has strong associations with dockland and there are many signs of its busy freight past. On the Down side of the section on to Canning Town the spur into Plaistow & West Ham goods was still there in 1984 but the old Canning Town LNW depot had disappeared beneath a vast pile of scrap metal. Canning Town station (5 m 57 ch) started life in 1847 on a site further south and with the name Barking Road. Following re-siting north of the road additional facilities were added on the Down side for the Victoria Park service. Further changes were made around the turn of the century but now only the centre island platform is used.

Next on the Up side comes the site of Canning Town South, once a very busy goods depot with a connection over Bow Creek into the north side of the East India Dock. Now the area is covered with rubbish as far as the sluice gates on Bow Creek. Past these are rusting scrapyard sidings and the line to the entrance to Bow Creek which developed from a timber depot to a steel import terminal for Instone Lines and then into a steel railhead. From the old Thames Wharf Junction (6 m 10 ch) the original route to North Woolwich survived as a spur off the branch tracks for over a century after the diversion to the present course to accommodate the building of the Royal Victoria Dock. The eastern pair of tracks

diverged into the dock nearby and their course is still visible although the former Tidal Basin junctions have disappeared.

When the Victoria Docks opened in 1855 the diverted North Woolwich branch, now passing along their north side, was given a new station called Victoria Docks, Custom House. This survives as plain Custom House (6 m 72 ch) but Tidal Basin (6 m 33 ch), opened three years later, was closed on 15 August 1943. Today Custom House has been attractively rebuilt in the same style as the other new/renovated stations and includes a substantial single-storey ticket, staff and waiting area building on the Down side. The station footbridge parallels the footbridge entrance to Royal Victoria Dock which until the end of PLA rail traffic on 1 May 1970 spanned busy exchange sidings where PLA locomotives fussed around hundreds of vans containing every kind of import or export traffic. On the opposite side of the road the Seaman's Mission building sports the flying angel as another reminder of the maritime connections of this area of East London.

From Custom House signal box (6 m 77 ch) the section on to North Woolwich becomes a single line operated on the One Train basis. The Down line is used for this purpose, the Up line becoming an Electric Token freight line connecting with the end of what was the old Silvertown Tramway (and which, in turn, led through to North Woolwich Yard via the 'Third Line'). Diverging at the same point are the remains of the second route of the North Woolwich branch which became a PLA line when the GER line had to be diverted to a tunnel to accommodate the connection to the Royal Albert Dock opened in 1880.

From 7 m 23 ch, where Albert Dock East Junction signal box was located, there were formerly two other lines, the first to be opened (1872-3) and the last to survive being the single line via West Ham South Goods, Beckton Tramway Crossing signal box and Beckton station (8 m 73 ch) to

Beckton Gas Works. The route was opened by the gas company, which had brought its gas works into use in 1870, but was worked by the Great Eastern which ran passenger services for workmen from 17 March 1873 until closure on 28 December 1940.

The other line was the PLA railway to the hotel and liner pier at Gallions. The line was double and opened in 1880-1, the PLA running the shuttle service from a bay platform at Custom House and the GER and its successors providing through trains. By 1938 the service was starting at 7.20 am and operating for just over twelve hours with trains taking nine minutes for the 2¼ mile journey and calling at Connaught Road, Central, Manor Way and Gallions.

Returning to the North Woolwich line, this now passes underneath the waterway between the two 'Royal' docks by means of the 600 yd Silvertown Tunnel (7 m 29 ch to 7 m 56 ch), a dark curving bore with a steep drop and rise gradient and a 30 mph speed restriction. The junction between the 'over' and 'under' routes, the former now relieved of its connection to King George V Dock, follows the Silvertown By-Pass overbridge and is itself followed by Silvertown station (7 m 79 ch). Only the Down platform is now used but this, again, has a modern attractive ticket office plus waiting room building with barrier access. On the opposite side of the road stands Ind Coope's 'The Railway' but the locomotive on its sign is somewhat less than appropriate for the area in which it stands.

On the final section to North Woolwich we are back on the original 1847 route. The single line runs between the vessels using or laid up in King George V Dock and the reviving housing area behind Albert Road

Diesel multiple unit at Silvertown station on 31 August 1967.

to the north and the works and factories lining the banks of the Thames to the south. Only one rusting siding connection remains to commemorate the once-extensive traffic in sugar and other commodities fed in by the sidings and the single line (with three passing loops) that ran for 1 m 29 ch back eastwards along North Woolwich Road from Silvertown Tramway Junction (8 m 51 ch). In its last busy phase the various Silvertown Tramway sidings were worked by a 350 hp diesel shunter and a staff team made up of a Yard Inspector, a shunter and head shunter and two mobile crossing keepers. The Clyde No 1 sidings at the far end of the tramway were shunted about 11.00 am after the No 2 sidings nearer Silvertown Yard. The sidings off the 'Third Line' had been serviced between 8-9.00 am, the locomotive then returning from the tramway to provide extra trips to Keillers.

At North Woolwich (8 m 60 ch) the old Up platform is used although the Down one remains in existence. A new ticket office and entrance complex has been provided at the end of the former to release the solid, Italianate 1847 terminal building to become a Great Eastern Railway museum, a scheme sponsored by the London Dockland Development Corporation and with displays coming from the Passmore Edwards Museum Trust.

The new museum makes a fitting end to a journey on this fascinating line now enjoying a new lease of life. The new interval service trains follow a public service tradition inherited from the Fenchurch Street and Palace Gates workings and also give excellent views of St Pancras and Kings Cross, an insight into the complexities of Stratford and a tour of London's dockland. At North Woolwich it is also possible to enjoy the Royal Victoria Gardens which originated as pleasure gardens to stimulate

traffic on the line or one can cross the Thames on the historic Woolwich Free Ferry which crosses from the nearby pier to South Woolwich.

N.16   Norwich

Terminus of Liverpool Street-Norwich line. 124 m 9 ch from Liverpool Street

Norwich is a fine city where modern shopping and other facilities harmonize well with a great deal of history—the Norman Cathedral, the castle of Robert Bigod, the Strangers' Hall, city walls and gates, narrow streets and timbered buildings. And the BR station lives up to the high standards of its surroundings. The approach from the city, across the River Wensum, gives a good view of the two-storey main building with its red brick construction, stone dressings and central dome rising 76 ft above the ground. The large forecourt, used for car parking and bus interchange, leads via the

arches of the *porte-cochère*, to the central booking hall and travel centre and then on to the concourse which gives access to the six main platforms, the longest accommodating thirteen bogies.

The original station at Norwich was opened on 30 April 1844 to serve Norfolk's first railway line, that from Yarmouth. It was located on the site of the later freight depot and comprised two bays with a covered roof, two goods lines and a loading bank, the booking office and the boardroom of the Yarmouth & Norwich Railway. The station was enlarged to cope with the addition of the trains from the Brandon line which were extended from the temporary terminus at Trowse from 15 December 1845 following the provision of a swing-bridge across the River Wensum. The present station was opened in 1886, the work of John Wilson and in the grounds of a private mansion adjacent to the former Norfolk Railway premises.

The station complex includes a parcels activity and the area in the bend of the river embraces freight yard, diesel depot and car-

The original station at Norwich Thorpe.

A more recent view of Norwich Thorpe pre-electrification.

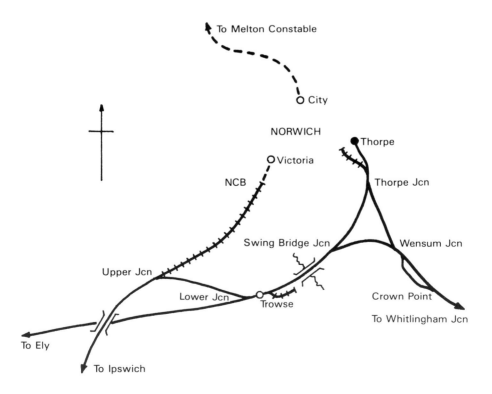

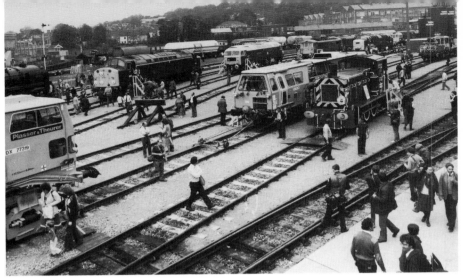

An open day at Crown Point depot.

riage sidings. This area, once alive with the movements of steam locomotives and the loading and unloading of freight traffic—steel, timber, coal, agricultural commodities and requisites—has now been largely superseded by the modern maintenance depot at Crown Point. Beyond the fuel tanks and fuelling point the tracks, controlled by Norwich Passenger signal box (123 m 72 ch) but due for radical alteration under the electrification scheme, come together to pass under Carrow Road Bridge and then at Norwich Thorpe Junction (123 m 56 ch) separate into the routes for Lowestoft/Yarmouth/Sheringham and Ipswich/Ely.

Pre-electrification Absolute Block signalling applied on all routes with an extra 'No Block' Down line between Trowse Swing-Bridge and Norwich Thorpe Junction. The London and Yarmouth routes are linked by a spur from Swing Bridge Junction (123 m 43 ch) to Wensum Junction (54 ch) and enclosing the former Crown Point Yard, now used primarily by the engineer's department.

On the London routes, trains leaving Norwich cross the Wensum by means of Trowse Swing-Bridge, a traditional swing-bridge incorporating its signal box (123 m 40 ch) in the main structure. It is due to be replaced by a new, electrically-worked single line bridge on a new, parallel alignment which will allow higher speeds. Past the former carriage cleaning and fish van and cattle dock areas on the Up side, now survived only by an aggregate depot, the route comes to the platforms and flint buildings of Trowse station after Trowse

Yard box (123 m 19 ch). At Trowse Lower Junction (123 m via Ipswich, 113 m 68 ch via Ely) the Ely route stays on the level while the Ipswich line rises sufficiently steeply to warrant provisions for the use of banking engines where necessary and as far as Trowse Upper Junction (112 m 67 ch). From this point it starts a long curve which will take it over the Ely route and its surrounding water meadows and then off to the south.

The connection to Norwich Victoria Goods Branch is made at Trowse Upper Junction. The branch was the route of the original Eastern Union line to Norwich which reached the city on 12 December 1849 but made no connection with the ECR route until 1852. It is now just a means of access to the coal concentration depot at Victoria Goods (114 m 9 ch). Single and limited to a maximum speed of 15 mph, the branch is worked on the One Train basis with no staff but with authorization to operate trains with a locomotive at each end. The facing junction in the Down direction formerly provided the connection to Kings private siding where many ex-BR steam locomotives were taken for scrapping, and to Harford market where new livestock facilities were provided in 1960 but soon fell into disuse as railways lost their livestock business to road haulage.

Victoria station, where once geese arrived by rail from the Continent and were then driven down St Stephens to the poulterers, closed to passengers on 22 May 1916 after lengthy negotiations with the City Corporation. Next to close, on 5 September 1939, was the station at Trowse, although the first station there had been displaced when the Brandon line was extended across the river.

The M&GN line into Norwich, opened by the Eastern & Midlands Railway on 2 December 1882, had about eight trains each way daily at the end of the 1930s, more on Thursdays and Saturdays. Some ran only to or from Drayton but the through trains from Melton Constable took 31 minutes for a non-stop journey, or 45 minutes if calling at Hindolvestone (2 m), Guestwick (4½ m), Whitwell & Reepham (8¼ m), Lenwade (10¾ m), Attlebridge (12¼ m), Drayton (16¾ m) and Hellesdon (19 m) before arriving at Norwich (City) (21¼ m). This station was one of the victims of the heavy wartime bombing suffered by Norwich, its buildings being completely destroyed by enemy action in 1942. They were replaced by single-storey utility buildings but then lost their passenger trains on 2 March 1959. Norwich (City) remained in use as a freight depot and then as a coal concentration depot for another ten years, reached by a new route created by linking the Coltishall and Melton Constable lines by means of a new Themelthorpe Curve.

On the other main route out of Norwich, Wensum Junction signal box (54 ch) is followed by the new Crown Point depot. This was opened on 27 October 1982 and the 12-acre site includes reception and departure sidings, maintenance and servicing bays, a carriage fuelling and washing plant and staff and administration accommodation. Initially the £10 million depot took over responsibility for 53 dmus, 16 locomotives and a number of coaches but it will also be fully capable of servicing electric stock when electrification takes place.

This then is Norwich, now about to enter a new era. The loss of 'The Norfolkman' and 'The Broadsman', the absence of 'Clauds' loping in from the Dereham line, no more 'Round the World' services or Col-

Norwich Thorpe with semaphore signal gantry and route indicator.

man's mustard vans, no excursions round the curve from Trowse to Wensum Junction or protective signals on City goods shed, no more Royal Show traffic... but all amply compensated for by electric-hauled services from Liverpool Street which will put London and the capital of East Anglia within a travelling time of only 100 minutes.

N.17   Norwich-Yarmouth Line

From Whitlingham Junction on the Sheringham Branch, via Acle, to Yarmouth. 16 m 39 ch

There are two routes from Norwich to Yarmouth, the original one leaving the Norwich-Lowestoft line at Reedham and travelling via Berney Arms and the later one leaving at Brundall and taking a more direct course via Acle. The latter is the busier and although by 1985 the through London workings were down to one train a day plus some extras on Saturdays the dmu services continued to be well patronized, especially by commuters and schoolchildren. Additional capacity is provided in the summer months for the increased use made of the route by holidaymakers.

By 1843 the Eastern Counties had experienced great difficulty in getting as far as Colchester, never mind reaching Norwich and linking it with Yarmouth. Disillusioned, the Norfolk shareholders promoted their own Yarmouth & Norwich Railway to improve communications generally and to protect the Norfolk textile industries. The new railway was incorporated in 1842 and with the Stephensons as surveyors, nice flat terrain to pass through, Peto as resident engineer and Grissell & Peto as contractors, it is no surprise to find it opening for public traffic on 1 May 1844 after official feasting on the previous day. Shortly afterwards the Yarmouth & Norwich and the sister Norwich & Brandon were united as the Norfolk Railway.

After leaving Norwich the route picks up the course of the River Yare, bridging its old course twice before coming to Whitlingham Junction (1 m 70 ch), where the Sheringham branch (*qv*) departs. The first dmu stop is Brundall Gardens (4 m 66 ch) where the two modest timber platforms serve the western end of the growing Brundall community. The line is now following a bend in the river which has become a boat building and hiring centre, Brundall station (5 m 63 ch) having boatyards flanking its Up platform. The station has staggered platforms, large square brick buildings on the Down side, gated crossing and footbridge. The signal box is at the country end overlooking Brundall Junction (5 m 71 ch) where the single line via Acle rises away from the double track on to Reedham.

Track Circuit Block applies over the single line all the way to Yarmouth via Chapel Road manned and gated crossing (7 m 55 ch), Lingwood station (7 m 78 ch) and Station Road crossing (8 m 3 ch) there, Acle station (10 m 33 ch) and Acle Damgate LC (11 m 6 ch). This section dates from 1883, the Acle-Brundall portion being opened on 1 June of that year and the remainder to Breydon Junction on 12 March. Lingwood has just a single platform on the Down side with a simple red brick station house plus ticket office and canopy. Acle is a block post with a 40 SLU passing loop, another red brick station house and adjacent ticket office, and with the old goods shed still in existence. The small signal box stands on the platform and the GER initials can be seen in the canopy support spandrels.

Acle is not far from the River Bure and back in Saxon times the sea would come up as far as the village. Now the marshes have been drained and until relatively recently the Acle cattle market was kept busy with handling cattle brought from Ireland by rail and then fattened on the marshes prior to eventual slaughter. After Acle the cuttings and embankments of the modestly graded section from Brundall Junction give way to a flat course across Acle Marshes, dead straight apart from the slight bend at Stacey Arms and with just the River Bure and its windmills, the A47 and its motorists and the marshes and their cattle for company. There used to be a physical junction with the route via Reedham at Breydon Junction (17 m 16 ch) but the two single lines now run parallel, but separate, to Yarmouth signal box (18 m 12 ch) and then Vauxhall station (18 m 29 ch).

The route has a maximum line speed of 60 mph with further speed restrictions at

Brundall Junction, through Acle crossing loop and approaching Breydon Junction. It has semaphore signalling and is closed on Sundays in winter. The basic traffic levels remain constant but hardly matching the days when even a bright summer evening would bring hundreds from Norwich to the firm sands and bright lights of Great Yarmouth.

N.18   Nunnery Junction—*see Sheffield*

O.1   Oakleigh Park

East Coast main line, between Finsbury Park and New Barnet. 8 m 30 ch from Kings Cross

The station was opened on 1 December 1873 and today comprises two island platforms served by the Welwyn Garden City emus. Standard Telephones and Abbots Packaging had sidings on the Up side.

O.2   Ockenden—see   Upminster-Grays Line

O.3   Old Street—see Moorgate Line

O.4   Orton Mere—see Peterborough

O.5   Oulton Broad North—see Brundall Junction-Lowestoft Line

O.6   Oulton Broad South—see East Suffolk Line

O.7   Oxcroft—see Chesterfield-Rotherham Line

P.1   Palmers Green—see Hertford Loop

P.2   Parkeston   Quay—see   Harwich Branch

P.3   Peascliffe Tunnel—see Grantham

P.4   Peterborough

East Coast main line, junction with Ely and Leicester lines. 76 m 29 ch from Kings Cross

Peterborough was one of the 'railway towns' of the Great Northern Railway although the first metals to arrive there were those of the London & Birmingham's branch from Blisworth via Northampton and the Nene Valley. Over these the first public railway services for the citizens of Peterborough began on 2 June 1845, using a station east of Fair Meadow built by the Eastern Counties Railway in readiness for the link on to Ely—opened for goods on 10 December 1846 and for passengers on 14

The new station at Peterborough pictured in March 1973.

January of the following year.

As one of the manoeuvres in the Midland v Great Northern conflict George Hudson pushed ahead the line from Syston towards Peterborough, with the Stamford-Peterborough portion opening on 2 October 1846 and through services from Stamford, via Peterborough and Ely, running to London from the following January. Two years later the through route to Syston was completed and then, on 17 October, came the first GNR services with trains running from the ECR station, over the Midland metals to Werrington and then along the newly-opened GNR route via Boston to Lincoln and Grimsby.

The advent of the Great Northern's direct line from London, celebrated on 8 August 1850, had a major impact on the earlier lines and their traffic. This became even more marked with the opening of the

Another view of Peterborough's new station. The previous Up platform is on the right.

main line northwards through Grantham on 1 August 1852 and using a new Peterborough station on the site of a medieval tithe barn. Peterborough's railway map was completed by the opening of the MR's Peterborough, Wisbech & Sutton Bridge Railway (which became part of the M&GN from 1893) on 1 August 1866, although the LNWR's Wansford-Seaton link had given the developing city a quicker route to Rugby from 1 November 1879.

In its railway heyday Peterborough was a complex and busy place. In addition to passenger services in all directions—north and south, Rugby and Leicester, Cambridge and Norwich, Kings Lynn and Yarmouth, Boston and Grimsby—the freight activity, especially coal, livestock and bricks, was considerable. All kinds of agricultural traffic was handled and at one period all the competing companies were encouraging the barging of Fenland traffic to and from their own particular wharves. In addition to the main East and North stations, each company had its own goods depot and there were loco sheds at East, Spital, Woodston and New England, the latter for local passenger workings, freight trips and pilot workings and for re-engining main line goods workings. The extensive

marshalling yards at New England exchanged traffic between the main line and the routes east and west and behind lay several streets of railway housing. There were numerous private sidings, especially for timber and engineering products.

The first closure to affect Peterborough occurred quite early and was that of the modest Crescent station which lasted only from 1858 to 1866. Then, post nationalization, the M&GN route lost its passenger services out through Eye Green and Thorney on 28 February 1959 and the regular services to Northampton ceased on 2 May 1964, just a year after a dramatic fire had destroyed the wooden bridge at Stanground on the approach to Peterborough East from Whittlesea. The Rugby line closed on 6 June 1966 with East station also closing to passengers in favour of its old rival, but becoming a parcels and Brute train handling point, preserving the odd layout and elevated signal box for a little longer.

Peterborough itself is a fine city where the dignity of the cathedral preserves a sense of timelessness amid a very progressive reshaping by the Peterborough Development Corporation. British Rail kept pace with the changes around it, the 1970s seeing the beginning of a round of major improvements. In 1972 came the new power signal box and a realignment of the curves which had slowed down ECML trains for years and even featured in the LNER's pre-war Square Deal campaign. Another momentous year was 1978 when work began on building the new 'North' station and the first HST arrived.

The main line approach to Peterborough from the south changes back from two lines to four beyond the old Yaxley & Farcet station and the surviving emergency cross-

Peterborough goods depot in 1959 showing the concrete 'barrel' roof.

over (72 m 50 ch) there. The section which follows stands above a layer of Fletton clay which stretches north-east and gave rise to the vast areas of brick-making around the GN main line, the Stanground-Whittlesea line and the M&GN route through Dogsthorpe and Eye Green. The dry, powdered clay, itself highly combustible, helped to produce a kiln temperature of 1,000°C and the process of pressing four times gave the London Brick Company the brand name Phorpres for its Fletton bricks. Most of the yards kept the names of their original owners—Beebys, Hicks, Plowmans etc— long after they became part of the LBC, NBC or Redland groups. More recently the yards which once displayed an immense variety of tub and bucket conveyors and turned out the bricks which built many a GN station have been rationalized and many pits filled in and returned to other uses.

Inwards fly ash for the infilling process moved largely by rail and via Fletton Junction (75 m 20 ch) where the 1 m 60 ch branch from Orton Mere joins on the Down side. This was formerly a loop to the LNWR line at Longville Junction and serving the BSC factory and it is now also a link with the Nene Valley Railway which operates from Wansford station. The branch is worked on the One Train basis and has a 10 mph restriction.

After Fletton Junction the main line uses a substantial bridge to pass over the line from Ely (which formerly continued west to Woodston Wharf and Wansford), then over Fair Meadow and another bridge over the Nene, past carriage sidings and on to link with the Ely-Stamford route at Crescent Junction (76 m 25 ch). The new station follows (76 m 29 ch) with platform lines to the two islands and two fast lines between. There is a coach link from the station to Kings Lynn and the Great Northern Hotel stands opposite.

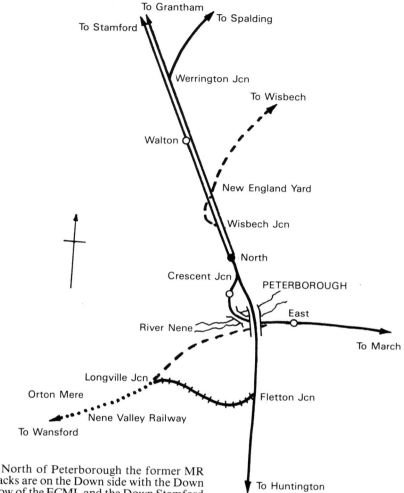

North of Peterborough the former MR tracks are on the Down side with the Down Slow of the ECML and the Down Stamford combined until the Stamford lines depart at Helpston Junction (81 m 75 ch). On the opposite side are the North and South Arrival lines for freight, parcels and GPO traffic. From the panel box (74 m 47 ch), now controlling the 46 route miles from Sandy to Stoke, there is a series of leads and crossovers past Eastfield (77 m 2 ch) and New England Ladder Crossing (78 m 6 ch) to Werrington Junction (78 m 6 ch) where the original GNR route to Spalding departs.

This section has lost its former signal boxes, private and departmental sidings, the Norwich-Birmingham services flash past the sites of Walton and Helpston stations and the days of the huge LMS Garratts and the coaling plant that fed them are just memories. Two Up lines once interlinked, as opposed to joined, through Walton's old level crossing and on a lucky day for the railway devotee an M&GN train might cross over all the remaining lines to approach the station parallel with a train from Leicester and a main line arrival from Scotland, the North-East or the West Riding. Level crossings survive at Marholme (69 m 78 ch) and Woodcroft (81 m 32 ch).

Peterborough, a traditional railway centre which has kept abreast of the times, has an excellent passenger service which puts it within 54 minutes of Kings Cross, 100 minutes of York and under four hours of Edinburgh.

The superb station frontage of the former Stamford East station.

P.5   Peterborough-Leicester Line

Branch from East Coast main line at Helpston. 12 m 60 ch to regional boundary

After running parallel with the East Coast main line from Peterborough northwards, this double track east-west artery swings away at Helpston LC (16 m 71 ch) and heads for Stamford, the regional boundary at Luffenham Junction (4 m 11 ch) and then on to Manton Junction, Melton Mowbray and Leicester. It carries an important service of through Norwich/Ipswich-Birmingham trains supplemented by some local workings.

In addition to the stations at Walton (49¾ m from Leicester) and Helpston (46½ m) alongside the GN main line, there was formerly a station at Uffington & Barnack (42¾ m) but all of these closed at various dates in the 1960s and the line now runs direct to Stamford via Maxey CCTV LC (16 m 9 ch), Bainton Green AHB LC (15 m 33 ch), Bainton AHB LC (14 m 20 ch), the signal box, crossing and old station at Uffington & Barnack (12 m 75 ch) and then

Ketton station looking east in a 1967 view.

the 35 mph section through the 341 yards of Stamford Tunnel (10 m 36 ch to 10 m 20 ch). On the last section it is possible to spot the overgrown trackbed of the 8½-mile branch from Wansford by way of Wansford Road (1½ m), Ufford Bridge (4 m) and Barnack (5 m) to Stamford (Water Street). Prior to closure on 1 July 1929 this quiet backwater had only three trains each way daily and at least one of its station masters is said to have made his inspections on horseback.

Stamford itself is a delightful Lincolnshire town of mellow buildings and a sense of history now, thankfully, relieved of the Great North Road which once ran through its centre and possibly pleased that the Great Northern Railway chose a route through Peterborough instead. The first railway came to Stamford from Peterborough on 2 October 1846 as part of George Hudson's plans for a link with the Eastern Counties Railway, the section to Melton (and thus the link to Saxby) being completed on 1 May 1848. Stamford as a whole had not been keen on having the GN main line through the town, hoping instead to retain its ancient coaching trade. The Marquis of Exeter had felt obliged to share in this opposition but when its wisdom became increasingly doubtful he had become the leading light in the building of a branch to the GNR at Essendine. This had

Ryhall, former intermediate station between Essendine and Stamford.

opened on 1 November 1856, with the Wansford branch following on 9 August 1867.

Today Stamford's surviving operational station (10 m 11 ch) has a long approach road which gives time to appreciate the splendid arcade and turret which Sancton Wood designed in local stone. The station house is at one end of the complex and the tower at the other, the latter topped by a weather vane embodying the initials of the original Syston & Peterborough Railway. From the booking hall and Down platform a footbridge leads to the Up, formerly with a bay at its outer face. The signal box is at the Syston end (10 m 1 ch) and, between, the old goods yard—once busy with mighty loads of round timber—has a dock and several interesting buildings.

A walk from the ex-Midland Railway station, along the River Welland, leads to the former Great Northern Railway Water Street station. Still in existence, this is an exceptional building in the Tudor style by William Hurst and owing much to the patronage of Lord Exeter. The terminus

The original, later 'Town', station at Stamford.

was the headquarters of the 'Marquis of Exeter's Railway' and its offices led off a gallery above the booking hall. There is an excellent model of the station in Stamford Museum which also gives details of the occasion when a GN engine was derailed into the river and, although rescued, earned itself by this action the nickname of 'The Welland Diver'. The signal box at Water Street station, later Stamford East, backed onto the river and was often used for a quiet spot of fishing between the working of the branch sets, the goods trips to Blackstone's sidings or the visits of the district inspectors.

At the end of the Great Northern era Stamford Water Street had nine Down and eight Up trains on the Essendine branch, the first train leaving at 7.45 am and the last one getting back at 7.25 pm. On the 4-mile journey a call was mde at the only intermediate station, Ryhall (1¾ m from Stamford). As Stamford East, the terminus was closed on 4 March 1957 with the branch trains then running into Stamford Town (via the connection still visible east of the tunnel) until they too ended on 15 June 1959.

On the remaining section of the ex-MR route to the regional boundary lies the old Ketton & Collyweston station, complete with belfry and with a crossing and signal

Priory Sidings at Stamford in 1967 and looking towards Ryhall.

box (6 m 60 ch) surviving, along with the siding to the important Ketton Cement Works.

P.6   Pitsea

Fenchurch Street-Shoeburyness line, junction with Tilbury Loop. 26 m 42 ch from Fenchurch Street

Pitsea station has platforms to each of the two-track routes which join at Pitsea Junction (26 m 52 ch) at its country end. The signal box stands there and there is a modern ticket office at the London end, between the two sets of platforms.

After reaching Tilbury in 1854, the original LT&S line pushed on towards Southend via Pitsea, reaching Leigh in 1855 and Southend in 1856. There was a proposal for a branch to Rettenden ten years later but what is now the main line did not arrive at Pitsea until 1 June 1888, shortening the distance to Fenchurch Street by 6 m 5 ch. The distances on the loop are Pitsea Hall CCTV LC (32 m 24 ch), Pitsea (32 m 37 ch) and Pitsea Junction (32 m 43 ch).

Ponders End station looking north and before its modernization.

Pitsea got a new station when the main line opened in 1888 and this served Basildon New Town until the latter got its own station. But Pitsea remains busy and has a basic half-hourly service on each route. The station still has some of the blue Gill Sans signs and there is a milepost on the Down platform.

P.7   Ponders End

Liverpool Street-Kings Lynn line, between Tottenham Hale and Broxbourne. 9 m 71 ch from Liverpool Street

Ponders End, one of the original stopping points on the 1840 Northern & Eastern line, has been modernized and simplified to a basic combination of Up and Down platforms, modern ticket office and waiting shelters. Its former crossing has gone, together with a once considerable goods activity.

The half-hourly Liverpool Street-Hertford East emus call.

P.8   Ponsbourne Tunnel—see Hertford Loop

P.9   Potters Bar

East Coast main line, between Finsbury Park and Welwyn Garden City. 12 m 57 ch from Kings Cross

Potters Bar stands at the summit of an 8-

mile climb at 1 in 200 from Wood Green. Today's trains hardly notice the bank and its three tunnels but before the quadrupling was completed on 3 May 1959 any heavy train which had to wait on the Slow line for a free path over the bottleneck section between New Barnet and Potters Bar might be in for a long, hard struggle which could delay a dozen succeeding trains.

The first station at Potters Bar opened in 1850 but the complex was remodelled in 1955 in advance of the widening scheme and now consists of island platforms serving the pairs of Up and Down lines and with ticket office and car park below. It derives an excellent commuter service from the Kings Cross-Royston and Moorgate-Welwyn Garden City electrics.

The 1,214 yd Potters Bar Tunnel (11 m 25 ch to 12 m) stands on the approach to the station with Fast to Slow line connections between the two.

P.10 Prittlewell—see Shenfield-Southend Line

P.11 Purfleet

Tilbury Loop, between Barking and Tilbury. 16 m 2 ch from Fenchurch Street

The double line of the Tilbury Loop approaches Purfleet across the low flat grassland of the north bank of the Thames. The rifle range visible to the south was served by Purfleet Rifle Range Halt until its closure on 31 May 1948 and there is still a Purfleet Rifle Range CCTV crossing (15 m 26 ch) before the tank farm which precedes Purfleet station. This was one of the original stations on the line opened by the LT&S from Forest Gate to Tilbury on 13 April 1854 but today the old overbridge has gone and the station has a modern, single-

The Esso asphalt plant at Purfleet in the 1960s.

storey ticket office on the Up side. It is followed by Purfleet barrier crossing with the signal box nearby.

To the south of the station a number of wharves line the bank of the river. Adjacent to Harrisons Wharf, reached through the Esso bitumen storage depot, Luximax ore used to be landed and ship boiler cleaning carried out. Purfleet Deep Wharf, long a rail user with its own motive power, still deals with steel and newsprint traffic and both Esso and Shell have oil storage installations on either side of the BR line. Powell Duffryn and Thames Matex operate the oil and petrochemical storage complexes.

Although the Thames Board Mills activity has now ended there is still a Thames Board Mills LC (16 m 36 ch), followed by Deep Wharf LC (16 m 67 ch) and then Jurgens LC (17 m 9 ch). The margarine firm's siding connection was little used by 1984 but that of Proctor & Gamble remained available for coal and general traffic. Lafarge Cement were also rail connected and a new facility has been brought into operation for Foster Yeoman aggregates.

Purfleet has changed much over the years. The Tilbury tanks have given way to today's half-hourly emu service, the saw mills have gone, the War Office Siding closed and traffic is no longer transferred from barge to rail at Cory Wharf. But Purfleet Deep Wharf is still active with rail business and operates its own motive power to handle it and many a train of rail tanks still moves to and from the Purfleet sidings.

Q.1 Queens Road Tunnel—see Clapton

R.1 Rainham

Tilbury Loop, between Barking and Tilbury. 12 m 54 ch from Fenchurch Street

Like Purfleet, Rainham was one of the original 1854 LT&S stations. Its half-

hourly trains approach the station complex of twin platforms, high footbridge and modern ticket office via Manor Way CCTV LC (12 m 2 ch) and Rainham LC and signal box then follow (12 m 60 ch). At one time Rainham dealt with timber traffic from the Phoenix Timber Company premises on Frog Island, one of the pioneers of mechanical handling of loose timber which made it easier to load to rail in pipe or tube wagons.

R.2 Rauceby—see Grantham-Skegness Line

R.3 Rayleigh—see Shenfield-Southend Line

R.4 Rectory Road—see Enfield Town Branch

R.5 Reedham—see Brundall-Lowestoft Line

R.6 Retford

East Coast main line, junction with Cleethorpes-Sheffield line. 138 m 49 ch from Kings Cross and 64 m 32 ch from Manchester (London Road)

Retford's railway complex changed dramatically in 1965 with the opening of a re-routed section of the former Great Central line to take it beneath the Great Northern main line instead of crossing it on the level. And so ended 113 years of inconvenience, no longer acceptable with increasing traffic and speeds on the ECML and more coal trains on the GC route.

The Sheffield & Lincolnshire Junction/ MS&L line between Sheffield and Gainsborough was opened on 16 July 1849, just before the GNR route from Sykes Junction to Doncaster which trains started using on 4 September. The notorious and much-photographed crossing then came into being on 15 July 1852 with the opening for goods traffic of the GN's direct line from Peterborough, used by passenger trains from 1 August of that year. Allowing the Sheffield & Lincolnshire Extension Railway/MS&L running powers into Lincoln from Sykes Junction brought the GNR reciprocal rights on the line towards Sheffield and these were exercised from 1859 when a connection was installed between the two routes, diverging from the GN main line at North Junction and curving west to Whiskerhill Junction on the Sheffield line. This was the route taken by the GN's Manchester and Sheffield expresses and the MS&L/GC trains calling at Retford also passed via Whiskerhill and North Junc-

tions to enter the station from the north, rejoining their own line towards Gainsborough at South Junction.

In the 1920s, the approach to Retford was via Grove Road, Ordsall Lane and the GC crossings and then by the 7½ ch South Junction curve, Retford station, North Junction, Retford Goods and Babworth, Canal and Botany Bay signal boxes. The two pre-grouping railways each had its own loco shed and each its own goods depot, Babworth, with a 10-ton crane and which the GN shared with the LNW, and Thrumpton where the GC had a 5-ton crane. The passenger station at Thrumpton had closed in 1859 with the opening of the curve to the GN station but the goods depot lasted until 1970, four years longer than the one at Babworth.

Today the double track ECML arrives at Retford via Gamston Emergency Crossover (136 m 28 ch) and Grove Road LC (137 m 37 ch) and there are then extra Up and Down platform lines, the latter continuing as the Down Slow as far as Retford Emergency Crossover (139 m 69 ch). Northwards lie CCTV crossings at Botany Bay (140 m 53 ch), Sutton (141 m 55 ch) and Torworth (143 m 17 ch) and the remains of Barnby Moor station. On the ex-Great Central route Mansfield Road CCTV LC (62 m 24 ch) is followed by Rushey Sidings LC (62 m 44 ch) and then the separate divergence of the Up and Down single line connections to the ECML. The Up connection from Thrumpton West Junction leaves at 63 m 29 ch and the Down one joins at 63 m 46 ch, both joining the ECML at Retford Western Junction (64 m 29 ch).

Following this modern replacement of the 1859 Whiskerhill-North curve comes the 1965 low level Retford station provided with concrete shelters and footbridge and located on the east side of the ECML above. Retford Thrumpton signal box (63 m 46 ch) is then followed by a bridge across the canal and Gringley Road RC LC (65 m 4 ch). The old goods yard is visible near the Up and Down Goods Loops.

In addition to the Sheffield-Retford/ Lincoln/Cleethorpes trains the former GC line carries a considerable volume of coal to the local power stations, frequently using the new Class '58' locomotives. On the East Coast main line the Doncaster trains call at Retford plus some longer distance services and the journey time to Kings Cross is now under two hours, about the same as the GN's 'Breakfast Car Express' used to achieve with four fewer stops but half an hour better than the average LNER service.

R.7   Ripple Lane—see Barking

R.8   Rochford—see Shenfield-Southend Line

R.9   Romford

Liverpool Street-Norwich line, junction for Upminster Branch. 12 m 30 ch from Liverpool Street

Romford has an excellent train service, derived from the 20-minute all-stations Gidea Park trains, the half-hourly South-end emus and calls by the Colchester and Witham/Braintree trains, the latter running non-stop to Liverpool Street and taking 17 minutes. There is also a half-hourly service Mondays to Saturdays on the Upminster branch.

The present station dates from an LNER reconstruction in 1931 and comprises centre island and two outer platforms with brick buildings and tiled ramps and stairs down to street level. The first Romford station was just a single island platform which was the terminus of the Eastern Counties Railway's original line from 20 June 1839 until the route was extended on to Brentwood on 1 July of the following year. The LT&S branch to Upminster, conceived mainly to keep the Great Eastern away from Tilbury, took ten years between authorization and completion but was eventually opened on 7 June 1893. It was linked by an exchange gallery with the GE station but had a separate entrance until 1934.

Today Romford consists just of the station plus preceding signal box (12 m 11 ch) and DGL and of the following Romford Junction (12 m 39 ch) where the single line branch departs. At one time, however, it had a considerable goods activity with an Up side goods yard, a steeply inclined gas works siding with trap points and limited to six wagons and another which passed beneath the main line to the brewery on the Down side.

R.10   Romford-Upminster Line

From Liverpool Street-Norwich line at Romford to Fenchurch Street-Shoebury-ness line at Upminster. 3 m 27 ch

As indicated in the previous entry, this line opened on 7 June 1893 as part of an LT&S route to Tilbury via Upminster and Grays and to forestall any Great Eastern hopes of tapping the Tilbury traffic. In LT&S days some trains ran through to Grays and others to Tilbury Riverside, the number of the latter increasing under the LNER when the service was mainly Romford-Upminster or Romford-Tilbury.

The intermediate station at Emerson Park (1 m 64 ch) was opened in1909 and provided with a passing loop but the route is now just a One Train single line, operated with dmus and subject to a maximum of 30 mph once clear of the curve by the former goods yard following Romford Junction.

R.11   Rossington—see Doncaster

R.12   Rotherham

Midland main line, junction with Chester-field-Rotherham line. 162 m from St Pancras

On 1 November 1838 the Sheffield & Rotherham Railway opened a line from Sheffield to a terminus in Rotherham later known as Westgate. A short coal branch north to Greasborough was opened from Holmes in the following year and in 1840 a link from Holmes to Masborough allowed the newly arrived North Midland trains from Derby to work through to Sheffield over the S&R. The North Midland opera-

Romford station from the Upminster branch platform.

A 2-4-0 with a train of four-wheeled stock passes through Rotherham Masborough (Lens of Sutton).

tions began on 11 May and its route was extended north to Leeds on 1 July.

The other main railway route through Rotherham was that of the South Yorkshire Railway which evolved from a Tinsley-Rotherham section of 1 August 1868 to a through line to Mexborough over which passenger services began running on 3 April 1871. This eventually became part of the Great Central system but was closed to passengers on 5 September 1966 as part of the elimination of the age-old duplication between the Midland and Great Central systems. Current PTE-linked proposals would restore the GC route in preference to the MR one, with services using a new Holmes Chord to reach a re-opened Rotherham Central and then continuing north through the Don Valley via Swinton Town and the old spur towards Mexborough.

On the main line from Sheffield, Holmes Junction CCTV LC (163 m 43 ch) is followed by the junction itself and the commencement of the Rotherham Down Goods line. The juncion formerly had a curve round towards the Chesterfield line and still adopts its mileage of 161 m 77 ch in place of the via-Sheffield one of 163 m 74 ch, but the physical line between the two routes is now at Rotherham Station North Junction (162 m 24 ch). The line from Chesterfield has arrived via Masborough Sorting Sidings South Junction (160 m 61 ch) and Masborough Station South Junction (161 m 73 ch) and both routes pass through the station proper.

The original Westgate station at Rotherham lasted until 6 October 1952 and the Midland station at Holmes until 19 September 1955. On the GC line, Meadow Hall and Rotherham Road closed in 1953 and Central in 1966. The surviving Masborough station consists of a centre island with two outer platforms and with its main buildings, single-storey, in brick and with some relieving gables and facings, on the Up.

In addition to local trains on the Doncaster and York lines some of the longer distance east/west services call at Rotherham and some of the North-East/South-West trains. There is also a local service to and from Sheffield.

R.13 Roydon

Liverpool Street-Kings Lynn line, between Broxbourne and Bishops Stortford. 20 m 9 ch from Liverpool Street

Roydon is a modest station in a rural riverside setting and with two Bishops Stortford emus calling each hour. The platforms are staggered, there is a barrier level crossing and a small modern ticket office on the Up side.

R.14 Royston

Hitchin-Cambridge line, between Baldock and Shepreth Branch Junction. 44 m 72 ch from Kings Cross

The brave scheme for a line from Cambridge via Royston, Hitchin, Luton, Cheddington, Aylesbury and Thame to Oxford was authorized by Parliament only in respect of the Hitchin-Royston section which was duly opened on 21 October 1850. Worked by the Great Northern Railway, the line was extended to Shepreth on 1 August of the following year with a connecting omnibus service into Cambridge. From the completion of the junction with the ECR on 1 April 1852 the latter took over the Royston & Hitchin on a fourteen-year lease after which it again came under GNR control under arrangements which eventually gave that company full access to Cambridge.

Above *View of the Shell oil terminal at Royston on 31 January 1967.*
Below *Royston, with an Up emu about to depart and grain wagons in the Down sidings.*

Royston has changed quite a bit in recent years notably as a result of the 1977-8 electrification which made the station a turn-round point for the emu service from Kings Cross. The hourly Fasts cover the journey in 48 minutes with the Slows taking 62 minutes. Both platform lines are bi-directional to facilitate the use of either platform and the handling of the Cambridge shuttle service of dmus at the country end of the Up platform.

Royston had private sidings connected with its agricultural surroundings and this tradition is perpetuated by the Down side facility for Grainflow wagons. There is also a traditional grain warehouse opposite the light, airy and modern ticket office on the Up platform.

Litlington AHB LC (43 m 13 ch) precedes Royston which lies in pleasant heathland countryside the undulations of which create the 1 in 120 falling gradient towards Meldreth.

R.15   Rye House—see Hertford East Branch

S.1   St Botolphs—see Colchester

S.2   St James' Street—see Chingford Branch

S.3   St Margarets—see Hertford East Branch

S.4   St Neots

East Coast main line, between Hitchin and Huntingdon. 51 m 58 ch from Kings Cross

A typical Great Northern station, St Neots has a long approach road which rises from the main Cambridge road to the small booking and parcels office building on the Down side. There are some railway houses opposite and, to the north, the coal yard and pathway to the former station master's house. The main goods yard and shed are also on the Down side, south of the booking office and still dealing with some van traffic.

Access to the station's two island platforms is by footbridge and the basic service is provided by the hourly dmu workings between Hitchin and Huntingdon. South-bound these give access at Hitchin to the electric trains to Kings Cross and north-bound every second service connects with a Doncaster HST at Huntingdon.

The four main lines run straight from the CCTV LC which marks the remains of Tempsford station (47 m 38 ch), through No 55 R/G LC (48 m 16 ch) and past the erstwhile sidings of Little Barford power

station to St Neots. They then continue through two more R/G LCs, No 63 (54 m 7 ch) and No 65 (55 m 52 ch), to a stretch alongside the Great Ouse and the level crossing at Offord & Buckden (55 m 72 ch). The curves on this section, now eased, formerly checked trains' speeds quite severely.

Tempsford station used to deal with wartime traffic for Tempsford aerodrome which flew the lonely missions carrying agents to occupied Europe. St Neots used to have a small bus from the Cross Keys Hotel to meet all the important trains and Offord & Buckden had a siding for the produce firm Superior International.

S.5   Salhouse—see Sheringham Branch

S.6   Sandy

East Coast main line, between Hitchin and Huntingdon. 44 m 10 ch from Kings Cross

Early GNR plans included a scheme for a line from Melton Mowbray to Sandy but the latter acquired its junction status in a more modest way. Seven years after the opening of the main line, a local celebration marked the inauguration of services on the Sandy & Potton Railway, a single coach being hauled from Potton to Sandy and back behind 0-4-0WT *Shannon* which was named after the ship of Captain Sir William Peel, the instigator of the project. A sailor, writer and explorer of considerable stature, Captain Peel was the third son of Sir Robert Peel and this local railway, often known as Captain Peel's Railway, was built largely on Peel land. Among the banners at the opening of the 3½-mile line was one inscribed 'In remembrance of the live Shell, October 18th 1854', referring to Peel's exploit in throwing back a Russian shell which had landed with its fuse still burning.

The Sandy-Potton line was mainly for goods traffic and its trains called at local farms on the way from the terminus on the south side of Potton to the station in the GNR goods yard. The two engines also managed four passenger trains a day, probably in the form of mixed trains, despite signalling by red flag. Services ceased at the beginning of 1862 as most of the route was absorbed into the LNWR-backed Bedford & Cambridge Railway which opened to the public on 7 July 1862. This eventually became part of a cross-country route running from Cambridge via Lord's Bridge (5¼ m), Old North Road (10½ m), Gamlingay (15¼ m), Potton (17¾ m), Sandy (21½ m), Girtford Halt (for which passengers travelled in the special car with retractable steps), Blunham (23¾ m), Wil-

Cambridge-Oxford service dmu crossing over the GN main line at Sandy.

lington (26 m), Bedford St Johns and then on to Bletchley. In LNWR days the route was from Oxford to Cambridge and at one period BR had plans for its development as a major freight artery, despite the single line section between Sandy and Bedford, but it was eventually closed on 1 January 1968.

Prior to the closure of its cross-country route Sandy station consisted of a centre island used by main line Up trains and Cambridge-Bletchley services and then outer platforms on each side, the one nearest the town accommodating the GNR offices and station house. Both the GNR and LNWR companies, and their successors, had a goods yard and shed, the former having two Sandy signal boxes and the latter a small one on the island platform which also housed a mobile canteen for the war period and some time after.

Beyond the LNER North box, where the LMS line rose to cross over its main line companion, there was a siding to a small brickyard. Further on still was a spur between the two routes used for wartime traffic. Sandy was also the terminal point of pipelines from Avonmouth and Stanlow and between 6 September 1943 and 31 August 1944 despatched the equivalent of 54,791 tank wagons of fuel to service East Anglian airfields.

Until 1978 Sandy was a bottleneck where the four main lines reduced to two for the passage through the station. This created a lot of difficulty in steam days, especially as Sandy was a major loading point for market garden produce, but the problem was swept away with remodelling which kept the GN Down platform but used the former LNWR area to make space to accommodate all four tracks through the station.

Like St Neots, Sandy is served by the Hitchin-Huntingdon dmus. The old LNW route is still visible both north and south of the station, as are the abutments of the skew bridge which caried it over the main line. On the latter Everton LC (46 m 31 ch) lies between Sandy's sand hills and the former station at Tempsford.

S.7 Sawbridgeworth

Liverpool Street-Kings Lynn line, between Broxbourne and Bishops Stortford. 26 m 56 ch from Liverpool Street

A pleasant station in a period setting, Sawbridgeworth has a modern ticket office in light brick on the Down side and a shelter plus a good example of a traditional signal box with gates on the Up. A service of two trains an hour each way is given by the Liverpool Street-Bishops Stortford emus.

Maltings and granary buildings adjoin the station, one now housing light industry. There is another set of gates, plus signal box, at Spelbrook (28 m 19 ch).

S.8 Saxilby—see   Spalding-Doncaster Line

S.9 Saxmundham—see   East   Suffolk Line

S.10 Scunthorpe

Barnetby-Doncaster   line,   between Wrawby Junction and Thorne. 22 m 54 ch from Doncaster

The first Scunthorpe furnace began work in 1864 with others following rapidly and the complex expanding steadily into today's massive BSC steelworks. The first railway to serve the developing heavy industry was a private scheme which was overtaken by the Trent, Ancholme & Grimsby project of the MS&L and South Yorkshire companies. This was opened from the former's existing line at Barnetby to the Trent at Althorpe and across to meet the SY's line from Thorne, goods traffic commencing on 1 May and passengers on 1 October 1866.

On 19 January 1900 a Light Railway Order was confirmed to North Lindsey Light Railways for a line north towards the Humber. Opening followed in sections, from the main line to West Halton on 3 September 1906, to Winteringham on 15 July 1907 and to Whitton on 1 December 1910. Passenger services lasted only until 13 July 1925 and consisted just of one morning and one early afternoon train each way with an extra working on Saturdays. The departures from Scunthorpe served Winterton &

Thealby (5 m), West Halton (6 m), Winteringham (8½ m) and/or Whitton (11 m).

From the direction of the Trent the double track of the Doncaster-Grimsby line approaches Scunthorpe along a brick-walled viaduct and comes first to the passenger station dating from 1928 and with well-kept brick buildings and country end bays. The North Lindsey station had closed three years earlier but the separate line to Normanby Park still commences at Scunthorpe West Junction (23 m 15 ch) with the signal box just beyond (23 m 27 ch). Its east-facing leg joins the GC line at Trent Junction (23 m 51 m) and there are now Up and Down Goods lines and a Transfer line for the BSC network which lies to its south. Crossovers at North Lincoln Junction (25 m 10 ch) follow and eventually Scunthorpe Foreign Ore Branch Junction (25 m 34 ch) with its connection to the BSC Foreign Ore Terminal. In between are Santon Slag Sidings and the Santon Ore Terminal line.

The North Lindsey line remains in existence as a BR line as far as Winterton & Thealby, worked primarily by the BSC and with a branch from the north end of the quarry area west to Flixborough Works and the Trent. The main route commences at Scunthorpe West Junction (3 ch) and runs west via Scunthorpe Goods Yard LC (18 ch) to Dawes Lane Junction (25 ch) where there is a signal box and the 28 ch line from Trent Junction joins. The double line then heads north through Crosby Warren to Crosby Mines box (1 m 45 ch) and on via Normanby Park South (2 m 6 ch) to Normanby Park North (2 m 60 ch). Beyond the works the route continues as a single line to Roxby Siding Ground Frame and Winterton & Thealby (4 m 42 ch).

In addition to the inwards movements of ore and coal Scunthorpe deals with a considerable volume of outwards business including not only the obvious flows, like the 100,000 tonnes of coil rod a year, but also significant supplies of bulk cement from the Rugby Portland Cement Company. The passenger station is served by the Doncaster-Cleethorpes dmus with some calls by longer distance trains.

S.11   Seven Kings

Liverpool Street-Norwich line, between Ilford and Romford. 8 m 45 ch from Liverpool Street

In the same style as its neighbours, Seven Kings comprises centre island plus two outer platforms with stairs up to the ticket office above. The location, which got its first rail services from 1 March 1899, is now served by the Liverpool Street-Gidea Park emus.

S.12   Seven Sisters—see Enfield Town Branch

S.13   Sheffield

Midland main line, junction with Manchester, Leeds, York, Doncaster and Retford routes. 158 m 30 ch from St Pancras

Sheffield had some early wagonways but its first conventional railway was that of the Sheffield & Rotherham which opened its 5¼-mile line from Sheffield (Wicker) to Rotherham on 1 November 1838. Then the North Midland's route from Derby to Leeds was opened as far as Rotherham on 11 May 1840 and connected there with the S&R to give Sheffield its first railway route to London.

The route west across the Pennines to Manchester was built by the Sheffield, Ashton-under-Lyne & Manchester Railway which opened the Sheffield (Bridgehouses)-Dunford Bridge section on 14 July 1845 and was able to run a through service following the completion of the Woodhead Tunnel on 23 December of the same year. In 1849 the Sheffield & Lincolnshire Junction took the route east to Woodhouse Junction (12 February) and then Gainsborough (17 July) to create the future Great Central east-west route. Great Northern trains reached Sheffield via the MS&L route in 1850 with the latter company opening Victoria station in the following year.

There were three other major railway schemes still to affect Sheffield. On 1 August 1868 the South Yorkshire Railway paralleled the Midland access from Rotherham along the valley of the Don, completing the northern portion to Mexborough three years later. By that time the Midland itself had at last provided direct access from Chesterfield by opening the line up the valley of the Sheaf on 1 February 1870. Another significant new railway was the Midland's route from Dore & Totley to Chinley which was opened for goods on 6 November 1893 and for passengers on 1 June 1894. Six years later the Sheffield District Railway link from Treeton Junction to Brightside brought the LD&EC to join the considerable band of railway companies serving Sheffield.

The opening of the Great Central Railway's London Extension brought a major change in the pattern of Sheffield services but it continued as a vast and complicated railway centre with a complex permutation of through and local passenger services.

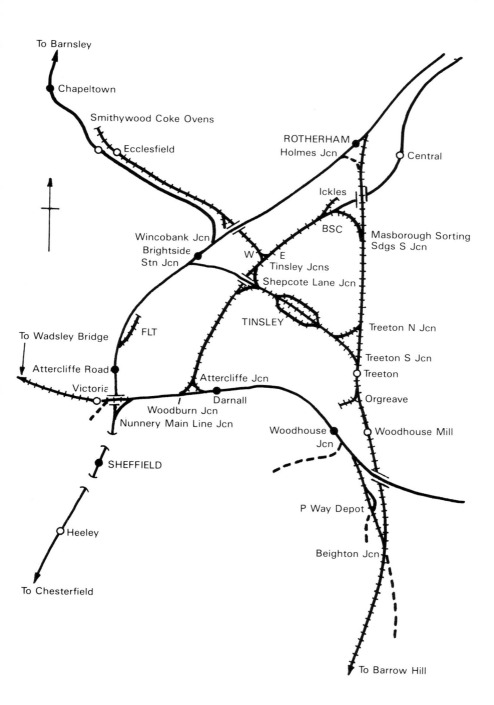

To Barnsley

Chapeltown

Smithywood Coke Ovens

Ecclesfield

ROTHERHAM
Holmes Jcn   Central

Ickles

BSC

Wincobank Jcn   Masborough Sorting
Brightside   Sdgs S Jcn
Stn Jcn   W   E
                 Tinsley Jcns
                 Shepcote Lane Jcn

To Wadsley Bridge   TINSLEY

FLT   Treeton N Jcn

Attercliffe Road   Treeton S Jcn
Victoria   Treeton
         Attercliffe Jcn
         Darnall   Orgreave
    Woodburn Jcn
Nunnery Main Line Jcn   Woodhouse   Woodhouse Mill
                          Jcn
SHEFFIELD

                          P Way Depot

Heeley

                          Beighton Jcn

To Chesterfield

                                 To Barrow Hill

New signalling centre at Sheffield.

There was also a massive freight activity, not only dealing with coal, steel and other heavy products, largely through private sidings, but also a high volume of full loads and of small consignments of general goods.

In the post-nationalization era the first round of changes came in 1954 when electric trains started running between Manchester and Sheffield via the new Woodhead Tunnel from 20 September. Previously, on 5 July, the original North Midland line had lost its passenger services.

The 1960s brought both development and rationalization to Sheffield. The Sheffield District Railway route became the home of an impressive modern marshalling yard at Tinsley which used the latest in techniques, including multiple Dowty retarders for slowing down wagons in the sorting sidings. As part of the same scheme the 1,500 volt electrification was extended to Rotherwood yard and a number of new access routes and junctions created. Freight traffic was then generally concentrated on Tinsley and a new Grimesthorpe freight terminal, and the Midland passenger station increasingly took over the passenger workings starting with the ex-Great Central services after Nunnery Curve was put in during 1965 and traffic concentrated on the old S&R line to Rotherham a year later. Sheffield Victoria closed on 5 January 1970 when the Huddersfield services were diverted, but in May 1983 these were re-routed again via Barnsley and the Woodhead route was finally truncated in favour of its younger Hope Valley rival.

The process of local station closure had begun back in 1927 with Attercliffe GC station leaving the local business to its Mid-land counterpart. Further GC closures included Neepsend, Tinsley, Wadsley Bridge and West Tinsley and on the Midland lines, Beauchief, Heeley, Millhouses, and Wincobank. Very early closures had included Grimesthorpe Bridge (S&R) in 1843, Bridgehouses (MS&L) in 1851, Wicker (Mid) in 1870 and the first Woodhouse station (MS&L) in 1875.

Sheffield ER today is very different from the Sheffield of the past. Its signalling has been concentrated on a modern panel and the old Pond Street station site handles all the passenger services—HSTs to and from St Pancras, NE/SW trains via Derby and Doncaster, local PTE services and through workings east to Cleethorpes and west to Manchester. On the freight side there is a Freightliner terminal and full loads of coal, steel and scrap remain important. The latter is dealt with in the main yard at Tinsley, which also has Speedlink and special/transfer traffic at the west end and a loco and dmu depot at the Treeton end.

From the south the former Midland main line is joined to the Hope Valley line at Dore South Junction (153 m 73 ch), the station (154 m 20 ch) then following before the Dore Station Junction (154 m 50 ch) meeting point for trains bound for Sheffield. These then continue along the Sheaf Valley, past the former stations at Beauchief, Millhouses and Heeley to the short, 80 yd East Bank Tunnel (158 m 1 ch to 158 m 5 ch) and former underpass. The 1904 station at Sheffield, recently refurbished, comprises the main Down platform with No 1 Platform Line, Through Line, No 2 Platform Line, two Through Lines and Platform Lines 5-8. Overall the total is Down platform plus two islands with through lines between and with bays at both ends.

Immediately beyond the station comes a cutting and Nunnery Main Line Junction (158 m 77 ch) where the GC and MR routes split before passing through the 109 yd Broad Street Tunnel (158 m 76 ch to 159 m 1 ch) and separating. Along the road, rail and water corridor to Rotherham the main line now passes through the simplified suburban station at Attercliffe Road (159 m 34 ch) and by the wire coil and Freightliner depots to come to Brightside Station Junction (161 m 6 ch/162 m 35 ch). This gives access to the former Sheffield District Railway route via Shepcote Lane Junctions (161 m 24 ch to 161 m 13 ch), Tinsley Park (160 m 65 ch) and the BSC lines, Tinsley Yard (160 m 2 ch) and Catliffe Junction (159 m 15 ch/25 ch) to the triangular Treeton Junctions with the Chesterfield-Rotherham line. From the Shepcote Lane Junctions connections are made to the triangle of Attercliffe, Darnall West and Woodburn Junctions on the GC route to the south and via the Tinsley Junctions to the Smithywood line and to the GC route via Ickles and Rotherham to the north.

Back on the main line Brightside station (161 m 27 ch) comprises just platforms and shelters in a cutting and is followed by Wincobank Junction (161 m 52 ch) where the Chapeltown route departs.

On the route from Sheffield to Cleethorpes the 1965 curve links up with the former GC route from Victoria at Nunnery Junction (159 m 33 ch), alongside the Nunnery carriage sidings and with a mileage change to 41 m 68 ch. Woodburn CCE shops then precede Woodburn Junction (42 m 29 ch) and the freight route to Rotherham via Attercliffe Junction (28 ch), Broughton Lane Junction (1 m 38 ch), the Tinsley Junctions (2 m 22 ch to 2 m 68 ch) and Ickles (3 m 49 ch). Trains from this route join at Darnall West Junction (43 m 4 ch) where there is also a complex of yard, engineers' and carriage and wagon activities.

Darnall station (43 m 23 ch) has islands and out-of-use brick buildings. Four tracks here have now reduced to two and the signal boxes at Orgreave Colliery (45 m 10 ch) and Rotherwood (45 m 70 ch) have both had their work transferred to the Sheffield panel. Woodhouse station (46 m 18 ch) retains its gabled buildings in red brick and is followed by the junction (46 m 52 ch) with the Chesterfield line which the route then crosses over after Beighton permanent way depot and before Brookhouse Colliery.

This, then, is Sheffield. Its surviving single station is an attractive one with a pleasant arched entrance and services to many main centres. It lies near to the city centre, well placed to carry the thousands that use the PTE/BR local services or the businessman who will be carried to London in around 2½ hours. The slimming down process has been accompanied by modernization which has placed 180 route miles under the control of the signalling centre and kept the most important and appropriate of the freight flows. All a long cry from Sheffield's railway beginnings on a branch line from Rotherham!

S.14   Shelford

Liverpool Street-Kings Lynn line, between Audley End and Cambridge. 52 m 32 ch from Liverpool Street

Shelford might have been the junction between the 1845 ECR main line to Norwich and the Royston & Hitchin Railway but it had, in fact, to wait twenty years for junction status. It then came with the opening of the GER's route from Sudbury, completed on 1 August 1865 after the Shelford-Haverhill section had opened on 1 June of that year. Pre-war there were five weekday trains each way to and from Cambridge, calling at Shelford (3¼ m), Pampisford (7¾ m), Linton (10¼ m), Bartlow (12 m), Haverhill (18¼ m) and on via Long Melford (31¾ m) to Marks Tey (46½ m) and Colchester (51½ m), a journey of nearly two hours. The route was operated by dmus from 1959 but the Shelford end closed to freight on 31 October 1966 and to passengers on 6 March 1967.

The station is preceded by Sawston LC (50 m 46 ch) and Dernford R/G LC (51 m 36 ch) and then has its own crossing after the trackbed of the former Colchester route has come alongside the main line. The two platforms with modest two-storey buildings on the Up are followed by Grahams LC (52 m 64 ch) and are served by the Bishops Stortford-Cambridge dmus.

S.15   Shenfield

Liverpool Street-Norwich line, junction with Southend line. 20 m 16 ch from Liverpool Street

Important since 1888-9 as the junction with the Southend line, Shenfield was the eastern turnround point for the 1,500 volt dc electrification initiated by the LNER and completed in the first years of nationalization. Now the electric trains operate at 25 kv ac and continue along the main line to Colchester and beyond and on the branch to Southend Victoria.

Class 315 electric multiple unit set seen at Shenfield on introduction in December 1980.

The four-track section of the main line from Liverpool Street ends at Shenfield, with Fast to Slow and Slow to Fast crossovers preceding the combination of centre island and two outer platforms, provided with red brick buildings and traditional canopies and with tiled stairs to the Down side ticket office block. Beyond the station where the old wartime HQ control building is still in existence on the Up side, the Southend lines depart, the single Down line passing beneath the main line before rejoining the Up side pair.

In addition to the Southend trains, the Witham/Braintree and Colchester services call at Shenfield which also originates and terminates the early and late all-stations services to Liverpool Street.

S.16   Shenfield-Southend (Victoria) Line

Liverpool Street-Norwich line, branch from Shenfield. 21 m 17 ch

The Great Eastern Railway did not reach Southend until over thirty years after the LT&S had arrived there. However, a branch from the main line at Shenfield was finally opened in 1889, passenger trains

reaching Wickford on 1 January and Southend on 1 October. The route was doubled twenty years later.

From Shenfield Junction (20 m 22 ch) the Down side 'Southend Loop' is a bi-directional single line as far as Mountnessing Junction (21 m 32 ch) where it joins the two Up side lines. The first station on the branch is then Billericay (24 m 28 ch), a conventional location with two-storey buildings on the Down side and a former London end bay. Wickford (29 m), the junction for Southminster since 1 July 1889 (goods 1 June), formerly had three bays. It still uses the two at the country end, Up trains from the branch either running into the Down side bay or through the crossover by the signal box to get to the Up side one. Wickford's main Down side buildings are traditional but have a modernized ticket office.

In a field on the Down side of the Southend line, before it reaches Rayleigh, a marker still records the spot where two World War I aeroplanes crashed after colliding in mid-air. There is also an R/G level crossing on this section at Wick Lane, 37 ch after Wickford Junction (29 m 13 ch) with the Southminster line.

Rayleigh itself has a windmill for company and is a straightforward station of Up and Down platforms with canopies, underbridge and red brick buildings on the Up side. Hockley (36 m 10 ch) is similar except that it has a footbridge.

Rochford (38 m 54 ch) has a Down side dock and country end bay in addition to the main Down side buildings. In the same way that the old smelting works is now active again at Hockley, Rochford's former goods shed is again serving a useful purpose, as a community centre. The half-hourly train services give a good view of Southend airport before coming to Prittlewell (40 m 67 ch) which stands on a curve and has a short Up platform.

S.17   Shepcote Lane Junctions—see Sheffield

S.18   Shepreth

Shepreth is on the Hitchin-Cambridge line, 49 m 63 ch from Kings Cross and Shepreth Branch Junction (55 m 26 ch) is where that line joins the Liverpool Street-Kings Lynn line (53 m 4 ch from Liverpool Street)

Following Meldreth Road AHB LC (49 m 37 ch), Shepreth station has a traditional complex of platforms, station buildings—including house with bow window—and former goods shed. It is served by the Royston-Cambridge dmus.

Shepreth Branch Junction is preceded from the Hitchin direction by Hauxton

AHB LC (54 m 1 ch) and on the Liverpool Street line by Grahams LC (52 m 64 ch). The Down Hitchin line trails into the Down Cambridge but Up Hitchin trains cross From Up main to Down main before diverging onto the Up Hitchin line.

An omnibus service operated from Shepreth to Cambridge after the Royston & Hitchin line was extended to that point on 1 August 1851 but from the completion of the through line in the following year the ECR trains served the station until its fourteen-year lease expired.

S.19   Sheringham Branch

Norwich-Yarmouth line, branch from Whitlingham Junction. 28 m 29 ch

The Sheringham branch, linking Norfolk's capital city with the coast, has a basic service of thirteen trains each way on weekdays and three on Sundays, the dmu sets taking an hour for the journey and calling at seven intermediate stations. The main traffics are commuter and local with extra travel in the summer months, especially on the coastal portion and to Cromer and Sheringham.

The route is that of the former GER Cromer branch as far as Cromer Junction and then that of the Norfolk & Suffolk Joint Railways Committee between Roughton Road Junction and Newstead Lane Junction to give access to the former M&GN Cromer Beach station, trains completing their journey by means of the M&GN line along the coast to Sheringham. This arrangement dates from 1954 when

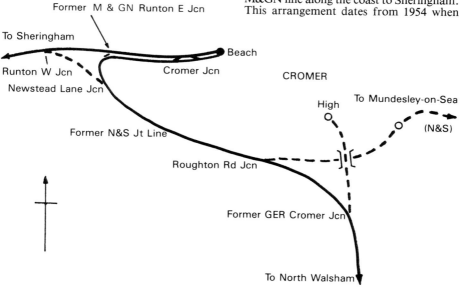

passenger services were diverted from the former GER Cromer High to the more convenient Cromer Beach station. Absolute Block working applies over the double track portion as far as Wroxham, Electric Token working on the single line thence to Cromer and One Train operation on the final single line portion to Sheringham.

At Whitlingham Junction (1 m 71 ch from Norwich Thorpe) the double line branch turns north away from the Yarmouth line and climbs, initially at 1 in 80, towards Salhouse via AHB crossings at Norwich Road (4 m 20 ch), Great Plumstead (4 m 50 ch) and Rackheath Road (5 m 20 ch). This section to North Walsham was opened by the East Norfolk Railway on 20 October 1874 after ten years of financial problems. It includes some of the brick and wood crossing houses which are a distinctive feature of the route. Salhouse station (55 m 71 ch) lies on a long straight section and comprises Up and Down platforms with wooden Down side buildings and closed brick buildings with canopy opposite.

Wroxham station (8 m 61 ch), whose traffic increased with the popularity of the Broads holidays for which it is a centre, is heralded by a curved cutting and three overbridges. Then comes the bridge over the River Bure, with a 35 mph speed limit and a movable centre section, followed by the station itself raised high above the B1354 Potter Heigham-Coltishall road. Beyond its brick, canopied buildings lies the Up side yard with its fertiliser warehouse and grain loading point and then Wroxham Junction (8 m 70 ch) where the signal box stands.

The East Norfolk opened a branch from Wroxham Junction to County School in five stages between 1879 and 1882. One could, in fact, travel from Norwich and back to Norwich via this line and its stations at Coltishall (11½ miles from Norwich Thorpe), Buxton Lamas (14¼ m), Aylsham (17¾ m), Cawston (22 m), Reepham (24 m) and Foulsham (28¾ m) but the 38½ mile journey from Norwich to Dereham took 85 minutes and gave the route its 'Round the World' soubriquet. The Wroxham-County School line closed to passengers on 15 September 1952 and was cut between Reepham and Foulsham, but the eastern section was linked to a portion of the M&GN line into Norwich city from 12 September 1960 via a new 'Themelthorpe Curve'. In turn this was cut back to Lenwade in 1969 but the 23 m 77 ch 'One Train' single line light railway used to service Anglian Building Products at that

point was out of use by 1983 with sleepers blocking the visible trackwork remaining at Wroxham Junction.

Having dropped to the Bure Valley at Wroxham the branch proper, now reduced from double to single track, begins to rise again as it continues north past the gated crossings at Tunstead Market Street (10 m 45 ch) and Sloley Church Lane (12 m 17 ch) to Worstead (13 m 9 ch). The station here is a simple one—just traditional brick buildings plus canopy on the Up side with two gated LCs and the disused Down platform and signalbox (bought by one of its previous signalmen)—but it serves a village of considerable historical significance. The Flemish weavers who brought their skills over in Norman times were to make Worsted cloth world famous while, on a different plane, Worstead was the birthplace of John the Dyer who became a leading light in the Norfolk peasants' rebellion and created himself 'King of the Commons' until Henry le Despenser defeated John's peasant army and hung, drew and quartered its leaders.

From historic Worstead the railway line rises in four stages of 1 in 80/180/247/440 to North Walsham (15 m 75 ch), where Nelson went to school, and a block post where the tablets are exchanged at the signal box at the commencement of the passing loop. The surviving station, formerly North Walsham Main, has canopied brick buildings, those on the Up side still incorporating the 'General Waiting Room' lettering in a glass door panel. North Walsham Town, the M&GN station, stood opposite its Great Eastern neighbour until its passenger services ceased on 2 March 1959. The two goods yards were subsequently combined and an oil terminal plus wooden goods shed, track and docks survive on the Up side of the main line.

The M&GN line had originally reached North Walsham from Stalham as part of the Yarmouth & North Norfolk Railway on 13 June 1881, with the Eastern & Midlands portion from Melton Constable completing the new through route between Kings Lynn and Great Yarmouth on 5 April 1883. The branch to Mundesley was opened on 1 July 1898 and extended on to Cromer on 3 August 1906 under the auspices of the N&S Joint Railways Committee formed by the GE and M&GN companies. The second section closed on 7 April 1953 and the North Walsham-Mundesley portion on 6 October 1964, ending forever the chance to make the former 42 minute trip via Paston & Knapton (3½ m), Mundesley-on-Sea (5¼ m), Trimingham (7¾ m), Overstrand

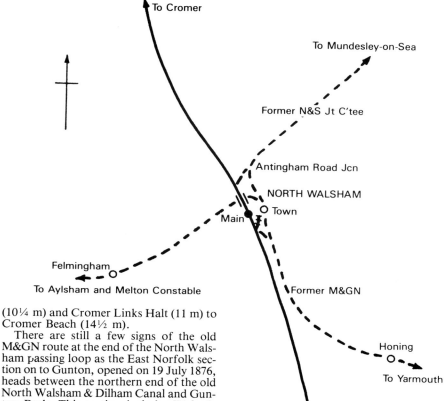

To Cromer

To Mundesley-on-Sea

Former N&S Jt C'tee

Antingham Road Jcn

NORTH WALSHAM

O Town

Main

Felmingham

To Aylsham and Melton Constable

Former M&GN

Honing

To Yarmouth

To Wroxham

(10¼ m) and Cromer Links Halt (11 m) to Cromer Beach (14½ m).

There are still a few signs of the old M&GN route at the end of the North Walsham passing loop as the East Norfolk section on to Gunton, opened on 19 July 1876, heads between the northern end of the old North Walsham & Dilham Canal and Gunton Park. This section includes Walpole gated crossing (18 m 67 ch) and two lesser crossings—all with crossing keepers' houses. At Gunton (19 m 62 ch) itself, formerly a passing loop, the Up platform is now used, the old station buildings on the Down side having been adapted for use as a private dwelling.

The hills around Cromer are reputed to be amongst the oldest places of habitation in the British Isles, but this feature of interest could hardly have been of any consolation to those who had to make the long walk and climb from the town to catch a train at the old Cromer High station. This part of the original route was completed by the East Norfolk Railway on 26 March 1877 but access to the pleasant Norfolk resort was improved when the Eastern & Midlands opened Beach station just west of the town centre ten years later (16 June 1877), BR services being concentrated on the latter following the closure of the GER station on 20 September 1954. Subsequent rationalization produced the present single line approach from Cromer Junction (46 m

27 ch), round the town via the old N&S route and then over the M&GN portion into the surviving terminal. Traces of all the former routes can still be spotted on this final approach to Cromer.

The surviving Cromer station is approached by separate single lines from the North Walsham and Sheringham directions, these eventually terminating either side of a single platform with the station buildings beyond the buffer stops and some coal and timber activity now occupying the old goods yard on the seaward side. The truncated roof still has the E&MR motif in its support spandrels. At the other end of the platform are the approach crossovers and the signal box where the ET tablet is exchanged for the OT section token while the dmu driver holds the deadman button in a feat requiring some dexterity.

From Cromer signal box (46 m 35 ch) the 55 mph single line to Sheringham runs near the coast via West Runton (44 m 39 ch) and

Mundesley station as it was in 1960 and with camping coaches on the left.

its single platform on the Down side. At Beeston Regis the main level crossing (43 m 69 ch) has a separate crossing to the 600-year-old church overlooking the sea. Beyond the crossing is the single platform of the simple station built as Sheringham (42 m 61 ch), the preservation society having taken over the traditional station provided by the E&M when it opened on 1 October 1884.

The distances on this final section are measured from Kings Lynn which was originally the headquarters of the M&GN system. On the approach to Cromer the mileage changes from 23 m 73 ch to 11 m 53 ch (from North Walsham via Mundesley) at what was originally Cromer Junction and from 13 m 48 ch to 45 m 64 ch at what was originally Runton East Junction. The link between the two single lines on the approaches to Cromer station now bears the name Cromer Junction (46 m 27 ch).

It is difficult to imagine that the Cromer/Sheringham line once carried trains like the 'Cromer Express' and the 'Norfolk Coast Express' in which the Great Eastern Railway took such pride. By 1938 the 9.45 am Saturday train from Liverpool Street was reaching Cromer at 1.35 pm (Sheringham 1.51 pm) and while the best service from Kings Cross took 46 minutes longer, the old M&GN route was carrying a substantial number of through services from such places as Leicester, Derby and Manchester. The responsibilities later carried by trains like the 'Norfolkman' now rest more humbly with the dmu units but the branch continues to fulfil a useful function and is of considerable scenic and railway interest.

S.20   Sherwood-Shireoaks Line

Cleethorpes-Sheffield line, branch from Shireoaks Junctions. 12 m 60 ch

This 1875 Midland Railway route formerly carried a Mansfield-Worksop passenger service calling at Mansfield Woodhouse (1-½ m), Shirebrook (4½ m), Langwith (6 m), Elmton & Creswell (8¾ m) and Whitwell (10¼ m). Today it is a freight-only route carrying important flows of coal traffic.

Recognizing the MR origins, the distances for the ER portion of the line commence at Sherwood Colliery Sidings South (LMR) (141 m 50 ch) which are followed by Shirebrook Sidings (144 m 7 ch), the LMR/ER boundary point, and then Shirebrook Station (144 m 79 ch). The connections to the old LD&ECR route, still surviving eastwards as the High Marnham branch, are still marked by Shirebrook Junction (145 m 14 ch) leading to the Warsop Junction line and Shirebrook East Junction (145 m 62 ch) leading to the Shirebrook South Junction line. After Norwood LC (147 m 71 ch) Elmton & Creswell Junction (149 m 37 ch) provides a link towards Barrow Hill and then comes the 544 yd Whitwell Tunnel (150 m 3 ch to 150 m 28 ch), Whitwell signal box (150 m 45 ch) and Steetley Colliery Sidings (152 m 31 ch). From Woodend Junction (153 m 71 ch) there is a single line to Shireoaks West Junction (154 m 36 ch) and a double one to Shireoaks East Junction (154 m 30 ch).

S.21   Shippea Hill

Birmingham-Norwich line, between Ely and Thetford. 77 m 25 ch from Liverpool Street

Shippea Hill lies on the long, straight section of the route opened by the ECR on 30 July 1845. In addition to meeting the rail transport needs of the agricultural community of the fertile South Bedford Level fenland, the station came to serve Mildenhall air base, away to the south along the A1101. It was known as Mildenhall Road until 1 April 1885 and then became Burnt Fen until 1 May 1905, a name not inappropriate in view of the dark rich soil of its sur-roundings. The present name derives from a sandy hillock in this otherwise flat part of Cambridgeshire.

On the approach from Ely Padnal signal box, a level crossing (73 m 17 ch) and an emergency crossover mark the site of the former agricultural siding closed on 13 July 1964. They are followed by Mile End AHB LC (74 m 76 ch) and then the station which comprises Up and Down platforms with shelters, traditional brick signal box plus gates, two railway cottages and the nearby 'Railway Tavern'. Despite its lonely loca-tion the latter used to be a favourite haunt of the Cambridge district inspectors and was capable of serving a meal very nearly up to Great Eastern Hotel standards.

Ely-Norwich dmus serve Shippea Hill station which is followed by Chivers open LC (78 m 54 ch). Near the latter there used to be a Drainage Board railway and a line out to Shrubhill farm and brickworks. Hiam's tramway ran south from the station and a Fens Light Railway link was proposed with the Wissington line.

S.22 Shirebrook—see Sherwood-Shire-oaks Line

S.23 Shireoaks

Cleethorpes-Sheffield line, between Ret-ford and Woodhouse Junction. 54 m 56 ch from Manchester (London Road)

The Sheffield-Retford trains service Shire-oaks, some extended on to Lincoln or Clee-thorpes. The station itself comprises Up and Down platforms with gabled buildings, signal box, level crossing and crossover and to the east lies the triangular junction with the Shirebrook line.

S.24 Shoeburyness

Terminus of Fenchurch Street-Shoebury-

Shoeburyness emu depot in 1983.

ness line. 39 m 40 ch from Fenchurch Street

After reaching Southend in 1856 the LT&S was not extended to its present terminus until 1 February 1884. This now comprises a simple two-platform station with wooden buildings and an Up side bay. After the built-up route through Southend the loca-tion seems very rural but the Down side sig-nal box (39 m 23 ch) controls access to a major carriage depot and signing on point which provides the stock for the emu service of three trains an hour off peak and nine in the peak.

The army gunnery school which con-stituted one of the reasons for the original extension of the route developed into a major MoD location with extensive sidings. A connection still remains.

S.25 Silver Street—see Enfield Town Branch

S.26 Silvertown—see North Woolwich Branch

S.27 Silverwood Colliery Branch

Doncaster-Sheffield line, branch from Thrybergh Junction. 2 m 54 ch

A portion of the old GC&Midland line sur-vives to serve Silverwood Colliery. With a 25 mph limitation the single line is operated on the One Train basis and runs from Thry-bergh Junction (13 m 13 ch) to Silverwood Junction (11 m 8 ch) and the end of the branch at 10 m 39 ch.

S.28 Six Mile Bottom

Cambridge-Ipswich line, between Cam-bridge and Newmarket. 7 m 63 ch from Coldham Lane Junction

The first station was called Westley and lay on the 1848 line opened by the Newmarket Railway to the ECR main line at Great Chesterford. After losing its battle with the larger company the Newmarket closed its

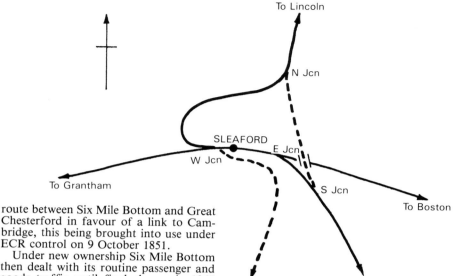

route between Six Mile Bottom and Great Chesterford in favour of a link to Cambridge, this being brought into use under ECR control on 9 October 1851.

Under new ownership Six Mile Bottom then dealt with its routine passenger and goods traffic until final closure in 1967 (goods 1964). Even then the signal box and level crossing remained active and the goods shed and station buildings remain in existence. It is also possible to spot the route of the old Newmarket main line.

S.29 Sizewell Branch—see East Suffolk Line

S.30 Skegness—see Grantham-Skegness Line

S.31 Sleaford

Junction of Nottingham-Skegness and Spalding-Doncaster lines. 120 m 53 ch from Kings Cross

The Great Northern, in the guise of the Boston, Sleaford & Midland Counties Rail-

Main Down side station buildings at Sleaford.

way, reached Sleaford from the main line on 16 June 1857 and pushed on to Boston on 13 April 1859. Sleaford then became a junction on 2 January 1872 when the route to Bourne was opened. By linking the latter point with Cambridge the Great Eastern had in mind its cherished ambition of a separate route to the North but Parliamentary approval was not forthcoming and this had to wait until 1882 when the GN&GE joint line arrived from Spalding on 6 March and was connected to Lincoln from 1 August.

With only local traffic the meandering Bourne line needed only four trains each way daily, starting with the 8.20 am from Sleaford which called at Aswarby & Scredington (3½ m), Billingborough & Horbling (8 m), Rippingale (11¾ m), Morton Road (14¾ m) and then Bourne (17½ m). Its pas-

senger services lasted only until 22 September 1930 but a truncated freight activity was maintained from the Spalding end after the northern portion was closed entirely in 1956.

More recent rationalization at Sleaford has closed the GN&GE Avoiding Line and singled much of the trackwork except that through the station proper. The Nottingham-Skegness dmus approach the latter via Sleaford West signal box (120 m 33 ch) where the 2 m 8 ch single line from Sleaford North Junction trails in. There is a UKF depot nearby and a grain warehouse behind the station which is a distinctly Great Northern affair with main buildings on the Down side and an island on the Up. Sleaford East Junction signal box (120 m 58 ch) operates the barrier crossing over the main road into the town, the singled line then continuing east past the siding area which once served substantial grain and seed warehouses. From Sleaford East Junction (121 m 21 ch) there is a 43 ch single line spur to Sleaford South Junction leaving the Boston line to continue through Kirby Laythorpe LC (122 m 52 ch). On the joint line Sleaford South Junction stands at 62 m 13 ch from Huntingdon and Sleaford North Junction at 63 m 48 ch, the latter also having a level crossing in addition to its signal box.

S.32   Soham—see Newmarket-Ely Line

S.33   Somerleyton—see Brundall-Lowestoft Line

S.34   Southbury—see Churchbury Loop

S.35   Southend

Southend Central and Southend East are on the Fenchurch Street-Shoeburyness line, 35 m 55 ch and 36 m 47 ch respectively. Southend Victoria is on the line from Liverpool Street via Shenfield, 41 m 39 ch from the former.

Southend's early traffic demands were met by steamer and the GSN sailings from Tower Bridge continued to be popular as part of a day's outing for Londoners. To secure a share of the growing business the Eastern Counties and London & Blackwall partnership opened its LT&S line to Southend in 1855-6. From 1 March 1856 until 1 February 1884, when the route was extended to Shoeburyness, the Southend station was a terminus and it was to continue to act in this capacity for thousands of day, half day and evening excursion trains right up to electrification.

The former LT&S route runs parallel to and not far from the shore line of the estuary and at Southend Central crosses the main road to the sea front. The station comprises two through lines and platforms with additional London end bays on both the Up and Down sides. Only one of these is now in use as part of a patterned emu service which, off-peak, consists of a Fenchurch Street-Shoeburyness train every twenty minutes and half-hourly slower starting/ terminating trains via the Tilbury Loop. The substantial, and quite stylish station buildings are on the Up side and the modern panel signal box (35 m 49 ch) on the Down.

Southend East now uses only the two main line tracks and platforms, although the extra Up side track, yard and parcels areas are still evident. The station (36 m 47 ch) caters for commuters and local journeys and has the same service as Shoeburyness. The large wooden signal box is still standing but is not needed now that the East station no longer stables excursion train stock.

The other route to Southend, opened on 1 October 1889, was built to satisfy the Great Eastern's need for independent access to the resort and as part of a wider scheme of exploitation of the whole area. Although a typical GER terminus of 1889, Victoria station needed to keep up the standards set five years earlier by the LT&S and has some pleasant features. Nearby an escalator now rises to the Victoria Shopping Centre, a feature well in keeping with the station remodelling.

Although not a major scheme, the remodelling of Southend Victoria included some track and signalling alterations but the latter were accommodated within the existing Up side signal box (41 m 22 ch). On the Down side prior to the four-platform terminus stand a coal concentration depot, the carriage washing plant and a GPO depot on the site of the old loco shed. There are carriage sidings on both sides of the main line and supplying sets for the three trains an hour which makes up the basic service.

S.36   Southminster Branch

Shenfield-Southend Victoria line, branch from Wickford. 16 m 48 ch

The Great Eastern Railway opened its branch from Wickford to the Crouch estuary and on to Southminster on 1 July 1889 (goods 1 June). This was part of an expansion package which included not only separate access to Southend but also a branch from Woodham Ferrers to Maldon West opened on the same day as the South-

The connection from Maldon East to Maldon West by way of the viaduct over the Blackwater Estuary, pictured in 1959.

end line (1 October 1889) and connecting at Maldon with the 1848 branch from Witham.

The Maldon branch ran from east of Woodham Ferrers, through Cold Norton (3½ m) to Maldon West (7¼ m) and then round through a tunnel to Maldon East (8¾ m). The five daily trains of GER days had become six by 1938 and were calling at Baron's Lane and Stow St Mary halts but business was not sufficient to stave off the closure to passengers on 10 September 1939. Freight continued until 1954 when all but the connection at Maldon was abandoned.

In contrast to its Maldon subsidiary the Southminster branch flourished to become a candidate for a simple electrification scheme which will give through emu services to Liverpool Street by May 1986. As

Burnham-on-Crouch in 1967.

Balfour Beatty started putting in the masts at the beginning of 1985 the traffic on the branch warranted fourteen daily dmu workings each way plus a service on summer Sundays and a residual freight activity for the sand from Southminster and Bradwell nuclear power station traffic.

From Wickford Junction (29 m 13 ch) the single line of the Southminster branch turns away from the Southend line and starts a climb to the single platform at Battlesbridge (31 m 40 ch). Woodham Ferrers (34 m 51 ch) which follows was also a passing loop but now uses only the Down platform although this has a station house and canopy. The traditional level crossing is to become automatic under the electrification scheme.

Some rising and falling now brings the branch to Fambridge (37 m 27 ch) and the end of the first of the two Electric Token sections. The passing loop and token exchange is controlled by a conventional signal box complete with decorative barge boards. Althorne (40 m 27 ch) now has only a single platform plus level crossing and the latter is also scheduled to become automatic. Burnham-on-Crouch (43 m 24 ch) is

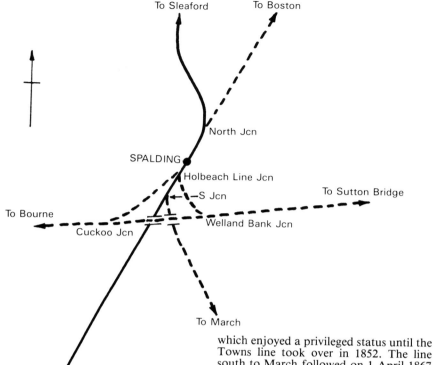

To Sleaford

To Boston

North Jcn

SPALDING

Holbeach Line Jcn

To Sutton Bridge

S Jcn

To Bourne

Welland Bank Jcn

Cuckoo Jcn

To March

To Peterborough

similar to Woodham Ferrers but with the large brick goods shed still extant. Then comes the terminus at Southminster (45 m 42 ch), 42 ch after its traditional signal box and comprising a single platform, platform line, out-of-use run-round line, conventional station buildings and booking office, goods shed and old loco area. The lifting gantry for the Bradwell traffic stands in the old goods yard.

S.37 South Tottenham—see Upper Holloway-Barking Line

S.38 Spalding

Werrington Junction - Spalding and Spalding-Doncaster lines. 92 m 77 ch from Kings Cross

The South Lincolnshire market town and agricultural centre of Spalding was the focus of several early east-west railway ambitions and then featured in a long Great Northern struggle to keep other railways out of its territory. The first trains to arrive were those on the Great Northern's line from Peterborough to Boston and Lincoln

which enjoyed a privileged status until the Towns line took over in 1852. The line south to March followed on 1 April 1867 but owed as much to thwarting Great Eastern ambitions as to traffic prospects.

The Great Northern controlled and/or operated the Norwich & Spalding Railway opened from Spalding to Holbeach on 15 November 1858 and on to Sutton Bridge on 1 July 1862 and also the Spalding-Bourne enterprise which came into use on 1 August 1866. With the Lynn & Sutton Bridge these all became part of the Midland & Eastern Railway in that same year with the GN having to accept an increasing Midland Railway presence in the area. This went further after the Saxby-Bourne line was opened on 5 June 1893 (1 May 1894 for passengers) and created the basis of the M&GN system linking the East Midlands with Norfolk and its coastline.

By that time the Great Northern had also had to admit the Great Eastern's ambitions for a route to the coal areas in the form of the Great Northern & Great Eastern Joint enterprise which gave Spalding a new line, to Lincoln and beyond, from 1 August 1882. It also had a long siding connection to the BSC factory in later years.

Until the period of railway closures Spalding was a busy railway junction handling the Kings Cross-Peterborough-

Boston-Grimsby services, a lot of M&GN trains (although the summer Saturday services used the direct line, avoiding the station) and both passenger and freight workings on the GN&GE route. Its domestic goods business was quite considerable and the station received many passengers for the Spring bulbfield tours.

The line from Werrington Junction approached Spalding via the Hawthorn Bank AHB LC (92 m 8 ch) and its tiny brick cottage. The route of the M&GN Avoiding Line is visible before South Junction (92 m 58 ch) where the recently-closed joint line from March joined (44 m 7 ch from Huntingdon). A surviving single line at Holbeach Junction (44 m 11 ch) marks the route used by the Spalding-Holbeach trains and then Spalding No 1 box (44 m 13 ch) is followed by the crossing and station. This is the 1848 original with the main buildings on the Up side but now only using two of the previous four platform lines. The goods yard and shed follow as the route continues to Spalding No 2 box (44 m 42 ch). At North Junction (44 m 53 ch) the Boston and Sleaford lines used to separate but by 1984 track was being lifted on the former and trains could no longer continue on to Surfleet (96 m 74 ch), Algarkirk & Sutterton (100 m 54 ch), Kirton (103 m 38 ch) and then Boston. Along the Sleaford line Park Road LC (44 m 65 ch) is followed by Mill Green signal box (44 m 74 ch).

The ER section of the M&GN started 1 m 40 ch from Saxby Junction and then ran as a single line with passing loops through Edmondthorpe & Wymondham (2 m 34 ch), South Witham (6 m 74 ch), Castle Bytham (11 m 16 ch), became double at Little Bytham Junction (13 m 12 ch) to pass through the 330 yd Toft Tunnel and come to Bourne (18 m 11 ch), where the station house was reputedly haunted. The truncated Sleaford route, from the run-round loop at Billingborough, joined the M&GN line just east of Bourne station. In the 1950s this was a regular turn for a Spalding guard who used his own brake van, fitted to carry his gun and do a bit of strictly irregular shooting during the course of a very peaceful and rural day's work.

After Twenty station (3 m 54 ch from Bourne) the M&GN route singled through Counter Drain (5 m 18 ch) and North Drove (7 m 5 ch) but was double from Cuckoo Junction (8 m 3 ch), where the Spalding station connection had departed to Welland Bank Junction (9 m 32 ch) where it rejoined. Shortly after this the line singled again to continue to Sutton Bridge via

Weston (11 m 67 ch), Moulton (13 m 27 ch), Whaplode (14 m 33 ch), Holbeach (16 m 53 ch), Fleet (18 m 58 ch), Gedney (20 m 2 ch) and Long Sutton (21 m 15 ch).

Although freight spurs to Bourne and Holbeach remained after the M&GN closure from midnight on 28 February 1959, Spalding was never to be quite the same place and today it is rather a shadow of its former self with no sugar beet permits to process, no busy telegraph office, no Manchester-Lowestoft service on the Avoiding Line and no through trains to Kings Cross. Even so, access to the ECML at Peterborough plus the dmu workings north to Lincoln and Doncaster still give the town some very useful rail facilities.

S.39   Spalding-Doncaster Line

From Werrington Junction-Spalding line to ECML via Decoy Junction, Doncaster. 73 m 20 ch

As described in earlier entries, the Great Eastern Railway's ambitions for an outlet to the industrial north were finally realized with the opening of the Great Northern & Great Eastern Joint Line in 1882, made up of existing lines from Huntingdon to March and Spalding, a new line to Lincoln and then over the GNR line to Doncaster. For a century this was to be an important artery, especially for freight after the opening of Whitemoor in 1929, but with the closure of the March-Spalding section today's services are basically dmu-operated and comprise through trains taking just under 2½ hours plus Cambridge/Peterborough-Lincoln, Sleaford-Lincoln trains, some through longer distance workings in summer and a few other permutations.

From March the line formerly ran via Guyhirne (3¼ m), Murrow (6¼ m), French Drove & Gedney Hill (9 m), Postland (12½ m) and Cowbit (16¼ m) on the 19½ miles to Spalding. This GNR line of 1867 was then extended by a new line opened to Ruskington on 6 March 1882 and on to Lincoln on 1 August 1882.

Beyond Spalding the GN&GE joint line takes a level course through agricultural countryside and via a succession of level crossings at Blue Gowts (45 m 42 ch), Cherry Holt (46 m), Flax Mill (46 m 66 ch), Bearty Fen (47 m 22 ch), No 94 Water Drove (48 m 9 ch), Cheal Road (48 m 31 ch), Gosberton (49 m 26 ch), Brewery Lane (50 m 19 ch), Quadring (51 m 10 ch), Church Lane (51 m 47 ch), Golden High Hedges (51 m 58 ch), Malting Lane (52 m 29 ch) and Blotoft Siding (56 m 25 ch). The four station sites at

Pinchbeck, Gosberton, Donington Road and Helpringham are still obvious, Gosberton with a signal box (49 m 13 ch) and Down Goods Loop, another signal box at Blotoft Siding (55 m 25 ch) and then at Helpringham (58 m 13 ch).

At Sleaford the Avoiding Line from Sleaford South Junction (62 m 13 ch) to North Junction (63 m 48 ch) is now closed and the joint line trains take an 'S' course through the station and round the town (see separate entry). Having completed this they then continue through Leasingham Moor LC (64 m 68 ch) to Ruskington where the wooden signal box (65 m 57 ch) precedes the short, simple platforms, with the original station buildings and house on the Down side. There are overbridges as the line rises to Rowston LC (69 m 33 ch) and continues to Scopwick LC (70 m 48 ch) where the location still has its brick goods shed and 1888 gabled station buildings. Via Martin Road LC (72 m 9 ch), the route next comes to Blankney LC (72 m 79 ch) and Metheringham station (73 m 3 ch). This, like Ruskington, has been revived with county council support and has short wooden platforms with the older buildings behind. The lattice post of the Down starter signal is topped by a Great Northern finial.

The stations on the remaining section to Lincoln—Nocton & Dunstan, Potterhanworth and Branston & Heighington—are closed but still intact and the signal box at Potterhanworth (76 m 70 ch) is followed by the 60 yd Branston & Washington Green Cross Roads Tunnel (79 m 44 ch to 79 m 47 ch). A deep cutting and a significant down gradient then mark the final approach to Greetwell Junction (81 m 25 ch) and Lincoln (see separate entry).

The route out of Lincoln is surrounded by evidence of former railway activity, including the sites of the loco depot and Pyewipe Yard. Clear of this, the route takes its waterside course to the signal box at Kesteven Sidings (87 m 41 ch) where both box and signals are typical of a whole era of railway signalling. Saxilby (88 m 51 ch) remains open and the station, with its Up side gabled buildings, is served by trains on both the joint line and on the Lincoln-Sheffield route. The latter no longer take the cut-off line to Clarborough Junction although after the crossing house and gates of Sykes LC (89 m 15 ch) Sykes Junction signal box (90 m 4 ch) still controls the single freight line to Torksey although it is locked out of use and with the signals off except when access is required.

Stow Park LC and signal box (93 m 13 ch)

lie at the bottom of a dip and the location has a gabled station house and a goods shed with attractive leaded windows. Lea Road signal box (98 m 3 ch) comes after a succession of cuttings and overbridges and stands at the end of Lea Road station's long platforms, the joint route then joining the Cleethorpes-Sheffield line at Trent East Junction (98 m 56 ch) and leaving it at Trent West Junction (98 m 69 ch).

The Lincoln-Gainsborough line had originally opened on 9 April 1849 but had then closed between Sykes Junction and Gainsborough between 1864 and 1867 when the new line to Doncaster opened on 15 July. On the latter there used to be stations at Beckingham, Walkeringham, Misterton, Haxey, Park Drain and Bessacarr Halt plus a goods siding at Stockwith and the junction north of Haxey with the Isle of Axholme Light Railway (leading to Goole and the Hatfield Moor Depot branch).

Leaving the Retford line after the crossing of the River Trent, the joint line resumes its northerly course and comes to Beckingham LC (100 m 78 ch) where the station house and goods shed survive and there are Up and Down Goods Loops. After Tetheringress Lane LC (101 m 54 ch) comes Walkeringham LC (102 m 52 ch), again with surviving station house and goods shed, the former and the station buildings to a nice design in light brick and with decorated windows. At Misterton there are more station buildings in the same vein and also a rusting Down side siding.

The route now crosses the Chesterfield Canal and, after North Carr LC (104 m 66 ch), comes to Haxey CCTV LC (105 m 58 ch). The joint line veers west here and the station lost its passenger service on 2 February 1959. Haxey Junction, the Axholme station, had closed to passengers on 17 July 1933 along with Haxey Town which lay about 1½ miles to the north. On through Park Drain CCTV LC (108 m 52 ch) and Beech Hill AHB LC (109 m 73 ch), another CCTV LC at Wroot Hall (111 m 53 ch) then precedes Finningley where all the old station trappings remain intact, including platforms, out-of-use signal box, station house and buildings and the operative level crossing (112 m 8 ch).

From Auckley AHB LC (112 m 73 ch) the line rises through a succession of cuttings to come to the R/G level crossing which marks the former Bessacarr Halt (115 m 48 ch). The junction with the ECML is made after Bessacarr Junction (115 m 72 ch), Flyover East Junction (116 m 20 ch) and Flyover

West Junction (116 m 46 ch)—at Decoy
South Junction (116 m 71 ch) and Decoy
North Junction (117 m 46 ch).

S.40   Stainforth & Hatfield

*Barnetby-Doncaster line, between Scun-
thorpe and Doncaster. 6 m 40 ch from Doncaster*

The station comprises two platforms with
shelters and a footbridge to the small brick
ticket office, and the service is provided
mainly by the Cleethorpes-Doncaster
trains. East of Stainforth station is Stainforth Junction (6 m 27 ch) where the Bram-
with freight route departs westwards.

S.41   Stallingborough

*Cleethorpes-Sheffield line, between
Grimsby and Habrough Junction. 104 m 72
ch from Manchester (London Road)*

The Barton-on-Humber branch dmus call
at Stallingborough with its signal box,
gated level crossing and small, but quite
stately buildings. The old goods shed survives and there is an AHB LC at Little London (103 m 56 ch).

S.42   Stamford—see   Peterborough-
Leicester Line

S.43   Stamford Hill—see Enfield Town
Branch

S.44   Stanford-le-Hope

*Tilbury Loop, between Tilbury and Pitsea.
27 m 21 ch from Fenchurch Street*

Stanford-le-Hope lies on the flatlands
north of the Thames and was reached by the

original LT&S in 1854 as part of its extension east from Tilbury towards Southend.
The station is an uncomplicated one—two
platforms with shelters, footbridge, signal
box and gated level crossing—served by the
half-hourly Tilbury Loop trains.

S.45   Stanstead

*Liverpool Street-Kings Lynn line, between
Bishops Stortford and Audley End. 33 m 27
ch from Liverpool Street*

Just a small station with period buildings
and served by the Bishops Stortford-
Cambridge dmus and with extra services
during the peak hours.

S.46   Steetley Colliery—see Sherwood-
Shireoaks Line

S.47   Stepney East

*Fenchurch Street-Shoeburyness line, bet-
ween Fenchurch Street and Barking. 1 m 48
ch from Fenchurch Street*

Stepney East was one of the original
London & Blackwall Railway stations,
opened on 6 July 1840 and attaching its own
separate coaches to the cable which formed
the basis of the line's operations. From
Stepney the L&B line then continued its
raised course, over Regents Canal and
Limehouse Cut, across the neck of the Isle
of Dogs and finally to Blackwall, where
passengers connected with the river
steamers. The route now taken by the main
line dates from 1849 when a link to the ECR

*The crossing gate at Stanford-le-Hope are
opening for an Up train.*

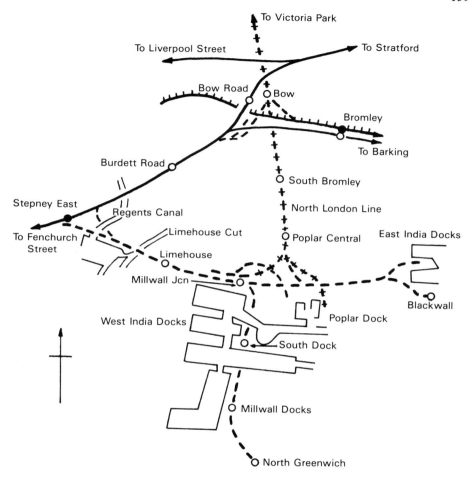

at Bow ended the Blackwall Railway's isolated existence and was accompanied both by an abandonment of cable working and a reduction of some four inches in gauge to bring it into line with the standard 4 ft 8½ in adopted by its neighbour.

The station at Stepney East straddles Cable Street and Commercial Road. Access is from street level, where the ticket office is situated, to the two platforms above where the canopies intersperse the tie rods across the top of the bridge members. Behind the Up platform the route of the original line is still visible as it heads for the former Limehouse station. Passenger services to Limehouse (2¼ m), West India Docks (2½ m), Millwall Junction (3 m), Poplar (3¼ m) and Blackwall (3½ m) ended on 4 May 1926 but freight continued into the 1960s, the section overlooking Regents Canal Dock being

used for loading traffic to and from ship and for scrap traffic.

The whole of the original line from Fenchurch Street was roofed with either iron or slate 'so as to prevent annoyance to the neighbourhood by the noise arising from the said railway'. Beyond Stepney further roofing was added in 1849 to prevent the newly-introduced locomotives setting fire to sailing ships in the dock. At Stepney the two routes were also linked by a spur from Salmons Lane Junction to Limehouse Junction, disused from 5 November 1962 and closed completely from 10 May 1963.

The four-track section of the main line from Fenchurch Street ends at Stepney East Junction (1 m 48 ch) and the surviving two tracks then curve through the station towards Gas Factory North Junction (2 m 57 ch). Here the connecting line to Bow

Although the London & Blackwall's line was not affected by the fire and explosion, this Illustrated London News *item does reveal the line's elevated course.*

Junction (3 m 39 ch) begins. It is controlled from Fenchurch Street box but carries no regular services. The triangle is completed by the LT lines from Bow Road, but the link from Burdett Road to the North London line is partly covered by housing and the old depot has long since lost its form. Burdett Road passenger station closed in 1941.

Stepney East has a basic service of four trains each way each hour with additional trains in the peaks. Under the Light Rail Transport plans of the GLC and the London Docklands Development Corporation for a revival of the route (from Tower Hill) of the old L&B and the Millwall Extension Railway there could again be a train service from Stepney East to the Isle of Dogs by 1987.

S.48   Stevenage

East Coast main line, between Welwyn Garden City and Hitchin. 27 m 45 ch from Kings Cross

The old Stevenage gave way to a new community as a result of the development under the New Towns Act of 1946. The needs of the latter then brought the present station

into being, as a joint project between BR and the Stevenage Development Corporation and with a capital grant from the Department of the Environment towards the cost. Work started on the scheme at the end of 1971 and on 26 September 1973 Mrs Shirley Williams officially opened the new station with its two 800 ft island platforms and purpose-built access to and from the town centre and adjoining industrial area.

To cater for its local needs the modern Stevenage station derives three services an hour—one of them fast and reaching Kings Cross in 27 minutes—from the Royston electrics and, in addition, has calls by a number of longer distance main line trains to give direct links with such important centres as York, Hull and Newcastle.

In the Down direction Stevenage is preceded by Langley Junction and the former Langley Goods Siding just north of the junction. The goods siding closed on 2 November 1970 and the Langley box has gone, along with Stevenage North and South boxes, the latter once controlling Ellis & Everard's coal siding and the former the Down side sidings at Wymondley (29 m 69 ch). After Wymondley box closed, train guards took a key from Stevenage North to gain access to the sidings and then carried on to Hitchin South, but this ended with the closure of the Wymondley location on 4 May 1964. The old station at Stevenage closed when the new one opened.

S.49 Stocksbridge

Branch from Nunnery Junction, Sheffield.
8 m 33 ch

With the May 1983 timetable the surviving passenger service over the former GC main line was diverted to run via Barnsley and the great Pennine route, opened by the Sheffield, Ashton-under-Lyne & Manchester Railway pioneers in December 1845, was destined to become just a freight-only single line serving BSC Stocksbridge and carrying occasional football specials to Wadsley Bridge. A classic and difficult route, struggling steeply up the Don Valley out of Sheffield, this GC main line not only carried the through services from Manchester to Marylebone and to the East Coast but also services originating at Penistone and local trains from Deepcar to Sheffield and Doncaster, calling in the Don Valley at Oughty Bridge, Wadsley Bridge and Neepsend. Despite its electrification the route was a costly one and had a duplication of trans-Pennine facilities, these factors leading to the closure of the section beyond Deepcar through Thurgoland Tunnel to Huddersfield Junction and the singling of the remaining portion from Nunnery Junction (41 m 68 ch) via Sheffield Victoria, Wadsley Bridge (38 m 36 ch) and Oughty Bridge (36 m 23 ch) to Deepcar (33 m 35 ch).

The clean lines of the station at Stevenage in a view looking south.

S.50 Stoke

East Coast main line, between Peterborough and Grantham. 99 m 61 ch from Kings Cross

Soon after Helpston (18 m 71 ch), where the Stamford line departs, the East Coast main line starts to climb, gradually at first but then for 4½ miles at 1 in 200 and soon for another 3 miles at 1 in 178 to the summit site of Stoke box. Stoke Tunnel then lies on the five mile descent at 1 in 200 which could occasionally give drivers a real problem in stopping at Grantham.

The CCTV LCs at Maxey (82 m 38 ch) and Lolham (83 m 33 ch) are followed by R/G LC No 115 (84 m 6 ch) and the crossing (84 m 64 ch) marking Tallington's former station and the Dow-Mac/Redland sidings. After another CCTV LC at Greatford (87 m 8 ch) comes the site of Essendine station, once with branches to Stamford and Bourne but now just marked by the old dock and a hand crane. On the Up side trees mark the route of the former branch via Braceborough Spa (2½ m), Thurlby (4½ m) and then the West Junction meeting with the M&GN before Bourne proper (6½ m).

Little Bytham (92 m 22 ch) still has its old goods shed, station house and a siding but the M&GN route from Saxby, which crossed the GN main line just before the station, is now marked only by bridge abutments. After passing the old station

'Essendine, change for Stamford and Bourne Branches' looking north (Lens of Sutton).

area at Corby the ECML changes from quadruple to double track before Stoke Emergency Crossover (99 m 65 ch) and then plunges into the 880 yd Stoke Tunnel (100 m 39 ch to 100 m 79 ch).

Great Ponton, on the steep drop to Grantham, was formerly the controlling station for the High Dyke mineral line network which lay to the west and which collected great quantities of iron ore to be moved to Scunthorpe and other steelworks. From High Dyke Junction (101 m 31 ch) the single line ran to Skillington Junction (4 m 62 ch) and split there for Stainby (5 m 73 ch) and Sproxton (7 m 70 ch). On the isolated parts

Essendine station has lost its platforms in this 1967 view but the outline is still clear.

of these lines some less than conventional shunting often took place.

Other railway interest on this section of the East Coast main line derives from the former private Bytham & Edenham Railway and from its role in the quest for high speeds, notably the establishment of *Mallard*'s world steam record here.

S.51 Stoke Newington—see Enfield Town Branch

S.52 Stowmarket

Liverpool Street-Norwich line, between Ipswich and Haughley Junction. 80 m 54 ch from Liverpool Street

Stowmarket was provided with a railway by the Ipswich & Bury Railway and owes its handsome station to that company's architect Frederick Barnes. The 1846 complex is a Grade Two listed building and this has been recognized in the £¼ million renovation which has been carried out in readiness for electrification. In the

platform lengthenings and other alterations recognition of the past has retained the old filigree brackets despite having to move the canopy support columns back from the platform edge.

The station comprises Up and Down platforms and its buildings are decorated in moulded brickwork. The goods shed and former yard lie at the London end, a barrier crossing at the country end and Regent Street LC at 80 m 68 ch.

S.53 Stratford

Liverpool Street-Norwich line, junction with North Woolwich branch and lines to Copper Mill Junction and Dalston. 3 m 75 ch from Liverpool Street

Stratford and Liverpool Street together made up the heart of the old Great Eastern empire, the former providing the main locomotive works, extensive carriage sidings and the largest steam shed, and hosting many smaller functions from the C&W depot to the modest goods yard and the

market sidings at Stratford Market. To the north of the complex lay Temple Mills, the GER's London marshalling yard, to the west the link to the North London line via Victoria Park Junction, to the east the Forest Gate junction with the LT&S and Goodmayes Yard and to the south Thames Wharf where traffic to and from the docks was collected or distributed.

The area was a rural one when the ECR line opened from Devonshire Street to Romford on 18 June 1839. It became a junction on 15 September of the following year when the N&E abandoned its ideas of a separate terminus and joined its Broxbourne line to the ECR route instead. In the junction between the two routes, on a site known as the Polygon, the first part of Stratford Works was begun and some railway housing and other developments soon followed. The line to North Woolwich and the Thames Wharf branch opened on 14 June 1847, the Victoria Park-Stratford Market link being opened for goods on 16 October 1854 and the Loughton Branch

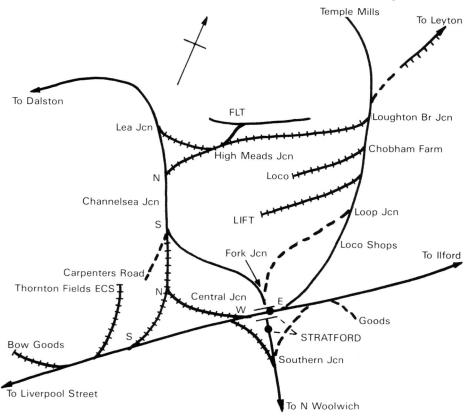

Junction-Loughton section following on 22 August 1856.

Stratford Locomotive Works produced many notable locomotive designs, not only the famous ones like the Claud 4-4-0s and the 0-10-0 *Decapod*, but standard Great Eastern workhorses like the 'E4' and 'F5' Classes. The locomotive depot was, at one time, the largest in the country with an allocation of 350 engines, from 'B1's, 'B12's and 'B17's to the diminutive 'Y' Classes. In addition to providing for the main line workings, the depot engined services on the Epping/Ongar line and from Palace Gates to North Woolwich, it catered for the main line freight workings out of Temple Mills and dozens of local freight trips and also provided pilots for all the local depots as well as for Liverpool Street station.

The nine Stratford platforms later became thirteen with the Down side curved platforms, virtually a separate station for the old N&E route, going out of use when London Transport took over the Loughton line. This had previously carried an intensive train service out through Leyton (5 m), Leytonstone (6 m), Snaresbrook (7 m), South Woodford (7¾ m), Woodford (9 m), Buckhurst Hill (10¼ m), Loughton (11½ m), Chigwell Lane (13 m) and Theydon Bois (15 m) to Epping (16½ m). For a while the line on through North Weald (19 m) and Blake Hall (21 m) to Ongar (22¾ m) had then had a separate steam service.

The arrival of the Central Line trains at the ER Stratford station on 4 December 1946 necessitated modifications which produced the present interchange platforms and below are those of the North Woolwich route. The entrance is via a long tiled subway.

Within the Stratford complex the maintenance depot and carriage sidings remain

important but the more traditional activities have been replaced by the LIFT inland freight terminal and by the Freightliner depot.

On the Down approach to Stratford there are nine lines from Carpenters Road South Junction (3 m 50 ch), Cambridge, main and electric pairs plus the No Block goods lines and the Up Fenchurch Street. The route continues to Central Junction West (3 m 70 ch) and Central Junction East (3 m 75 ch) with Stratford box (4 m 3 ch) then following. From the North London line direction the double route distances are Lea Junction (15 ch), Channelsea North Junction (64 ch), Channelsea South Junction (65 ch), the 77 yd Stratford Low Level Tunnel (1 m 16 ch to 1 m 20 ch), Stratford Low Level (1 m 20 ch), Southern Junction signal box (1 m 28 ch), Southern Junction (1 m 30 ch/4 m) and then on to North Woolwich.

The distances on the other links are (a) Lea Junction (51 ch), High Meads (65 ch); (b) Channelsea North Junction (0), High Meads Junction (15 ch), LIFT/R&M AOCL LC (50 ch), Loughton Branch Junction South (59 ch); (c) Stratford Central Junction West (0), Carpenters Road North (25 ch), Stratford Channelsea South Junction (29 ch).

All local train services call at Stratford which, because of its LT interchange facilities, also originates and terminates trains during emergency or engineering work periods. It is less complex than of old but the location remains busy and important in terms of its traction maintenance, carriage stabling and servicing and freight (unit loads and private sidings) as well as for the sheer volume of its local and interchange passenger business.

S.54 Sudbury Branch

Liverpool Street-Norwich line, branch from Marks Tey. 11 m 61 ch

Known as the Stour Valley line, this branch takes its title from the course it takes and

Sudbury station buildings, now in use as a museum.

The ornate 'Great Eastern' public house at Sudbury.

from the Colchester, Stour Valley, Sudbury & Halstead concern that originated the project. This company had considerable ambitions in the area between the two main lines but, like many others, found railway construction a costly business. As a result the line opened from Marks Tey to Sudbury on 1 July 1849 was leased to and worked by the Eastern Union Railway right from the outset.

On 9 August 1865 the Stour Valley line was extended from a new station at Sudbury to Long Melford and north to Bury St Edmunds. At Long Melford it met the route from Shelford via Haverhill (1 June) in an attempt to thwart the ambitions of the Colne Valley Railway concern. The latter had taken over the C,SV,S&H's Halstead ambitions with a line which opened from Chappel to that point on 18 April 1860 and was then extended in stages to reach Haverhill by 10 May 1863.

From Sudbury (16¾ m from Colchester) the EUR/GER line ran to Long Melford (19¾ m), noted for 'The Most Haunted House in England', with the Bury line then continuing through the pretty village of Lavenham (25 m), Cockfield (28½ m), Welnetham (31½ m) and then coming to Bury St Edmunds (30¼ m). West from Long Melford, which even had a refreshment room at one time, the 'main line' to Cambridge served Glemsford (22¼ m), another pretty village at Clare (26¼ m), Stoke (28¼ m), Sturmer (31¼ m) and then Haverhill North (33¼ m). From Chappel, the Colne Valley Railway's independent line ran via White Colne (2 m) and Earls Colne (3½ m) to Halstead (6 m) and on via Sible & Castle Hedingham (9 m), Yeldham

(12 m) and Birdbrook (16 m) to Haverhill (19 m). Each had five trains a day in the 1930s.

The Long Melford-Bury line was the first to close, on 10 April 1961, with the Colne Valley route following on 1 January 1962. Four years later the last freight traffic was dealt with on the route via Clare and then passenger services west of Sudbury ended on 6 March 1967. Though full of character these lines had never been very busy. They were all single with passing loops, Clare even having a Tyers No 6 instrument, the one where the signalman could not 'cancel' and either had to avoid mistakes or pay the penalty of passing the token through the section.

Curiously two railway preservation activities survive on this network, at Chappel and at Sible & Castle Hedingham. Even better, BR services survive on the Marks Tey-Sudbury section to the tune of eleven dmu workings each way, most running to and from Colchester. Operation is on the One Train basis with a token taken at Marks Tey station, the route then being single throughout and subject to a maximum permissible speed of 50 mph.

From the curved branch platform at Marks Tey (46 m 63 ch) the line turns west and, after the Home and Starter signals, takes a tree and shrub-lined climbing course beneath a succession of overbridges to come to the massive Chappel Viaduct and then Chappel & Wakes Colne station (50 m 18 ch). This was formerly a passing loop but now only the Down platform, with its traditional brick house and buildings, is in use. The whole of the Up side is given over to the preservation activities of the Stour Valley Railway Society.

Immediately beyond the road bridge the junction for the Colne Valley line can be identified and then the route presses on, rising to a deep cutting and then dropping with views of the Vale of Dedham and Stoke-by-Nayland church to the signals, cottage and gated crossing at Mount Bures (52 m 61 ch). A mound nearby is perhaps the burial place of Queen Boadicea.

Bures station (53 m 45 ch) has a single platform and shelter and serves new housing nearby. Not far away is the spot where Edmund was crowned King of East Anglia in 855. From the railway there are more views of the shallow Stour Valley as the line heads through the countryside immortalized by Thomas Gainsborough to Cornard LC (57 m 42 ch) and then Sudbury (58 m 38 ch).

The solid station buildings are now the home of Sudbury Museum and the former through line has buffer stops at the end of the single curving platform. The route of the original line, which became the goods yard when the through line was opened, is still apparent. There are also surviving signs of the sidings which crossed Great Eastern Road and on the corner of that road the public house still carries the marks of its railway affiliations in the form of a Sinclair 2-2-2.

S.55 Swinderby—see Newark-Lincoln Line

S.56 Swineshead—see Grantham-Skegness Line

S.57 Sykes Junction—see Spalding-Doncaster Line

T.1 Tapton Junction-see Chesterfield-Rotherham Line

T.2   Temple Mills

On Stratford-Copper Mill Junction line, between Temple Mills East and Temple Mills West

A water mill said to belong to the Knights Templar gave Temple Mills its name but the first railway line did not arrive until the N&E opened its route from Stratford to Broxbourne on 15 September 1840. The yard then developed from an early siding into a reserve goods depot for Stratford and then from 1877 expanded steadily as a shunting yard in its own right. By 1930, when the Cambridge Yard became a hump yard, there were altogether eight yards and

Two views of Temple Mills yards, one before and one after its reconstruction.

28 reception sidings with a total capacity of 6,500 wagons.

Temple Mills was a target for several wartime bombing raids but even before these ended it was looking forward again and experimenting with diesel-electric shunting locomotives. Ten years later these were to become standard and then, in 1959, the new marshalling yard became operational, completely modernizing the old complex and taking over the work of a number of small peripheral yards.

The change in BR's freight business to fast, through, high-capacity wagon services has meant only a modest role for Temple Mills now but in the 1960s it was a showpiece which Yardmaster Dan Rose, something of a legend in the area, was proud to display. The main yard, following the remodelling, comprised reception sidings leading to two single lines over the hump, the main one then dropping through two primary and eight secondary retarders to the sorting sidings. After the incoming engines had been released and the cuts prepared, trains would be propelled over the hump at 1½ mph with the separated wagons then being divided to pass first over one of the primary retarders and then one of the secondary eight. Trains could arrive into the reception sidings from either direction and made up trains depart from the sorting sidings either north via No 2 Departure Line, Temple Mills West (6 m 8 ch) and Lea Bridge (6 m 25 ch) to Copper Mill Junction (7 m 13 ch) or south via Temple Mills East (4 m 54 ch), Loughton Branch Junction (4 m 45 ch) and Stratford Central Junction East (3 m 75 ch). Most trains were drawn down to the departure sidings beyond Manor Yard box and the East Yard rather than slow the sorting process which was targeted to shunt 1,000 wagons an hour.

In addition to the main yard at Temple Mills, lying east of the through lines, the East Yard was sited between the departure sidings and the Loughton line and the West Yard below the hump. On the other side of the main line lay the wagon works and body works, with the Road Motor Engineer's workshops opposite the Yardmaster's office and the huge guards' dormitory building nearer Stratford.

T.3   Thames Haven Branch

Tilbury Loop, branch from Thames Haven Junction. 4 m 3 ch

The Thames Haven branch, which forwards huge quantities of oil traffic for Shell

and Mobil, recently made news with the provision by Shell of a new £12 million computer-controlled wagon loading facility. The branch, which leaves the Tilbury Loop at Thames Haven Junction (26 m 41 ch), becomes a single line at signals L37/42 and is then under the control of the Thames Haven supervisor as it runs via Shell No 1 Ground Frame (28 m 46 ch) at Curry Marsh, Shell Pump House LC (28 m 75 ch), West End Gate AOCL LC (29 m 30 ch) and No 43 Gate AOCL LC (30 m 44 ch) to the Thames Haven Terminus Ground Frame (30 m 44 ch). There is a maximum speed of 40 mph.

This part of the Thames shoreline was used by Danish longships and Roman galleys, and in the war of 1667 the Dutch fleet anchored here to blockade the Thames. The oil business dates from 1875 when the Thames Haven Petroleum Wharf Company started operations, Shell opening at Shell Haven in 1916 and the Vacuum Oil Company taking over the Coryton Refinery after the Second World War.

Thames Haven got a railway as a result of City merchants dreaming of a down river port for goods, fish and cattle. The branch was opened on 7 June 1885 and worked by the LT&S under an agreement by which the Thames Haven Dock & Railway Co abandoned its original plan for a link with the ECR at Romford.

Until 1880 there were summer trains from Fenchurch Street and Chalk Farm to connect at Thames Haven with the steamers to Margate. The marshes had long been a venue for prize fighting and on the occasion of the last great bare knuckle championship between Jem Mace and Tom King on 26 November 1862, a special train left Fenchurch Street at 6.00 am loaded with enthusiasts who were to see King triumph after 21 rounds.

From the mid-1860s until 1892 Thames Haven dealt with an appreciable volume of livestock imports, carrying the animals forward to Maiden Lane by rail. Even after the regular boat trains ceased some rail plus steamer workings continued to use the eight-line terminus and its passenger platform; various types of workmen's service also existed.

At the end of the last century the Corringham Light Railway came into being to carry munition workers to the Kynochtown works. A connection was made to the LT&S line (at 30 m 15 ch) which continued in use when the Mobil Oil Co took over the light railway.

Today cattle traffic and steamer excur-

Roudham Junction in 1962 with the old platforms surviving and the Watton branch on the left.

sions are just memories and the prime business of the branch is its valuable oil traffic.

T.4   Theobalds Grove—see Churchbury Loop

T.5   Thetford

Birmingham-Norwich   line,   between Brandon and Wymondham. 93 m 50 ch from Liverpool Street

Thetford lies on a great loop added to the original Norwich & Brandon line instead of the proposed branch connection. A month after the N&B became part of the Norfolk Railway the line from Norwich met that of the ECR from Newport on 30 July 1845 to create a through railway link from London

Thetford was served by the Norwich & Brandon Railway rather as an afterthought.

to Yarmouth.

Thetford was subequently to become a junction for cross-country routes to Swaffham and Bury St Edmunds. The 1866 Thetford & Watton Railway opened its line to Watton in 1869 with the Watton & Swaffham extending the route to meet the Kings Lynn-Dereham line six years later. The Bury St Edmunds & Thetford concern was incorporated a year before the Thetford & Watton but did not open until 1 March 1876 when it was worked by the latter. By 1880 the three small companies had been leased by the GER and the potential north-south route became just two branches from Thetford, the Great Eastern abandoning the spur from the Bury line towards Roudham Junction and with it the through service between Bury and Swaffham.

The approach to Thetford is via the AHB crossing at Two Mile Bottom (91 m 16 ch) which follows the site of the old signal box and siding (for pit props and fertilizer). The curving woodland route then follows the course of the Little Ouse River and rises for

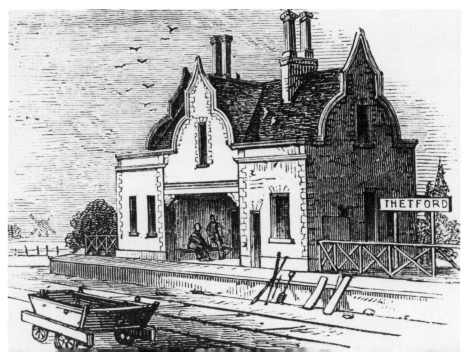

two miles at 1 in 267 to come to Thetford where the ancient mound of Thetford Castle gave its owners command of the Icknield Way near the meeting of the Little Ouse and the Thet.

Despite its excellent railway facilities, including a new station in 1890, Thetford remained little more than a market town and the home of the Burrell steam engine factory. A London overspill development has now lifted the population dramatically and added extensive housing and light industry to the area.

Thetford is well served by the Ely-Norwich dmus plus Birmingham-Norwich trains and the surviving through London services. It has Up and Down platforms with main buildings of flint, ornately gabled on the Up side and with a signal box on the Down.

At the country end of the station a newish housing estate occupies the site of West Junction and its signal box, where the Bury line departed until 1960 (see Bury St Edmunds entry). On the main line the summit is reached near Croxton AHB LC (96 m 45 ch) and some surviving Down side cottages which mark the site of Roudham Junction (TL 920 876).

In the 1930s the Swaffham line carried a service of five trains each way daily calling at Wretham & Hocking (6¾ m), Stow Bedon (10¼ m), Watton (13¼ m), Holme Hale (18¾ m) and Swaffham (22¾ m). Roudham Junction itself officially closed on 1 May 1932 although thirty years earlier it had been reduced to an exchange station and lost its regular main line trains from 1920. The rest of the branch closed on 15 June 1964 apart from the Swaffham-Watton portion where freight services last for another ten months.

T.6   Thoresby Colliery—see High Marnham Branch

T.7   Thorne

Barnetby-Doncaster line. Thorne Junction with the Goole line is 8 m 8 ch and Thorne South 9 m 41 ch from Doncaster

Using its favourite method of avoiding an approach to Parliament by building its railway lines on its own or other private land, the South Yorkshire Railway originally opened from Doncaster to the waterway at Thorne in 1856. Thorne got a new station with a similarly-based extension to Keadby three years later. The present Thorne South dates from 1866 with a proper line from Doncaster to a junction with the NER's Staddlethorpe line coming in 1869 by which

time the South Yorkshire had become part of the MS&L.

Only the South Humberside line concerns this volume, the Hull trains continuing via Thorne Junction to Thorne North and Goole. On that line the junction is preceded by Hatfield Colliery Bunker Loading Sidings ground frame where the old private siding for coal traffic has now been replaced by an overhead loading facility over an Up side siding.

Beyond the junction the Grimsby line comes to Kirton Lane Crossing CCTV LC (8 m 47 ch) where the four tracks reduced to two, cross the canal and come to Thorne South. This comprises an approach footbridge, platforms with brick shelters and the old goods yard area behind. Thorne No 1 (10 m 12 ch) and Thorne No 2 (10 m 35 ch) AHB level crossings follow.

Thorne South is served by the Cleethorpes-Doncaster trains.

T.8   Thornton Abbey—see Barton-on-Humber Branch

T.9   Thorpe Bay

Fenchurch Street-Shoeburyness line, between Southend Central and Shoeburyness. 37 m 73 ch from Fenchurch Street

A traditional station serving a residential area of Southend and with a twenty-minute interval service in both directions.

T.10   Thorpe Culvert—see Grantham-Skegness Line

T.11   Thorpe-le-Soken—see Colchester-Clacton Line

T.12   Three Horse Shoes

Birmingham-Norwich line, between Peterborough and March. 91 m 5 ch from Liverpool Street

The location is now just a block post with a Down side signal box and gated level crossing. The goods shed and siding area is still apparent but not the 4½-mile single line agricultural traffic branch which formerly ran south to Benwick. This was opened halfway on 1 September 1897 and completed on 2 August of the following year and ran via passing/loading loops at Quakers Drove (72 ch), West Fen Drove (1 m 42 ch), Burnt House Drove (2 m 2 ch), Jones' Drove (2 m 61 ch) and White Fen Drove (3 m 39 ch) to Benwick (4 m 41 ch). Closure dates from 13 July 1964.

T.13   Thrumpton Junctions—see Retford

T.14 Thrybergh Junction—see Silverwood Colliery Branch

T.15 Thurcroft Sidings—see Brancliffe-Kirk Sandall Line

T.16   Thurston

Cambridge-Ipswich line, between Bury St Edmunds and Haughley Junction. 32 m 52 ch from Coldham Lane Junction

The Ipswich & Bury's line of 24 December 1846 runs as straight as an arrow from Bury St Edmunds to Thurston and then on to Elmswell, great tree-lined cuttings and embankments keeping the gradients short and modest. Thurston itself, about ¾ m west of the village, has a modern shelter on its Up platform but on the Down side retains one of the delightful examples of Frederick Barnes' work in the Tudor style. The lower storey is below platform level and the gabled upper storey, with the centre section surmounted by a weather vane, is self contained from the platform side but completes the pleasantly elaborate frontage when viewed on the approach. Coal in the old goods yard and a former grain warehouse nearby complete the period picture, with the excellent dmu service on the line representing the current and functional side of the location.

T.17   Tilbury

Tilbury Loop. Tilbury Town is 21 m 48 ch from Fenchurch Street and Tilbury Riverside 22 m 45 ch

The original LT&S line opened between Forest Gate and Tilbury on 13 April 1854, inspired by the London & Blackwall's interest in the steamer business and the ECR's involvement in the North Woolwich branch. These two railways not only launched the new company but also provided the first trains which ran from Bishopsgate and Fenchurch Street, joined at Stratford and then carried their passengers on to Tilbury and the steamers for Gravesend and beyond. Between 1854 and 1856 extension eastwards to Southend also brought that growing resort's excursion business to the new railway.

At the beginning of the 1880s the LT&S acquired a monopoly of the Gravesend ferry traffic and with it the West Street Pier. In the same decade came the development of Tilbury Docks and the opening of Tilbury Docks station, on 15 June 1885. The LT&S made an agreement with the dock company under which the former provided a goods depot at Commercial Road, near Fenchurch Street, and the latter

guaranteed a minimum level of business for carriage between the two locations. Shortfalls on the 'guaranteed tonnage' were to be a continuous problem between docks and railway concerns right up to the days of the Line Traffic Manager's organization at the end of the 1950s.

The railway links into the docks produced a vast variety of business until relatively recent years, from easy packaged cargoes to the hard-to-handle hides and skins. Now the traditional pattern has changed for both dock and railway and the latter has a Freightliner terminal for the receipt and forwarding of container traffic. The passenger business has also altered somewhat although the boat train tradition is maintained by specials connecting with the Gdynia Line cruises. There is also a Tilbury Grain Terminal producing railway grain business and a Rugby Portland Cement terminal.

In the 1950s, prior to the era of railway, docks and handling rationalization, the railway activities at Tilbury required 120 BR staff and another 125 to operate the five twin-screw ferry vessels. The latter then handled nearly 4 million passengers a year and the former not only 571 special trains (in 1953) but also 209,610 tons of goods traffic, 18,000 packages of stores and 17,000 consignments of baggage.

Following the connection to the Freightliner terminal inside the docks area the double line of the Tilbury loop continues round the latter, through the simplified Tilbury Town (formerly Docks) station and comes to Tilbury West Junction (2 m 6 ch). A triangle starts here, the cut-off line continuing ahead to Tilbury East Junction (22 m 30 ch) and the other pair of tracks turning to South Junction and Tilbury Riverside panel box (22 m 30 ch) and then terminating at Tilbury Riverside station. The triangle is completed by the 25 ch link between the South and East junctions.

Tilbury Riverside has originating and terminating trains in the peak, some to Fenchurch Street and others to Barking. A few loop trains reverse at the station but the main service is provided by the half-hourly Grays/Upminster trains, passengers changing at Tilbury Town for Fenchurch Street.

Although Riverside station now only uses platforms 1 and 2 and it has been much simplified, there is still a special air about its sizeable circulating area and riverside location. From the ferry pontoon nearby there are 39 daily 'sailings' across to Gravesend and back.

Ellingham station on the Waveney Valley line.

T.18   Tinsley—see Sheffield

T.19   Tivetshall

Liverpool Street-Norwich line, between Diss and Norwich. 100 m 60 ch from Liverpool Street

This final section of the main line to Norwich was originally opened in December 1849 and soon plans were being made for a branch to Bungay. The first section of the Waveney Valley Railway's route east from Tivetshall was not, in fact, opened until 1 December 1855 when ECR-operated trains reached Harleston. Another five years were to pass before the extension to Bungay was completed on 2 November 1860 and by the time the route had linked with the East Suffolk Railway at Beccles, on 2 March 1863, the ECR working had been dispensed with and the Waveney Valley company was running its own trains.

The Waveney Valley line figured in several schemes for grandiose east-west routes but nothing came of these and the line settled down to a very modest existence, losing some of its stations quite early on. By 1938 the service consisted of six trains each way daily, with additional trains on Wednesdays and Saturdays and a skeleton service on Sundays. On the branch itself they called at Pulham Market (17¼ m from Norwich), Pulham St Mary (18¼ m), Harleston (20¾ m), Homersfield (23½ m), Earsham (26½ m), Bungay (27¼ m), Ditchingham (28¼ m), Ellingham (29¾ m), Geldeston (31¼ m) and then Beccles (34 m). The line had quite a busy time in both wars but then lost its passenger services on 5 January 1953. Although operated as a light railway from 1954 to

1960, the centre section of the WVR was closed on 1 February 1960 with further cutbacks following until final closure came on 18 April 1966.

By 1984 only a rusting loop around the old island platform at Tivetshall remained as visible evidence of the Waveney Valley line although the signal box was still called Tivetshall Junction. In addition to this and the gated crossing, some station buildings survived and the old goods shed was in use by a plant hire firm. The casual observer could be forgiven for not suspecting that this had once been a location of some importance as a junction and for its main line water troughs.

T.20   Torksey Branch

Spalding-Doncaster line, branch from Sykes Junction. 2 m 76 ch

Originally opened on 4 September 1849, the Sykes Junction-Clarborough Junction line is now severed into two branches, this one serving the Shell depot at Torksey. Operated on the One Train basis and with a maximum speed of 20 mph, the line runs from Sykes Junction (76 m 46 ch) via TMO level crossings at Sykes Lane (75 m 16 ch) and Torksey (74 m 46 ch) to the exchange point (73 m 50 ch) and end of the line. For access to the reach wagon used when moving tanks in the sidings a set of stop blocks are unlocked by the trainmen.

T.21   Totley Tunnel

Hope Valley line, between Dore and Regional Boundary. 155 m 20 ch from St Pancras

The 1894 Hope Valley line, now carrying both a local Sheffield-New Mills service and through trains from Cleethorpes and the Doncaster direction to Manchester, leaves the Midland main line at Dore West Junction (154 m 16 ch). Then, after Totley Tunnel East signal box (154 m 62 ch), comes the 3 m 950 yd Totley Tunnel (155 m 20 ch to 158 m 63 ch), the larger of the two substantial tunnels needed to cross through the Pennine range. Grindleford station (158 m 70 ch) and signal box (159 m 6 ch) follow as the route passes into the LM Region.

T.22   Tottenham Hale

Liverpool Street-Kings Lynn line, between Copper Mill North Junction and Broxbourne. 6 m from Liverpool Street

Tottenham Hale is now an important point of interchange with the Victoria Line and the Bishops Stortford trains stop there, in addition to the Hertford East all-stations emus, for just that purpose. Before the station comes the 42 ch link from Tottenham South Junction to the T&H line and then Tottenham Hale itself comprises Up and Down platforms with the main, substantial and traditional buildings on the former.

Tottenham was one of the original 1840 Northern & Eastern stopping points but the GER entrance and booking office were closed in 1968 in favour of a combined entrance with London Transport. There is a gradient post on the platform and an old siding area in front of the present LT depot and former furniture factory site.

T.23   Trent   Junctions—see   Gainsborough

T.24   Trimley—see Felixstowe Branch

T.25   Trowse—see Norwich

T.26   Turkey   Street—see   Churchbury Loop

T.27   Tuxford

East Coast main line, between Newark and Retford. 131 m 50 ch from Kings Cross

Tuxford now is notable only for the 40 mph Up to Down emergency crossover at 131 m 48 ch and that from Down to Up at 131 m 53 ch. In the past, however, the LD&ECR route from Chesterfield to Lincoln crossed the GN main line here from its opening on 8 March 1897 to closure on 19 September 1955. Tuxford Central station (GC) was closed completely on this date, Tuxford North (GN) having closed on 4 July 1955 (although remaining open for goods until 1964) and the Dukeries Junction station to the south—something of a failure as an interchange point—five years earlier on 6 March 1950.

The progression through Tuxford was Dukeries Junction signal box, Dukeries Junction station, Tuxford Junction box, Tuxford Junction, Tuxford North station and Tuxford box. The spur between the two lines—still apparent on the Down side—was used for freight traffic exchange, Down trains giving two whistles when passing Carlton box if they had wagons for the Dukeries line.

U.1   Ulceby—see   Barton-on-Humber Branch

U.2   Upminster

Fenchurch   Street-Shoeburyness   line, between Barking and Pitsea. 15 m 20 ch from Fenchurch Street

Between Barking and Upminster BR trains now run non-stop, flashing through the stations at Becontree (1926), Dagenham East (1885) and Hornchurch (1885) and past the LT-served island platforms at Upney, Dagenham Heathway, Elm Park and Upminster Bridge. As the pairs of LT and BR lines approach Upminster they are joined by the single line from Romford which has had its own platform at Upminster since 20 May 1957.

The direct LT&S line from Barking reached Upminster on 1 May 1885 with the section westwards coming into use in the following year and the lines to Grays and Romford in 1892 and 1893 respectively. Reconstructed in 1932, when the sidings for the Metropolitan District trains were provided and the main entrance became from the London end overbridge, Upminster now consists of a main Up side platform—with traditional buildings and a bay for the trains to Grays and Tilbury—an island for BR Down and LT Up trains, another island for LT trains and then the Romford line platform. The 1959 LT depot at the country end is opposite East Junction (15 m 38 ch signal box, 15 m 39 ch junction) where the Grays branch is linked to the main line, the Romford   branch   having   no   such connection. There is also a siding off the Grays branch for track machines and a crossover at each end of the station.

Upminster has a half-hourly service off-peak, with connections into and from the four-car sets working the route to Tilbury Riverside. The Romford-Upminster service is also half-hourly.

U.3   Upminster-Grays Line

Fenchurch   Street-Shoeburyness   line, branch from Upminster to West Thurrock Junction. 6 m 53 ch

South Tottenham looking west and showing the signal gantry controlling the junction between the T&H and Enfield Town lines.

From the branch platform at Upminster, the single line opened by the LT&S on 1 July 1892 quickly veers off south and heads for its one intermediate station at Ockendon (3 m 11 ch). The station has a long passing loop and a typical LT&S set of buildings—station house, ticket office and staff etc accommodation—on the Down side.

Beyond Ockendon the line is again single as far as 6 m 33 ch and then double past West Thurrock Junction LC and signal box (6 m 46 ch) to the physical link with the main line at West Thurrock Junction (6 m 53 ch). A reversible 'third line' exists on the Down side from the signal box to Grays station.

Controlled by Track Circuit Block and subject to a maximum line speed of 70 mph, the line has a few curves and earthworks at the south end. It carries a half-hourly Upminster-Tilbury service which turns round at Riverside and connects, at Tilbury Town, with the Down Tilbury Loop trains.

At one period some of the through Romford-Tilbury Riverside services had a connecting ferry link to West Street Pier at Gravesend.

U.4   Upper Holloway to Barking Line

From Gospel Oak LMR to Fenchurch Street-Shoeburyness line at Barking. 10 m 42 ch

The 'Tottenham & Hampstead' route, as it is popularly known, links the former Midland and LNW systems at its west end with the former Great Eastern and LT&S systems to the east of London. It takes a long, looping route through the capital's eastern suburbs with the ER portion commencing

at milepost 3, between Upper Holloway and Crouch Hill, and then running for another 10 m 42 ch to Barking, Tilbury Line West Junction. On the way the route has links with the East Coast main line, with the Enfield Town and Lea Valley lines and with the main line from Liverpool Street to Ipswich and Norwich.

The route grew up piecemeal, the first section to open being that brought into use by the LT&S from Forest Gate Junction on the ECR main line to Barking (and on to Tilbury) on 13 April 1854. By an Act of 19 July 1862 the Tottenham & Hampstead Junction company built the section from Tottenham to Highgate Road and opened it on 21 July 1868, twenty years then elapsing before the extension west to Gospel Road. The route was completed on 2 July 1894 (9 July for passenger trains) with the opening of the Tottenham & Forest Gate Railway portion from South Tottenham Junction (East) to Woodgrange Park where the LT&S provided a new station.

Nowadays the western end of the line is represented by platform 3 at Gospel Oak, the two-car dmu sets then passing via Junction Road Junction and Upper Holloway station (2 m 71 ch from St Pancras) to enter the Eastern Region territory midway between that point and Crouch Hill (3 m 65 ch). This section is in a cutting, as is Crouch Hill station where stairs down from the overbridge lead to the two platforms, each with a brick shelter. The 90 yd Crouch Hill Tunnel (4 m 1 ch to 4 m 5 ch) follows and then Harringay Park Junction (4 m 15 ch) where there is a brick, flat-roofed signal box, crossover and the single line connection up to the Down side of the East Coast main line route.

After passing under the ECML and over the New River, the route rises to cross Green Lanes and reach the elevated platforms of Harringay Stadium (4 m 61 ch), now shortened but still serving the adja-

South Tottenham looking east and with the line to Tottenham South Junction straight ahead.

cent stadium via the red brick ticket office on the Up side. The old St Ann's Road station, which stood on the next stretch, closed on 9 August 1942 and the route continues its elevated suburban course undisturbed until it comes to the Enfield line where the course of the former spur towards Stamford Hill can still be spotted.

The spur from Seven Sisters, running for 12 ch to South Tottenham Junction West (5 m 65 ch), was at one time used by Palace Gates trains. Now the single line sees little traffic and the points levers in the signal box on South Tottenham's Up platform are rarely pulled for its use. The station (5 m 69 ch) has modern buildings on its short platforms, the ticket office standing below in Stamford Hill High Road. South Tottenham East Junction (5 m 73 ch) sees the original T&H route go straight ahead as a double line connection to the Lea Valley line at Tottenham South Junction while the Tottenham & Forest Gate line rises to cross the GER route and then take an elevated viaduct course across the reservoir area surrounding the River Lea.

After the railway and its companion Forest Road have squeezed between the reservoirs the former comes to the modern Black Horse Road station (7 m 32 ch) with its concrete slab platforms, modern brick shelters and footbridge to the adjacent ticket office. It is a good example of what BR/GLC/local authority investment has done for a number of stations on the line and contrasts with the remains of the old station beyond the following overbridge. At Walthamstow (8 m 11 ch) the old brick ticket office remains on the Up side but the traditional station has been generally spruced up to a simple but adequate standard.

Walthamstow is preceded by a group of ten skew bridges and followed by another, smaller group which is interspersed with steel cross members to retain the cutting walls. Then the line rises past the old Queens Road signal box (8 m 35 ch), which still provides a reminder that there was once a busy goods activity here with quite a lot of overlapping of cartage boundaries between the rival railways and not infrequent disputes as a consequence. A stretch along a high, walled embankment with typical arches below now takes the route first to Leyton Midland Road (9 m 22 ch), with its long wide platforms and vast booking office subway below, and then to Leytonstone High Road (10 m) which was modernized early in BR days but no longer uses its signal box.

Wanstead Park (11 m 15 ch) is another older station which has been simplified and it is followed by 40 mph and 30 mph sections as the route descends over the Norwich main line to meet the connection therefrom at Woodgrange Park Junction (11 m 79 ch), just past the old goods depot on the east side and 10 ch before the controlling signal box (12 m 9 ch) on the unused Barking end portion of Woodgrange Park's platform. The box, a traditional one, has some excellent barge boards.

From the GE main line the route on to Barking Station Junction (13 m 12 ch) where the passenger workings then head into their own station terminating line, and to Barking Tilbury Line Junction West where the LT&S connection is made, is equipped with overhead electric power supply.

Originally a Midland and Great Eastern enterprise, the T&H has carried a variety of

Operating simplicity derived from the use of emus means that only the Down side platform is now needed at Walton-on-Naze.

services over the years. There was a lavish steam service between St Pancras and East Ham/Barking for a long period, a GER service from Cambridge to St Pancras for a time and a variety of workings to and from the LT&S, including Southend excursions and St Pancras-Tilbury boat trains. Other services used part of the route eg, Palace Gates-North Woolwich, and the freight traffic has always been heavy, particularly to and from Little Ilford until Ripple Lane was built and for/from the Tilbury Loop. The line is still important for the latter and also carries a half-hourly dmu service between Gospel Oak and Barking.

W.1 Wadsley Bridge—see Stocksbridge Branch

W.2 Wainfleet—see Grantham-Skegness Line

W.3 Waltham Cross

Liverpool Street-Kings Lynn line, between Tottenham Hale and Broxbourne. 12 m 63 ch from Liverpool Street

Today's station of platforms, shelters and footbridge is the third and dates from 1969. Its traditional predecessor had been opened by the Great Eastern in 1885, replacing the original 1840 Northern & Eastern station. The Hertford East emus serve the modern station and then continue north via Trinity Lane LC (13 m 22 ch).

Waltham Cross formerly had a substantial freight and parcels activity, not only catering for the market garden produce of the area but also contributing traffic to the

Lea Valley Enterprise service. It was the base for relief cartage and cranage resources for the area.

W.4 Walthamstow Central—see Chingford Branch

W.5 Walthamstow Queens Road—see Upper Holloway-Barking Line

W.6 Walton-on-Naze Branch

Colchester-Clacton line, branch from Thorpe-le-Soken. 4 m 78 ch

The Tendring Hundred Railway completed its line to the modest Victorian watering place at Walton on 17 May 1867. Business grew steadily until the era of Clacton's expansion and Frinton got a station in 1888 and Kirby Cross a passing loop in 1899. For many years trains to and from Liverpool Street were split/joined at Thorpe-le-Soken into Clacton and Walton portions but now the workings are confined to the branch except for some business period trains to and from St Botolphs.

After Thorpe-le-Soken the single line of the branch rises and turns north away from its Clacton junior. There is an AHB crossing at Pork Lane (66 m 55 ch) and then Kirby Cross (67 m 52 ch) where the signal box stands 7 ch ahead of the typical THR buildings, shelter and canopies of the station proper. At Frinton-on-Sea the station is of a different style and uses only the Up platform which is followed by a gated crossing. Part of the section on to Walton had to be re-sited in 1929 as a result of coastal erosion fears for the original alignment.

The station at Walton-on-Naze (70 m 10 ch) stands on a cliff top not far from the beach. Only one platform remains in use, with traditional buildings beyond the buffer stops and the 'Station Lounge' public house now occupying the large block in front of the terminus. Walton used to have a small loco depot but this is now a coach park.

W.7   Wanstead   Park—see   Upper Holloway-Barking Line

W.8   Ware—see Hertford East Branch

W.9   Warren   Hill   Tunnel—see   Newmarket

W.10   Warsop—see   High   Marnham Branch

W.11   Waterbeach

Liverpool Street-Kings Lynn line, between Cambridge and Ely. 61 m 1 ch from Liverpool Street

A small station with simple two-storey buildings, traditional gates and signal box and serving the nearby Air Force base. There are level crossings either side, at Milton Fen (59 m 10 ch), Bottisham Road AHB (61 m 47 ch), Bannolds AHB (62 m 72 ch) and Dimmocks Cote AHB (66 m 25 ch).

W.12   Weeley—see   Colchester-Clacton Line

W.13   Welbeck Colliery—see High Marnham Branch

W.14   Welwyn Garden City

East Coast main line, between Hatfield and Hitchin. 20 m 25 ch from Kings Cross

Welwyn Garden City has a substantial commuter and local travel activity catered for by the station opened to serve the growing township on 20 September 1926. From the Down side ticket office complex in red brick a footbridge leads to the two island platforms which are served by the Kings Cross-Royston trains and Welwyn Garden City's own emus to and from Moorgate. With electrification came the provision of a flyover south of the station so that Down side arrivals could cross to the Up without fouling the main lines. The location has carriage stabling and servicing accommodation and a goods yard area on the Up side.

Eight years after the opening of the Great Northern's main line a second railway came to the Welwyn area in the form of the Hertford & Welwyn Junction's line which opened to Hertford (Cowbridge) on 1 March 1858. Later in the same year amalgamation with the Hertford, Luton & Welwyn Junction concern produced the Hertford, Luton & Dunstable which exten-

ded the western end of its line from Luton to Welwyn on 1 September 1860. The Great Northern then absorbed the two branches and extended the Dunstable line south to Hatfield in 1868 and the Hertford one in 1876.

The Hertford line closed to passengers on 18 June 1951 and lost its final activity, the refuse trains from Finsbury Park to Holwell, on 23 May 1966. The Dunstable line, from Welwyn Garden City (2½ from Hatfield), had run via Ayot (4½ m), Wheathampstead (9½ m), Luton Hoo (12 m), Luton (15 m) and Dunstable Town (19¼ m) to Dunstable proper (20 m). Passenger services ended on 26 April 1965 but freight continued via a new connection at Welwyn for a while longer.

Welwyn gave its name to 'Welwyn Block', a signalling modification deriving directly from a bad accident at Welwyn Garden City on 15 June 1935. Confused by a succession of trains, a signalman gave 'Out of Section' for the second believing it to be the first, and thirteen people died when the third train ran into the second at speed and under clear signals.

W.15   Welwyn North

East Coast main line, between Welwyn Garden City and Hitchin. 21 m 20 ch from Kings Cross

Welwyn North station lies between Welwyn Viaduct and the two Welwyn tunnels. The great forty-arch viaduct over the valley of the tiny River Mimram was completed in 1851 and its original narrow parapet is reputed to have been used by Blondin as a practice ground for his Niagara tightrope feats. The viaduct now leads a rather less exciting life carrying the Up and Down lines of the East Coast main line.

Immediately after crossing the valley the double track route passes through the two platforms of Welwyn North station, a simple traditional type of location where the former coal drops still remain visible. The service is provided by the Kings Cross-Royston trains.

The 446 yd Welwyn South Tunnel (22 m 11 ch to 22 m 31 ch) is closely followed by the 1,046 yd Welwyn North Tunnel (22 m 44 ch to 23 m 12 ch) after which the 105 mph top speed rises to 115 mph and the Slow lines restart near Woolmer Green Emergency Crossover (23 m 20 ch/23 m 73 ch).

W.16   Werrington Junction-Spalding Line

East Coast main line, link to GN&GE joint

line at Spalding. 13 m 30 ch

The double line route from the East Coast main line at Werrington Junction (79 m 34 ch), north of Peterborough, to Spalding was on the first section of the Great Northern Railway to be opened on 17 October 1848. With some local authority support it survives to carry a local service of five trains each way on weekdays plus some longer distance workings.

Once clear of Werrington Junction the dmus take a north-easterly course through a fruitful agricultural landscape, passing via the gated level crossing at Fox Covert (80 m 73 ch) to the site of Peakirk station (81 m 58 ch). Surviving here are the large brick goods shed and the station house which John Taylor designed with an imposing three-storey tower portion as the station master's accommodation.

Soon after Peakirk the line, running absolutely straight, crosses first the Maxey Cut waterway and then the River Welland. The next former station, St James Deeping, survives as a block post with a mixture of semaphore and colour light signals, a gated level crossing (83 m 38 ch) and the modest station house. Via Stowgate AHB crossing (84 m 37 ch) the route continues through the flat, rich landscape to the third former station at Littleworth, again with signal box, level crossing (87 m 61 ch), large brick goods shed and surviving station buildings.

From Littleworth the route remains as straight as an arrow not only to Spalding, but through and beyond it, a clear reminder of the reasons the infant GN had for tackling this part of its mammoth task first. On the final section into Spalding there are further level crossings at Lucks Road AHB (90 m 1 ch), South Drove AHB (90 m 63 ch), London Road AHB (91 m 61 ch) and then Hawthorn Bank AHB (92 m 8 ch).

W.17 West Burton—see Gainsborough

W.18 Westcliff-on-Sea

Fenchurch Street-Shoeburyness line, between Leigh-on-Sea and Southend. 34 m 66 ch from Fenchurch Street

Five trains call hourly in each direction, a level of service which led the Line Traffic Manager (LT&S) to offer local Southend single fares of 3d for one station, 6d for two, 9d for three and 1/- for four when electrification was first introduced—much to the chagrin of the local bus authority! The station, with a road bridge over and a concrete footbridge has good, gabled buildings plus canopies with the LTSR legend in the support brackets.

W.19 Westerfield—see East Suffolk Line

W.20 West Ham—see North Woolwich Branch

W.21 West Horndon

Fenchurch Street-Shoeburyness line, between Upminster and Pitsea. 19 m 15 ch from Fenchurch Street

From opening on 1 May 1886 when the line from Upminster arrived (and was then extended on to Pitsea on 1 June 1888) until 1 May 1949 the station here was called East Horndon. It lies in a flat, agricultural setting and although once busy with wagons from the Brown & Tawse siding now has only its passenger services plus an occasional trip to and from the engineers' siding on the Down side. The main buildings—sizeable but to the LT&S standard pattern—are on this side, with a brick shelter and integral decorated canopy opposite. There is an emergency crossover at the London end and a ground frame for the siding at the country end.

West Horndon has a half-hourly off-peak service which puts Fenchurch Street within 28 minutes.

W.22 West Runton—see Sheringham Branch

W.23 West Thurrock Junction—see Grays

W.24 White Hart Lane—see Enfield Town Branch

W.25 Whitemoor

Birmingham-Norwich line, access via March. Whitemoor Junction is 86 m 18 ch from Liverpool Street

By the mid-1920s the LNER was beginning to feel the effects of competition from the growing road haulage industry. Small businesses were hungry for traffic and the protection of the 1933 Road & Rail Traffic Act was yet to come. Great Eastern section receipts were being held up by the establishment of the new sugar beet industry but some action had to be taken to protect the general freight business and the LNER directors opted for a new traffic control office at Cambridge and a new mechanized marshalling yard at Whitemoor. Work began in 1925 with the Up Yard being completed four years later at a cost of £285,000. The Down Yard was added in 1933.

Whitemoor Yard was in a very accessible spot and it embodied the latest technology.

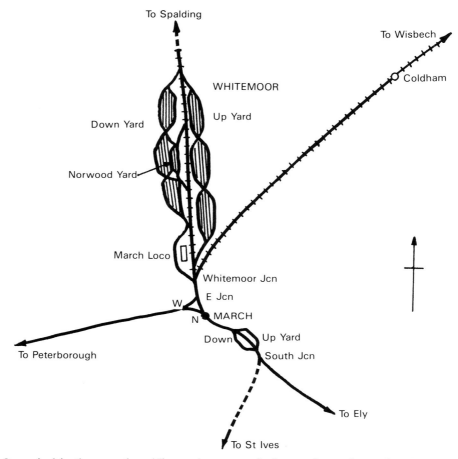

On arrival in the reception sidings a 'cut card' was prepared according to the forward destination of each wagon and the train then cut, ie, uncoupled, accordingly. Shunting locomotives duly propelled the train up to and over the hump which was designed to allow the cuts to separate sufficiently for resetting the points between each as it descended to the destination sorting siding. The weight of the descending wagon, its type and load, the length it had to run and the skill of the retarder operators were then combined to determine the amount of hydraulic pressure to be exerted by the retarder bars in order to let the wagon run accurately and safely into the chosen siding. If necessary wagon chasers, adept at riding on a brake stick wedged in the axle box frame, would use the wagon brakes to increase the slowing down process. When enough traffic had been accumulated for each forward service it would be coupled up and drawn forward to the departure sidings, there to be engined, provided with a brake van from the brake 'kip' and then sent on the next stage of its journey.

Fragile traffic, livestock and other special loads all varied the main process and Whitemoor also had a small 'knuckle' yard which dealt with non-standard activities. One such was the task of shunting the season's incoming fruit vans which left the local stations as late as possible in order to give growers the maximum picking time and then had to be shunted at a very fast pace in order to catch the evening departures from the Down Yard. The shunters of Norwood Yard who dealt with these movements were at the top of their branch of railway working.

Like the other big yards, Whitemoor has been affected by the changes in BR's freight movement business. Its Up Yard has continued in use for Speedlink movements and the Down Yard has been used for scrap stock destined for Snailwell but if the work passes elsewhere the site may eventually be used for a prison.

From the triangle between March station and loco, Whitemoor Junction leads to Grassmoor Junction, standing between the Up and Down sides of the yard and where the mileage changed from 87 m 3 ch from Liverpool Street to 25 m 58 ch from Huntingdon. The north end of the Whitemoor complex ended at Twenty Feet River signal box and level crossing (26 m 50 ch).

W.26 White Notley—see Braintree Branch

W.27 Whitlingham Junction

Junction of Norwich-Sheringham and Norwich-Yarmouth lines. 1 m 71 ch from Norwich Thorpe

Whitlingham station, Norwich side of the junction, closed to passengers on 19 September 1955 but a signal box remains to control the two routes. On 10 September 1874 a serious accident occurred near Thorpe Mental Hospital when the 5.00 pm ex-Liverpool Street and the 8.40 pm from Yarmouth were both given authority to proceed onto the single line section and collided head-on with the loss of 25 lives and 73 people injured.

W.28 Whittlesea

Norwich-Birmingham line, between March and Peterborough. 94 m 56 ch from Liverpool Street

From the March direction Whittlesea is pre-

ceded by Eastree AHB LC (93 m 28 ch) and the station LC (94 m 61 ch) is then followed by more crossings at Harts Grove R/G (95 m 2 ch), Ramsey Road AHB (95 m 28 ch), Black Bush AHB (95 m 34 ch), Star and Victory (96 m 46 ch), Kings Dyke LC (96 m 73 ch) and Funthams Lane CCTV LC (97 m 16 ch).

The former traditional station is now just a functional location with short, staggered platforms and served by the Cambridge-Peterborough dmus and some longer distance services. There is also a wooden signal box, some rusting sidings and a UKF depot. On the Up side of the line there are brickyards on either side of Kings Dyke signal box.

W.29 Whittlesford

Liverpool Street-Kings Lynn line, between Audley End and Cambridge. 49 m 1 ch from Liverpool Street

In the Down direction Whittlesford is preceded by the connection installed to the Ciba-Geigy works under the Section 8 grant arrangements and by AHB level crossings at Hinxton (47 m) and Duxford (47 m 60 ch). The station itself has just modest brick buildings on the Down side and a wooden shelter on the Up but the goods yard is still in use for grain and end dock traffic. Northwards after the URS and DGL comes Sawston LC (50 m 46 ch) and Dernford R/G LC (51 m 36 ch) with the site of Spicers' former sidings between the two.

W.30 Whitwell—see Sherwood-Shire-oaks Line

W.31 Wickford—see Shenfield-Southend Line

W.32 Wickham Market—see East Suffolk Line

Hump shunting at Whitemoor with a single wagon 'cut' descending towards the primary retarders.

W.33 Winchmore Hill—see Hertford Loop

W.34 Winterton & Thealby Branch—see Scunthorpe

W.35 Wisbech Branch

Birmingham-Norwich line, branch from March. 7 m 42 ch

Only ten miles south of the Wash and linked to the sea by the River Nene, Wisbech has a long tradition as an inland port and by the 1840s was dealing with quite a significant volume of business, especially timber. In 1847 the Wisbech, St Ives & Cambridge Junction Railway reached Wisbech from March, the first trains arriving on 3 May of that year. On 1 February 1848 the East Anglian line from Watlington arrived at a separate station (later to become Wisbech East) and a link was established between the two.

The East Anglian company, being slowly strangled by the Eastern Counties, had turned to the Great Northern which was not averse to a lease which would give it access to the rich fenland of which Wisbech was a centre. However, the ECR blocked the connection between the two railways at Wisbech and the GNR failed to secure an injunction for its removal. The latter's plans for development at Wisbech thus foundered and the East Anglian concern was swallowed up by its Eastern Counties neighbour. The balance was redressed by the arrival at Wisbech of the Peterborough, Wisbech & Sutton Bridge Railway on 1 June 1866 (1 August for passengers), this line later becoming part of the M&GN system.

Wisbech itself continued to grow, under the influence of general economic expansion and the resultant dividends for agricultural activity. In addition to the two railways and their links to the riverside quays, Wisbech had a modest canal and also the Wisbech & Upwell Tramway. This was a roadside line, opened alongside the earlier canal to Outwell on 20 August 1883 and extended to Upwell on 8 September 1884. At one time the enclosed tram engines of the branch also handled passenger traffic but this ended on 2 January 1928 and the tramway concentrated on the collection of agricultural produce into Wisbech for onward movement to Whitemoor.

Although the Wisbech & Upwell Tramway lived long enough to be dieselized it finally closed on 23 May 1966, the year in which the Harbour East branch closed on 12 September. The Harbour North branch

had already closed on 4 January 1965. Passenger services on the M&GN line, which had run via Wisbech St Mary (16 m 73 ch from Peterborough), Wisbech North (19 m 25 ch), Leverington Road Crossing (19 m 43 ch), Goods Loop Junction (19 m 70 ch)—for the 70 ch harbour branch—and then on to Sutton Bridge, had ended on 2 March 1959. The passenger service on the GER line ran via Coldham (89 m 27 ch), Waldersea box (90 m 35 ch), Goods Junction (93 m 30 ch)—for the 37 ch goods branch—Wisbech East (93 m 52 ch), with the single line tramway leaving from behind the Up island platform and the Harbour East branch departing from Harbour Junction, 27 ch further on. The branch was 1 m 13 ch long with a 20 ch spur while the tramway ran from Upwell Tram Junction (93 m 44 ch) via Elm Depot (1 m 56 ch), Boyce's Depot (3 m 26 ch), Outwell Basin (4 m 11 ch) and Outwell (5 m 9 ch) to Upwell (5 m 74 ch from Upwell Tram Junction).

After the main closure period a 25 mph, One Train, freight-only single line remained in existence from Whitemoor Junction (86 m 18 ch) to Wisbech Goods Yard (93 m 60 ch) for the conveyance of Spillers pet-food, Metal Box and coal traffic. The line starts with two AHB crossings, at Elm Road (86 m 60 ch) and Chain Bridge (87 m 31 ch), continues with TMO crossings at Coldham (89 m 21 ch), Waldersea (90 m 29 ch), Redmoor (92 m 9 ch) and New Bridge (92 m 46 ch) and concludes with Weasenham Lane LC, the whole being controlled by the Whitemoor Junction signal box.

W.36 Witham

Liverpool Street-Norwich line, junction for Braintree branch. 38 m 48 ch from Liverpool Street

Braintree, Colchester and Clacton trains call at Witham to give the station an excellent service and put it within 39 minutes of Liverpool Street. After a two mile descent at 1 in 178 and then both facing and trailing crossovers, the station proper consists of an access via footbridge from the Down side ticket office to the two island platforms around which the passenger loops pass.

Beyond the country end of the Down platform the four-car sets for Braintree, separated from the companion set which has worked down as an eight-car formation, veer off along the course of the River Brain. The signal box stands opposite and by it the surviving trackbed of the line which followed the River Blackwater to Maldon.

Witham station looking north, with the signal box on the right and the Braintree branch veering off left.

Both of Witham's branches were opened for goods traffic on 15 August 1848 and for passengers on 2 October of that year, the original Maldon, Witham & Braintree Railway by then having been taken over by the Eastern Counties. It is curious that of the two branches one should have survived to enjoy electrification while the Maldon line, via Wickham Bishops (2½ m) and Langford (4½ m) to Maldon (East) & Heybridge (5¾ m), should have kept its passenger services only until 7 September 1964; despite the fact that it enjoyed nine trains each way daily before the last war.

W.37   Wivenhoe—see Colchester-Clacton Line

W.38   Woodbridge—see East Suffolk Line

W.39   Woodgrange Park—see Upper Holloway-Barking Line

W.40   Wood Green

East Coast main line, junction with Hertford Loop. 4 m 78 ch from Kings Cross

The station, opened as Wood Green on 1 May 1859 but several times renamed and reconstructed, has now taken the name Alexandra Palace in recognition of its situation below that notable building. Although remodelled for electrification in 1976 it remains typical of the Up and Down island plus footbridge access design that the Great Northern made standard on four-track routes. Situated at the north end of the Bounds Green carriage depot complex, Alexandra Palace formerly had a Great Eastern neighbour in the shape of the terminus of that company's line from Seven Sisters.

At Wood Green the two junctions for the Hertford Loop are Wood Green Junction Down (4 m 68 ch) and Wood Green Junction Up (5 m 7 ch). The 706-yd Wood Green Tunnel (5 m 41 ch to 5 m 73 ch) then lies to the north.

A concrete cutting taking the outer Down line round the outside of the Down Hertford flyover line, now infilled, used to be known as the 'Khyber Pass'. It was also possible to transfer between the GN and GE sections by reversal at Wood Green.

Off-peak six trains an hour call at Wood Green.

W.41   Woodham Ferrers—see Southminster Branch

W.42   Woodhouse—see Sheffield

W.43   Wood Street—see Chingford Branch

W.44   Worksop

Cleethorpes-Sheffield line, between Ret-
ford and Woodhouse Junction. 56 m 58 ch
from Manchester (London Road)

Worksop derives an hourly service from the
PTE-supported dmus which operate from
Sheffield to Retford and beyond. The
passenger station retains its 1849 MS&L
buildings, the main ones comprising a long
single-storey structure in Steetley stone and
remarkably enhanced by extra storeys,
superb gables and tall decorated chimneys.

On the freight side considerable evidence
of the coal traffic activities is apparent.
There are extra Permissive lines between
the signal box at Worksop Sidings (56 m 6
ch) and the one at Worksop West (56 m 42
ch), Worksop Yard and mgr depot lying
between the two. Beyond the station the
next signal box is at Worksop East LC (56 m
66 ch) as the route continues via the link
with Manton Wood Colliery and on to Retford.

W.45   Worstead—see   Sheringham
Branch

W.46   Wrabness—see Harwich Branch

W.47   Wrawby Junction—see Barnetby

W.48   Wroxham—see   Sheringham
Branch

W.49   Wymondham

Birmingham-Norwich line, between Thet-
ford and Norwich. 113 m 72 ch from Liver-
pool Street

Two Down side sidings survive in advance
of the Wymondham signal box (113 m 65
ch) and South Junction (113 m 70 ch) where
the freight-only single line from North
Elmham trails into the Down main. Then
comes the station with its three-leg footbridge and main buildings of unknapped
flints on the Down side. The goods yard
comes next, still in use for Ketton cement
traffic, then the trackbed of the former
branch to Forncett and then another level
crossing, at Browick Road (114 m 35 ch).
Like the station house, the latter has a cottage in flint, one of the features of the buildings of the original Norwich & Brandon
Railway.

The 6¾-mile branch from Forncett,
through Ashwellthorpe to Wymondham
was opened by the Great Eastern Railway
on 2 May 1881, more as a relief route than
for local traffic. In addition to seven local
trains each way daily it did carry services to
and from the Dereham line from time to
time and there was some through goods

train working, especially during the First
World War. Passenger services ceased on
10 September 1939 and freight on 4 August
1951 although some track was left in situ at
the Wymondham end for wagon storage.

The line from Wymondham to Dereham
was a Norfolk Railway branch opened for
goods traffic on 7 December 1846 and for
passengers on 15 February 1847. It was
extended north to Fakenham on 20 March
1849 with the Wells & Fakenham Railway
completing the link to the coast at Wells on
1 December 1857 and later adding a harbour branch there. Although carrying a fair
amount of traffic on the Norwich-Kings
Lynn route once the through connection
was established at Dereham, the Wells
route was never terribly busy despite its
links with the West Norfolk Railway to
Heacham and the East Norfolk Railway at
County School.

Passenger services ended on the Wells
line on 5 October 1964 and on the Kings
Lynn line on 9 September 1968. One year
later the final section from Wymondham to
Dereham carried its last passenger and
remained open only for freight from 6
October 1969. After the dmus left this area
of Norfolk some freight activity continued
but this has now shrunk to the 21 m 5 ch
from Wymondham to North Elmham.

The surviving single line is operated on
the One Train basis with a speed limit of 30
mph and control by the single signal box at
Wymondham South Junction (6 ch). From
there the line runs north via Church Lane
LC (60 ch) to the former station at Kimber-
ley Park (TMO LC 3 m 53 ch), through
another at Hardingham (5 m 39 ch) to the
third at Thuxton (TMO LC 6 m 73 ch).
Then comes Gaverstone TMO LC (7 m 39
ch), former station and TMO LC at Yaxham (9 m 35 ch) and AOCL LCs at Yaxham
Road (10 m 75 ch) and Hall Lane (10 m 79
ch).

Dereham station was preceded by a triangular junction with the line to Swaffham
via Wendling, Fransham and Dunham. At
11 m 31 ch the station followed the South/
West/Central Junction layout and was
itself followed by Norwich Road (11 m 33
ch) and Neatherd Road (11 m 52 ch), both
of which survive as TMO crossings. More
TMO crossings—Swanton Road (11 m 71
ch), Hoe (13 m 61 ch) and Worthing (15 m
16 ch)—bring the surviving line to its 1984
terminus at North Elmham, once a forwarding station for large quantities of milk
traffic and latterly, with the UKF depot at
Dereham, keeping the line open with its
grain business.

The Wells line had continued on from North Elmham via County School (17 m 39 ch), a passing loop as well as the junction for Aylsham, Ryburgh (21 m 5 ch), a bridge over the M&GN and then Fakenham East station (23 m 42 ch), Walsingham (28 m 40 ch), Wighton Halt (30 m 20 ch) and finally Wells-next-the-Sea (33 m 5 ch). Cockles from Wells and pilgrims to and from Walsingham's shrine and slipper chapel were among the other businesses of the line which was completely blocked in the 1947 snows.

Y.1 Yarmouth

Norwich-Yarmouth line. 18 m 29 ch from Norwich Thorpe

The Romans knew Yarmouth and provided forts at Caister and Burgh Castle to guard the inlet which led to the waters of the Bure, Yare and Waveney rivers. The title of Great Yarmouth derives from the charter of 1272 and the town's importance as a port from the provision of a deep channel by the Dutch engineer Joost Jansen in the 16th century. For many years Yarmouth was one of the home ports of the East Anglian fishing fleet and some trawlers are still based there, but today's shipping activity has more to do with container movements and with supplying the North Sea oil and gas rigs. Yarmouth's long, sandy beaches continue to lure thousands of holidaymakers each year, especially from London and the Midlands.

Yarmouth's first railway was that of the Yarmouth & Norwich enterprise which began its public services on 30 April 1844, the shorter route to Norwich via Acle opening as far as that point on 12 March 1883

and on to a junction with the 1844 route at Brundall on 1 June of the same year. The latter is now the main rail access route to the Norfolk resort, carrying a good dmu service with connections into and out of the hourly London trains.

The opening of the line across the marshes to Brundall in 1883 was accompanied by another piece of railway excitement for Yarmouth, already blossoming as a resort and with much of the steamer traffic on its rivers and along the coast from the Thames transferring to the steadily improving rail communications. This other event was the completion of the link to the Midland and Great Northern companies' lines via the route which was later to become the M&GN Joint Railway and to bring thousands of visitors from Central England. At the Yarmouth end the route had originated in 1876 as the Great Yarmouth & Stalham Light Railway, opening its first section to Ormesby on 1 August 1877 and extending by stages and with a change of title to Yarmouth & North Norfolk Railway to reach North Walsham on 13 June 1881.

To the south Yarmouth enjoyed a second rail route to London via the Yarmouth & Haddiscoe and the East Suffolk systems from 1 June 1859. The resort's last route was that of the Norfolk & Suffolk Joint Committee along the coast from Lowestoft and opened on 13 July 1903. In addition to the connection into Yarmouth (South Town) there was a line round the inland side

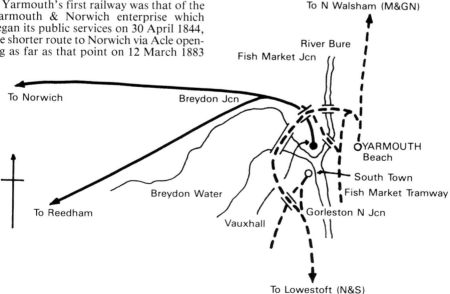

On a wet morning in January 1959, 43145 stands at Yarmouth Beach with the 10.02 train to Peterborough.

of the town, over the GER route into Yarmouth (Vauxhall) and then into the M&GN (Beach) station. The section for 22 ch from 74 m 17 ch was single for crossing Breydon Water by means of a swing-bridge and the connection with the Beach station line was then made at Lowestoft Line Junction (72 m 63 ch). At Caister Road Junction (73 m 25 ch) the M&GN lines were linked with the Quay Tramway.

The flood year of 1953 not only saw South Town station under water but also brought the closure, on 21 September, of the link across Breydon Water via the swing-bridge. Six years later came more closures with the M&GN line into Beach station going on 2 March and the Haddiscoe-South Town section on 2 November. Trains to and from the East Suffolk line then reversed at Lowestoft and used the N&S route between that point and Yarmouth until that option, in turn, ended on 4 May 1970.

The last Yarmouth closure, on 1 January 1976, was that of the tramway to the quays and fish wharf. From Fish Market Junction (18 m 9 ch from Norwich) outside Vauxhall station this led for 37 ch to a loop where the 50 ch link from Caister Road Junction joined. In addition to the 7 ch of the loop itself, the single line continued for another 1 m 26 ch (with three more loops and an 8 ch spur) to the fish wharves on the east bank of the inlet channel. The route was worked by an enclosed tram engine until diesel shunters took over and special operating instructions included scotching the rails and pro-

viding additional brakevans and shunters for trains on the incline where the route bridged the River Bure.

The approach to Yarmouth's surviving station is from the old Breydon Junction. Formerly the single lines via Acle and via Berney Arms joined here and the junction and signal box at 17 m 13 ch was followed by Fish Market Junction and the tramway connection at 18 m 3 ch. Now the two approach lines remain separate past the little-used carriage sidings and washer as far as the junction and main signal box (18 m 12 ch) preceding the station.

Yarmouth station proper has two main platform lines plus an extra line to the outer face of the Up platform and a shorter bay on the Down side. There is still a line to the Up side shed and to the yard beyond but although this was still being used in 1983 for coal traffic and pipe storage there was a closure proposal in the offing. On the Down side approaches the tramway route is still visible with the old locomotive shed and adjoining N&S route embankment apparent opposite.

When the Yarmouth & Norwich Railway received the Royal Assent on 18 June 1842 it provided for a capital of £150,000 and borrowing powers of £50,000. In a curious footnote to this it was revealed at a 1958 valuation court in Yarmouth that the brewery capital contribution to the original line had been part of a deal to provide a pub near most stations and to prohibit the opening of a competing refreshment room at Vauxhall. The fish and carriage sidings at the latter were badly bombed in May 1943 and rebuilt in 1959-61.

Y.2 Yorkshire Main Sidings—see Brancliffe-Kirk Sandall Line

SECTION 4

Route summaries

East Coast main line, Kings Cross-Doncaster

From Lewis Cubitt's Kings Cross station, its severity now modified by the modern approach area additions, the East Coast main line has to rise at 1 in 107 through two tunnels to get to Finsbury Park where the Moorgate line emus join. On this section, once with a Holloway ticket platform, 'car carrier' depot, carriage sidings and Clarence Yard goods activity, the route passes under the North London line and the Freight Terminal connection joins.

On either side from Finsbury Park to Wood Green, where the Hertford Loop departs, there is the paraphernalia of train support in the shape of the Ferme Park/ Bounds Green maintenance, cleaning and stabling areas. The route then climbs for another eight miles, this time at 1 in 200 and with five more tunnels, to get to the

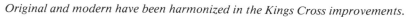

Original and modern have been harmonized in the Kings Cross improvements.

summit at Potters Bar. Hatfield, now modernized and with little trace of its former branches, is followed by the Welwyn Garden City flyover and the station complex which acts as turnround point for an intensive electric train service to and from Moorgate.

The track, which has so far been quadruple, becomes double to cross Welwyn Viaduct and pass through the Welwyn tunnels. There are four lines again by the time the Hertford Loop rejoins at Langley Junction and the main line continues through Stevenage to Hitchin, junction with the Cambridge branch. Formerly there were connections with the LMS system at Hitchin (for Bedford) and Sandy where the loss of the Cambridge-Bletchley line has allowed station remodelling and the elimination of one more bottleneck.

Leaving Biggleswade/Sandy market gardening areas behind, the main line has the Ouse as companion beyond St Neots and through Offord where another round of ECML improvements has eased the once notorious curves. After Huntingdon, now without its Kettering-Cambridge route and no longer the commencing point of the GN&GE joint line distances, the ECML rises at 1 in 200 and then falls again to a flat section through Holme, once the junction for the Ramsey North branch. Next comes the brickyard area which heralds the approach to Peterborough.

The cathedral city of Peterborough, itself much remodelled, has a new station complex to match and is an important junction with the Norwich-Birmingham route. The lines to Northampton/Rugby and to Kings Lynn have gone, but Peterborough retains its services to Spalding and beyond and has a coach link to Kings Lynn.

The original section of the GNR main line departs at Werrington Junction leaving the 'Towns' line to head for the South Lincolnshire heights via Helpston where the Stamford line leaves and Essendine which once had branches to Stamford and to Bourne. The record-breaking territory of Stoke Bank involves 4½ miles at 1 in 200 which then steepens to 3 miles of 1 in 178 to the summit and Stoke Tunnel. The High Dyke connection with the former ironstone lines to the west lay on the 5 miles of 1 in 200 down to Grantham.

Grantham is another important ECML junction where trains connect with the

Down HST speeds through Hitchin in 1984.

A Down HST on the East Coast main line just north of Werrington Junction.

Nottingham-Skegness service. The Nottingham line departs just north of the station and the Skegness line at Barkston, just beyond Peascliffe Tunnel and with a direct connection to the Nottingham line. Lincoln trains no longer travel via Barkston and Honington Junction but passengers continue on to Newark and link up there with the Nottingham-Lincoln-Cleethorpes trains.

The Nottingham-Lincoln line crosses the ECML on the level beyond Newark Northgate station and the Trent valley then produces nearly six miles of level running before a further slight rise to the former Dukeries Junction and Tuxford links with the LD&ECR system. Retford is the next significant junction and gave the infant GNR its access to Sheffield over MS&L metals. It is still an interchange point with the Sheffield-Lincoln/Cleethorpes trains although these now have their own platforms below ECML level, part of a remodelling which was also designed to facilitate the flow of mgr coal trains to the power stations of the area.

Coal is also increasingly in evidence on the final stretch into Doncaster which is preceded by a maze of yards and junctions which largely survive for the freight-only lines servicing this valuable BR business. The joint line from Lincoln and the Sheffield line join the ECML south of Doncaster's busy station and to the north the Humberside and West Riding trains take their separate courses. 'The Plant', which produced the great Stirling, Ivatt and Gresley designs, lies just west of the station and is still an active BREL location.

Much has changed on this southern section of the East Coast main line. The branches and the old Ferme Park and New England yards have either gone or changed beyond recognition but so have the bottlenecks and curves to leave today's HST sets free to attain their 125 mph potential over much of the distance from Kings Cross to Doncaster.

K.4	Kings Cross	H.33	Holme LC (69 m 28 ch)
G.2	Gasworks Tunnel (22 ch)		Fletton Junction (75 m 2 ch)
C.28	Copenhagen Tunnel (65 ch)	O.4	Orton Mere Branch
M.19	Moorgate Line		Crescent Junction (76 m 25 ch)
F.5	Finsbury Park (2 m 41 ch)	P.4	Peterborough (76 m 29 ch)
H.11	Harringay (3 m 32 ch)		Werrington Junction (79 m 34 ch)
H.36	Hornsey (4 m 4 ch)	W.16	Werrington Junction-Spalding Line
W.40	Wood Green (4 m 78 ch)	H.21	Helpston LC (81 m 71 ch)
H.23	Hertford Loop	P.5	Peterborough-Leicester Line
	Wood Green Tunnel (5 m 41 ch)	S.50	Stoke (99 m 61 ch)
N.10	New Southgate (6 m 35 ch)		Stoke Tunnel (100 m 39 ch)
B.6	Barnet Tunnel (7 m 42 ch)	G.9	Grantham (105 m 38 ch)
O.1	Oakleigh Park (8 m 30 ch)		Nottingham Branch Junction (106
N.4	New Barnet (9 m 12 ch)		m 8 ch)
	Hadley Wood South Tunnel (10 m	G.10	Grantham-Nottingham Line
	21 ch)		Peascliffe Tunnel (107 m 65 ch)
H.6	Hadley Wood (10 m 46 ch)	B.4	Barkston South Junction (109 m
	Hadley Wood North Tunnel (10 m		56 ch)
	60 ch)	G.11	Grantham-Skegness Line
	Potters Bar Tunnel (11 m 25 ch)	B.34	Newark South Junction (119 m 73
P.9	Potters Bar (12 m 57 ch)		73 ch)
B.47	Brookmans Park (14 m 37 ch)		Bottesford-Newark Line
H.14	Hatfield (17 m 54 ch)	N.2	Newark Northgate (120 m 8 ch)
W.14	Welwyn Garden City (20 m 25 ch)	N.3	Newark-Lincoln Line
W.15	Welwyn North (22 m)		Newark Crossing (120 m 63 ch)
	Welwyn South Tunnel (22 m 11 ch)	C.6	Carlton LC (126 m 25 ch)
	Welwyn North Tunnel (22 m 44 ch)	T.26	Tuxford Crossover (131 m 50 ch)
K.10	Knebworth (25 m 3 ch)	A.12	Askham Tunnel (134 m 37 ch)
L.3	Langley Junction Up (26 m 45 ch)	R.6	Retford (138 m 49 ch)
	Langley Junction Down (26 m 61	B.12	Bawtry (148 m 55 ch)
	ch)	R.11	Rossington LC (151 m 29 ch)
S.48	Stevenage (27 m 45 ch)		Decoy North Junction (154 m 13
H.30	Hitchin (31 m 74 ch)		ch)
	Cambridge Junction (32 m 11 ch)		Balby Bridge Tunnel (155 m 34 ch)
B.23	Biggleswade (41 m 13 ch)		South Yorkshire Junction (155 m
S.6	Sandy (44 m 10 ch)		58 ch)
S.4	St Neots (51 m 58 ch)	D.7	Doncaster (155 m 77 ch)
H.38	Huntingdon (58 m 70 ch)		Marshgate Junction (156 m 28 ch)

Liverpool Street-Colchester-Ipswich-Norwich Line

The Great Eastern Railway's great complex of London terminus and headquarter offices is changing entirely in a scheme that will close Broad Street and re-route its trains via Hackney and will replace the present Liverpool Street layout with a new combined station and office block development. Part of the changes involves an improved access over the section between Liverpool Street and Bethnal Green, still revealing much evidence of the past in the shape of the East London Line route, Bishopsgate Low Level and the Spitalfields/Bishopsgate goods route.

At Bethnal Green the Enfield/Chingford/Lea Valley routes depart leaving the main line to continue via the Devonshire Street/Mile End sites and the Bow Junction link to Fenchurch Street and then come to the Stratford approaches. Stratford used to be the heart of the GER empire and although the works activity

Up train arriving at Marks Tey. The Sudbury branch is on the extreme left.

has now gone it remains important as an interchange station with the Central Line and with the route from Richmond (SR) to North Woolwich. It also has important functions as a traction and rolling stock maintenance depot, for carriage stabling and servicing, as a Freightliner and LIFT terminal and for some specialized freight activities.

After Stratford comes Forest Gate Junction with the LT&S section and then Ilford with its flyover and maintenance depot but no service now to Woodford. The route continues past the sites of the former Up and Down yards at Goodmayes to Romford which has a single line branch to Upminster. After Gidea Park, turn-round point for inner suburban services, comes Harold Wood and then the 1 in 103 start to Brentwood Bank which caused the infant Eastern Counties Railway such a great deal of money and trouble in the construction period.

Once over Ingrave summit today's trains descend to Shenfield, junction for the Southend line, and then continue gently down to Chelmsford. Easy gradients continue all the way to Colchester through Witham, where the Braintree line survives from the two former branches, Kelvedon, no longer with its quaint branch out to the pier at Tollesbury, and Marks Tey, junction for the Sudbury branch. Colchester itself is both an important railhead and the junction with the route to Clacton and Walton.

Electrification has now spread north from Colchester as the main line heads on to Manningtree where it sheds the Harwich branch at the neck of the Stour estuary. This section originated with the Eastern Union Railway which had taken over the ambitions of the exhausted ECR and completed the line from Colchester on to Ipswich via Manningtree and Bentley which at one time had a branch inland to Hadleigh. A tunnel heralds the approach to Ipswich station where passengers

Liverpool Street.

change for the Bury St Edmunds, East Suffolk and Felixstowe lines, the last two leaving at East Suffolk Junction just north of the station.

The Ipswich & Bury Railway took the route on via a typically attractive station at Needham to Stowmarket and then the junction at Haughley, once also a junction for the very individualistic Mid-Suffolk Light Railway. The remaining straight and easily graded section on to Norwich was built in stages by the EUR and passes through Mellis which used to have a short branch to Eye, the railhead at Diss, Tivetshall which had water troughs and was the junction for the Waveney Valley route to Beccles, and Forncett which had a cut-off link to Wymondham on the Norwich-Ely line.

There is a high level approach to Norwich, shedding the branch to the original EUR terminus at Victoria and then descending to join the Ely route at Trowse, continue via the swing-bridge over the Wensum, join with the Lowestoft/Yarmouth/Sheringham routes beyond Crown Point and then come to an end at the elegant Norwich terminus.

L.15	Liverpool Street	S.11	Seven Kings (8 m 45 ch)
B.26	Bishopsgate Tunnel (27 ch)	G.4	Goodmayes (9 m 23 ch)
B.21	Bethnal Green (1 m 10 ch)	C.7	Chadwell Heath (9 m 79 ch)
B.36	Bow Junction (2 m 69 ch)	R.9	Romford (12 m 30 ch)
S.53	Stratford (4 m 3 ch)	R.10	Romford-Upminster Branch
M.11	Maryland (4 m 39 ch)	G.2	Gidea Park (13 m 41 ch)
F.8	Forest Gate (5 m 21 ch)	H.10	Harold Wood (14 m 76 ch)
	Forest Gate Junction (5 m 63 ch)	B.43	Brentwood (18 m 16 ch)
M.4	Manor Park (6 m 19 ch)	S.15	Shenfield (20 m 16 ch)
I.1	Ilford (7 m 28 ch)	S.16	Shenfield-Southend Line

Liverpool Street-Cambridge-Ely-Kings Lynn

The southern portion of this route was part of the Northern & Eastern Railway's dream of a main line to the north, but the railway abandoned its plan for a separate London terminus in favour of a link with the Eastern Counties at Stratford and was eventually swallowed up by that company. Nevertheless the N&E beginnings had the distinction of being part of the first route between London and Norwich

Modern ticket office and circulating area grafted onto the three-storey main block at Bishops Stortford.

Kings Lynn before completion of its improvement scheme.

and for many years carried combined Norwich and Kings Lynn trains which divided and joined at Ely.

The route commences at Liverpool Street but leaves the Norwich main line at Bethnal Green to follow the course of a later cut-off route to the original N&E line at Copper Mill Junction. It caries the trains for Enfield Town and for Cheshunt via the thrice-opened Churchbury Loop as far as Hackney Downs and main line trains share the section on to Clapton Junction with the Chingford emus. From that point on they traverse the original N&E Lea Valley course, through an area once dominated by furniture making, various heavy industries and market gardening activity but now equally notable for the recreational activities based on the river and adjoining land. There used to be a marshalling area at Northumberland Park and a single line from Angel Road to Lower Edmonton; both these have gone but Tottenham Hale remains an important interchange point with London Transport and there is still a junction with the Tottenham & Hampstead route. At Cheshunt the Churchbury Loop rejoins the main line south of the station and there is an interchange facility at Broxbourne between the Bishops Stortford and Hertford East services, the latter leaving at Broxbourne Junction.

The gradual rise which started back at Tottenham continues through the new station at Harlow and then Bishops Stortford, once a junction for Dunmow and Braintree and subsequently a turnround point for North East London emus and for the dmus working intermediately to Cambridge. The Anglia West electrification will take the overhead wires on from Bishops Stortford to Cambridge, with trains climbing up to the summit at Elsenham which once had a modest light railway branch out to Thaxted. Audley End was formerly the junction for Saffron Walden and the descent then continues through the ornate Audley End Tunnel and the following Littlebury Tunnel to Great Chesterford. This was the starting point

A Down train discharges its passengers at Cambridge.

for the Newmarket Railway's main line until that company was swallowed up by the Eastern Counties. On the final section to Cambridge, the trackbed of the former route from Sudbury joins at Shelford, the GN's access to Cambridge joins at Shepreth Branch Junction and the old LNW route from Bletchley joined just before Cambridge itself.

Cambridge remains distinctive for its single long platform with central crossovers and bays for local services. It has a modern panel box and a large maintenance depot and then north of the station comes Coldham Lane Junction where the dmus for Newmarket, Bury St Edmunds and Ipswich depart. Immediately after is the site of the junction for the old Mildenhall branch and then Chesterton Junction where the large permanent way depot and a surviving freight-only line remain, the latter from the one-time route for trains via St Ives to March and Kettering. After a level section of some twelve miles comes Ely where a branch from St Ives formerly joined just south of the present junction with the line from Chippenham Junction, Newmarket. Beyond the station there are excellent views of the cathedral and of Ely's boating activities and the route then comes to the series of junctions with the Norwich and Peterborough routes.

The route on to Kings Lynn, now simplified, takes a course through rich fenland countryside to Denver where the Stoke Ferry branch used to join, bringing with it wagons of produce off the rambling Wissington Light Railway system. Next comes Downham and then Magdalen Road where the Wisbech branch used to join. Finally comes Kings Lynn proper, not only the headquarters of the M&GN system for a long period but also the birthplace of the lines which made up the East Anglian Railways. Now only the main line remains of former routes north to Hunstanton, east and west over the M&GN from South Lynn, to Wisbech and to Norwich via Swaffham and Dereham.

L.15	Liverpool Street	S.7	Sawbridgeworth (26 m 56 ch)
B.21	Bethnal Green Junction (1 m 20 ch)	B.27	Bishops Stortford (30 m 27 ch)
		S.45	Stansted (33 m 27 ch)
C.2	Cambridge Heath (1 m 61 ch)	E.6	Elsenham (35 m 49 ch)
L.16	London Fields (2 m 35 ch)	N.9	Newport (36 m 69 ch)
H.3	Hackney Downs (2 m 78 ch)	A.16	Audley End (41 m 55 ch)
E.13	Enfield Town Branch		Audley End Tunnel (42 m 70 ch)
Q.1	Queens Road Tunnel (3 m 19 ch)	L.13	Littlebury Tunnel (43 m 27 ch)
	Clapton Tunnel (3 m 53 ch)	G.13	Great Chesterford (45 m 56 ch)
C.18	Clapton (3 m 78 ch)	W.29	Whittlesford (49 m 1 ch)
	Clacton Junction (4 m 38 ch)	S.14	Shelford (52 m 32 ch)
C.14	Chingford Branch		Shepreth Branch Junction (53 m 4 ch)
C.29	Copper Mill North Junction (4 m 74 ch)	C.1	Cambridge (55 m 52 ch)
	Tottenham South Junction (5 m 41 ch)	C.25	Coldham Lane Junction (56 m 24 ch)
T.21	Tottenham Hale (6 m)		Chesterton Junction (57 m 55 ch)
N.11	Northumberland Park (6 m 73 ch)	F.4	Fen Drayton Branch
A.8	Angel Road (7 m 57 ch)	W.11	Waterbeach (61 m 1 ch)
P.7	Ponders End (9 m 71 ch)		Ely Dock Junction (69 m 79 ch)
B.45	Brimsdown (10 m 61 ch)	N.8	Newmarket-Ely Line
E.12	Enfield Lock (11 m 65 ch)	E.9	Ely (70 m 30 ch)
W.3	Waltham Cross (12 m 63 ch)		Ely North Junction (71 m 72 ch)
	Cheshunt Junction (13 m 71 ch)	L.14	Littleport (76 m 2 ch)
C.16	Churchbury Loop		Denver Junction (84 m 32 ch)
C.11	Cheshunt (14 m 1 ch)	D.9	Downham (86 m 4 ch)
B.49	Broxbourne (17 m 17 ch)	M.1	Magdalen Road (90 m 74 ch)
	Broxbourne Junction (18 m 35 ch)		Kings Lynn Harbour Junction (95 m 25 ch)
H.22	Hertford East Branch		Kings Lynn Junction (96 m 54 ch)
R.13	Roydon (20 m 9 ch)	M.16	Middleton Towers Branch
H.9	Harlow Town (22 m 59 ch)	K.5	Kings Lynn (96 m 75 ch)
H.9	Harlow Mill (24 m 36 ch)		

Fenchurch Street-Shoeburyness

Like its neighbour Liverpool Street, Fenchurch Street is undergoing modernization and remodelling activity but the development scheme provides for the retention of its imposing frontage. The station was the City terminus of the London & Blackwall Railway which originated as a cable-worked line seeking a share of the traffic carried by steamer down river from Tower Bridge. The London & Blackwall was a partner with the Eastern Counties Railway in the opening of the original LT&S section from Forest Gate Junction to Tilbury and to cater for docks traffic and London deliveries a number of goods depots and warehouses were established immediately outside Fenchurch Street at Royal Mint Street, Haydon Square and Commercial Road.

The route is four-track as far as Stepney East where the original line continued on past Regents Canal Dock. Its route is planned to come to life again as part of the Dockland Light Railway scheme. Beyond Stepney the LT&S route has a connection to the Norwich main line and also used to connect with the North London Line which it passes over. Then it takes as its companion the Metropolitan District metals which accompany the LT&S route all the way to Upminster. The latter's intermediate stations are now served by LT trains, the Abbey Mills connection with the North Woolwich branch has gone and Plaistow Works and loco shed became redundant when the line was electrified. This also produced the Electric Traction Depot between East Ham and Barking and finally put an end to the former's tradition of services to and from the T&H route and of the goods marshalling activities at Little Ilford yard.

Above *The station platforms at Basildon.*

Below *A visit of an HST to the LT&S line for the Southend 125 anniversary celebrations.*

Shoeburyness terminus of the line from Fenchurch Street.

The work of Little Ilford had been taken over by a new mechanized yard at Ripple Lane, Barking, the station there also being completely rebuilt to give easy interchange between LT&S and LT line trains and with the services on the Upper Holloway route. Beyond Barking the Tilbury Loop turns away towards the Thames, skirting Ripple Lane yard and then passing the Ford car plant and on through an industrialized area to Tilbury. The later main line takes a level course and comes to Upminster where the single line branch from Romford joins on the Down side and the one from Grays on the Up. There is a dip beyond Upminster which leads eventually to the line's summit at Laindon and then down through Basildon New Town and its modern station to the junction at Pitsea where the Tilbury Loop rejoins.

Now back on the original metals which were pushed forward from Tilbury to tap the Southend excursion traffic, today's emus push on through flat, Thames-side scenery to the three stations serving the western end of the Southend complex and then come to the former terminus at Southend Central. Near the front and the shops, Central is now a through station with four of its six-hourly trains continuing on to Shoeburyness which was originally opened for its artillery range traffic but is now more notable for the sizeable emu depot there.

F.3	Fenchurch Street	B.10	Basildon (24 m 48 ch)
S.47	Stepney East (1 m 58 ch)	P.6	Pitsea (26 m 42 ch)
	Gas Factory North Junction (2 m 57 ch)		Pitsea Junction (26 m 52 ch)
		B.17	Benfleet (29 m 11 ch)
	Barking Tilbury Line Junction West (7 m 5 ch)	L.7	Leigh-on-Sea (32 m 43 ch)
		C.8	Chalkwell (34 m 2 ch)
B.2	Barking (7 m 42 ch)	W.18	Westcliff-on-Sea (34 m 66 ch)
	Barking East Junction (8 m 11 ch)	S.35	Southend Central (35 m 55 ch)
U.2	Upminster (15 m 20 ch)		Southend East (36 m 47 ch)
U.3	Upminster-Grays Line	T.8	Thorpe Bay (37 m 73 ch)
W.21	West Horndon (19 m 15 ch)	S.24	Shoeburyness (39 m 40 ch)
L.1	Laindon (22 m 69 ch)		

Stamford-Peterborough-March-Ely-Norwich

The Eastern Region section from Ketton through to Norwich represents the eastern end of a through route carrying a service between Birmingham and Norwich via Leicester and Peterborough, through services from Harwich, Ipswich and Cambridge to the routes beyond Peterborough and local dmu services on the Ely-Norwich, Ely-Peterborough and Peterborough-Stamford sections. The section from Ely to Norwich was part of the Eastern Counties Railway's original main line to the Norfolk capital, that from Ely to Peterborough part of its links with the Hudson empire, and the Peterborough-Stamford portion a part of Hudson's Syston & Peterborough concern.

From the Birmingham direction trains come on to the Eastern Region near the Ketton Cement premises and then call at the attractive station at Stamford. This pleasant town had a second station, for the branch connection to Essendine, and this too survives, albeit in private hands. Along with the tunnel portals, both were built in Barnack stone.

The intermediate stations on the section on to Peterborough are now closed, as is the former branch to Wansford, so trains run direct to Helpston and then parallel with the East Coast main line to Peterborough. After calling there they drop down to pass over the River Nene, beneath the main line and through the area of the first station at Peterborough, near Fair Meadow and in later years called East.

Once over Stanground Creek the line passes through a brickyard area as it heads for March, formerly a considerable railway centre but now without its St Ives, Wisbech and GN&GE joint line services. On the way is Three Horse Shoes, once the junction for the Benwick goods branch.

Between March and Ely only the waterway bridges lift the railway above the fertile fenland plain and then north of the cathedral city comes the loop plus trident junction configuration which allows trains to go into Ely and reverse or join the Kings Lynn or Norwich routes direct. On the latter there is over ten miles of level track on the section to Brandon which has the first of the flint buildings which are a feature of the Norwich & Brandon Railway section.

As trains enter Norfolk they also enter forest scenery and this continues to Thetford which was placed on the route as something of an afterthought and involves a long sweep south. From Thetford there used to be branch services to Bury St Edmunds and to Swaffham, the latter departing north at Roudham Junction where the main line resumes its direct course towards Norwich. There is a summit before Roudham and another beyond Wymondham, formerly the junc-

Birmingham-Peterborough dmu at Stamford in 1967.

tion for the line to Wells and Kings Lynn via Dereham and for a modest link to the Ipswich line at Forncett.

From Ketteringham and then Hethersett the line drops at 1 in 129 to the water meadows which precede the union with the Ipswich line at Trowse and the entry into Norwich station via the swing-bridge over the Wensum and the junction with the Sheringham/Yarmouth/Lowestoft routes.

P.5	Ketton (6 m 60 ch)	B.42	Brandon (86 m 32 ch)
S.42	Stamford (10 m 11 ch)	T.5	Thetford (93 m 50 ch)
S.20	Helpston LC (16 m 71 ch)	H.8	Harling Road (101 m 38 ch)
	Peterborough (see ECML)	E.3	Eccles Road (104 m 39 ch)
	Crescent Junction (100 m 66 ch)	A.15	Attleborough (108 m 19 ch)
W.28	Whittlesea (94 m 55 ch)	S.40	Spooner Row (111 m 27 ch)
T.11	Three Horse Shoes (91 m 5 ch)		Wymondham South Junction (113
	March West Junction (86 m 17 ch)		m 70 ch)
W.25	Whitemoor	N.12	North Elmham Branch
W.35	Wisbech Branch	W.49	Wymondham (113 m 72 ch)
M.6	March (85 m 76 ch)	H.25	Hethersett (117 m 73 ch)
M.2	Manea (80 m 13 ch)	T.24	Trowse Lower Junction (123 m)
	Ely West Junction (72 m 39 ch)		Swing Bridge Junction (123 m 43
	Ely North Junction (71 m 65 ch)		ch)
E.9	Ely (70 m 30 ch)		Norwich Thorpe Junction (123 m
S.21	Shippea Hill (77 m 25 ch)		56 ch)
L.2	Lakenheath (82 m 44 ch)	N.15	Norwich (124 m 9 ch)

Cleethorpes-Sheffield

The two Great Central routes between its heartland around the Pennines and its port and playground on the East Coast both survive, although the original line via Retford and Gainsborough has now surrendered most of its through services to the later route via Doncaster and Scunthorpe. In the former case the Down direction is from Cleethorpes westwards and this also applies on the Doncaster line as far as Kirk Sandall. In addition to the through services on both routes there are heavy flows between Sheffield and Doncaster and towards Retford, a good dmu service between Doncaster and Cleethorpes and a Sheffield-Lincoln service.

The station at Cleethorpes is right on the front and is 112 m 37 ch from Manchester (London Road). The line then runs behind Grimsby's dock area to Grimsby proper where the East Lincs line from Boston and Louth used to join. The local service on the section on to Habrough Junction is then provided by the Barton-on-Humber trains which leave the main line at a triangular junction, which is also the access route to Immingham's port and refineries and formerly led to New Holland and the paddle steamer service across the estuary to Hull Corporation Pier. The other leg of the triangle joins the main line at Brocklesby Junction.

Just beyond Barnetby, at Wrawby Junction, the single route from Cleethorpes divides into three, two heading for Sheffield and the third to Lincoln, Newark and Nottingham. On the original route to Sheffield only two stations remain open on the first section to Gainsborough, Brigg on the flat plain and Kirton Lindsey high on the wold. Reaching the latter involves a 3½ mile climb at 1 in 125/6 and passage through Kirton Tunnel with its magnificent turreted portal.

Its situation on the Trent made Gainsborough the target for the railways which were to form the Manchester, Sheffield & Lincolnshire company and our route met there the line from Sheffield and what later became the Great Northern & Great Eastern Joint line. The two pass over the great river together and the Sheffield route then continues to Clarborough Junction (and tunnel) where the former direct line from Lincoln survives in part to serve Cottam power station. Then comes the link with the East Coast main line at Retford, now remodelled to provide separate platforms for the ex-GC route.

There is a good dmu service, PTE supported, on the remainder of the route which rises in steps through the superb station at Worksop and on to the coal traffic areas and a summit at Kiveton Bridge. Over three miles of 1 in 115 down gradient follows to Woodhouse Junction and the Sheffield approaches.

On the other route to Sheffield, probes east from Doncaster to the Trent were joined with early Scunthorpe lines and one west from Barnetby to create the through link, now always busy with passengers and freight to and from Scunthorpe. After the great steelworks complex there, including the surviving stub of the Flixborough/Whitton route, Cleethorpes-Doncaster trains cross the Trent via the dog-leg created by the building of a new bridge and continue, under the old Isle of Axholme route, to Thorne Junction and the junctions with the freight routes from Stainforth and Kirk Sandall.

On the other side of Doncaster, described earlier, the route resumes its westerly course in company with the River Don, reunited with the Avoiding Line and climbing to Conisbrough Tunnel before dropping again to the Mexborough junctions and the link towards Wath. The two former routes south to Rotherham and Sheffield are being progressively rationalized so that they will not only carry Inter-City trains but will also more effectively serve the local communities. The process will remodel the junctions at the Mexborough/Swinton end and use these instead of the interchange at Thrybergh, south of which the ex-GC route will come back into its own with a new station at Rotherham. The remaining section into Sheffield, with its links to the original North Midland line, to the Barnsley line and to Tinsley Yard will stay broadly as it is.

Cleethorpes-Gainsborough-Retford-Sheffield

C.21	Cleethorpes (112 m 37 ch)
N.5	New Clee (110 m 79 ch)
	Grimsby Docks (110 m 12 ch)
G.15	Grimsby Town (109 m 20 ch)
M.10	Marsh East Junction (108 m 8 ch)
	Marsh West Junction (107 m 69 ch)
G.14	Great Coates (107 m 19 ch)
H.17	Healing (105 m 75 ch)
S.41	Stallingborough (104 m 72 ch)
H.1	Habrough Junction (101 m 7 ch)
B.9	Barton-on-Humber Branch
	Brocklesby Junction (99 m 39 ch)
B.46	Brocklesby (99 m 33 ch)
B.4	Barnetby (94 m 56 ch)
W.47	Wrawby Junction (94 m 12 ch)
B.5	Barnetby-Lincoln Line
B.44	Brigg (91 m 1 ch)
	Kirton Tunnel (85 m 72 ch)
K.8	Kirton Lindsey (84 m 65 ch)
N.13	Northorpe (82 m 14 ch)
G.1	Gainsborough Central (74 m 42 ch)
S.39	Spalding-Doncaster Line
	Trent East Junction (73 m 24 ch)
	Trent West Junction (73 m 11 ch)
C.19	Clarborough Junction (68 m 32 ch)

C.30	Cottam Power Station Branch
	Clarborough Tunnel (67 m 79 ch)
R.6	Retford (64 m 32 ch)
	Thrumpton West Junction Down (63 m 46 ch)
	Thrumpton West Junction Up (63 m 29 ch)
W.44	Worksop (56 m 58 ch)
	Shireoaks East Junction (55 m 62 ch)
S.20	Sherwood-Shireoaks Line
S.23	Shireoaks (54 m 56 ch)
B.40	Brancliffe East Junction (53 m 59 ch)
B.41	Brancliffe-Kirk Sandall Line
K.9	Kiveton Park (51 m 53 ch)
K.9	Kiveton Bridge (50 m 34 ch)
	Woodhouse Junction (46 m 56 ch)
W.42	Woodhouse (46 m 18 ch)
	Darnall (43 m 23 ch)
	Woodburn Junction (42 m 29 ch)
N.16	Nunnery Junction (41 m 68 ch)
	Change of mileage to 159 m 33 ch
	Broad Street Tunnel (159 m 1 ch)
	Nunnery Main Line Junction (158 m 77 ch)
S.13	Sheffield (158 m 40 ch)

Cleethorpes-Doncaster-Sheffield

W.47 Wrawby Junction (33 m 34 ch)
E.7 Elsham (31 m 33 ch)
Scunthorpe Foreign Ore Branch
Junction (25 m 34 ch)
North Lincoln Junction (24 m 10 ch)
Trent Junction (23 m 51 ch)
Scunthorpe West Junction (23 m 15 ch)
S.10 Scunthorpe (22 m 54 ch)
A.6 Althorpe (19 m 21 ch)
C.33 Crowle (15 m 43 ch)
T.7 Thorne South (9 m 41 ch)
Thorne Junction (8 m 8 ch)
S.40 Stainforth & Hatfield (6 m 40 ch)
Stainforth Junction (6 m 27 ch)
K.7 Kirk Sandall Junction (3 m 27 ch)
Bentley Junction (1 m 3 ch)
Marshgate Junction (3 ch)
D.7 Doncaster
South Yorkshire Junction (22 m 57 ch)
St James West Junction (22 m 35 ch)

H.25 Hexthorpe Junction (20 m 76 ch)
C.27 Conisbrough Tunnel (19 m)
Conisbrough (18 m 13 ch)
M.15 Mexborough (15 m 71 ch)
Mexborough East Junction (15 m 64 ch)
Change of mileage to 10 m 17 ch
Mexborough South Junction (9 m 75 ch)
T.14 Thrybergh Junction (7 m 73 ch)
S.27 Silverwood Colliery Branch
A.2 Aldwarke North Junction (7 m)
Change of mileage to 164 m 48 ch
Masborough Station North Junction (164 m 24 ch)
C.13 Chesterfield-Rotherham Line
R.12 Rotherham (162 m)
Wincobank Junction (161 m 52 ch)
B.38 Brightside (161 m 27 ch)
Brightside Station Junction (161 m 6 ch)
A.14 Attercliffe Road (159 m 34 ch)
S.13 Sheffield (158 m 40 ch)

SECTION 5

Traffic and operation

Like most of the other BR Regions, the Eastern Region is an area of contrasts and in its Southern Area these will be heightened as further electrification covers the main line to Norwich, the Kings Lynn line as far as Cambridge, then the East Coast main line, and smaller schemes for the Southminster branch and the Camden Road Junction-Stratford route. Already being transformed by electrification, the Norwich main line still retains at its extremity a simple One Train operation scheme for the final portion of the Sheringham Branch (S.19). When the panel box at Colchester takes over its full workload it will cover the main line as far as Norwich itself, yet not that far away—on the Grantham-Skegness line

The ticket and information office at Basildon.

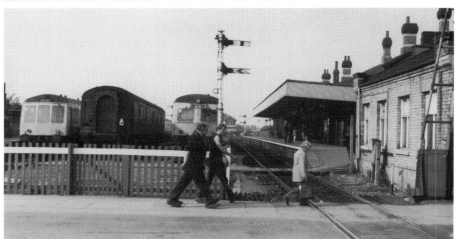

(G.10)—there are still some surviving examples of the GN somersault signals.

The East Coast main line has been transformed in recent years and is now busy with HST sets clocking up 1,000 miles a day or more and with top average speeds nearing the 90s. In contrast, the ER's coal and steel business may be less obvious but an HST passenger passing through Retford (R.6) could easily catch sight of a new Class '58' locomotive with a merry-go-round train on the remodelled GC line below. And within the freight business itself there are further contrasts, between the oil and ore activity of Immingham (I.2), the motor industry traffic of the Tilbury Loop (D.1), the supplies for and products of Scunthorpe (S.10), the multi-facet activity of an area like Sheffield (S.13) and the grain flows of East Anglia (F.11, N.12), the fertiliser depots (K.5, N.12, W.28), the cement works and terminals (G.11, P.5, S.18, W.49) and special distribution schemes such as that of Dagenham Storage (B.2).

The extension of control from new panel boxes (C.1, C.23, D.7, P.4, S.13) has still left plenty of areas and routes covered by traditional Absolute Block signalling, such as the GN&GE joint line (S.39), but as more routes are simplified, eg, Grantham-Skegness (G.10), Barnetby-Lincoln (B.5) and Ely-Kings Lynn the number of Electric Token or Tokenless block single line schemes increases. Simplification is usually the keynote for freight access with key access to minor freight-only routes (S.57) and most crossings operated by the train crew. Paradoxically the simplification process involves new techniques and sophisticated equipment in examples such as the radio control scheme being applied on the East Suffolk line (E.1).

Some of the operational activity of the Region is there for all to see and some is less obvious. The elimination of the 6.25 kv sections around Liverpool Street (C.14) leaves little evidence now that the work has been completed but a visit to Royston (R.14) or Bishops Stortford (B.27) provides an interesting study of interchange between emu services and dmu services. The timetable relationship between services is also of interest between the two routes of the LT&S, between the Lea Valley and Hertford East services at Broxbourne (B.49) and on the Colchester-Clacton line (C.24) while centres like Doncaster (D.7) and Sheffield (S.13) are always full of fascinating insights into operational systems and practices.

The physical and operational profile of the Region is still changing although little alteration is likely in its overall network. The Sheffield area, already greatly changed as part of the process of eliminating duplication which had been assiduously built up by rival Midland and Great Central activity, is likely to change further under the Holmes Chord scheme which would produce new commuter stations between Sheffield and Mexborough. Lincoln loses one of its inconvenient crossings as traffic is concentrated on Central station and Norwich is to get a new swing-bridge across the Wensum at Trowse. The process of station reopening and refurbishing, well under way with examples like Metheringham (S.39) and Homerton (N.14) where there has been a joint approach with the local authorities,

Top left *East Coast main line improvements have included a realignment at Peterborough and the provision of this new station there.*

Above left *The new connection into Lincoln Central, one of the many pieces of ER rationalization, eliminates one of the level crossings at Lincoln, seen here at St Marks station.*

Left *Until completion of the Anglia West electrification to Cambridge, dmus connect with emus at Bishops Stortford.*

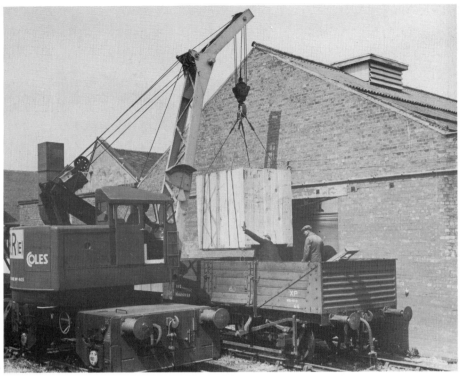

Above *A typical scene of traditional railway freight activity.*

Below *Typical crossing gate and GNR housing, on the Peterborough-Grantham section of the main line.*

Above *The Ford traffic became one pioneer of the change to company train and bulk goods traffic movements.*

Below *Another major bulk traffic is fertilizer in high capacity, pallet-carrying wagons.*

The delightful architecture of the original Syston & Peterborough Railway section at Stamford.

is likely to continue and the joint examination and action on level crossings will remain an important area for progress.

Backing the train running activity is an extensive and modern maintenance function, now supplemented by the new depot at Crown Point (N.15). On the passenger side the 'Customer First' approach of the Region embraces staff training, computer-based reservation facilities, the latest techniques in electronic information display (P.4) and recorded and self-service information systems to back up the travel centre work.

SECTION 6

Civil engineering

For the past decade the permanent way side of the Eastern Region's civil engineering function has, in the south of the area, been much concerned with improvements to the East Coast main line and with simplification in several other areas. The former GN main line, now laid with continuous welded rail, resignalled and with a significant portion suitable for running at or near 125 mph, has been transformed. The Kings Cross (K.4) 'throat' has been simplified, the bottlenecks at Arlesey and Sandy (S.6) have gone, the Offord curves have been eased and the awkward layout at Peterborough (P.4) totally revised. At the other end of the spectrum track rationalization in the form of partial closure and/or singling has been applied to routes like the East Suffolk line (E.1), the Grantham-Skegness line (G.10) and the Kings Lynn main line north of Ely.

Each of the track rationalization schemes has involved additional features such as resignalling and/or the provision of automatic half barrier and open crossings. In the case of Sleaford (S.31) the direct 'avoiding' line has been closed and at Lincoln (L.11) a new connection has enabled trains to be concentrated on one station instead of two. In addition to the overall schemes there have been many interesting individual alterations such as the bridge renewal at Barkston (B.4), the provision of slab track through Ipswich Tunnel (I.4) and the earlier remodelling at Retford (R.6). Ahead lie such things as the replacement of one of the Norfolk swing-bridges, that over the Wensum at Norwich (N.15).

Typical traditional railway bridge, in this case on the M&GN at Potter Heigham and after closure.

Felixstowe Town before the station buildings were incorporated into a supermarket development.

The railway engineers of the Eastern Region are now becoming increasingly immersed in a fresh round of electrification. On the Anglia East scheme ten realignment schemes had been completed by the beginning of 1985, 35 bridges had been reconstructed and 66½ miles of the total of 186 had been provided with masts for the overhead wiring. To cope with this work the traditional permanent way depots at places like Chesterton Junction (F.4) have been supplemented by new locations such as the one established on the old station site at Ipswich (I.4).

The alterations to track and bridges are accompanied by resignalling to enable full exploitation of the advantages of electric traction and in the case of the North Woolwich (N.14) scheme an external partner is involved. This is the GLC who are adding up to £9 million towards electrification to the £1½ million already spent on the provision of new stations on the line.

External partners are also involved in the major remodelling schemes at Fenchurch Street (F.3) and Liverpool Street (L.15) which will virtually give the latter a

Lincoln Central with crenelated tower, secondary turrets and tall chimneys.

Stevenage, a new station in modern materials and style.

new station. With Kings Cross (K.4) already given a new frontage and many suburban stations being modernized and generally smartened up, the London scene is already much more convenient and attractive for the commuting public. In the provinces new stations for new towns at Basildon (B.10), Harlow (H.9) and Stevenage (S.48) and major remodelling schemes such as that at Peterborough (P.4) have gone hand in hand with making the best of existing structures by the use of modern techniques and materials.

In the process of bringing the ER's buildings up to modern standards sight has not been lost of the intrinsic attraction and architectural merit of traditional stations. Among the many examples remaining are:

—the ornate Ipswich & Bury Railway stations (B.57, E.4, N.1, T.15);

—the stations on the Newark-Lincoln line (N.3);

—Lincoln itself, both Central and St Marks (L.11);

—the matching styles of Norwich Thorpe (N.15) and Hertford East (H.22);

—the traditional, staid GNR approach at Biggleswade (B.23) and St Neots (S.4) and the out-of-character three storeys at Peakirk (W.16);

—Cambridge with its surviving example of a long, single platform (C.1);

—the clearly identifiable styles of the Tendring Hundred Railway's stations (C.24);

—the gabled and mullioned attraction of Brocklesby (B.46);

—the warm stone of the original station at Stamford (P.5);

—the use of flint by the Norwich & Brandon Railway (B.42);

—the gatehouses on the East Suffolk line (E.1);

—the ogee windows on the Grantham-Nottingham line (G.9);

—Sheffield's surviving, centralized and nicely cleaned station (S.13);

—the delightful gables and chimneys at Worksop (W.44).

SECTION 7

Early and closed lines

The rural nature of the Eastern Counties produced more light agricultural lines than early wagonways. Such of the latter as lie within the ER territory covered by this book were to be found in the industrial areas, especially around Sheffield and Doncaster. These early wagonways were generally displaced by the advent of conventional railways whereas the rural railways co-existed happily and largely by the courtesy of their bigger neighbours. They were, however, the most vulnerable to the rising tide of road competition and a number of rural lines lost their passenger services in the 1920s and '30s, usually closing at the end of the summer to take a final dividend from the modest upsurge in business brought by the better weather.

In the 19th century the Newmarket Railway's line from Great Chesterford to Six Mile Bottom closed when that company lost its battle with the enveloping Eastern Counties system. Another closure before the inter-war period was that of the Churchbury Loop, but this was destined to reopen not just once but twice more. The northern part of the Hertford Loop, closed on 11 September 1939 to passengers, was also destined to come back to life again.

After nationalization the first major victim was the M&GN system and the revisions at the beginning of the 1970s removed a considerable mileage in East Lincolnshire. Otherwise the closures have tended to occur piecemeal but, even so, have removed from the railway map such large areas as North Norfolk and the gentle countryside between Colchester and Cambridge.

The closures have borne hard upon the east-west links with not only the M&GN

The M&GN station at Potter Heigham, two years after closure.

going but also the Colchester-Cambridge, Cambridge-Bedford, Cambridge-Kettering, Peterborough-Rugby/Northampton and Lincoln-Chesterfield routes. The last major surgery, in 1982, cut out the March-Spalding portion of the GN&GE joint line route which the old Great Eastern had worked so hard to establish.

The main passenger closures of the pre-nationalization period were:

1925	13 July	North Lindsey Light Railway
1926	4 May	Stepney-Blackwall and Millwall Extension Railway
1928	2 January	Upwell Tramway
1929	12 April	Southwold Railway
	1 July	Stamford-Wansford
	2 December	Doncaster-Dinnington
1930	22 September	Ramsey East Branch
		Sleaford-Bourne
		Stoke Ferry Branch
1931	2 February	Mellis-Eye
		Ely-St Ives
1932	29 February	Hadleigh Branch
1933	17 July	Isle of Axholme
1939	10/11 September	Angel Road-Lower Edmonton
		Finchley-Edgware
		Forncett-Wymondham
		Spilsby Branch
		Woodham Ferrers-Maldon
1940	29 December	Beckton Branch
1947	6 October	Ramsey North Branch
	30 November	Ilford-Woodford

And then, of the BR era:

1951	7 May	Tollesbury Branch
	18 June	Hatfield-Hertford
		Essendine-Bourne
	1 October	Hatfield-St Albans
	5 November	Lincoln-Louth
1952	3 March	Bishops Stortford-Braintree
	2 June	Heacham-Wells
	28 July	Haughley-Laxfield
	15 September	Thaxted Branch
		Wroxham-County School
	1 November	Framlingham Branch
1953	5 January	Tivetshall-Beccles
	7 April	Mundesley-Cromer
	8 June	Thetford-Bury St Edmunds
	21 September	Yarmouth, South Town-Beach
	7 December	Newark-Leicester
1954	5 July	Finsbury Park-Alexandra Palace
	12 September	Horncastle Branch
1955	19 September	Lincoln-Chesterfield
1957	18 November	Stratford-Loughton (last steam train)

1959	2 March	M&GN system
	15 June	St Ives-Huntingdon
		Stamford-Essendine
	2 November	Haddiscoe-Yarmouth South Town
1960	1 February	Tivetshall-Beccles
	5 December	Louth-Mablethorpe
1961	10 April	Long Melford-Bury St Edmunds
1962	1 January	Chappel-Haverhill
	18 June	Cambridge-Mildenhall
1963	7 January	Palace Gates Branch
	17 June	Goxhill-Immingham
		Woodhall-Boston
1964	15 June	Brightlingsea Branch
		Thetford-Swaffham
	7 September	Audley End-Bartlow
		Maldon East Branch
	5 October	Dereham-Wells
		North Walsham-Mundesley
	16 November	Buntingford Branch
1965	26 April	Dunstable Branch
	13 September	Ely-Newmarket (local traffic)
	1 November	Honington-Lincoln (local—10.9.1962)
1966	5 September	Sheffield-Rotherham (GC route)
	12 September	Aldeburgh Branch
1967	6 March	Sudbury-Shelford
1968	9 September	Dereham-Kings Lynn
		March-Wisbech
1969	5 May	Kings Lynn-Hunstanton
	6 October	Dereham-Wymondham
1970	5 January	Sheffield-Huddersfield
	4 May	Lowestoft-Yarmouth South Town (N&S)
	5 October	Bellwater Junction-Lincoln
		Boston-Lincoln
		Cambridge-March
		Firsby-Grimsby
		Spalding-Boston
		Willoughby-Mablethorpe
1982	16 November	March-Spalding
		Lincoln and Sleaford avoiding lines

Gorleston station in August 1963.

SECTION 8

Preservation and non-BR lines

On 1 May 1970 the exchange of rail wagons between British Rail and the Port of London Authority ceased, closing an era in which many major rail siding networks had been operated as an adjunct to the main line system. Along the north bank of the Thames there had been large private siding installations at Dagenham Dock (Fords and Samuel Williams), at Purfleet (Purfleet Deep Wharf, the oil companies, Thames Board Mills etc) and Grays (the cement companies, Thurrock Chalk & Whiting, Proctor & Gamble etc).

This large scale private railway activity, often with large steam locomotive studs, had also existed in other port and colliery areas and some remnants survive, using diesel traction, at the major steelworks and coal loading points. Felixstowe, for example, still has its own motive power. With the availability of Section 8 grants private sidings have increased again in recent years but in many cases BR now does the wagon positioning.

The change in the BR freight situation has meant that private railway activity is now largely the preserve of the preservation societies. In the area covered by this book there are two major operational locations, that of the Nene Valley Railway along the old LNW line from Wansford towards Peterborough and the North Norfolk Railway's line which uses Sheringham station as its starting point. Among the more modest lines is that of the Lincolnshire Coast Light Railway group near Cleethorpes.

In addition to the operating lines there are sizeable steam centres at Chappel & Wakes Colne (Stour Valley Railway Centre), Castle Hedingham (Colne Valley Railway) and Bressingham (Bressingham Steam Museum). Musems include the recently-opened collection in the former North Woolwich station building, the former Royal Waiting Room at Wolferton, the East Anglia Transport Museum (Carlton Colville) and the Lincolnshire & Humberside Railway Museum in Mount Pleasant Windmill at Kirton-in-Lindsey.

There are further preservation schemes for the Dereham-Fakenham and Louth-Grimsby lines with interest being shown in some other locations as well. In the sphere of non-standard rail traction Southend has a cliff railway.

The Eastern Region since 1986

A major event on the organisational front since 1986 has been the separation from the old York-based Eastern Region of a new Anglia Region. The York headquarters retains control of King's Cross, the East Coast Main Line and its branches, but from 29 April 1988 the lines from Liverpool Street and Fenchurch Street came under the operational control of Anglia Region. The rapid growth in business on these lines, now accelerated by the extension of electrification, has led to the need to recognise the separate nature of the old Great Eastern Railway territory and give it, once again, a separate identity.

The Anglia Region falls largely within the Network South East business sector which the British Railways Board created with effect from 10 June 1986. Like the InterCity sector, it is much involved with change, and in the Eastern and Anglia Regions much of the change has been associated with electrification. The erection of overhead equipment has been pushed forward ahead of schedule on the East Coast Main Line and on 11 May 1987 electric services were extended north as far as Peterborough, using Class 317 multiple units. The Class 317/2 sliding door version had been put to work on the suburban services out of King's Cross in 1986 after an initial £24 million BREL order for 24 four-coach sets and more to follow for the Peterborough services. Another event of some note in the Peterborough area was the erection of the first 140 mph speed indicator boards near Werrington Junction and Stoke Tunnel. By the middle of 1989 these were applying to regular electric services to the West Riding.

On the Great Eastern side the first of the electrification extensions came into public service with the new timetables on 12 May 1986. These were on the Southminster branch, and on the main line north from Colchester to Manningtree and then through Parkeston Quay to the coast at Harwich. Further north on the main line, stations were being altered, bridges lifted and signalling modified in readiness for the extension of electric traction to Norwich.

The main event of 1987 was the extension of the North East London electrified network from Bishops Stortford to Cambridge. Planned for implementation with the new timetables on 11 May, the scheme had been finished early and some regular passenger services were able to begin on 19 January. This route is to get new Class 321 units in 1989, and the first of 46 new four-car sets began trial running on 15 September 1988. They are built by BREL, with Brush traction equipment, and are capable of 100 mph. Some will also be used on the services to and from Southend Victoria.

After the end of the pre-electrification works, passengers on the Cambridge line would be aware of further civil engineering activity north of Stansted. The Bill for the 4½ mile branch to Stansted Airport received the Royal Assent in 1987 and construction work began soon after. When the rail access to the airport is completed, passengers will be conveyed to and from Liverpool Street in Class 322 sets. These are special vehicles with more generous seating and extra space for luggage, and an order for five four-car sets was placed with BREL during 1988.

Another 1987 event was the linking of Liverpool Street to the EuroCity network. A musical launch took place on 1 June 1987 when the two new named trains entered service between Liverpool Street and Parkeston Quay. Given the names *Benjamin Britten* and *Admiraal de Ruyter*, the services are part of a rail and sea link from London via Parkeston Quay and the Hook of Holland to Amsterdam and joined a network of 64 pairs of trains serving 200 major centres in 13 European countries.

The great hurricane of October 1987 did considerable damage to electrification works in the Anglia area, but not even the forces of nature were to be allowed to delay the main event of 1988, electrification through to Norwich. The regular service of electrically-hauled trains began on 11 May 1988 but had been preceded on 5 May by a celebratory run from Norwich to Liverpool Street and back. The locomotive was 86 220 which was named *The Round Tabler* as part of the occasion. Its non-stop return journey achieved a remarkable timing of 83 minutes 22 seconds — 83 mph start to stop.

One of the new Class 321 units after completion by BREL. These trains were then destined for use on the Cambridge and Southend Victoria lines.

At Norwich Thorpe station the pre-electrification works included a simplification of the approaches near Carrow Road bridge. The station concourse was extended at the expense of the old ticket barriers and the whole complex was tastefully redecorated. Especially notable among the changes in the area was the conversion of the old swing bridge crossing of the Wensum to a new, modern equivalent. The first example of a swing bridge in an electrified area, the new bridge is single track and uses fixed power supply sections.

Both Norwich and Ipswich benefit considerably from electrification and from new cross-country Sprinter services. Originating at Cambridge, Parkeston Quay or Yarmouth/Norwich, these run via Peterborough, Grantham and Sheffield to Manchester/Liverpool/Blackpool. Added to the workings to and from Birmingham, they have dramatically improved the scope and quality of cross-country travel and, in the process, have made Ely an important interchange point.

The electrification of the main line to Norwich rather overshadowed other developments in 1988 but a smaller scheme, the closing of the gap between Royston and Cambridge, was nevertheless of some significance. The 10 mile section between the outer limit of the King's Cross emu workings and Cambridge had previously been operated by dmus, necessitating a change at Royston for through passengers. The completion of the electrification works in time for the new May 1988 timetables enabled the Class 317s from King's Cross to continue on through Meldreth, Foxton and Shepreth to Cambridge.

Another aspect of the electrification picture is BR's decision to convert two 6.25 kV sections on the Fenchurch Street-Shoeburyness line to the standard 25 kV. The 6.25 kV system was originally adopted to reduce flashovers in areas of bridges and tunnels with low clearances, but this has proved unnecessary. This decision to standardise on 25 kV in a scheme costing £936,000 and to be implemented in 1988-89 is a prelude to the introduction of Networker units on the ex-LT&S line in 1991-2.

There have been some contractions, like the withdrawal of freight facilities from such places as Broxbourne, but the general picture has been one of expansion, and freight traffic has been able to justify its own piece of electrification. From the beginning of 1988, regular electric haulage began over the route from Stratford to Camden Road Junction, producing substantial savings by eliminating a diesel traction gap for freight services to and from Ripple Lane, Dagenham, Tilbury and the Ipswich line.

Electrification preparations have affected the northern part of the region where Grantham has been renovated and Doncaster has become a major centre for both electrification works and maintenance. It will become more apparent still as test running to the West Riding is converted to a public service in 1989. Meanwhile, more local services have been worked by Sprinter units improving the activity on all lines in the East Midlands and Lincolnshire, except for Barnetby-Gainsborough which was proposed in 1988 for closure.

The other major change is the reconstruction work at Liverpool Street. Following the closure of Broad Street, its services were diverted to its neighbour via a new curve at Graham Road. By then, the massive Liverpool Street redevelopment scheme was under way, starting with the renovation of the western train shed and followed by the building of a raft over the eastern one. By 1988 the disruption had reached its worst and signs of better things to come were beginning to emerge.

Ahead lies electrification from Cambridge to Kings Lynn. Transport Secretary Paul Channon has announced approval for a £20.1 million scheme covering 41 route miles and involving the purchase of seven four-car Class 321 sets.

Gazetteer update

Aldwarke Junctions

These junctions link the former Midland and Great Central routes north of Sheffield. Traffic through them has already been affected by the opening of the Holmes Chord to the south, and the closure of Rotherham Masborough in favour of a new Central station at Rotherham. A further scheme, orginated jointly by BR and the South Yorkshire Passenger Transport Executive, plans to close the GC route north of Aldwarke in favour of the MR line and install a connecting curve from the latter to Mexborough East. The scheme also provides for a new station at Swinton.

Arlesey

The old Arlesey station, closed to passengers on 5 January 1969, was a notorious bottleneck but the main line here is now four-track and the new station, opened on 3 October 1988, will not suffer the same stigma. Costing £630,000, the new Arlesey consists of two platforms with shelters and linked by footbridge to the ticket office and car park area.

Baldock

The traditional appearance of Baldock has been altered by an improvement scheme and the replacement of its platform buildings but the main station building has been retained and a new ticket hall and ticket office installed within it.

Berney Arms

After a long period of insecurity, the future of Berney Arms and the secondary route between Yarmouth and Reedham became more secure on 29 April 1987. On that day a special train called at the tiny station for

the signing of a contract between British Rail and local interests which, by a form of underwriting, would ensure the line remaining open for a further five years.

Biggleswade

This typical Great Northern station has been the subject of an improvement scheme involving the installation of a new ticket hall and ticket office within the main street level building. The 1987 works also provided a new parcels office there.

Bottesford-Newark

This line was part of a joint GN&LNWR enterprise for a route south from Newark to Melton Mowbray and Leicester. After its closure to passengers, it was retained for freight traffic but the petroleum movements to and from Nottingham routed over it ended in 1986 and the route fell into disuse. Lifting of the track was completed in 1988.

Brigg

The future of Brigg station became uncertain in 1988 when BRB announced that it was seeking the approval of the Secretary of State for Transport for the closure of the line from Wrawby Junction at Barnetby to Trent Junction at Gainsborough. The intention was to substitute buses for the three trains serving the intermediate stations at Brigg and Kirton Lindsey.

Broxbourne

As part of the pattern of reducing the number of freight terminals, freight facilities were withdrawn from Broxbourne in 1987.

Cambridge

Cambridge was the subject of a major station refurbishment operation in 1986-7. The work included cleaning Francis Thompson's original frontage and repainting its colourful crests of colleges and prominent local citizens. The forecourt has been remodelled, with extended parking and landscaping, and the rest of the station re-signed and re-painted. Funding of the improvements was by BR's Network South East, the Railway Heritage Trust and Cambridge City Council, and a plaque was unveiled on 23 March 1987 to mark the event.

Chelmsford

The traditional appearance of Chelmsford station has been radically altered by a £1.4 million rebuilding scheme. Former period buildings have been replaced by a new com-plex, modern in function and appearance, but harmonising with the Victorian viaduct which carries the Norwich main line here.

Downham Market

Freight facilities were withdrawn in 1987.

East Suffolk Railway

Trains on the East Suffolk line were embraced in the new radio-controlled elec-tronic signalling scheme from 1985. The system is based on a new signalling centre at Saxmundham and operates with computer

This impression of the new station at Chelmsford shows how the design has been matched to the elevated viaduct level used by the main line here.

controlled solid state interlocking which precludes the issue of more than one token to a train.

Felixstowe

Traffic through the port of Felixstowe has continued to expand. Sharing in the expan-sion, the volume of rail traffic warranted the completion in February 1987 of a 1½ mile freight line from south of Trimley station to a second container terminal at Felixstowe.

Freightliners switched their European shipping movements from Felixstowe to Parkeston Quay to create more room for the exploitation at the former point of the deep sea container traffic potential.

Fenchurch Street

Prior to its redevelopment, Fenchurch Street had changed little since the age of the Til-bury tanks. Now it has been completely re-furbished with a modern ticket office, escalators to the platform level and tiled walls up to the concrete raft which supports the office development above. The original frontage has been retained.

Just beyond the station platforms the Docklands Light Railway now commences with a small modern station of arched metal and glass, the line then occupying the site of the second pair of former LT&S tracks out as far as Limehouse. The DLR extension to Bank will drop steeply underground from a junction between the present terminal and the surviving Minories wagon hoist building.

Finsbury Park

Finsbury Park, which had been getting steadily more seedy, got a long overdue facelift in 1985. The scheme embraced London Regional Transport, the GLC and other interested parties and has provided the station with a new ticketing area, improved and redecorated subways and platforms, a small bus station, and retailing units.

Gainsborough

At Gainsborough Lea Road a long-standing siding is still in use. This is the modest line down to Paul & Sandars mill, originally used to transfer traffic between Trent shipping and the railway system. Serving the area of the mills and wharves alongside the river, the line is still in use for Grainflow traffic.

Grantham

This is another location where BR civil engineering staff have tackled the difficult problem of achieving station improvements without creating a conflict in appearance between new works and those parts of the older structures which are retained. Grantham's 1986 renovation work included the complete reconstruction of the buildings on the Down island and refurbishment of those on the Up side. To ensure harmony, new canopy supports were made from period moulds.

Great Chesterford

New Up side ticket office and staff accommodation was completed in 1988.

Harwich Branch

Stations on the branch were renovated and re-signed in readiness for its electrification. On 24 March 1986 the current was switched on to allow testing and trial running prior to the introduction of the full public service from 12 May 1986.

Although BR has withdrawn from the Harwich-Zeebrugge ferry service, Parkeston Quay remains busy, Freightliners European shipping operation being switched there to allow development of more deep sea container business through Felixstowe. Parkeston Quay has also been given a new ticket office and has three named trains, *The Loreley* operated by a Sprinter set to the North West, and the *Benjamin Britten* and *Admiraal de Ruyter* which link Liverpool Street and Amsterdam via the Hook of Holland as part of the EuroCity network.

King's Cross

From 16 May 1988 King's Cross got a new station on the old King's Cross (Met) site, to be used by trains of the Thameslink service from the Bedford line to the Southern Region via Farringdon and Blackfriars. The changeover from overhead to third rail current collection is made at Farringdon, with the SR territory then commencing at the

The latest improvements at King's Cross have been at the suburban station where the renovation work has included a new platform 11 pictured here.

north end of the 800 yard section of revived railway through Snow Hill Tunnel. The Thameslink station at King's Cross is 350 yards from the main line one.

The year 1988 also foreshadowed further developments in the King's Cross area. BR sought Parliamentary approval for a possible additional Channel Tunnel terminal at King's Cross and also for a link that would allow Peterborough and Cambridge trains to run to and from St Pancras. The latter was connected with the major development proposals for the whole King's Cross and St Pancras area. After considering submissions for the use of the 122 acres available, the majority of it owned by BR, the London Regeneration Consortium was chosen to develop the idea of a linked rail complex as part of a much wider exploitation of the area.

Kirton Lindsey

In 1988, BRB announced that it was seeking the approval of the Secretary of State for Transport for the closure of the line from Wrawby Junction, Barnetby, to Trent Junction, Gainsborough. Buses would be substituted for the three daily trains serving the two intermediate stations at Kirton Lindsey and Brigg.

Liverpool Street

At the end of 1988 Liverpool Street was still a scene of orderly confusion with bulldozers

The extensive changes at Liverpool Street have had to be carried out while running a normal train service. This view of the east side gives some idea of how it has been done.

levelling the site of what had once been the Continental Traffic Manager's headquarters at Harwich House. However, the first signs of fulfilment of the dramatic new station depicted on the posters began to emerge, albeit in the form of new lavatories. Work on the £100 million redevelopment scheme had started in 1985 with the repair and renovation of the western train shed. At the same time the plans for the closure of Broad Street and its complete obliteration by a new Broadgate development were about to be implemented, and those plans have now been carried through with some North London line services transferred to Liverpool Street via a new curve at Graham Road, Hackney.

By the beginning of 1989 the eastern train shed at Liverpool Street had gone, replaced by a raft over the platforms in readiness for upward development. Work was also taking place to remodel the platform lines.

The Liverpool Street alterations include an improvement in the track approaches from Bethnal Green and work to ease the congestion at the platform approaches. The opportunity is being taken to lengthen the platforms so that 15 of the 18 will be able to take eight-car trains and eight of them 12-car trains. The revised layout will be under the control of a new signalling centre housed in a building near Worship Street and which was handed over by the contractors on 9 June 1988.

London Fields

After closure due to a serious fire on 13 November 1981, the station buildings at London Fields were demolished in 1985 preparatory to rebuilding and reopening in 1986.

North Woolwich Line

Between 5 and 16 November 1984 the branch was closed to permit the laying of a third rail in readiness for electrification. This was part of the Crosstown Linkline scheme which provided a new through emu service from Richmond with the May 1985 timetables.

The Great Eastern Railway Museum had opened in the old North Woolwich station building on 22 September 1984 and was visited by HM the Queen Mother and LNER No 4472 *Flying Scotsman* in the following month.

Norwich

Electric services to Norwich began on 11 May 1988 after a 'preview' ceremonial run on the 5th which had achieved an 83 mph start-to-stop speed. The new electrically-hauled trains approach Norwich Thorpe over a new swing bridge across the River Wensum and a simplified track layout between Carrow Road bridge and the station itself. In readiness for the occasion, the latter had been pleasantly redecorated and its

concourse had been extended by the removal of the old ironwork ticket barriers. The approaches to Norwich are also marked by the new Crown Point servicing depot, resited from its old location beside the Yarmouth line to an area adjacent to the curve between the Yarmouth and Trowse routes.

Unusual in its status as a swing bridge on an electrified route, the one over the Wensum is a single line bridge on a site just upstream from the 1906 bridge which was itself built on the foundations of the 1846 original. Rigid overhead power supply sections have been used on the bridge proper and the lineside power and communication cables ducted beneath the river. The new bridge was commissioned between 13 and 15 February 1987.

Peterborough

Shortly after electric train services between King's Cross and Peterborough began with the May 1987 timetable, a new Electrification Fixed Equipment Maintenance Depot was opened there on 14 July 1987. Established on the former cattle dock area, the new depot will eventually maintain 315 miles of wiring between Hitchin and Newark.

Potters Bar

The station buildings are to be replaced in a property development scheme costing £2½ million and including the erection of a five-storey office block.

Potters Bar is getting a new station as a result of a development scheme arranged by the BR Property Board.

Romford-Upminster Line

A decision was taken in 1984 to electrify the single line branch from Romford to Upminster and the work was completed in 1986.

Rotherham

The Holmes Chord line was installed in 1987 with a South Yorkshire PTE ceremony to mark the completion of the project on 8 April 1987. This was followed by the opening, on 11 May, of a new Rotherham Central, replacing the Great Central Railway station closed in 1966, and comprising two concrete platforms reached by ramp from the brick station building at street level. The latter houses the ticket and parcels offices plus public facilities and has a clock tower in the best railway tradition.

With the rerouting of the York-Sheffield service via Rotherham Central, the Masborough station at Rotherham was closed on 2 October 1988.

St Neots

Like its neighbour Biggleswade, St Neots has received a facelift. Costing £250,000, the improvement scheme has provided a new booking hall, Up side waiting accommodation and improvements to the car parking accommodation in the old coal yard on the Down side.

Sheffield

The last working remnant of the Great Central route out from Sheffield to Penistone saw its final train on 1 July 1988. A section of line had been retained for freight as far as Deepcar and had latterly carried waste trains between there and Stocksbridge Steelworks. The last such train on 1 July also marked the end of the once extensive Stocksbridge Railway system.

Southminster Branch

After the erection of overhead electrification equipment on the branch in 1985, the current was switched on from 17 March 1986. The tests went well which permitted some public running from 14 April with full electric services from 12 May.

Stansted Airport

The Bill for the 4½ mile spur from the Cambridge main line to Stansted Airport was given the Royal Assent in 1987. By the third quarter of the following year work had progressed sufficiently for the engineers to lay in first the South Junction (just north of Stansted station) and then the North Junction.

East of the main line the new railway passes beneath the M11 and then runs below the airport runways to a three-platform station below the terminal building. Concurrent with the building of the new line, work was going on at BREL to meet an order for five four-car Class 322 sets for use between Liverpool Street and the airport.

Stepney East

Stepney East has been renamed Limehouse. Behind the station the route of the old London & Blackwall Railway past Regents Canal Dock and West India Dock sidings is now used by the Docklands Light Railway.

Stevenage

Although a relatively new station, Stevenage was the subject of further improvements in 1988. These include new terrazzo flooring and new ceilings for the booking hall, overbridge and stairs access.

Ware

A sum of £173,000 was spent on renovation work at Ware in 1986 although there was some difference of opinion between BR and the local council over the retention of the station's period buildings. These have, in fact, been spared.

Welham Green

A site ceremony on 3 March 1986 marked the start of work on a new station between Brookmans Park and Hatfield. Duly opened on 29 September 1986, Welham Green consists of two six-coach platforms with shelters and steps to a ticket office on the Dixons Hill overbridge.

Welwyn Garden City

Changes on the Up side include a new international road/rail freight terminal opened on 28 January 1986. The main initial movements were trainloads of petfoods from Melton Mowbray.

On the opposite side of the line, work has begun on the Howard Shopping Centre. When completed in 1990, the complex will incorporate a new station ticket office and parcels office at first floor level.

Wymondham

The 4½ mile freight line from Dereham to North Elmham was closed on 25 January 1989 with closure of the 11½ miles from Wymondham to Dereham following in June. A Wymondham & Dereham Rail Action Committee has been formed to consider preservation prospects.

Routes, operation, closures and preservation since 1986

The main changes in the route network of the Eastern and Anglia Regions derive from the steady increase in the number of electrified lines. From 12 May 1986 electric trains began operating over the Southminster branch and to Harwich via Manningtree, followed in 1987 by the extension of electric operation on the East Coast Main Line. From 11 May of that year, electric multiple units began a regular service between King's Cross and Peterborough, bringing considerable benefits to the intermediate stations north of Hitchin. On the same day the full electrification timetable became operational between Liverpool Street and Cambridge where some electric trains had been running since 19 January.

The process continued in 1988. After a preview run on 5 May, the train services on the main line to Ipswich and Norwich were electrically hauled from 11 May with a standard timing of 1 hour 55 minutes over this difficult 115-mile route. At the same

This design of dynamic track stablising machine enables the civil engineer to return track to full operation without the need for penal speed restrictions.

time the 10-mile gap in the electrified system between Royston and Cambridge was filled and the King's Cross Class 317s took over from the previous dmu workings through Meldreth, Foxton and Shepreth to Cambridge. The following year produced ECML electric services to Leeds and the announcement of a Cambridge-Kings Lynn scheme.

On the closure front, the little-used route between Bottesford and Newark has been closed and the line between Barnetby and Gainsborough proposed for closure. The process of eliminating route duplication north of Sheffield continues with a new curve at Swinton completing the process begun with the Holmes Chord. Rotherham has gained a better-placed station and Swinton is to have a new one as part of these changes. The old North London terminus at Broad Street saw its last trains on 27 June 1986 with the line from Dalston Junction then closing. From 30 June the Richmond-North Woolwich route included some services from Watford Junction to Liverpool Street via a new curve at Graham Road, Hackney. In East Anglia, the remnants of the old Wymondham-Wells line closed in 1989.

The North London line development brought with it a change of current collection, the Class 313 dual voltage emus changing from third rail dc to overhead ac current at Dalston Kingsland. The Thameslink services also perform a current change, at Farringdon, and King's Cross gained an extra station — at the former King's Cross (Met) location — when they were introduced in 1988. New stations have also opened at Arlesey and at Welham Green.

The preparation work for electrification has generally included some track remodelling and resignalling, and pushing back the areas of semaphore signalling to the branch lines and rural locations. Cambridge now has a modern panel signal box and Liverpool Street will get a new signalling control centre as part of the wholesale changes which are taking place there. In rural contrast, the full radio-controlled electronic signalling system now operates on the East Suffolk line with a modern signalling centre at Saxmundham, radio links with the trains and computer-controlled solid state interlocking.

In the sphere of non-BR lines, the 1986 Spring Bank Holiday saw the Nene Valley Railway extend 1½ miles to a site near Fair Meadow at Peterborough. Using an area once occupied by the LNWR loco shed, the extension gives the railway a presence near the city centre as well as an 8 mile run along the course of the River Nene to Wansford. The Southend Pier Railway was reopened on 2 May 1986 after complete rebuilding. This 1¼ mile, 3 ft gauge line is operated by two push-pull sets with diesel hydraulic locomotives.

The principal preserved railways and steam centres are now:

Audley End Miniature Railway, Estate Office, Audley End, Saffron Walden, Essex CB11 4JG. 1½ mile, 10¼ in gauge line.

Bressingham Steam Museum, Bressingham, Diss, Norfolk IP22 2AB. Four lines totalling 5¼ miles; four different gauges.

Colne Valley Railway, Castle Hedingham Station, Halstead, Essex. 1 mile, standard gauge line.

East Anglian Railway Museum, Chappel Station, Chappel & Wakes Colne, Colchester, Essex CO6 2DS. Short standard gauge line.

East Anglia Transport Museum, Chapel Road, Carlton Colville, Lowestoft, Suffolk NR33 8BL. Narrow gauge line.

Kessingland Miniature Railway, Suffolk Country & Wildlife Park, Kessingland, Lowestoft, Suffolk. 2 miles of 10¼ in gauge.

Knebworth & Wintergreen Railway, Knebworth Park, Stevenage, Herts. 1 mile

Above *One of the many facets of the Nene Valley Railway is its 'Continental' flavour, demonstrated here by a Peterborough-Wansford train headed by Swedish Class S1 locomotive No 1928* (Jim Wade/Nene Valley Railway).

Above right *A train of the Docklands Light Railway (see page 229) approaching All Saints Station.*

Right *A train for Tower Gateway leaves South Quay Station.*

Below *The Docklands Light Railway uses platform 4 at Stratford. An Island Gardens train stands there, with a Liverpool Street train in platform 5.*

circuit of 2 ft gauge line.

Nene Valley Railway, Wansford Station, Stibbington, Peterborough, Cambs PE8 6LR. 8 miles of standard gauge line.

North Norfolk Railway, Sheringham Station, Norfolk NR26 8RA. 5¼ miles of standard gauge line.

Wells & Walsingham Light Railway, Wells-next-the-Sea, Norfolk. 4 miles of 10¼ in gauge line.

Other developments include the Fakenham & Dereham Railway Society which has started work on a heritage centre, which will include some track, at County School. The Lincolnshire Light Railway does not now appear to be operating, but that county has new museums at Goxhill and Burgh-le-Marsh stations as well as the activities of the Grimsby-Louth Railway Preservation Society. The former royal waiting room

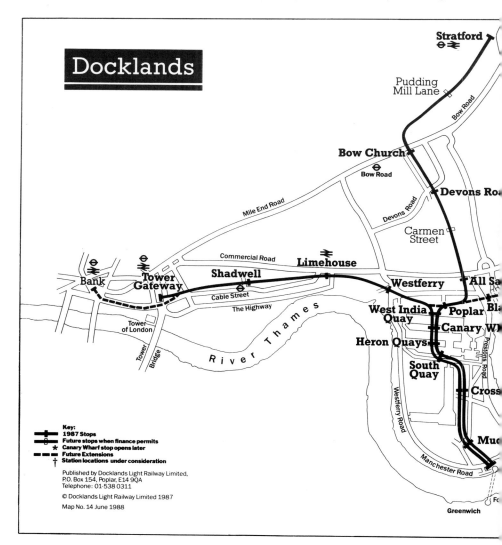

at Wolferton station houses a museum and the Museum of Lincolnshire Life has some narrow gauge locomotives.

The most significant non-BR development has been the introduction of services on the Docklands Light Railway which had an advance royal opening ceremony on 30 July 1987. Trains start from Tower Gateway station, near Fenchurch Street, and run over the old London & Blackwall route to Poplar and thence to either Island Gardens or No 4 platform at Stratford. The system uses an overhead current supply, centralised operational control and machine-issued tickets. It has been so successful that the stations have had to be altered to accommodate two-car trains and construction has started on an extension underground to Bank.

Map of the Docklands Light Railway.

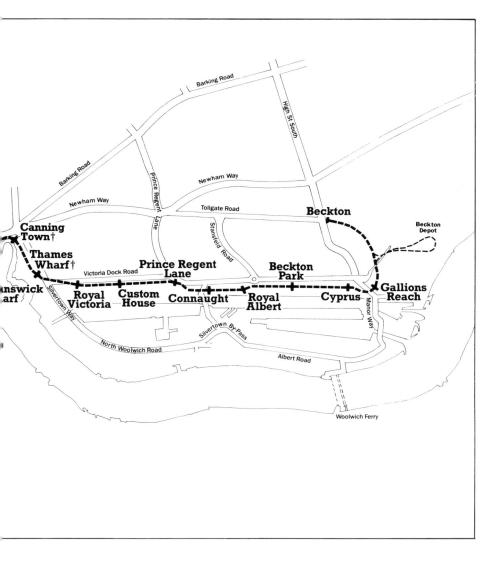

230

Bibliography and sources

The sources for a book of this sort are numerous and largely fragmentary. Official items, like the Sectional Appendix to the Working Timetable, make a significant contribution but much comes from minor documents eg, the LNER's pre-war freight publicity, old timetables and personal records. Nevertheless there are quite a few standard works available to add to the reader's knowledge and understanding of the southern part of the Eastern Region.

Among those books giving an overall coverage a few stand pre-eminent. George Dow's work on *The Great Central Railway* provides a definitive history of that company and John Wrottesley does the same for the GNR in his three-volume treatment of *The Great Northern Railway* (Batsford). Charles H. Grinling's *The History of the Great Northern Railway* (Allen & Unwin) was originally published in 1898 and gives an excellent insight into the earlier years, something that Cecil J. Allen's 1955 *The Great Eastern Railway* does for the lifespan of that rural and metropolitan concern. Ian Allan have added *The Great Eastern Since 1900* to their GER coverage and have also published a number of books on the LNER and BR eras, the latter including *The Eastern Since 1948*. In area, as opposed to company, terms the volumes in David & Charles' 'Regional History of the Railways of Great Britain' are invaluable and include Volume 3 *Greater London* by H. P. White, Volume 5 *The Eastern Counties* by D. I. Gordon, Volume 8 *South and West Yorkshire* by David Joy and Volume 9 *The East Midlands* by Robin Leleux.

A number of excellent books deal with the smaller companies, like John Wrottesley's treatment of *The Midland & Great Northern Railway* (David & Charles). The Oakwood Press again makes a contribution with works on the *London, Tilbury & Southend Railway, East Suffolk Railway,* and several of the individual lines.

Books on traction are legion but some on other specialized subjects are worth separate mention. George Dow's *Railway Heraldry* (David & Charles) is usefully supplemented by the Ian Allan work *Railway Liveries LNER*. Stations and their architecture are treated in detail in *Victorian Stations* (D&C) by Gordon Biddle and D&C also published *Great Northern Suburban* as well as contributing *East Anglia* in the 'Forgotten Railways' series. Depth treatment of one spot is given in *Rail Centres: Peterborough* (IA) and the various map and gradient data works are both useful and interesting.

Supplementary Index

An open day at Stratford in 1979.